LABOR
IN
RETREAT

SUNY series in American Labor History
Rober Asher and Amy Kesselman, editors

LABOR IN RETREAT

Class and Community among Men's Clothing Workers of Chicago, 1871–1929

YOUNGSOO BAE

State University
of New York
Press

Published by
State University of New York Press, Albany

Printed in the United States of America

For information, address State University of New York Press,
90 State Street, Suite 700, Albany, NY 12207

Production by Susan Geraghty
Marketing by Jennifer Giovani

Library of Congress Cataloging-in-Publication Data

Bae, Youngsoo.
Labor in retreat : class and community among men's clothing workers of Chicago, 1871–1929 / Youngsoo Bae.
p. cm. — (SUNY series in American labor history)
Includes bibliographical references and index.
ISBN 0-7914-5117-8 (alk. paper) — ISBN 0-7914-5118-6 (pbk. : alk. paper)
1. Men's clothing industry—Illinois—Chicago—Employees—History. I. Title. II. Series.

HD8039.C62 U637 2001
331.7'687'0977311—dc21

00-066142

10 9 8 7 6 5 4 3 2 1

To my mother

CONTENTS

LIST OF TABLES

LIST OF MAPS

ACKNOWLEDGMENTS

No one can complete a book alone. This was especially true of this book. The notes and bibliography show how much I have benefited from the work of individual scholars. Here, I would like to give thanks to those individuals and institutions that came to my aid in other ways, although I cannot list them all.

First of all, I am grateful to those institutions that provided financial support for my research. This book is primarily based on my doctoral thesis, a study made possible by the Harvard-Yenching Institute, the Korean-American Educational Commission, and the Charles Warren Center for Studies in American History, Harvard University. Subsequent research, sponsored by Seoul National University and the Korean Ministry of Education, was done at Newberry Library, which kindly helped me concentrate in an unforgettable atmosphere in 1994–1995. Without the generosity of these institutions, my research could not have been completed as planned.

I am also thankful to many archivists and librarians for their kind and competent assistance. A number of documents critical to my project were located by the staff of the following archives and libraries: Labor-Management Documentation Center, Catherwood Library, Cornell University; Chicago Historical Society; Newberry Library; Widener Library, Harvard University; Schlesinger Library, Radcliffe College; Harvard University Archives; Special Collections, Main Library, University of Illinois at Chicago; Downtown Library, Roosevelt University; Illinois State Archives; Chicago Municipal Reference Library; Chicago Public Library; Regenstein Library, University of Chicago; University Library, University of Illinois at Urbana-Champaign; Northwestern University Library. Some archivists deserve particular mention; Richard Strassberg was considerate enough to take an interest in my research at Cornell's Labor-Management Documentation Center, and Archie Motley called my attention to uncatalogued items at the Chicago Historical Society.

Special thanks go to those who allowed me to use their cherished stories and materials. I feel very much obliged to the Amalgamated Clothing and Textile Workers' Union, now merged into the Union of Needletrades, Industrial and Textile Employees. Henrietta Dabney, ACTW Director of Research, provided me with the permission to examine the Amalgamated Clothing Workers of America Papers, including the minutes of the General Executive Board meetings. At the Chicago ACTW organization, Joe Costigan guided me to the basement storage, where I discovered invaluable materials that it had kept from the 1910s. He also introduced me to old-timers, in particular my interviewees: Marie Aliotto, Sol Brandzel, Rose Falk, Frank Hanus, and Albert Wadopian. I am beholden to Hartmarx Corporation, where Sherman Rosen and Max Hart kindly allowed me to study the work process instituted there as well as the papers of Hart, Schaffner and Marx, forerunner of the corporation.

I have incurred more debts than most historians trying to publish a monograph. The readers of my manuscript, which is written in my second language, took pains to check numerous grammatical errors and awkward expressions as well as to make many suggestions about the substance of my arguments. Stephan Thernstrom, my mentor ever since I first met him in 1984, read the entire manuscript at various stages and has always been reassuring while criticizing specific points. Eric Arnesen, with his expertise on labor history and with his enthusiasm, meticulously read earlier versions and gave me precious advice. David Brody was so kind as to read a later version and make instructive comments with encouraging words. Jim Ralph carefully read the manuscript at several stages and made insightful critiques, cheering up my faltering spirit. Jim Grossman, Elliott Gorn, Tim Spears, Tim Gilfoyle, and Terry Toulouse read part of the manuscript in its later stages and made a variety of useful comments. At its last stage, Robert Asher and anonymous readers made constructive comments to improve my arguments, and Priscilla Ross and Susan Geraghty, my editors at SUNY Press, took pains to have my sentences corrected and polished. In addition, Lizabeth Cohen and Steven Fraser pointed out important sources when my research took shape.

I am deeply indebted to my teachers at Seoul National University, Byung-Woo Yang and Suk Hong Min, in particular, who led me to the study of history and to the world of scholarship. Oscar Handlin, Bernard Bailyn, and David Herbert Donald, my teachers at Harvard, have inspired me, above all, by bestowing their confidence on an ungifted student. If this book shows them anything, it will be that I keep trying.

Finally, I would like to say thanks to my wife and daughters, whose love has sustained me in the long, arduous process of completing this book. Words are inadequate to convey my feelings.

INTRODUCTION

This book presents a pair of ironies: First, although the Amalgamated Clothing Workers (ACW) of America had once appeared to represent progressive unionism, in sharp contrast with the type preached by Samuel Gompers, they were in fact becoming a business union in the early 1920s; second, while studying the ACW, I found myself starting from radical postulates, formulations often leading to a rosy future, but eventually arriving at pessimistic inferences. These ironies seem to be entangled with each other, and implicated, to some degree, in the transformation that occurred in the world over the decade during which I worked on this book; the collapse of the Soviet bloc and the changing direction of the labor movement in South Korea, where I live, compelled me to question my premises and rethink labor history in general. In retrospect, however, I realize that these ironies came into being when I discovered that my postulates were not entirely appropriate and began to modify them for my subject. Their seed was there, in a sense, in the ultimate question I had always hoped this study would answer.

The central question of the book is, Why did the American labor movement decline so drastically in the 1920s? At first, it appeared to be a clearly-specified question that would have narrow implications. Like most historians, I believed that the labor movement, though occasionally slowed in its progress, had made steady advances since the end of the nineteenth century. The aberration represented by the twenties seemed interesting. The movement had surged near the end of World War I, but then dramatically faltered. The American decline appeared particularly striking in comparison with Europe. Although the United Kingdom presented a parallel to America, with the miners' strike there crushed in the mid-1920s, labor maintained its strength in Germany and in France. To be sure, it had retreated from the radical and militant movement that existed following World War I, but it was powerful enough to secure a distinct voice in the political economy.

A number of American historians have addressed themselves to this broad question, but one of its most important aspects has remained almost untouched. Irving Bernstein has attributed the "lean years" after World War I to a combination of economic, political, and social factors: Despite general prosperity, many industries suffered chronic recessions;

the political climate, along with conservative courts, favored business over organized labor; and American workers remained divided along lines of race, ethnicity, and skill. David Brody has focused on welfare capitalism, which he has argued might have stabilized labor relations in the United States had there not been the Great Depression. But this line of examination stresses structural factors—that is, circumstances that faced the workers—and neglects other significant questions, such as how workers coped with their circumstances and what role they played in the waning labor movement. David Montgomery has addressed these questions, but, by focusing largely on the workplace, he fails to explain why organized labor retreated after all the shop floor struggles. More recently, Lizabeth Cohen has claimed that under welfare capitalism workers formulated a moral view of the American political economy. She suggests that in the 1920s they showed an accommodative tendency to the established order, which might be a key to the "lean years." Chiefly interested in the New Deal era, however, Cohen has not developed this suggestion into a full-blown explanation.

Amid the breadth of historiography examining American labor in the 1920s, the ACW deserves closer scholarly attention. The union represented the workers in the men's clothing industry. Although this industry now occupies a peripheral place in the American economy, it was an important sector in the early twentieth century; in 1910 it employed some two hundred thousand workers, a figure equal to two-thirds of the workforce engaged in all branches of the iron and steel industry. Created in 1914 as an industrial union—an entity that labor radicals assumed to be the organizational basis for a revolutionary movement—the ACW at first lived up to its founders' assumption; launched as an alternative to the United Garment Workers, a craft union that secured staunch support from the conservative leadership of the American Federation of Labor (AFL), it conducted a series of aggressive campaigns to organize men's clothing workers across the country, and by the end of World War I had won a firm foothold in the industry. The ACW led the postwar progressive labor movement, cooperating with employers through arbitration and scientific management, venturing into unemployment insurance, labor banking, and cooperative housing, and supporting both independent labor politics at home and Soviet Russia's economic development. At the same time, however, the union also experienced setbacks; it suffered from a shrinking membership and, although initially an industrial organization, gradually turned into an AFL-type business union, seeking exclusive control over jobs and bureaucratic rule over the rank and file.

The decline of the ACW in the 1920s has yet to be analyzed from the perspective of the rank-and-file membership. Contemporary observers held contrasting views of the ACW. At the end of World War I, John Commons praised the arbitration machinery instituted at Hart, Schaffner and Marx, a Chicago-based men's clothing firm that was the largest in the world. In the late 1920s, however, Selig Perlman asserted that the union was in fact following in the AFL's footsteps because of the wage-earners' "job consciousness" in addition to the constitutional and political order in the United States. Subsequent commentators have inclined toward the first explanation, paying attention to the ACW leadership, Sidney Hillman in particular. Three biographies—the first one written by George Soule during the Great Depression, the second by Matthew Josephson in the midst of the McCarthy era, and the last by Steven Fraser during the late doldrums of organized labor—stress Hillman's inspiring personality and constructive vision in dealing with frustration and confusion that American workers felt in adverse circumstances. Social historians such as Susan Glen or Jo Ann Argersinger have recently investigated the workforce engaged in the men's clothing industry, and touched on the decline of the ACW in the twenties. Focusing on gender and ethnicity as well as class, however, they do not seem to offer an opinion essentially different from the prevailing interpretation of labor history during the decade. In regard to the question I wish to raise in this study, therefore, the most helpful approach would be to review Perlman's observation.

Such a review calls for further investigation into the workforce in the men's clothing industry. For this, Chicago is a particularly interesting locale. Second only to New York in the production of men's clothing, Chicago was representative of the national landscape, both in the ethnic composition of its workforce and in the development of the labor process. In New York, one ethnic group, the Jews, was predominant in the numerous small shops which relied on a relatively simple division of labor. But in Chicago the workforce was composed of diverse groups such as Czechs, Poles, and Italians in addition to Jews, with the majority working at large factories that operated with a more sophisticated labor process. Women were visible, constituting nearly three-fifths of the workers at the Chicago factories around the turn of the twentieth century. And union members there, comprising roughly one-fourth of the entire ACW membership, maintained stable relations with employers, helped to financially support their national organization, and made Chicago the citadel of the ACW.

In this study, my approach is derived from the late E. P. Thompson. Although I am less interested in consciousness than in organization, I believe that the labor movement can be best understood in terms of class. For the movement is an essential part of the historical process that Thompson called "class." He stressed that class happens when working men and women, "as a result of common experiences (inherited or shared)," understand their interests to be at once identical among themselves and different from others'. The experiences are largely determined by the relations of production. These relations, a concept that Thompson took for granted and did not probe, comprise a primary link between employers and employees, and a collateral connection among the latter. Therefore, class has two sides: On one side is the way working people regard their employers, and on the other the way they feel about each other.

It is on the latter side that I start to diverge from Thompson. He discussed this collateral connection, but loosely. Attacking the structuralist tendency, among Marxists and non-Marxists alike, to consider class as a thing, he took pains to show that class is not predetermined, but derives from how working people interpret their experiences. In other words, Thompson regarded experience as centering on exploitation at the point of production, which is based on the primary link between employers and employees. Hence, he was more interested in how this primary link influences the collateral connection than vice versa. As a matter of fact, Marxism, the basis of his work, has long been chiefly and very often exclusively concerned with the link. Class is, however, a relationship in power as much as in culture, and hinges on the way workers mobilize themselves and on the way they are connected with one another.

Reserving "class" for the specific process that Thompson defined, I will use the generic term social relations, so as not to dismiss the collateral connection among employees as incidental. This leads me to further diverge from him and stress social life beyond the workplace. Chiefly concerned with how consciousness develops from experience in the sphere of production, he did not elaborate on the ways in which the other sphere bears upon the relations of production; consumption was more often than not undifferentiated from production in the working-class households of industrializing England. I attempt to capture the unfolding relations on both spheres, keeping an eye on the way the collateral connection affects the primary link. I am particularly interested in social relations around the turn of the twentieth century, when life for working people was increasingly demarcated, both in time and in space, between the workplace and the community. In the sphere of production, I explore how the transformation of the labor process touched not only the primary link between employers and employees but also the collateral connection among employees. In the sphere of consumption, I concentrate on social life in the community, how it was organized, how it changed in the context of a larger society, which was also evolving, and how it helped to shape the contest at the workplace.

The sphere of consumption comprises more than simply the purchase and use of goods and services available at stores. No doubt it is important to investigate the way working people, in consuming a rapidly increasing number of commodified necessities and comforts, recast their lifestyle and identity in the changing world of commodities. No less significant is an attempt to understand how they rearrange their way of life based on different conditions in housing; housing is the commodity that constitutes both the principal item of expenditure and the major point of consumption. Housing is where people shape their social life outside the workplace and locate themselves in the social landscape. Social relations are significantly affected by the way people feel about and interpret their living environment, as expressed particularly in terms of residential patterns. In fact, urban settlement has undergone a notable change since the late nineteenth century: Population growth and geographical expansion have gone hand in hand with a functional reorganization of space that has separated business districts from residential ones; the latter districts have been further divided by social boundaries, as residents of inner city slum sections have moved into more decent neighborhoods, which themselves had been abandoned by well-to-do families fleeing to the even more respectable suburbs. Trying to understand the impact of these changes on the way of life among working people, I have become especially interested in the interrelationship between spatial structures and social relations. This is an issue foreign to most historians but familiar to geographers, who have explored this interrelationship since the 1960s. Many geographers agree that the space owned and used by people is a product of social processes, but they dispute whether and how space, once integrated into the processes, affects social relations. The controversy invites historians to search into the spatial context of history, in addition to the temporal one that characterizes our discipline. In this regard, I feel obliged to formulate my own perspective, but, for the convenience of my readers, I have relegated it to an appendix.

My approach has led me to organize this story of Chicago's men's clothing workers by subject as well as chronology. The first two chapters reveal the way in which the workers coped with the obscure but decisive forces shaping their world. Chapter 1 surveys how the workers, mostly new arrivals from eastern and southern Europe, rearranged their social life in a world that was American, urban, and capitalist. It argues that they endeavored to recreate the communities they had known in the Old World, in an effort to ward off the individualistic tendency that, embedded in the world of commodities, appeared to be ingrained in the American way of life, endangering their cherished values. Chapter 2 discusses the workplace and the social relations they formed there. In particular, it shows how the factory system led them to develop worker solidarity among themselves and brought them into conflict with their employers, while at the same time they restrained themselves from challenging the system itself and accepted the imperative of compromise.

Incorporating those contradictory forces working at the workplace and in the community, the next two chapters discuss the rise of labor organization in Chicago's men's clothing industry. Chapter 3 details the story of worker mobilization, culminating in a stubborn and violent general strike in 1910–1911, a turning point in the history of the industry. The following chapter examines how the workers organized Chicago at the end of World War I. The ACW, led by progressives and moderate leftists who could mobilize even unorganized workers chiefly by virtue of potent solidarity, proved its effective command of the workforce through a series of organizing campaigns, and succeeded in pressing the strike-ridden employers for a union agreement. These two chapters, reviewing events now familiar to labor historians, present previously unexamined details, with events placed in a new perspective. Unlike existing literature that separates the 1910–1911 strike from the sudden rise of the ACW, my narrative is designed to show how class consciousness, developing from the specific experiences of unskilled immigrants, helped them launch and build up an industrial union.

The last chapters detail how the Chicago ACW organization quickly turned into a business union in the 1920s. Focusing on the workplace, Chapter 5 analyzes how the imperative of compromise, which ACW leaders stressed in their policy toward management, helped them consolidate their bureaucratic rule over the union membership. Chapter 6 finally returns to the community. It examines changes in social relations there, and discusses the reasons that the ACW became a business union in such a sudden and ironic way. Established as a power representing and benefiting men's clothing workers in Chicago, the union found itself in an unresponsive community. Economic individualism, now pervasive and effective enough to overshadow the communal tradition, as indicated by the social life the workers shaped in postwar ethnic neighborhoods, restrained the leadership from mobilizing the rank and file and confronting management at the workplace.

The conclusion sums up my arguments concerning the rise of business unionism in the ACW. This chapter discusses why the union was in retreat after World War I, and stresses the significance of community. This term, which has two distinct meanings throughout this book, demands a brief comment here (for details, see note 16 to Ch. 1). I find the best-known concept, originally formulated by Ferdinand Tönnies and long accepted by most scholars, inappropriate. It refers principally to locality, and while this usage appears in this book, I do not apply it to personal relationships, instead employing "communalism" where necessary. Rather, the concept of community is here defined as a corporate entity that organizes into a formal structure a number of people who share a common interest—property—and at the same time common control over it; in this sense, the community has a material basis that goes back at least to the feudal world. This form of corporate community vanished under capitalism, leaving behind persistent traces in modern culture. The early history of the ACW suggests that during the "lean years" organized labor was losing both communal solidarity within its own fold and communal support from without. This conclusion, along with recent adversities facing organized labor in the industrialized world, has prompted me to rethink the conventional wisdom on the long-term trend of the American labor movement and eventually to arrive at a pessimistic conclusion, which I had not expected at the start.

CHAPTER 1

The Ethnic Community in the World of Commodities

Immigrant labor has long characterized the men's clothing industry of the United States. Immigrants already constituted the majority of its workforce when it became a sweating trade that employed poorly paid workers to make cheap work clothes in the mid-nineteenth century. However, the ethnic makeup of the workforce has frequently changed, roughly reflecting the historical patterns of immigration. When manufacturers of quality garments assumed leadership of the industry in the last decades of the century, modern men's clothing factories were relying chiefly upon immigrants from eastern and southern Europe. By that time, the workforce had taken on distinct traits, too, depending on locality. As the industry, typical of the labor-intensive sector, became concentrated in urban areas, each center of production found its workforce composed of different immigrant groups.

After identifying the groups represented in Chicago's men's clothing industry around the turn of the century, this chapter discusses the cultural changes that took place in the ethnic community. Social historians have written much about these changes. Those primarily interested in immigration have recently stressed continuity, pointing out that immigrants brought with them social networks and cultural baggage formed in the Old World. These historians note that the immigrants had already been exposed to a market economy in their native countries, that in America they often got their jobs through family and acquaintances, and that they practiced a "family economy" in which the income of children as well as parents was pooled together to ensure their survival. Labor historians have shown how, painfully and yet successfully, immigrant workers adapted themselves to new work patterns and factory discipline by taking advantage of skills they had learned in their homelands.

There also seem to have been unsettling experiences in their acculturation. In particular, immigrants were often shocked at the materialism they found rampant in American cities and palpably pervading their families and neighborhoods. The process of changing their old ways of life involved not only acclimatization to the American ethos, in particu-

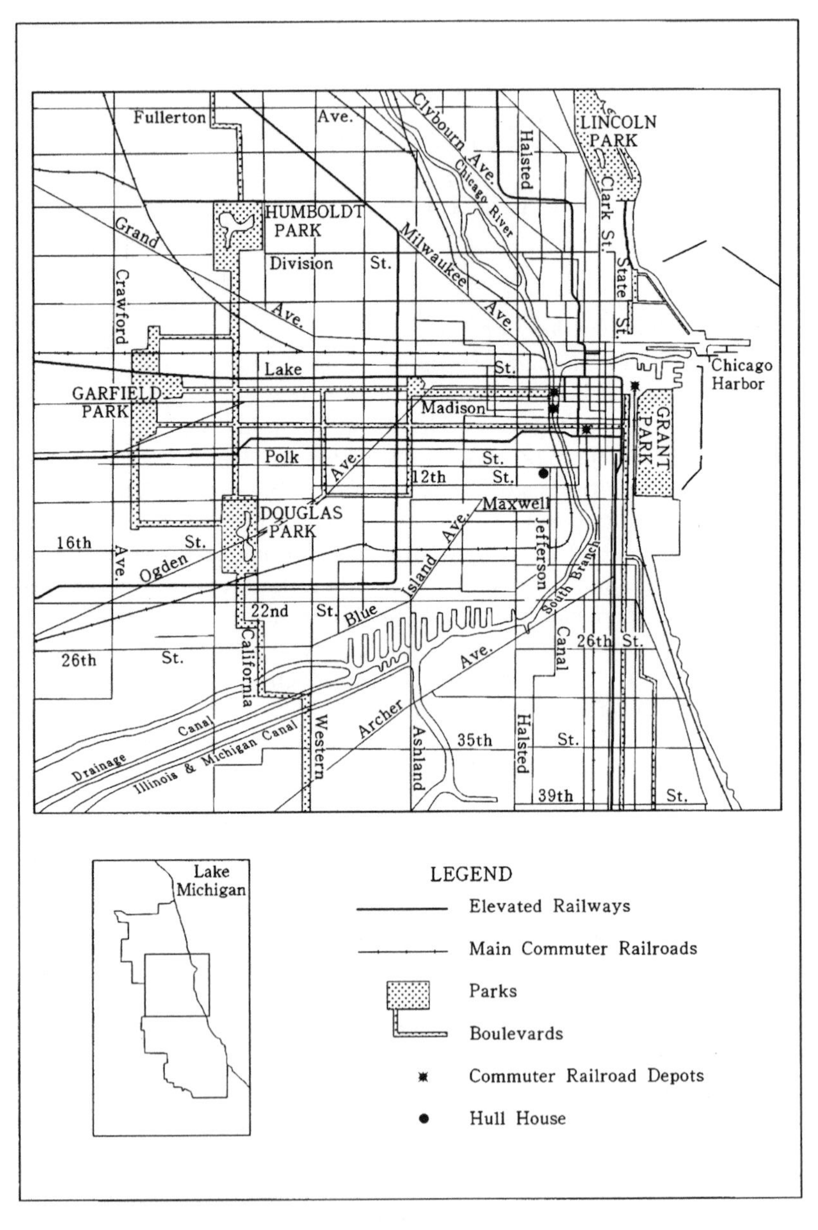

MAP 1.1
Central Chicago, 1915. Adapted from Harold M. Mayer and Richard C. Wade, *Chicago: Growth of a Metropolis* (Chicago: University of Chicago Press, 1969).

lar values emphasizing the individual achievement, but also readjustment to urbanism and capitalism. Both in the extent of its urbanization and in the advanced stage of its capitalist development, America constituted a different world from that which they had known in their homeland. In eastern and southern Europe, capitalism had begun to develop in urban areas by the late nineteenth century, bringing about profound changes; however, it was not mature enough to eclipse the ancient traditions of social life in those areas, which were often much smaller than American cities. On the other hand, Chicago had a population of one million dispersed over an extended space, a scale that bewildered even those immigrants who had experienced city life in Europe. In the United States, capitalism was almost full-fledged; production relied upon the labor of numerous workers, wage earners under the direction of an employer who controlled the worksite and machinery; consumption composed a separate sphere, in which people increasingly bought and used goods produced in the factory instead of the household. These differences in degree, in addition to the American ethos, required the immigrants to rearrange their social life. And they did so, often learning from painful experiences in the process.

This chapter focuses on how immigrant workers adapted themselves to this world of commodities, the capitalist social relationship in particular. It specifically discusses what social traditions they brought with them from their homelands, what problems they confronted while attempting to recreate their traditions in Chicago, and what cultural changes followed their efforts to adjust. These questions confronted more men and women than just the immigrants engaged in Chicago's men's clothing industry, but the evidence they left behind is fragmentary; they were not simply inarticulate, but also entertained vague and ambiguous ideas about cultural transformation, which was usually implicated in daily life episodes as they strove to accommodate to new realities. Furthermore, the questions reach back to the towns or villages in which they were born and brought up under cherished, though decaying, traditions. Therefore, this chapter covers long-term changes. It also details seemingly trivial episodes whose subtle implications reveal larger cultural trends in the ethnic community. In particular, it examines the mutual aid society, a center of social life that immigrant workers organized as a communal institution, but that they would eventually transform into a capitalistic one.

IMMIGRANTS IN THE MEN'S CLOTHING INDUSTRY

By the first decade of the twentieth century, immigrants dominated the men's clothing industry, though the proportional representation of each ethnic group is not known. In 1911, the U.S. Bureau of Labor investigated the employment of women and children in the industry and published its findings as the second volume of the famous *Report on Condition of Woman and Child Wage-Earners in the United States.* This study covered 244 factories employing 23,683 workers in five clothing centers: New York, Chicago, Baltimore, Rochester, and Philadelphia.[1] According to the bureau's investigation, many diverse ethnic groups were represented in Chicago's men's clothing factories (see Table 1.1).

TABLE 1.1
The Factory Workforce of the Men's Clothing Industry, Classified by Ethnicity, 1911

Ethnicity	*N.Y. (%)*	*Chi. (%)*	*Balt. (%)*	*Roch. (%)*	*Phil. (%)*	*Total (%)*
American	56 (0.9)	65 (1.4)	520 (16.4)	166 (8.7)	133 (7.9)	940 (5.4)
Czech	1 (0.0)	1,193 (25.7)	64 (2.0)	0 (0.0)	0 (0.0)	1,258 (7.3)
German	286 (4.8)	398 (8.6)	467 (14.7)	681 (35.7)	146 (8.7)	1,978 (11.4)
Italian	3,062 (51.6)	507 (11.0)	338 (10.7)	305 (16.0)	783 (46.7)	4,995 (28.8)
Jewish	2,139 (36.1)	700 (15.1)	1,233 (38.9)	390 (20.5)	458 (27.3)	4,920 (28.4)
Lithuanian	75 (1.3)	108 (2.3)	287 (9.1)	0 (0.0)	45 (2.7)	515 (3.0)
Polish	111 (1.9)	1,021 (22.0)	141 (4.4)	60 (3.1)	40 (2.4)	1,373 (7.9)
Scandinavian	1 (0.0)	423 (9.1)	0 (0.0)	0 (0.0)	0 (0.0)	424 (2.5)
Other	202 (3.4)	222 (4.8)	119 (3.8)	222 (16.0)	73 (4.3)	920 (5.3)
Total	5,933 (100.0)	4,637 (100.0)	3,169 (100.0)	1,906 (100.0)	1,678 (100.0)	17,323 (100.0)

Source: U.S., Congress, Senate, *Report on Condition of Woman and Child Wage-Earners in the United States*, vol. 2: *Men's Ready-Made Clothing*, S. Doc. 645, 61st Cong., 2d sess., 1911, 45–46.

In each of the other four cities one or two groups tended to dominate: Jews and Italians in New York and Philadelphia, Jews in Baltimore, and Germans in Rochester. In Chicago, however, Czechs, almost unknown in the other centers, were the most conspicuous group, comprising about one-fourth of the total workforce studied by the bureau. Poles, more than one-fifth of all, were the next largest nationality, although only a minor factor in the other four cities. Jews, though predominant in New York, occupied only the third place in Chicago's men's clothing factories, representing 15 percent of the total workforce. Italians, meanwhile, constituted about one-tenth of the factory employees. Other ethnic groups, especially Germans and Scandinavians, were also represented in Chicago.[2]

But these figures, to a certain extent, are misleading. The factories investigated by the Bureau of Labor were large establishments, each maintaining an average workforce of ninety-seven wage earners. On the other hand, the U.S. Bureau of the Census reported that in 1909 the average men's clothing establishment in the country employed only thirty-four workers.[3] If small shops had been taken into account, Italians and Jews would have occupied higher percentages than indicated by the investigation. As new arrivals, they frequently chose to work in small shops located in their own neighborhoods and managed by their countrymen. Besides, as long as there was another choice, Orthodox Jews would not work at large factories, which did not allow them to observe the Sabbath on Saturdays. And most Italian women, especially married ones, wanted to work inside their homes finishing garments, because their cultural tradition discouraged working outside.

Immigrant men's clothing workers were mostly new arrivals. In Chicago, according to the U.S. Labor Bureau's investigation, almost two out of three female factory employees were born in Europe. Nearly all the Jews and Italians and roughly one-half of the Czechs and Poles were immigrants (see Table 1.2). These proportions would have been higher if the investigation had adequately included workers in small establishments. This was equally true of the male workers. In the factories the men were older than the women. Among the employees investigated, only 42.7 percent of all the males were younger than twenty-five, as opposed to seven out of ten female workers.[4] This age difference does not necessarily mean that the men had lived in this country longer than the women. Although male adults did tend to immigrate a few years before the females in their families, young men frequently left the men's clothing industry for other work, while young women usually stayed until marriage. In Chicago, according to the U.S. Immigration Commission's report published in 1911, one-half of the foreign-born workers employed in the clothing industry had lived in this country less than five

TABLE 1.2
Nativity of Factory Workers Employed in the Men's Clothing Industry, Females Sixteen Years and Over, Chicago, 1911

		Foreign-born		*Native-born*	
	Total	*Number*	*Percent*	*Number*	*Percent*
American	48	0	0.0	48	100.0
Czech	967	422	43.6	545	56.4
German	352	115	32.7	237	67.3
Italian	435	403	92.6	32	7.4
Jewish	451	443	98.2	8	1.8
Lithuanian	90	88	97.8	2	2.2
Polish	839	446	53.3	393	46.7
Scandinavian	399	290	72.7	109	27.3
Other	170	134	78.8	36	21.2
Total	3,703	2,341	63.2	1,362	36.8

Source: Adapted from *Woman and Child Wage-Earners*, II: 48.

years and another 23 percent less than nine years. The commission pointed out that "immigrants direct from Europe" had entered the industry.[5]

It is not clear what occupations these immigrant men's clothing workers had had in their home countries. The Immigration Commission investigated the subject but offered a questionable result. It declared that 63 percent of the 6,219 immigrant men employed in all the branches of the clothing industry had been engaged in "the manufacture of clothing" in Europe; that 13 percent had been engaged in trade and 7 percent in handicraft; and that only 8 percent had been peasants or agricultural laborers. The commission reported more surprising findings about the 1,255 immigrant women employed in this industry: The occupation of about three-fourths (75.6 percent) was "sewing, embroidering, lace-making, etc."; and only one out of ten (10.8 percent) had worked on farms.[6]

These figures seem inaccurate when the level of skill required of the men's clothing workers is taken into consideration. Those engaged in "the manufacture of clothing" in their home countries must have been skilled workers, since the clothing industry of eastern and southern Europe was still under the control of masters and journeymen. But in the United States most men's clothing workers required few skills, because the labor process was extensively deskilled. By the second decade of the century, the men's clothing industry, led by large factories, recruited predominantly unskilled labor. Perhaps the sampling of the investigation was misleading. Selecting employees for study, the Immigration Commission apparently disregarded the fact that among various branches of the industry there were great differences not only in total output and the number of employees but also in reliance upon skilled labor. Moreover, the study ignored the sizes of the establishments employing the sample workers.

There were some men's clothing workers who had learned the trade in their home countries, but they were few and they usually did not join the ranks of the factory workers, or if they did, quickly left to establish their own businesses. For example, Maria Czarnecka's father came from a small town near Cracow, a big city in Austrian Poland, where he had learned tailoring. Settling down in Chicago at the turn of the century, he opened a coat shop. When fierce competition drove him out of business after a few years, he went to work at Kuppenheimer's.[7] In 1913, when Frank Catrambone arrived in Chicago, he was a nineteen-year-old journeyman who had already quit his master tailor. His skill caught the eye of the Hart, Schaffner and Marx management and after six or eight months at one of the factories he became an all-round tailor; soon he was an instructor and then a substitute section foreman. In 1918, however, Catrambone left Hart, Schaffner and Marx in order to start a custom tailor shop for himself.[8]

Probably the majority of men's clothing workers had been peasants in eastern and southern Europe. The U.S. Immigration Commission reported that on the whole the immigrants came largely from the rural population. Among the 6,701 foreign-born male heads of households in seven American cities, according to the commission, two out of five had been engaged in farming before coming to this country. There were great differences among immigrant groups: while only a fraction of the Jews and about one-fourth of the Bohemians and Moravians had earned their livelihood from farming, more than two-fifths of the southern Italians and nearly two-thirds of the Poles belonged to the peasantry. In Chicago alone, as many as one half of the immigrants had been engaged in farming in the old country; among the Italians and Poles of the city, more than three-fifths had worked on farms; on the other hand, only one in three Czechs had lived on tillage, while most Jews had earned their livelihood from endeavors other than farming.[9]

The biographies of several men's clothing workers also indicate that, except for the Jews, most originally came from the European countryside. Zofia Kowalczyk, who arrived in the United States in 1901 and eventually settled down in Chicago and worked at a Hart, Schaffner and Marx factory, was born in a village in the part of Poland that was then under Austrian rule. Her parents had worked a small piece of land with the help of their ten children, including Zofia.[10] Eugene Pomorski was born in a town not far from Warsaw, where his father, a peasant, sent him to learn tailoring when he was twelve years old. At a shop in the city, Pomorski worked as an apprentice for three years and as an unqualified journeyman for another. After master tailors tested him for three days, Pomorski became a qualified journeyman.[11]

On the other hand, the Jewish men's clothing workers had diverse occupational backgrounds. By the end of the nineteenth century, eastern European Jews, mostly living in urban areas, engaged in trade- and handicraft-related occupations, particularly those that involved manufacture of clothing and shoes.[12] Once in America, artisans in both trades typically entered the clothing industry. Sooner or later, many became sweaters, or foremen, distinguishing themselves from the ranks of the ordinary factory workers. Jewish men's clothing workers had more previous experience in wage working than others. For example, Pearl Spencer was born in Nemirov, Ukraine, where her parents engaged in trade. Before coming to the United States and working at a tailor shop in 1907, Spencer left home when she was only twelve years old and went to Odessa, where she stayed five years, working in a tea factory.[13] Their diverse backgrounds, particularly their industrial experience, later helped Jewish workers take the initiative in the labor movement in Chicago's men's clothing industry.

COMMUNALISM IN THE OLD WORLD

As indicated by their occupational backgrounds, those who found jobs in the industry had already been exposed to urbanism and capitalism. But they were not fully adapted to the new environment. Urbanism and capitalism constituted a strange order of things, to which they had to adjust their cherished ways of life both in fundamentals and in details. Their experience in Europe may be considered the initial phase of a long-range process of acculturation that would continue, in a complicated and amplified form, once they arrived in the United States. That phase reached back to the period in which they originally built up their social relations, to the tradition that later helped them shape their social life in America. In their home towns around the turn of the century, traditional social relationships were slowly and yet distinctly disintegrating. The community, an institution that had shaped their work and lives for centuries, was in the final phase of a gradual dissolution, although communalism remained a tenacious, though decaying, tradition on which they still relied to form and maintain their social relations.

In Bohemia, Poland, and southern Italy, the village community had remained a corporate entity well into the nineteenth century. In these regions, the emancipation of the peasantry and the development of industrial capitalism, the two most important forces undermining the community in western Europe, were late in coming. Various laws enacted in the sixteenth and seventeenth centuries reinstated an earlier and more rigorous form of serfdom. The seigneurs secured servile labor, with new laws forcing peasants to remain in bondage and toil on the large estates. Statute labor enabled the seigneurs to produce and sell agricultural commodities to the rapidly growing markets of western Europe. The eastern part of the continent and southern Italy were turned into "an agrarian reserve of the increasingly industrialized West,"[14] showing hardly any progress toward industrial capitalism by the beginning of the nineteenth century. In the process, the seigneur imposed feudal obligations as a lump sum upon the village community as a unit, not as an individual assessment upon each peasant's household. The community had to divide up the seigneurial charge among its members and became responsible for its payment in behalf of each member. This practice led the villagers to maintain the community longer than elsewhere in Europe, by compelling them to resort to communal regulation and cooperation.[15]

In these regions, the village community continued to be a corporate body with a formal structure. It acted as a body in dealing both with the seigneur, who was frequently a noble holding the estate that had been cultivated by the villagers, and with the state. The community maintained institutions such as the assembly, the headman, and the council. The communal assembly was constituted of the heads of those households whose landholding was above a specified size. In many places it met only a few times a year, discussing matters such as operations in the fields, management of the common properties, and the election of community officials. In Bohemia, Moravia, Poland, and Russia, the village headman acted as an intermediary between the community and the seigneur. Counselors advised the headman and maintained the assembly's authority between sessions. In spite of this apparently inclusive structure, however, communal institutions responded directly to the influence of the seigneur and the wealthiest villagers. As a result, peasants often found themselves involved in feuds. Tradition, custom, and laws limited power and influence that could threaten communal interests. In order to protect their interests, the villagers often united against the seigneur and strictly regulated the admission of outsiders because of the limited farmland and other resources.[16]

By the late nineteenth century, however, peasants were already on the move, leaving their village communities vulnerable to disruptive forces. A series of piecemeal reforms, which the monarchies ruling these regions hesitatingly undertook in the course of the first seven decades of the century, finally freed the peasantry. The reforms essentially focused on making serfs independent proprietors by giving them the title to their holdings, while leaving mostly untouched other obligations to the seigneur, particularly labor services and miscellaneous dues. Even so, the cost was high. While the Czechs and the Poles under Austrian rule had to pay only half of the indemnification to the seigneur, the Russian Polish peasants were required to pay the entire cost or to give up three-fourths of their holdings to the landlord.[17] At any rate, the reforms opened the road to freedom for the peasantry.

Furthermore, pressure of a growing population pushed a number of peasants out of the village community. The Czech, Polish, and southern Italian population grew steadily throughout the nineteenth century. For example, the population of the entire Polish territory jumped from nine million in 1800 to twenty-nine million in 1910. Besieged by the rapidly growing number of mouths to feed in their own households, peasants repeatedly parceled out their holdings to their children, which led to a reduction in the average size of the peasant holding. By the turn of the twentieth century four-fifths of the Galician peasants had fewer than fourteen acres, giving currency to the phrase "Galician poverty." Many had become landless. In Russian Poland, peasants without land comprised more than two-fifths of the total population, which was approaching two million in 1891. Those with a tiny patch of land or none at all began to move from Galicia to Bohemia, from Russian Poland to Germany, or from southern Italy to northern Italy, seeking employment, either seasonal or permanent.[18]

There were significant regional differences, depending on industrial development. In Bohemia, where textiles, metal working, and some other industries had notably developed by the early nineteenth century, many peasants found jobs in factories. In Poland and southern Italy, however, industrial development was retarded, and most peasants tried to make a living in rural districts. Big estates needed large numbers of cultivators, since the great landlords did not invest much in agricultural machinery. Partly because the land often remained unconsolidated, which made it difficult to mechanize operations, and partly because the growth of the rural population had led to an abundance of cheap labor, landlords preferred to rely on manpower. In Prussian Poland, for example, they managed their estates by employing a few resident farm hands in addition to many migratory day laborers. In Sicily and the Kingdom of Naples, landlords usually leased their estates to intermediaries, who dealt with the actual cultivators. With the rural population expanding on the one hand and with no long-term interest in improving the estates on the other, the intermediaries divided the land into small lots to sublet to peasants who owned no land or only tiny patches. Seeking quick profits, they preferred short-term contracts with the cultivators. Otherwise, they managed the estates with the help of day laborers.[19]

In the regions where freed peasants still earned their livelihood from husbandry, village communities often survived into the twentieth century. As Donna Gabaccia has recently argued, commercial agriculture and wage earning did not establish capitalism as a way of life in Sicily. "Subsistence production rarely disappeared," she maintains, "even in areas with large estates."[20] Although the communal lands and pastures were frequently shared out by the villagers or illegally enclosed by landlords, as they were in southern Italy, the communities still held common properties in many places. In Poland these commons often remained untouched while the villagers united against the landlords trying to enclose the property. Especially in the Polish territories under the Romanovs' rule, the Russian government kept the community organization alive and brought it under official supervision so that it could protect the peasants' landholdings from the nobles' encroachment.[21]

In villages where the corporate community had already disintegrated, its cultural tradition lingered in the way peasants cultivated the land. As independent proprietors, as some were, middling and small-scale peasants lacked the capital to introduce modern farming techniques. They continued to keep their holdings scattered, with one-half or one-third lying fallow each year.[22] In a Moravian village, which Emily Greene Balch visited to prepare *Our Slavic Fellow Citizens*, published in 1910, the peasants had decided to reapportion their holdings. For that purpose they made a survey. It showed that a typical villager's land consisted of eighteen strips scattered here and there, with one divided by the railroad running through the fields. In such places communal regulation and cooperation was still as essential to husbandry as in the past. "I have counted thirty men ploughing at the same time, each working his share of the same big, unbroken field,—open," Balch reported about another village, "for each man's share is marked, not by hedge, fence or wall, but only by a furrow some thirty centimeters (or about a foot) wide, which must not be planted."[23]

Communalism turned out to be stubborn even in the rural districts where a capitalist social relationship had already begun to develop. In southern Italy, for example, industry was too underdeveloped to attract the landless peasants freed from serfdom. Except for those employed in sulphur mines, handicraft workshops, and textile factories, peasants worked on large estates, or moved about looking for seasonal employment in the countryside. Whether working on their own or for an intermediary, they cooperated with each other from seed sowing to harvesting. On Sicily's estates, day laborers tilled the soil "in rows of eight or ten, one acting as leader and urging on the others by words and by example."[24] Apparently this method of work, to a degree, relieved peasants of fatigue and boredom as, stooping over, they hoed. When reaping they also worked "in groups of up to a dozen,"[25] sharing the food served in common and paying its cost from their wages.

The example of communalism in southern Italy indicates that the peasants of the region were not "amoral familists" who pursued the interests of the nuclear family at the expense of the community. In his influential book *The Moral Basis of a Backward Society*, Edward C. Banfield argued that southern Italian peasants were following one rule: "Maximize the material, short-run advantage of the nuclear family; assume that all others will do likewise."[26] While Banfield tried to explain why southern Italy of the 1950s lagged far behind the United States in adopting such organizations as the business corporation,[27] many scholars have projected his argument back to the turn of the century. In the nineteenth century, however, the Italian concept of family included not only parents and their children but also siblings, cousins, aunts, grandparents, and others such as godparents. Rudolph M. Bell has recently argued: "[T]he phrase 'nuclear family' had no place in popular language for the very good reason that the concept it refers to is not a motivational reference point as such."[28]

In southern Italy as well as in eastern Europe, therefore, communalism persisted in the countryside. But the culture had been losing its infrastructure, even in villages where the community survived as a corporate body. The corporate community was originally based on feudal relations of property. Feudalism assured a seigneur the authority to dominate both his estate and the people living there. He gave them a tenure to small or medium-sized holdings and in return exacted labor services or appropriated the surplus produced. And the people held their land as part of his integral estate, not as separate private property, thus constituting a body of villagers subject to the seigneur. The community was also based on feudal relations of control—a concept here devised to grasp the way in which control, not ownership, of property relates people to one another. The individual holdings consisted of scattered strips that were too narrow for a peasant to work on his own without trespassing on his neighbors'. So the villagers had to coordinate individuals' access to strips as well as grazing of cattle on fallow or harvested fields. Besides, the village held and managed common properties according to its specific rules about use. Such collective control over the land, which developed into compulsory communal tillage in some places, compelled the village to function as a corporate entity.[29] But these feudal relations of property and control, though reinforced early in the modern era, began to disintegrate after the first decades of the nineteenth century.

Emancipation enabled peasants to hold private property and to exercise individual control over it, which was a development to be completed by the maturing capitalist social relationship.

In late-nineteenth-century eastern Europe and southern Italy, however, the peasants did not understand that communalism had been losing its infrastructure. While some took advantage of the changing relations of property and of control, most clung to the surviving culture. They wanted their social relations, in both the fields and their neighborhoods, to be characterized by personal acquaintance, mutual assistance, and social control.[30] Although the village community was under stress, its physical dimensions helped them preserve their traditional personal interdependence. Their world was a *campanilismo*, whose land and the people within its boundaries lay within reach of the bell of the village church. But the world was also unstable, as the villagers were increasingly drawn into national and international life over the course of the nineteenth century.

This outline applies, to some extent, to eastern European Jews, who also organized their social lives into corporate communities characterized by binding personal interdependence. But they differed from the peasant communities in that their communal life was based on nationality, religion, and economic function. Mostly traders and artisans, the Jews had long lived in a hostile world. With their own religious needs to be satisfied in a host country that was anxious to control their activities, they maintained a semi-autonomous organization called the *kahal.* It consisted of communal institutions such as a governing board and a council, which Polish Jews had developed by the fifteenth century. With a rabbi participating on the board or employed as a staff member, these institutions regulated religious matters and educational activities within the Jewish settlements. In addition, the *kahal* controlled entrance into the membership, held jurisdiction over Jewish civil matters, collected taxes for communal purposes as well as for the state, and represented the Jewish community to outsiders.[31]

Under Russian rule the Jewish communal organization was gradually integrated into the state apparatus, until its official abolition in 1844. When Russia annexed a section of partitioned Poland in the late eighteenth century, it allowed Polish Jews, now the majority of the Russian Jewry, to keep the *kahal* intact as a tax-collecting and self-governing agency. In the first two decades of the nineteenth century, however, a series of statutes curtailed the autonomy of Jewish communities by forbidding the *kahal* to impose new taxes for communal purposes and by holding the Jews subject to the Russian authorities, except in religious matters. In 1835, anxious over the faltering assimilation process of the Jewish population, the empire forced many Jews into military service for twenty-five years from the age of eighteen, instead of letting them fulfill their military duty by paying a special tax, as they had done before. New responsibility for the draft did not simply make the *kahal* an imperial servant; the Jewish community also faced serious internal conflict, with impoverished Jews accusing *kahal* officials of favoring wealthy and educated coreligionists. Finally, in 1844 the Russian government condemned the *kahal* for hindering Jews' assimilation, and abolished it, subordinating Jews to the local authorities.[32]

Official abolition of the *kahal* did not ensure the end of Jewish communal life in Russia, however. The Jewish population of the empire was approaching one million, and most Jews lived in small towns within the Pale of Settlement, a region that extended from Lithuania to the Ukraine, including Russian-held Poland. Out of the 869 Jewish settlements, only three, Berdichev, Vilna, and Minsk, had more than ten thousand Jews; there were three hundred with between one and ten thousand and 565 with no more than one thousand. In these small settlements communal life was intimately organized around Judaism because the religion pervaded and guided every detail of Jewish life. As the house of prayer and study, the synagogue served as the center of the settlement, where the Jews discussed fund raising for relief, their relationship with the Russian authorities, or other common concerns. The whole settlement took pains to give an elementary education to every male child so that he could understand the Talmud and the Bible, while a rabbi performed ceremonies at births, marriages, and burials, and passed judgments on religious practices. In each settlement there were a number of voluntary associations called *hevras*. They were committed to studying the Law and running the synagogue, as well as pursuing charitable, educational, or other specific purposes. Some, such as the burial society and the tailors' association, were essentially guilds holding monopoly over certain crafts. The *hevras* survived the *kahal*, which had supervised their activities until its abolition in 1844, and kept the Jewish population organized in small and intimate circles.[33]

Communalism survived the demise of the corporate community. Jewish settlements retained a strong tradition of mutual assistance and social control. Believing that good works earned credits in heaven, the Jews kept round tin boxes in their homes, into which they dropped coins for the poor, old, or infirm. Probably the discriminatory environment encouraged the Jews to organize a number of *hevras* for charitable purposes and to provide for the least fortunate among their chronically impoverished population. However, the highest form of charity was money loaned to enable someone to make a living. As the population was largely engaged in trade and handicraft, loans were particularly effective in helping able-bodied persons temporarily in need. Besides relatives, friends, and neighbors ready to lend money, there were short-term loan associations that advanced community funds without interest. And the Jewish settlements also made sure that individuals complied with accepted behavioral norms. Like the peasants' village communities, the Jews resorted to social ostracism, censure, and gossip as punishments. In addition, communal institutions exercised sanctions against those who threatened their customs. Although the settlements lacked the official machinery to enforce the decisions of their institutions, they could always threaten excommunication as the ultimate tool of sanctioning power.[34]

Urbanism and industrial capitalism disrupted Jewish communal life as, in the latter half of the nineteenth century, eastern European Jews streamed into cities. The Jewish population, both urban and rural, steadily increased throughout the century. But their role as middlemen between the lords and the peasants declined after the 1861 emancipation of the serfs, and the Russian government drove them out of the villages, taking discriminatory measures that culminated in the infamous May Laws of 1882. Within the Pale, one-half of the 4.9 million Jews lived in cities by 1897, as compared to only 15 percent of the region's total population of nearly 126 million. Jews occupied more than 40 percent of the Pale's urban population. In the Russian northwest region alone, for example, seven cities had more than twenty thousand Jewish inhabitants, Minsk leading with 47,562. In the Polish territory under Russian rule, Lodz had nearly 100,000 Jews in 1897, and Warsaw 219,141 in 1891.

In such cities with expanding Jewish populations, Jewish artisans no longer belonged to as cohesive a *hevra* as before. Master tradesmen frequently turned their shops into factories, engaging in the production of commodities instead of dealing with individual customers. They forced journeymen and apprentices to work for meager wages in wretched conditions, leading their employees to rebel despite the well-known paternalistic relations in the Jewish shop. In addition, a growing number of young Jews without skills were hired in large factories that made hosiery, leather goods, brushes, cigarettes, and matches. These factory workers, in cooperation with socialist intellectuals, carried on waves of strikes against their coreligionist employers around the turn of the century. "Class struggle in the Pale," as a historian put it, the strike movement was a wedge into Jewish unity, which both the workers and the employers still valued.[35]

CALL FOR THE ETHNIC COMMUNITY

Exposed as they had been to urbanism and capitalism, immigrants referred back to their cherished traditions while endeavoring to settle in

Chicago. When they began to arrive en masse in the late nineteenth century, the city was already the second largest in the United States, with a population of one million dividing its neighborhoods along lines of power, wealth, and status. Such a defined structure channeled immigrant workers into certain districts. While middle-class citizens often occupied substantial houses in nearby suburbs, working people attempted to find apartments close to the Loop, the central business district with its offices, stores, and factories.[36] The West Side, fanning out both north and south from the Loop, attracted the majority of immigrants from eastern and southern Europe. By the early twentieth century, Czechs, Poles, southern Italians, and eastern European Jews had established their own enclaves in that area. No immigrant group monopolized any of the enclaves. While sharing with other nationalities, however, each group tended to concentrate in certain sections and set the tone there. The enclaves provided immigrants with favorable conditions in which they could recreate their communal traditions; despite the physically deteriorating environment that compelled many of them to leave at the first opportunity, high population density facilitated frequent and close social contact within their own groups.[37]

Sixteen thousand Czechs, immigrant or American-born, settled chiefly on the Southwest Side. They flocked together in Pilsen, a district shaped along Blue Island Avenue between Halsted Street and Ashland Avenue (see Map 1.1). Czechs became conspicuous in the district after the Great Fire of 1871, with their own churches, schools, gymnasiums, and meeting halls. Around the turn of the century, however, new arrivals from Russia, Poland, and Italy drove many of them farther to the west. Czechs carved out a new enclave between California Avenue and the western boundary of the city. Known as "Czech California," it contained the same ethnic institutions as the old Pilsen, but the Czech population was less predominant, dispersed over a much wider area. Most Czech men's clothing workers lived in the Pilsen or California districts. Czech contractors often moved along with their countryfolk; manufacturers, while increasingly building new factories in downtown Chicago, still retained their old establishments on the Southwest Side, particularly in Pilsen, where they could tap the cheap labor of recent immigrants in addition to experienced Czech hands.[38]

To the north of Pilsen was a large and crowded Jewish enclave that centered around the neighborhood of Jefferson and Maxwell Streets. This Near West Side ghetto, formed after the 1871 fire, was the first settlement for most of the estimated fifty thousand eastern European Jews who came to Chicago during the last decades of the nineteenth century; the others established themselves mainly on the Northwest Side. In the district bounded by Polk and Sixteenth Streets but extending from Canal

Street beyond Ashland Avenue, they frequented synagogues and Hebrew schools and patronized Yiddish newspapers and theaters. Before moving westward, chiefly to North Lawndale, starting in the second decade of the new century, most Jewish men's clothing workers lived in the ghetto; some chose to work at nearby sweatshops that allowed them to observe the Sabbath on Saturdays, while others found higher-paying jobs at factories on the West Side or in the Loop. The industry was dominated by their coreligionists from Germany, such as the Hart brothers of Hart, Schaffner and Marx, Bernard Kuppenheimer, and Julius Rosenwald, who had come to the United States in the mid-nineteenth century. But those from eastern Europe, most of whom abided by Orthodox Judaism, resented the German Jews' Reformist and gentile-like world.[39]

The Poles, numbering twenty-one thousand in 1910, settled in five districts, with one-half living on the Northwest Side. St. Stanislaus Kostka, the first Polish Catholic church, established a few blocks away from Milwaukee Avenue and Division Street in 1867, attracted immigrant Poles over the next four decades. The enclave was called Polonia, with prosperous small businesses, newspapers, and fraternal organizations providing for ethnic needs. Most Polish men's clothing workers lived in this settlement. There, Polish contractors replaced their German predecessors, and manufacturers established large factories, beginning at the turn of the century. St. Adalbert's Parish, another enclave roughly overlapping Pilsen, also had a number of men's clothing workers. The other Polish settlements, two on the South Side and one in South Chicago, were occupied mainly by those who worked in the stockyards or steel mills.[40]

Most southern Italians made inroads into either the Near West Side Jewish ghetto or the Northwest Side Polish enclave. Their countryfolk from northern Italy originally preferred the Loop, but moved west of the Chicago River, driven out by rapidly expanding business establishments in the city's inner core; many southern Italians followed, settling in the vicinity of Hull House. And a small northern Italian settlement on the Near North Side attracted southern Italians, who also infiltrated the Polish enclave across the north branch of the river toward the end of the nineteenth century. Latecomers encroaching on established enclaves from their peripheries, southern Italians failed to numerically dominate either settlement before World War I, but they did build ethnic institutions in each of the two districts. The settlements included most of Chicago's Italian men's clothing workers—not to mention home finishers—who were employed at Jewish or Polish contract shops or at factories on either side of the river.[41]

In all of these enclaves, personal interdependence was a binding element. Above all, acquaintance carried over from the old country weighed heavily among the immigrants, who found consolation and companionship among familiar faces. For example, eastern European Jews living in the same neighborhood used to get together whenever a *landsman*, a countryman from their hometown or province, arrived from Europe. Pearl Spencer, who later worked at a men's clothing factory in Chicago, met her future husband William that way. He was from Nemirov, the same Ukrainian town where Pearl was born. When fourteen years old, William had gone to Lodz, Poland, but eventually came to Chicago in order to avoid service in the Russian army. By the time Pearl arrived, he was already living in the neighborhood where her father had settled. On their way home from the station Pearl and her father saw William and invited him to come over in the evening. "It's the custom if you brought over somebody from Europe . . . you invited your country people to come and meet them," Pearl Spencer recalled, "because they wanted to have regards, did they see somebody from home, how was life there." She added: "Naturally in the evening my father called some other people and he made a little party and that way we [Pearl and William] met."[42]

The Old World tradition of communal social control was also alive in the ethnic neighborhoods. When someone deviated from the moral standards held in general by their group, immigrants would resort to gossip, social proscription, and even face-to-face censure, as they had in their native villages or towns. In the late 1910s an immigrant woman wrote in her reminiscences how such control worked in a circle of Czech youths. Shortly after coming to Chicago, she met young boys and girls from her hometown and its vicinity. Some twenty people gathered every Sunday to play games, sing songs, dance, and the like. In 1916 they organized an all-Czech club and their number continued to grow. Then they were joined by a second-generation Czech girl who not only "dressed in a very extreme and cheap, untasteful manner," but also "flirted, laughed ostentatiously and continuously chewed gum." One Sunday, at a party, the girl "flirted with a young man" and both had a good time, dancing together and going out for a walk. After a while a member reported that the couple "were kissing and embracing each other in the back yard." This apparently was too much for the Czech immigrants. "When the girl came in," recorded the writer of the reminiscences, "one of the old ladies told her that her behavior was ridiculous and that the members will not stand for anything like that." Then the writer noted: "She never appeared at the club again and the guilty man was ignored and disliked by all the girls."[43]

Immigrants also provided mutual assistance for those countryfolk in need. A death, sickness, or accident summoned the traditions of communal life. Mostly non-Protestants and aware that American missionaries sought to make converts by offering charity, immigrants established a number of charitable institutions for their own ethnic groups. However, unorganized help in their neighborhoods was more immediate and supportive, both materially and emotionally. Bertha Adamik, a Chicago-born tailor of Russian Polish parentage, had an indelible memory of this tradition. In 1907, when she was seven years old, her father, a factory worker, fell off the porch of the family's second-floor apartment and died, leaving his wife and six children destitute. Soon, people came to visit them and "helped out to bury him." A butcher gave them "odds and ends like lunch meat," bakers "day-old bread," and someone bought for Bertha Adamik "a pair of pretty slippers," which she would shine with a handkerchief.[44] The Italians, though they did not organize as many charity societies as other ethnic groups, were also active in neighborhood relief. Alfred Fantozzi, who came to the United States during the 1890s and worked at McCormick Works of Chicago, remembered how his countrymen helped each other in the neighborhood:

> [I]f somebody was down and out and [in] real bad shape, usually a few friends got together and made a collection for 'em, you might say. And they'd go around from house to house and solicit gifts or money preferred. And the family would give them fifty cents or a dollar. Maybe they'd get fifty or sixty dollars together and donate it to 'em to help 'em out. But it wasn't . . . an organized thing. It was just a friendly thing.[45]

Finally, ethnic leaders frequently appealed to the idea of community. Around the turn of the century, national consciousness was visibly developing among immigrants. In Europe, nationalism was growing, evident in independence movements among Czechs, Jews, and Poles, and in organized attempts to integrate the culturally diverse Italian population. In the United States, where a racial hierarchy was firmly and obviously established, these immigrants were believed to belong to distinct races and to form different nationality groups according to their shared languages and other cultural traits.[46] At the same time, they endeavored to reach beyond their provincial world. In order to secure jobs or satisfy social needs in this mobile and strange land, even those who intended to return home soon took pains to deploy personal networks rooted in kinship and neighborhood. Immigrants supported churches, synagogues, newspapers, and other ethnic institutions, often taking part in community-wide feasts organized by their own nationality. Yet they yearned for an organic form of social life like the corporate community in Europe, whose importance was stressed by their leaders.

This tendency to refer back to Old World order was particularly evident among Jews. They often compared Chicago with their home towns. Roughly twenty-five thousand Jews lived in Kovno, the capital of

Lithuania. In the early 1920s, this community maintained fifteen Jewish public schools as well as three *yeshivas* (Orthodox Jewish academies) and one rabbinical seminary, leaving the Chicago Jewry, with a population ten times as large, far behind. Conceding that there were various explanations for the contrast, the Orthodox *Daily Jewish Courier* stressed, "Then, of course, we must take into consideration that the Kovno Jews are communally organized, while the Chicago Jews are not."[47] Leaders of the Chicago Jewry often preached that in addition to synagogues, charity organizations, and other institutions, Jews should establish "a central authority to control the whole Jewish community life," as they had done in Europe.[48]

It was but a dream. The call for community in itself contradicted the reality that in America there was no corporate communal control over the individual. This was obvious when the New World was compared with the Old. "A community is helpless when it has no control over the actions of the individual," declared the *Courier*, "and since the Orthodox Jewish community of Chicago has no control over the Jewish individual even in matters affecting the fundamental laws of the Jewish religion, it is helpless, and as such cannot do anything that is constructive in nature."[49] Therefore, the new ethnic community was different in kind from that which immigrants had experienced in Europe. It was based upon their voluntary participation, not upon compulsory regulations and unavoidable cooperation dictated by economic or national necessity. Also, in America their communities were open-ended, admitting into membership any number of countryfolk, while Czech, Polish, and southern Italian villagers restricted admission of outsiders because the limited communal resources were at stake. Moreover, the ethnic community was not a corporate entity, as European villages and Jewish settlements had once been and still were in those places where there was communal property to manage.

The issue of the ethnic community involves an overarching interpretation of American immigration history. Specialists in this field, criticizing Oscar Handlin's pathbreaking study *The Uprooted*, have recently stressed that immigrants brought with them networks of kinship and acquaintances, traditional ways of living and thinking, and religious practices and institutions.[50] Such historians have also claimed that the Old World traditions turned into human and cultural resources to which immigrants resorted in their efforts to adjust to life in America. Synthesizing revisionist studies in his book *The Transplanted*, John Bodnar argues that capitalist development in Europe constituted a push factor that was more powerful than the pulling force of American industrial growth. The point is that immigrants had already been exposed to capitalist social relationships before arriving in the United States and that they were "willing to accept the wage economy."[51] This argument meshes with Daniel Rodgers's appropriate admonition that historians, when explaining immigrants' acculturation in industrial America, be cautious about the tradition-modernity polarity. Current revisionist studies appear to substitute an evolutionary model for Handlin's dramatic picture of immigration. The model is obvious, for example, in Ewa Morawska's richly detailed study on east central European immigrants. She claims that in the Old World peasants had already begun adopting a "market attitude," incipient economic behavior that became full-grown in America.[52]

However, the revisionist model tends to gloss over the disturbing experiences involved in acculturation, a long-range process reaching back to the period in which immigrants had been brought up in their home towns. This point emerges clearly when their native traditions are contrasted with the customs of the host society to which they had to adjust.[53] No doubt, tradition kept changing in Europe as well as in America; its invention is a process in which people continue to read new meanings from the past and try to reshape the present according to their reading.[54] The corporate community of Europe had been disintegrating, and its members becoming increasingly enmeshed in the capitalist world economy.[55] And yet they belonged to "the reserve army of capitalism."[56] Their everyday life still remained on the margin of capitalism; as Fernand Braudel argues in *Civilization and Capitalism*, they led their "material life"—production, consumption, and barter of goods and services to satisfy material needs—primarily outside the marketplace.[57] The immigrants did not fully adapt themselves to "market culture," which, according to William Reddy, developed much later even in advanced countries such as France.[58] In fact, they had been imbued with communalism in different forms and stages. On the other hand, American cities, undergoing rapid and expansive growth and attracting immigrants from overseas and migrants from the American countryside, ripened as capitalist markets. The cities composed the world of commodities, where everything, including labor power, tends to be commodified and everybody is treated as an individual seller and buyer. This world was what middle-class people had already recognized as a "conglomeration of detached individuals" in mid-nineteenth century Oneida County, New York.[59] The center of capitalism, dominated by private property and individual control, was barren soil for a community based chiefly on the integral estate and collective control. Immigrants around the turn of the century found themselves moving from the margins of capitalism into its center, suddenly plunged into the midst of a strange new world.

This movement amplified the process of their acculturation to urbanism and capitalism, which had already begun in Europe. This amplified process, also complicated by differences in language, beliefs, and customs, created disconcerting experiences when immigrants found money pervading their family lives. While in Europe few had had a chance to handle money, except to pay taxes to the state or rent and dues to the landlords,[60] in America the immigrants found almost every aspect of their lives touched by "the almighty dollar." Many were concerned about the threat that they felt money posed to the family. For instance, the Polish daily *Dziennik Chicagoski* voiced the fear that money encroached on familial relations. In an editorial titled "Our Materialism in America," published in 1892, the newspaper pronounced, "The desire for bettering one's condition in America, which has caused our brothers to emigrate from their homeland, has here developed into a feverish desire for gold." This "materialism" created "a slave of money" and hindered Polish nationalist causes, according to the editorial. Even worse, it stressed, "This materialism even destroys the family ties amongst us." While parents were delighted that their young children began to "work and pay 'board,'" they were warned, "You have gained a 'boarder' but have lost a child." The money children paid would take away love and respect for their parents, because each child had already become "an independent boarder." "The laxity of family ties leads these families and an entire nation to moral, financial, and political degradation," the newspaper bewailed, since "a family of that type is not a family [living] in accordance with the Divine will, but merely a 'boarding-house.'"[61]

The amplified process of acculturation also had a troublesome impact when immigrants were faced with accelerating commodification. This was the case in religion, a traditional guardian against the greed and egoism rampant in the market. The Jewish *Courier* called attention to the fact that on its advertising pages Jews offered themselves as circumcisers or marriage performers. This was a disgusting business.

> In no Jewish newspaper in Russia, Poland, Galicia, Rumania and Palestine, are there to be found such religious advertisements as are found in the Jewish newspapers in America, because in Eastern Europe and Palestine, where Jewish life pulsates strongly, the Jewish religion is not a business, circumcision is not a business, performing the matrimonial ceremony is not a business, and the burial of the dead is certainly not a business. Only here in America the Jewish religion is a business—and from birth until death the religious Jew is persecuted by the businessmen: circumcision has become a business, burial has become a business and even the prayer for the dead is now a business.[62]

While Judaism was "systematically commercialized," the *Courier* continued to deplore, "the leaders of the Kehilah [a community organization that dealt with charities and other communal affairs], as it seems, are already accustomed to this industrialization of the Jewish religion in America, and are not bothered by it any more."

How immigrants adjusted their social relationships to the world of commodities is, then, a significant question. Revisionist historians have explored the social networks transplanted from Europe and community-building efforts in America. Usually assuming that the ethnic community resembled the one to which immigrants had once belonged in Europe, however, these historians have been less interested in the means by which they rearranged their social relations while they endeavored to recreate their cherished traditions. Acculturation was also a collective process, which involved efforts to reconcile their changing social paradigms to the advanced capitalist culture. Although findings by revisionists have greatly enriched American social history, there still remain interesting questions, such as what problems immigrants faced while trying to recreate communalism, how they rearranged their old ways of social life, or how different their social life was in America.

These questions require a set of conceptual tools. As immigrants were adapting themselves to the workplace within the wage system, they also had to readjust their social relations in the community. They applied a different kind of social medium. Whereas in the corporate community men and women developed their extra-kinship networks chiefly by bartering labor or the products of labor, the world of commodities limited their opportunities to rely upon that medium of the field. Above all, immigrants who had lent a helping hand to a neighboring peasant confined to his bed found it impossible to go forth on behalf of a sick neighbor and work at his factory. Furthermore, foodstuffs, clothing, and other goods and services necessary to everyday life, which in Europe they had produced, consumed, and shared with their neighbors, were increasingly becoming commodities in American cities. In *Middletown*, the Lynds observed that since the 1890s more and more people bought baker's bread, commercially canned goods, and ready-made garments, and had them professionally mended or cleaned. These sociologists noted the increasing importance of money in everyday life.[63] With the medium of the field less and less effective in the world of commodities, immigrants needed more than that in order to form and retain their extra-kinship networks. In their social relations in America, they increasingly had to resort to money, the medium of the market that saturates the world of commodities. To a certain extent, this was true even of Jews, who as a group had had considerable experience handling money because of their traditional economic role; there had been no interest charged for the small loans made by synagogue associations,[64] which meant that money had not been treated as a marketable commodity within the Old World Jewish community. In the world of commodities, however, it became such a commodity. Once money was available within the ethnic community, it permeated social relationships, extending the cash nexus beyond the marketplace and the workplace.[65]

There is no simple set of sources that reveal the process through which immigrants rearranged their social relationships within the cash nexus; the process of adaptation and rearrangement was a matter related to such trifling details of everyday life, and dealt with in such a piecemeal manner, that the immigrants seldom, if ever, articulated their thoughts about it. Still, there is a window through which one can look into the process: The mutual aid society. A center of social life in the ethnic community, this society allows a glimpse at how immigrants dealt with the cash nexus and readjusted their communal traditions to the world of commodities. The society was essentially a voluntary association designed to cope with hazards rooted in capitalist social relationships, and thus a transmutable institution in accordance with the development of these relationships in the United States.

COMMUNALISM IN THE WORLD OF COMMODITIES

Mutual aid societies prospered in the ethnic communities around the turn of the century. Immigrants frequently banded together in mutual aid societies in order to take care of one another when any of them were in trouble because of death, sickness, or accidents. The societies proliferated in Italian and Jewish settlements of Providence, Rhode Island in the early twentieth century.[66] In Chicago, there were 313 such associations, according to Jacub Horak's study in the 1919 report of the Illinois Health Insurance Commission (IHIC) (see Table 1.3).

TABLE 1.3
Independent Mutual Aid Societies in Chicago, 1919

Ethnicity	*Societies estimated*	*Societies studied*	*Members studied*
Czech	91	58	3,012
Italian	80	33	3,569
Jewish	14	4	801
Polish	3	2	2,810
Other	125	64	10,832
Total	313	161	21,024

Source: Adapted from Jacub Horak, "Foreign Benefit Societies in Chicago," Illinois, Health Insurance Commission, *Report*, 1919, 523–531.

In fact, there were many more than the report indicates. Mutual aid societies were unstable. One-half of those studied by Horak had fewer than 100 members and another one-fourth between one hundred and two hundred, with a typical society consisting of about 130 members.[67] Smaller ones frequently became insolvent, disappearing as soon as they were created, so that it was never known exactly how many were in existence at any time. In 1915 there were about five hundred Czech societies in the city, either independent or affiliated with fraternal orders. Jews called such a society the *landsmanshaft*, a club organized by countryfolk from the same town or province in the old country. After World War I, there were about two hundred *landsmanshafts* in Chicago. The Poles of the city also organized mutual aid societies, which numbered about 750 in 1913, according to a Polish newspaper.[68] The Italians in Chicago had organized four hundred societies by 1912, though their consul reported there were only ten.[69]

These numbers probably included most of the city's lodges of fraternal orders, American or ethnic. Immigrants forming a society often joined an American fraternal order and constituted one of its lodges, or broke away as a group. An all-Italian lodge of the Woodsmen of the World appeared as its Illinois Camp No. 125 in 1907, and Chicago's first Italian lodge of the order followed several years later.[70] In these years, the Czechs who belonged to Lawndale Lodge No. 2034, Modern Brotherhood of America, withdrew from the order and associated with the Czech-American Foresters, while other Czech societies planned to depart from the Tribe of Ben Hur.[71] And fraternal orders established by ethnic groups were often less a hierarchy of lodges than a federation of mutual aid societies: The Polish Roman Catholic Union consisted of numerous bodies that remained so autonomous that they retained their own names, such as the Holy Trinity Society of St. Stanislaus Kostka Parish.[72] Even lodges affiliated with hierarchical ethnic orders enjoyed considerable autonomy, except in conducting rituals and financial matters. Poles belonging to the Polish National Alliance celebrated the anniversaries of their own lodges, and Chicago's four thousand Jewish members of the Workmen's Circle preferred to remain in tiny branches consisting of thirty to forty members rather than unite in a dozen large ones.[73]

With fraternal orders included, therefore, mutual assistance was extensively organized in the immigrant settlements. Indeed, Ernest Burgess, the sociologist who participated in the 1919 IHIC study, took into account fraternal orders in his survey contained there. According to this survey of insurance against accident, sickness, or death in more than three thousand Chicago's working-class families, three in four male household heads had their lives insured in some way (see Table 1.4).

TABLE 1.4
Life Insurance among Male Heads of
Working-Class Families of Chicago, 1919

Ethnicity of male heads of family	*Total no. of male heads of families*	*Kinds of insurance of male heads of working-class families*					
		Total no. insured	*Ordinary life*	*Industrial*	*Fraternal*	*Labor union*	*Other**
All families	2,756	2,022	240	607	1,071	122	58
U.S., white	577	462	92	161	189	47	6
U.S., black	229	200	5	140	28	3	27
Czech	218	174	11	45	106	7	2
German	206	147	28	47	69	7	2
Irish	102	84	10	26	55	4	3
Italian	199	88	2	18	42	2	2
Jewish	203	124	28	12	82	12	—
Lithuanian	111	71	1	9	80	1	—
Polish	503	391	23	73	264	16	12
Scandinavian	198	143	27	32	97	11	—
Other	210	138	13	44	59	12	4

*Independent mutual aid societies

Source: Adapted from Table 18 in Ernest W. Burgess, "A Study of Wage-Earning Families in Chicago," Illinois, Health Insurance Commission, *Report*, 1919, 179–317.

Among the 2,756 male heads of families covered by the survey, almost two out of five relied on fraternal orders (38.9 percent) and a fraction on mutual aid societies (2.1 percent), while fewer than one in ten held a policy with a regular life insurance company (8.7 percent). There were noteworthy differences by nationality. The proportion of fraternal members among the working male heads of families was very high among Poles (52.5 percent) and Czechs (48.6 percent). But it was average among Jews (40.4 percent) and lowest among Italians (21.1 percent). Jews could count on the still-viable tradition of communal assistance, particularly loan associations and various charitable institutions.[74] Chicago's Italians were relatively small in number, which accounted for their weak organizational basis, an obstacle that they tried to overcome in the 1920s.[75] Most of them had yet to establish a foothold in the United States and had been unable to save any money for a rainy day, as Burgess suggested in the survey. Many might have preferred small and unstable mutual aid societies, which were disproportionately under-represented in his survey.

Immigrants formed mutual aid societies for various reasons. There were obviously social needs to be satisfied, above all longing for congeniality. Barriers of language and customs restricted their contact with other nationalities. Even after learning to speak English, they found it difficult to express themselves well and to understand their friends from other corners of the world. Immigrants mingled with their countryfolk, finding it more secure and enjoyable to be among their own flock. Discussing the purpose of Polish societies, a Pole attributed their formation to a "lack of congenial social contact" in America. "Italians, Hungarians, Germans and other foreign groups were obliged to form societies and clubs of their own," this journalist added, "where they feel united and free from any outside influence, and where they can feel at home, express their thoughts in their own language, and enjoy their native traditions."[76]

Mutual aid societies amply provided such social contact according to diverse lines of affinity. There were societies based on trades within particular ethnic groups, such as the Educational Society of Czech Foundrymen in Chicago, the Polish Bakers' and Confectioners' Fraternal Benefit Society of Chicago, and Italian Barbers of Chicago.[77] Others were based on the church; Poles in particular preferred the church societies, most affiliated with the Polish Roman Catholic Union and some associated with an apparently independent Order of Foresters, as did many Italians, who formed, for instance, the Society of Mary and Jesus.[78] Still other societies were formed by countrymen or countrywomen who had come from the same village, town, or area in the Old World. This was the case not only with the *landsmanshafts* such as the Telzer Aid Society, comprising Jews from Telz, Russia, or the Kurlander Aid Society established by Jews from Riga and its vicinity;[79] Poles and Italians adopted the same organizing method, as evidenced by the Wielko Polanin Society, which was tied to greater Poznan, and the Arizi Society for Mutual Assistance, formed by people from Arizi, Italy.[80] In fact this method apparently was a favorite among many lodges affiliated with the large-scale fraternal orders that were open to anyone belonging to a specific national group. Hence, "among the Italians in the United States the desire to form mutual benefit societies turned into a veritable mania," observed an Italian journalist in the late 1920s, "which found a very fertile soil in the so-called 'campanilismo,' a form of chauvinistic attachment to the native village. . . ."[81]

The mutual aid society functioned as a social mechanism for its membership. It afforded immigrants a sociable world. It comprised a number of leadership positions to be filled by its members. There were officers such as presidents, vice-presidents, treasurers, financial secretaries, recording secretaries, and marshals. The society also had a board of trustees, a membership committee, and, if necessary, one or more committees in charge of visiting sick members or taking care of funerals.[82] Sometimes, particularly when the election of officers took place, the society became a battlefield among diverse factions led by the contenders. Despite its formal structure, it was a voluntary association oriented toward social contact. It usually organized a gathering in which the members talked about the old country, friends, and jobs over a game of cards, such as pinochle. A Czech society even declared in its constitution: "The purpose of this society is to promote brotherhood, social entertainment, mother tongue, and to strengthen the mind by education." In order to prevent disputes among Free Thinkers, Catholics, socialists, and nationalists, the society quickly added, "Political and religious discussions are entirely excluded."[83] In the mutual aid society, therefore, there was not much room for those arrogant and selfish leaders who, Rudolph J. Vecoli claims, were "presiding despotically over the meetings, marching in full regalia at the head of the society, and gaining economic and political advantage through their influence over the members."[84]

There was another reason many immigrants joined the mutual aid society: concern about funerals. The funeral ceremony was of special importance, because it was not only the rite of entrance into the next world but also the final consolation for the soul troubled in a strange land. Immigrants wished to be buried properly among their kin and familiar countryfolk, not in unhallowed ground among strangers.[85] Moreover, a funeral's cost was too heavy a burden for a working-class family. It was especially high when the deceased and the surviving family preferred an elaborate ceremony. After the funeral of his brother who died from an accident at a foundry, a Pole wrote to his family in the home country: "But I beg you, dear parents, don't weep and don't grieve, God willed it so and did it so. . . . He was buried beautifully. His funeral cost $225, the casket $60."[86]

Above all, economic insecurity compelled immigrants to form mutual aid societies. Oscar Handlin has stressed that the major impetus behind the societies was provision for the funeral,[87] but this assertion does not fit the harsh reality of living, which drove immigrants to do away with extravagances; the final ceremony indeed depended on economic security. John Bodnar depicts the mutual aid society as an ethnic middle-class institution.[88] Businessmen, doctors, and lawyers joined mutual aid societies, and they appeared to assume leadership roles when the societies were integrated into national fraternal orders, chiefly after World War I. But their leadership did not determine the general nature of the societies. Initially, workers, particularly skilled ones, had been usually the founders of these societies. And before the war, the majority of the membership had consisted of workers earning wages at the factory or engaged in peddling, ragpicking, organ grinding, and other occupations of a casual nature. Industrial capitalism made them wage earners but did not assure their families of uninterrupted income. A fatal or disabling accident, an employer's whim, or unforeseeable changes in the business cycle made their economic positions precarious. When a gas explosion in a Colorado coal mine claimed a number of workers' lives in 1910, the Polish National Alliance, paying $13,400 as death benefits, stressed: "The life of a worker is fragile; he is under constant fire, like a soldier at war. The life of a miner, however, is even more uncertain than that of others. He might be compared to a soldier in the front line, nearest to the enemy."[89] In June, 1877, *Hlas*, the Czech newspaper in St. Louis, published an article advocating the merger of independent mutual aid societies, noting that the societies helped working people at times of sickness or death, when labor unions were of no use to them.[90]

Immigrants felt all the more insecure because they had previously lived in the tradition of communal life, which sharply contrasted with the economic individualism dictated by capitalism. In the old country a peasant, when ill, could rely not only upon his own household but also upon other villagers' help. After he died, his family could keep making a livelihood, even though scant, from his patch of land, a transferable resource. Jewish artisans and traders had helped each other within a small circle based on their occupations, and the local Jewish community had taken pains to protect its population against misfortune. But in the United States immigrants were on their own. If they were dead or unable to work, their kin or countryfolk could not help their family earn a livelihood from the job they had held at a factory; nor did casual laborers, whether self-employed or not, have a stable source of income that could be secured with others' help.

To the immigrant workers coming from the communal society, therefore, economic insecurity in the world of commodities was particularly serious and often traumatic, leading them to seek collective protection. Bertha Adamik learned from experience how distressing it was for an immigrant family to be confronted with a breadwinner's misfortune. When her father, a factory worker, died after falling off the porch, his corpse was laid out at the family's apartment. Although only seven years old at that time, according to her recollection, she sat by the casket and watched the people coming to view the dead and console the living. At that moment, Bertha Adamik remembers, "first I thought, 'Oh, my God, what are we gonna do? He's not here, he won't be here. Who is gonna give us any money for living?'"[91] A Czech newspaper referred to exactly this kind of experience in its column titled "From Our Societies." It pressed the point that "a man must be well prepared for the vicissitudes of life," by arguing:

> If a man has a fortune, and a panic is not expected, then his child may not have to work. How many so situated are there among us? And how many who are just able to support their families decently, but who are not in a position to acquire a house, and own their own house? If not enough is left, the children frequently become beggars or vagrants.[92]

In fact, mutual aid societies were more concerned with economic security than with an elaborate ceremony itself. Out of the 161 mutual aid societies studied by Jacub Horak in the IHIC report, more than three-fourths provided death benefits, very often along with funeral coverage (see Table 1.5). This indicates that death benefits were intended to relieve the dead member's family of the inevitable pains involved in planning a new life. It is probably this essential feature that led Ernest Burgess to take into account fraternal orders in his 1919 survey of insurance among Chicago's working-class families. A Polish worker, identified as N. N., is a case in point. Having lived in America for twenty-two years, this immigrant died in an elevator accident in 1912 and left nothing for his wife and seven children but a small house with a mortgage of $300. They held a beautiful funeral with "the hearse and four white horses, casket for $120 covered with several high priced wreaths." A few days after the ceremony, the society to which the dead worker had belonged paid the widow a $1,000 death benefit. "For this amount the deceased was insured; very often he told his wife that in case of his death, she could pay off the mortgage and use the balance for the support of the children," related a reporter. "But the widow spent for her

TABLE 1.5
Benefits Provided by Mutual Aid Societies of Chicago, 1919

	Societies studied	*Death*	*Funeral*	*Sickness & accident*	*Medical care*
Czech	58	41	40	15	0
Italian	33	25	16	28	11
Jewish	4	3	2	2	0
Polish	3	0	1	1	0
Other	64	56	38	48	8
Total	161	125	97	94	19

Source: Adapted from Horak, "Foreign Benefit Societies," 524.

husband's funeral about $700, and with the $300 she paid off the mortgage," the writer pointed out, "but for living expenses for herself and the children there was nothing left." She remarried in four weeks.[93]

Obviously, the sickness and accident benefits, offered by almost three-fifths of the 161 societies, provided some economic security. Although a few societies paid the accident benefit alone, most covered both sickness and accident, industrial or nonindustrial. The amount did not usually exceed $5 a week, and the benefit period ranged from six to twenty-six weeks. After that a number of societies continued to pay the benefit at a reduced rate. And a handful of societies even provided for medical care[94] (see Table 1.5). All these benefits reflect the concern immigrants felt about their inability to earn a livelihood in the case of sickness or accident.

In order to protect against economic insecurity, mutual aid societies offered various amounts in death benefits. According to Horak's study in the IHIC report, the amount of death benefits, though much larger than any other benefits, was modest; in 1917 the 161 societies paid $36,308.73 on 250 claims in all, with a typical payment consisting of $145.[95] Again, the study is misleading. Burgess's survey, included in the same report, shows that the average amount of fraternal insurance was $769.16 for all male household heads. There were considerable differences by nationality. While the amount was high among Italians ($928.64), who perhaps belonged to the well-off segment of that nationality, and among Czechs ($864.62), it was low among Poles ($672.38), and very low among Jews ($409.38).[96] The discrepancies between the two studies were chiefly due to their different subjects; Horak concentrated on small societies, while Burgess dealt with large orders. The societies that Horak conceived of as independent of fraternal orders apparently offered smaller amounts. While self-reliant *landsmanshafts* such as Telzer or Kurlander paid $100 to $200 as their death benefit, large orders, such as the Czecho-Slavonic Benevolent Society (C.S.P.S.) or the Jewish National Workers' Alliance, offered $200 to $1,000, depending on a member's contribution.[97]

These disparate amounts presumably served different security needs. Larger benefits helped the survivors readjust themselves to their new situation, as indicated by the case of the Polish worker known as N. N. Smaller benefits were spent chiefly on the funeral itself, with the balance available for the family of the dead member to rearrange their living, affording them a few weeks or so. With meager incomes, many immigrants could not save much for tragedies. What they needed was to prevent death from completely draining their families of scant economic resources, and to help tide them over during the crisis.

The amounts of the benefits also changed over time, reflecting not simply long-term inflation but also the shifting policies of the mutual aid societies. The twenty-nine Czechs who formed the C.S.P.S. in 1854 had decided to allot twenty dollars for a member's funeral expenses and ten dollars for his wife. More significantly, they had agreed to pay five dollars a month, not a trivial sum at all at the time, to the widow until she remarried. If a widow had chosen to remain as such, then, the society would have had no choice but to continue to pay. They had also agreed to provide the sick with two dollars each week during the first year of illness. For the second year the Czechs did not reduce the amount but raised it by fifty cents, presumably because they thought the longer a member stayed bedridden the more he would need. So a member sick for two consecutive years would have received more than $230. In 1872, however, they decided to offer limited protection: The amount of the death benefit was for the first time fixed at $250; the sickness benefit also seems to have been curtailed, though the details are not available.[98] That year marked a momentous divide between familial care and limited protection.

Although there is no direct evidence that indicates how or why the society changed its policy, the original agreement among its founding members indicates that the Czechs were resolved to take almost unlimited responsibility in providing for a sick member or for a dead member's family. Their commitment possibly resulted less from innocence than from a fear of insecurity combined with a spirit of brotherhood, as indicated by their motto: "All for one, one for all!" Perhaps there was wishful thinking that a sick member would sooner or later leave his bed, or a commonsense understanding that if a widow did not want to remarry soon, the children, particularly sons, would someday be self-reliant enough to assume responsibility. Yet the Czechs were so serious about familial care that their original agreement was kept alive for almost two decades. The C.S.P.S. secretary, J. V. Lunak, in a lecture given at the sixtieth anniversary of the society, boasted of the "family spirit" prevalent in the organization at that time, as shown by the agreement.[99]

The shift to limited protection arguably came from perennial cases of large amounts withdrawn relative to contributions. In Chicago, the Czech Roman Catholic Society had to deal with a rather extreme case only one and a half years after its foundation in 1882. A member named Vaclav Burian caught a cold and received five dollars a week for a while. As his cold seemed to develop into pneumonia, however, the society decided to stop paying the sickness benefit by expelling Burian, accusing him "of quarreling with the wife of another member and being absent from the meeting." Burian appealed to the court and sought a mandamus against the society, asking for "the reinstatement as member of the brotherhood, and the $5 weekly sick benefit continuously until he is cured."[100] This kind of case apparently chafed at the spirit of brotherhood and led mutual aid societies to limit the amounts and durations, particularly the latter, of sickness and accident benefits or even to refrain from offering the benefits.

Such pains taken to replace familial care with limited concern were obviously due to the imperative that as a whole any benefit must be balanced against the member's contribution. At first, a rule-of-thumb method was enough. The mutual aid society managed on initiation fees and monthly dues, frequently one dollar and fifty cents each. When a member died or fell sick and could not work, the society simply assessed a certain amount upon each of the other members. If necessary, it did the same again and again. Indeed, it was often called the assessment society. As time went on, however, the benefit a member received would be so incommensurate to the contribution he or she made that the imbalance might brew discontent and undermine fraternity. One solution was to limit the amount of the death benefit, the major item of disbursement, as the C.S.P.S. did in 1872, and build a benefit fund with revenues from fees and dues. By the end of the nineteenth century, probably the majority of the mutual aid societies had adopted this solution, in addition to assessment, while the rest stuck to the older method. Another solution was to differentiate the amount of contribution according to the individual member's risk: The older a member was, the higher his or her dues were. The C.S.P.S. introduced this principle at the turn of the century. The principle that one contribute in accordance with one's risk made a society open its doors to individualism. When the Czech society began to collect different dues depending on age, it also decided to offer two kinds of death benefits, one of $500 and the other of $1,000.[101] This system of balancing benefit against contribution on an individual basis sooner or later spread among other societies. Limited concern would eventually lead to individualism within the fraternity.

The early experiences of mutual aid societies indicate that immigrants had to go through an unpleasant process while familiarizing themselves with the cash nexus. Ingrained in the tradition of mutual assistance and full of brotherhood on a strange soil, but afraid of economic insecurity in the world of commodities and unaccustomed to handling money matters, they translated the communal tradition in terms of cash. The mutual aid society was, so to speak, a cash translation of communal mutual assistance. This translation implicated an irony of history. Although immigrants forming a society initially committed themselves to familial care for each other, reality impelled them to rethink and accept that they must limit their responsibility to each other. For where labor, the medium of the field, is not unlimited, money is in essence a scarce resource. The conflict involved in allocating benefits taught immigrants, when dealing with matters related to money in the mutual aid society, not to be swayed by emotion but to adhere to reason and be careful and precise. The lesson helped immigrants adopt more complicated methods in dealing with their contributions. The new methods were applicable, however, only where they replaced familial care with limited concern in their social relations. Living in the world of commodities, therefore, they began to come to terms with the cash nexus by allowing communalism to give place to economic individualism.

The process of adapting to the cash nexus did not involve all of the immigrant groups at the turn of the century. Thanks to the Czech mutual aid societies and the American fraternal orders, there were already proven models available to the newcomers. Jews, Poles, Italians, and others could refer to these models, instead of having to take pains to figure out, by trial and error, how to operate mutual aid societies. But it does not necessarily follow that these groups easily reconciled themselves to the cash nexus. As a matter of fact, experiences such as the Czech societies had undergone were occasionally recounted in the ethnic newspapers, in articles that told of societies refusing to pay death benefits or that deplored the decline of brotherhood in fraternal orders. In the mutual aid societies around the turn of the century, therefore, traditional personal interdependence was painfully beginning to yield to modern social detachment.

This change led the mutual aid society to fierce competition with the life insurance company, an organization that provided commodified protection against economic insecurity on an individual basis. Indeed, the popularity of the mutual aid society led enterprising businessmen to launch a number of co-operative insurance companies that operated like fraternal orders. There were regular companies, too, trying to make profits in the field of life insurance. Almost from the start, the mutual aid society was an alternative to those companies, although ignoring actuarial principles and the necessity for a reserve fund to ensure its financial stability. By 1900, about three hundred fraternal orders throughout the country had a total of slightly less than six billion dollars' worth of insurance in force, which was more than three-fourths of the amount contracted by regular life insurance companies.[102] The fraternal orders were in fact serious competitors, from these companies' viewpoint. In 1877 Henry B. Hyde, head of the Equitable Life Assurance Society, declared, "We must make a sharp attack upon co-operatives, as we are being troubled by them a good deal."[103] Then he actually chose to work with his rivals, Mutual and New York Life, in order to launch a campaign attacking fraternal orders' encroachment on the life insurance business. Market competition was already pressing mutual aid societies to make major changes in their operating principles, which constitutes a separate topic to be discussed later in this book.

More significantly, adaptation to the cash nexus was not confined to the mutual aid societies. The societies formed a bridge between their members and the larger community. In order to have a balance of income and outlay, mutual aid societies conducted fund-raising activities in addition to collecting fees, dues, and assessments. The favorites were picnics, banquets, parties, and lotteries. Maria Valiani, an immigrant men's clothing worker, remembers such an activity of the Italian Working Ladies of Cicero:

> And we [Maria and her neighbors around Chicago's Oakley Avenue and 24th Street] used to . . . go their affairs . . . when they had tombola in the summer, thousand dollar tombola. That's lotto . . . tombola. They had eight hundred dollars for the first and two hundred dollars for the second . . . tombola. We all used to go to Cicero and have sandwiches over there . . . and buy the tombola tickets . . . so they'd make some money for . . . sick benefits.[104]

Selling tickets was such a common fund-raising practice that it sometimes annoyed outsiders. The Jewish *Courier* praised the Telzer Aid Society for avoiding the practice. "And the most remarkable feature about the whole thing is that the Telzer do not bother you every now and then to buy tickets for various benefits," the newspaper pointed out, "nor do they stampede editorial offices seeking free publicity for every bit of trivia."[105]

There was another side to the practice, however. Mutual aid societies repaid the favor of buying tickets by making substantial contributions to the ethnic communities. Charity was one of the major outlets. Each year the societies offered hundreds of dollars to orphanages, sanatoriums, or other charitable organizations. For example, in 1921 the Telzer Aid Society, with one hundred and fifty members paying their monthly dues, contributed $1,627 to charity.[106] Nationalist causes were another major outlet. In the five-year period between 1886 and 1891, the C.S.P.S. donated $4,995 to Czech schools alone, which was 1 percent of the total paid out in benefits.[107] Pointing out that the Polish National Alliance was annually contributing a quarter of a million dollars for charitable and educational purposes, in 1910 the Alliance noted that "our Alliance brethren did not deposit their hard-earned money for insurance purposes only."[108]

Mutual aid societies extended their helping hand to their countryfolk in trouble due to strike, depression, or natural disaster. The B'nai Moishe Ekatarinoslav Society, a Chicago *landsmanshaft* organized in 1912, came to the aid of the city's tailors conducting a strike in the middle of the decade. Previously it had weathered internal storms caused by members who thought of the society only as "a means of self-aggrandizement." After its stormy period the society became interested in "general Jewish problems." "No committee which approached them [the society] for a worthy cause was refused assistance," recalled a Jewish American, "and when the treasury was empty, individuals contributed from their own resources."[109] In these various ways, mutual aid societies functioned as community institutions.

Enmeshed in the ethnic community, the societies represented the process through which immigrants adapted to the cash nexus that pervaded American life. While many, feeling uneasy and unhappy in this harsh environment, chose to join rural communes or return to their homelands, most endeavored to succeed in the New World. As sellers of labor power in the workplace, these immigrants had little choice but to readjust their social relations in the community within that context. The immigrants discovered that they had to buy an increasing number of consumables instead of making the goods for themselves or borrowing from a neighbor; they had fewer opportunities to build communal personal interdependence through the medium of the field. And they often experienced the same unpleasant tensions as Czech mutual aid society members had, when they tried to restrain themselves from providing familial care for a neighbor in need of their help.

As a matter of fact, the tensions were symptomatic of the profound cultural transformation that immigrants had begun to experience. Taking pains to reconcile themselves to limited concern and ultimately to the cash nexus, they perhaps tried to bury those tensions deep down in their minds or even to put the experiences out of mind. But this does not necessarily mean that the process of adapting to the cash nexus no longer preoccupied them. Learning continued, forming a current at the depth of their consciousness that would eventually affect the labor movement. It was not a soothing but a nettlesome current; despite their efforts to transplant a familiar community, the immigrants around the turn of the century saw communalism waning at the same time that individualism was waxing in their settlements.

Men's clothing workers of Chicago lived in such settlements, which resembled villages, though the city was a metropolis with more than one million residents. Newly arrived from eastern and southern Europe, most chose to live within their own ethnic enclaves, close to those who originated from the same places. In congested enclaves, the workers coped with the economic insecurity that accompanied wage earning in the workplace. In order to provide against insecurity, they formed mutual aid societies, a translation of mutual assistance based on European communalism. Communal regulation, to which immigrants had long been accustomed, was also alive in the neighborhoods. More significantly, they built up extensive social networks beyond kinship, which they made efforts to adapt to the cash nexus.

The workers would not only bring these networks to the workplace but also resort to the networks in their contests with employers. Furthermore, they would, mostly unknowingly and only by degrees, modify their attitudes toward social relations at the workplace as well as in the ethnic community, as suggested by their efforts to accommodate to the world of commodities; although the workplace was increasingly differentiated in time and space from the community, in workers' consciousness it remained interlocked with the latter, not disconnected, as is sometimes assumed.[110] Their changing attitudes would eventually have a significant impact upon the labor movement in the men's clothing industry of Chicago. That impact was determined not only by individualism militating against communalism in the ethnic community; it ultimately resulted from an unstable complex of undercurrents that this changing balance created, together with the contradicting imperatives of conflict and compromise at the workplace.

CHAPTER 2

From the Sweatshop to the Factory

The men's clothing industry was undergoing significant structural changes when urban reformers engaged in a nationwide anti-sweatshop campaign in the 1890s. Although they battled the sweating system in a variety of light industries that were characterized by low wages, long hours, and unsanitary conditions, their campaign was chiefly aimed at the small shops producing men's or women's clothing. The men's clothing industry, producing ready-made suits, overcoats, and topcoats as well as work clothes and boys' garments, however, was already moving away from the sweatshop. No doubt, numerous sweaters tried to survive even in the twentieth century. But the notorious system was gradually but undeniably, though never completely, replaced by the factory system at the turn of the century.[1]

In the men's clothing industry, some cities saw the factory system on the rise earlier than others. In Rochester and Cleveland, a handful of large firms began to introduce the system beginning in the late 1870s, practically monopolizing local business and leaving only marginal room to small establishments. New York, where the sweating system had long dominated the industry, remained the home of small clothing shops that lived largely on the volume of business overflowing from large factories not only in the city but in other clothing centers such as Boston. Chicago was representative of the nationwide change. From the late 1890s large manufacturers in the city began to take over the production of men's clothing from a number of contractors and subcontractors who had once occupied a predominant position in this industry. It was there that the dynamics of industrial development clearly revealed itself around the turn of the century.

Those dynamics, as revealed in Chicago, involved profound changes on the shop floor. The labor process was transformed; artisanal skill was minutely subdivided into a great number of simple jobs, which were carefully coordinated under a central authority. The workforce was recast in terms of skill, gender, and ethnicity; the shop floor, once controlled by skilled men from a few ethnic groups, was increasingly occupied by unskilled women of diverse nationalities who represented the lower ranks of an informal job hierarchy. Work culture took on a different shape; while the sweatshop had provided a familial environment that emotionally tied workers to their employer, the factory turned into a schooling institution in which workers learned the rules of game at the workplace. All these changes, conjoined with shifting trends in the ethnic communities, constitute the background of the labor movement in the early twentieth century.

These changes concern the present chapter. After describing the early history of Chicago's men's clothing industry, this chapter explains why the sweating system was established in the 1880s and what culture was shaped in the sweatshop. It continues by discussing how and why the factory system developed in the last years of the nineteenth century and what impact this development had upon the structure of the industry there. Finally, it analyzes work culture in the factory by investigating the workforce, industrial disciplines, and social relationships. In other words, this chapter attempts to show how immigrant men's clothing workers of the city came to identify themselves as wage earners.

THE SWEATING SYSTEM

Anti-sweatshop reformers never clearly defined the sweating system. After studying sweatshops in the early 1890s, the Illinois Bureau of Labor Statistics (IBLS) identified the system with contracting and subcontracting. "In practice, sweating consists of the farming out by competing manufacturers to competing contractors the material for garments," declared IBLS, "which, in turn, is distributed among competing men and women to be made up."[2] The Committee on Manufactures (CM), which the U.S. House of Representatives authorized to investigate this notorious system, also defined it in a similar way. In its 1893 report the committee pointed out that the essence of the system lay in "the fact that the compensation of the contractor is the margin between the price he receives and the price he pays for the making of each garment." Then the CM added, "the subcontractor's compensation must be sweated in turn from [his] employés. . . ."[3]

In fact, however, the contract system was popular in some industries, such as machinery and arms, in which sweatshop conditions were never known to exist.[4] And in the nineteenth century there were a number of subcontractors engaged in the building and construction industries. The sweating system turned out to be viable in the production of clothing, shoes, cigars, and furniture, light industries that did not require large capital investment in machinery and equipment but needed intensive labor power. In such industries the sweating system was a type of production organization under which, in an effort to keep production costs down, manufacturers had the goods made up by contractors or subcontractors who were able to secure cheap labor in a simple form of division of labor.

In the men's clothing industry of Chicago, the system was established in the 1880s but had its origins in earlier years. Before the Civil War the industry had not flourished in the city. Developing as the hub of the national railroad network, and enjoying access to the Mississippi waterway system, Chicago soon became the distribution center for clothing for western pioneers and working people as well as for southern blacks. By 1870, output had expanded to well over $5 million, more than ten times that of a decade before, which made the city the fifth-largest men's clothing center in the country, behind New York, Boston, Philadelphia, and Cincinnati. The Great Fire of 1871 destroyed Chicago's men's clothing industry and a recession two years later hindered its fresh start. But the industry still grew in the 1870s, and its output in 1880 was more than $17 million, over three times that of the previous decade.[5]

The explosive growth was led by merchant-manufacturers who had accumulated capital and experience in the retail end of the clothing business and then ventured into making garments for their own wholesale outlets. In 1872 Harry Hart, who had worked at a clothing store as an errand boy, a stockboy, a salesman, and at last a clerk, opened a retail clothing store in downtown Chicago with his brother Max. They did not hit upon the idea of wholesaling until a downstate Illinois retailer, delighted at the quality of their stock, bought several suits from them. Although they had no experience in manufacturing, the Hart brothers rented a room near the store, hired cutters, and began to make men's clothing for sale. And so began the famous firm of Hart, Schaffner and Marx (HSM).[6] Bernard Kuppenheimer came to America in 1850 and peddled dry goods until he opened a retail clothing house in Terre Haute, Indiana, in 1852. His business grew steadily but he saw greater opportunities in Chicago and in 1866 joined Clayburgh, Einstein and Co., a wholesale clothing firm in the city. Ten years later, when the firm was dissolved, he established B. Kuppenheimer and Co., a leading manufacturer of men's ready-made clothes.[7] By 1880 other prominent firms such as Clement, Bane and Co., Charles P. Kellog and Co., and Kuh, Nathan and Fisher were engaged in both manufacturing and wholesaling.[8]

Merchant-manufacturers ran the so-called "inside shops," shops on their own premises. They usually rented a room or a loft near their downtown clothing store where they hired journeymen tailors to cut the material and repair, if necessary, the garments made up and returned by home workers. As the demand for ready-made clothing grew after the

Civil War, however, manufacturers secured large working spaces close to the tailors' neighborhoods and employed a number of tailors to work on garments, instead of collecting the completed goods from home workers. The size of the typical inside shop grew as a result, and a shop with two hundred to three hundred hands was not a rarity in the 1870s. But division of labor was so simple in the shop that tailors usually did the whole job, whether coats, pants, or vests, taking the material from the cutter and making up garments, doing both machine and hand work. The technology was still primitive; the sewing machine was not only clumsy and heavy but also run by foot power, though it had been continuously improved since its invention in 1846; the tailor's goose, heated on the stove or in a furnace, was used for pressing.[9] The inside shop was in fact a manufactory, dependent primarily upon human rather than inanimate sources of energy, even though contemporaries thought of it as a modern factory.

Merchant-manufacturers also relied on legacies of the putting-out system. Before the Civil War the material was usually cut on the firm's premises and then sent out to rural districts to be sewed together by farmers' wives and daughters, who worked by hand because sewing machines were not yet in general use. In New York, a metropolis with a population of well over 500,000 in 1850, the manufacturers tapped another source of cheap labor available nearby: working-class women. This practice was common in the production of work clothes, such as sailors' "slops" and overalls.[10] It was true of Chicago. The population of the city exploded from about 30,000 in 1850 to almost ten times that two decades later.[11] Working-class women, whose number had rapidly increased along with the population growth, sought work as a subsidiary source of income for the family. The women, relying on hand work rather than machines, worked on cheap clothes or did home finishing of better garments.

On the other hand, the better grades of men's clothing were frequently made under the so-called family system. The tailors working in the inside shop already brought home and made up the garments they could not finish during the day. Taking advantage of this practice, men's clothing firms now distributed cut fabrics even to tailors not employed in the inside shop so that they could make up garments with the help of their families. They worked on the material, leaving to their wives and daughters the less important parts of sewing machine operations and hand work such as button sewing and finishing. This system gave employment chiefly to immigrant tailors from England, Scotland, Ireland, and Germany.[12]

Between these home workers and the merchant-manufacturers were the middlemen, the forerunners of the contractors in the late nineteenth century. As an extension of their retailing experience, the manufacturers concentrated on marketing the goods, whether through jobbers or by sending out salesmen to retailers. When the busy season came, they found it difficult to hire tailors, distribute the material, and collect completed garments. These tasks were given to intermediaries who could recruit journeymen tailors or home finishers through a network of acquaintances. During the idle season when business was slow, the manufacturers, not obliged to maintain a large payroll even in the busy season, had their garments produced in the inside shop.[13]

The middleman turned himself into a contractor as soon as he acquired enough work to be able to afford to rent a room and have garments produced there under his own supervision. He did not need a large amount of capital because every journeyman tailor brought a sewing machine to work, either purchased or rented. Additionally, the contractor might buy a few sewing machines on the installment plan that Edward Clark, of I. M. Singer and Co., had already initiated as part of his aggressive marketing strategy in the mid-1850s.[14] On the other hand, a journeyman tailor working at home often secured more work than he and his family could do, and called in strangers to augment his own household workforce. Getting work at a certain piece rate from merchant-manufacturers, the tailor now became a contractor.[15] The shop, whether established by a middleman or a tailor working at home with strangers' help, was a contract shop. It was often called the "outside shop," as opposed to the inside shop, which the manufacturers had instituted on their own premises. By the late 1870s the contract system had taken a foothold in the men's ready-made clothing industry.[16]

It was into this industrial landscape that Scandinavian and Czech tailors entered. In addition to those from Germany and United Kingdom, hundreds of journeymen tailors immigrated from Sweden, Norway, and the Czech lands in the early 1880s.[17] In Chicago, Scandinavian tailors hired themselves out to German family shops. Settling down on the North and Northwest Sides of the city, where German tailors had already established themselves, Scandinavians, though few in number, began working on the ready-made garments. Soon, Swedish and Norwegian tailors became known as very good vest and pants makers and opened their own family shops. On the Southwest and Northwest Sides Czechs were recognized as excellent coat makers, and like their German predecessors they took in strangers and extended the family shops into contract shops. By the early nineties, Czechs and Scandinavians had a firm hold on Chicago's clothing industry, controlling more than one-half of all the clothing shops IBLS found in the city[18] (see Table 2.1).

TABLE 2.1
Clothing Shops of Chicago in 1892, Classified by Ethnicity of the Proprietors

Garment	*German*	*Scandinavian*	*Czech*	*Jewish*	*Polish*	*Other*	*Total*
Coats	50	15	200	30	47	0	342
Pants	35	43	19	0	24	1	122
Vests	7	79	3	2	0	0	91
Cloaks	1	6	0	50	2	3	61
Other	10	11	10	11	7	1	50
Total	103	154	232	93	80	4	666
No. of employees	1,366 (15.0)	2,690 (29.6)	2,682 (29.5)	1,241 (13.6)	1,092 (12.0)	26 (0.3)	9,097 (100%)

Source: Adapted from Illinois, Bureau of Labor Statistics, *Seventh Biennial Report*, 1893, 381, 382.

The enterprising Czechs and Scandinavians applied a simple form of division of labor. While manufacturers saved costs by installing steam power in the large inside shops where journeymen tailors completed whole garments with power-driven sewing machines, and while German tailors worked on clothes with the help of their wives and daughters, these newcomers took advantage of cheaper unskilled labor readily available in their ethnic neighborhoods. Dividing the work into several phases, they gave the important stages to a few skilled tailors and had simple jobs performed by unskilled helpers. Each employee concentrated on only one phase of the labor process and became dexterous at that task. The simple division of labor was not novel; it had been an established practice in the production of cheap garments, particularly work clothes, in antebellum New York, diluting artisanal skill and thus "bastardizing" the tailoring trade.[19] In Chicago it was introduced into better lines of pants, coats, vests, and overcoats, possibly in the 1870s, when the city began to compete with New York for the midwestern and southern markets. By 1892 IBLS agents found in the contract shops diverse job titles such as machine-hands (that is, sewing machine operators), hand-finishers, buttonhole makers, buttonhole finishers, basters, and pressers.[20] This simple division of labor gave a competitive edge to Czech and Scandinavian contractors, who in the course of the 1880s drove German family shops out of business and took an increasing share of the production of ready-made clothing.

The rise of the Czech and Scandinavian contractors changed the structure of the clothing industry. As the contractors bid against each other, manufacturers preferred distributing the work among them to producing garments in the inside shops. More and more firms kept their inside shops small, discharging tailors, who had constituted the majority of the employees. While some manufacturers, with a number of journeymen tailors on their payroll, had urgent orders filled by the inside shop, many others reduced their own shops to mere cutting rooms, sending out all the work to contractors. For example, Beifeld and Co., a Chicago women's clothing firm that had employed more than two hundred workers in its own shop, maintained only about seventy-five there by the early 1890s. Still others, such as Leigh Brothers, eliminated their entire workforce, finding it more profitable to rely entirely on contractors. In 1892, no fewer than 550 contract shops kept working on men's clothing even during the slack season in Chicago. Testifying before the Congressional Committee on Manufactures that year, John H. Prentis of Charles P. Kellog and Co. declared that the work was in general given out to contractors; few tailors took it directly from the firms to their homes.[21]

Relying upon the contract system, the men's clothing manufacturers of Chicago made the city the second-largest clothing center of this country, which caused them to be entangled in seasonal fluctuations of production. In 1890, 186 manufacturers produced more than $32 million worth of men's ready-made clothing, almost twice as much as a decade before. Their production left far behind the custom tailors, who that year made up and repaired garments worth only one-third of the total amount.[22] The manufacturers produced primarily suits and overcoats. Unlike work clothes, these generally sold at certain times of the year, such as Easter and Christmas. Since garments not disposed of in their proper season either had to be kept in stock until the next season came around or sold at a very cheap price, retailers tended to place orders immediately before the buying period began. To fill the orders, manufacturers began production earlier and had clothing stocked in advance of their sale to retailers. The spring season began in November, peaked during the winter, and slowed in March and April. The fall season began in May and ended in September, after a peak in July and August.[23]

Such fluctuations led to fierce competition among contractors. While each busy season offered a business opportunity to ambitious tailors, each slow season saw a number of contractors closing shop, and survivors trying to secure work from manufacturers by underbidding one another. Chicago contractors were also forced to compete with their counterparts in other cities. From the start the wholesale clothiers of the city campaigned painstakingly to drive a wedge into the western and southern markets that were the traditional territory of eastern seaboard manufacturers. By the early 1890s Chicago firms succeeded in selling three-fourths to seven-eighths of their products outside Illinois. But they still found themselves undersold by manufacturers from New York and Philadelphia, who took full advantage of skilled but cheap labor offered by new arrivals from eastern Europe. Chicago contractors became involved in nationwide competition, and some firms of the city, such as that of Henry W. King, one of the pioneers in the men's clothing business, chose to have their goods manufactured in New York because labor was cheaper there than in the Windy City.[24]

The intense competition divided contractors into two conflicting and yet symbiotic groups, original contractors and subcontractors. Manufacturers evaluated contractors according to their financial responsibility, workmanship, and probably even personal relationships. A good business rating enabled a contractor to secure steady work from one or several firms. He could enlarge his shop, installing steam engines and more sewing machines. By the early 1890s, many Czech and Scandinavian contractors were recognized as reputable businessmen. Enjoying direct and stable business relations with manufacturers, they operated more spacious shops with better working conditions, employed more experienced workers, and paid 10 to 30 percent higher wages than other contractors in the business. In 1892, IBLS reported that their shops could "hardly be called sweat-shops in the offensive sense. . . ."[25]

But the more substantial contractors did not wish to drive the less fortunate out of business. Just as manufacturers needed them, so they needed the small contractors, who in the busy seasons got enough work to aspire to establish themselves in the business, although they struggled to survive each slack season. Original contractors, with sizable investments in buildings and machinery and with dozens of employees on their payrolls, could not easily adjust their shops to the seasonally fluctuating volume of business. Some stabilized operations by securing work from several manufacturers, but most had to be cautious not to expand their shops to the size required by the busy season. These contractors chose to sublet that work that exceeded their productive capacity. The subcontractors at first occupied a marginal position in the production of ready-made garments. Keeping costs down, however, they gradually took over a significant part of the industry from the original contractors, who in turn bid lower contract prices for their work, allowing the manufacturers to enjoy lower production costs. In 1892, the CM estimated that throughout the nation about one-half of the work contracted out by clothing firms was given to subcontractors.[26]

The subcontractors were probably Jews and Poles, in addition to the Czechs and Scandinavians who ran tiny shops. From the late 1880s, new arrivals from Poland and Russia, later followed by Italians, entered Chicago's clothing industry. Tailors who had already learned the trade in the old country, though unable to speak English, found jobs in clothing shops, and sooner or later some opened their own businesses. Out of the 666 clothing shops canvassed by IBLS in 1892, Jews operated ninety-three, with 1,241 employees, and Poles had eighty, with 1,092 workers on their payrolls (see Table 2.1). These shops were the core of the sweating system, attracting the unskilled and inexperienced of their owners' ethnic groups.[27] The IBLS pointed out that "the system is chiefly spreading at present among the recently imported Russian Jews and Poles, who eagerly take in the cheapest work and execute it in the most squalid places."[28]

Subcontractors won a competitive edge by brutally slashing production costs, which quickly transformed their establishments and even many contractors' into sweatshops. With few financial resources, subcontractors invested as little as possible in machinery. They bought a few sewing machines on the installment plan, or required their machine operators to bring their own machines to the job. They also relied on foot powered machines, believing "leg power is cheaper than steam." A subcontractor could not afford power while running a small shop equipped with only a few machines.[29]

Sweaters, that is, subcontractors or marginal contractors, saved money by opening their shops in the worst buildings in the poorest neighborhoods of the immigrant settlements. In Chicago the sweatshops were located chiefly in the southwest, the northwest, and the northern districts, where newly arrived Poles and Jews were settled close to Czechs, Swedes, and Germans. On the Southwest Side there were a number of shops in the area tributary to Blue Island Avenue between Fourteenth and Twentieth Streets. They employed Czechs, Jews, and Italians, as well. On the Northwest and North Sides the shops of Germans, Czechs, Scandinavians, and Poles were concentrated in streets adjacent to Milwaukee Avenue, Division Street, and Clybourn Avenue.[30] These sweatshop districts were "the forgotten regions" overcrowded by newly arrived immigrants.[31] Streets were unpaved, sidewalk planks decayed, and drainage obstructed. The buildings were in general dilapidated cottages, shanties, or tenement houses, or brick structures built for temporary purposes after the Great Fire of 1871. Sweaters rented attics, basements, outhouses, or even stables, and converted the space to use as shops. Otherwise, they used the rooms next to their own living quarters in the tenement flats, which the CM found was a typical example of a subcontracting establishment.[32]

For sweaters, the most economical way to use the rented space was to pack the workroom with workers and machines and tools. In her testimony before the CM in 1892, Elizabeth Morgan, who investigated the sweating system for the Chicago Trade and Labor Assembly, said that a typical sweatshop employing a dozen people would be twelve by fourteen to sixteen feet. In the same year, the IBLS reported more favorable conditions; most frequently, that many employees worked in a space twenty by thirty feet in size.[33] Such a room was frequently integrated into the sweater's living space. A bed, removed during the working hours to make space for the employees, would be brought into the workroom at nights. To illustrate what a sweatshop was like, the IBLS reported:

> In another case seven persons were at work in a room 12 by 15 feet in dimensions and with but two windows. These people with the sewing machines of operators and the tables used by the pressers, so filled this meager space that it was impossible to move about. Charcoal was used for heating the pressers' irons, and the air was offensive and prostrating to a degree. Separated from this shop-room by a frail partition which did not reach to the ceiling was a bedroom about 7 by 15 feet in size, containing two beds, for the use of the family of the sweater.[34]

The shortcut to economy in operation was to "sweat" the employees, in other words, to pay the lowest wages possible and maximize the margin between the payroll and the contract price for the goods produced. Jewish, Polish, Czech, and Scandinavian sweaters took advantage of cheap immigrant labor by establishing shops chiefly in their own ethnic enclaves. Unmarried women were frequently taken in as learners without pay and then given a simple task such as finishing and button sewing. In 1901, a Polish Jew in Chicago told the U.S. Industrial Commission how he extracted cheap labor from the women. After a careful study of a Polish neighborhood, he opened a shop in the poorest section and hired only the newly arrived women. He lost money teaching them the trade, but for the long run the sweater had a practical plan, as he explained: "It will take these girls years to learn English and to learn how to go about and find work. In that way I will be able to get their labor very cheap."[35] Most of them were in their late teens, but girls under fourteen were also put to work in almost every shop. At first they sewed buttons on, prepared buttonholes, or pulled out basting threads. From these simple jobs they proceeded to operating machines or delicate hand sewing, learning from their more experienced fellows or the sweater himself.

Married women worked for lower wages in their homes. In pants and vest making, the garments were usually shipped out to have felling (stitching down the wider of the two edges left projecting by a seam) and button sewing done by home finishers after the machine operations and important handwork were completed in the shop. Bound to their homes by the exigencies of housekeeping and child raising, these women kept their names on more than one sweaters' lists, and sewed garments to supplement their husbands' incomes. In Chicago it was "only the poorest of the poor who finish garments at home, only the worst tenements being occupied by them, or the worst rooms of the better houses."[36] Working in their own homes, which often consisted of a single room that served as kitchen, living room, and bedroom, they could get help from their children; every member had to contribute to the family's livelihood.[37] To these women, whatever small amount they could earn was better than nothing.

Boys, few in number, were usually employed "as messengers or errand boys to carry goods to the buttonholer, or to the finisher, or to fetch beer." When they had nothing to do during working hours, boys occasionally learned the trade. Sweaters would exploit their labor by giving them garments to work on, without promoting them into regular shop hands for several months or even longer.[38]

Men occupied a better position in the sweatshops. Most of the men employed in the sweatshops were tailors who had recently arrived from Austria-Hungary, Poland, Russia, and Italy. Performing the parts of the production process that required skill and experience, these tailors tended to be paid better and employed more steadily than the women. For instance, in a sweatshop making boys' jackets where according to the IBLS report seven men and twenty-six women were employed, the three male machine operators were the best paid. Their weekly wages ranged from $7.50 to $10.00 and they worked for forty-eight to fifty-two weeks in the one-year period after May 1891. The other men were employed at rates of between $5.25 and $7.00 a week and worked all year round, except one machine operator. On the other hand, the three best-paid female machine operators in the shop earned only $6.00 to $7.50 a week, working for twenty-one, forty-two, and forty-eight weeks apiece in the same period. Only four of the remaining twenty-three women worked for more than forty weeks, at rates that ranged from $6.00 down to $1.50 a week.[39]

Skilled men, together with women workers, were sweated under the so-called task system. This notorious method of exploitation was not just confined to New York, where Jews from eastern Europe introduced it around 1880. Familiar with the labor process, these employers usually divided work into three phases, each performed by one "concentrator": In the coat shop the operator did all the stitching on the sewing machine, the baster put together the various parts of the coat, and the edge baster or finisher prepared the edge for the operator.[40] Assisted by a presser, a trimmer, and a few women who performed minor operations, a team of three worked in unison and turned out a specified number of coats each day, the number having been set as a task for the team. The team was paid at a normal day rate, regardless of how much time it took to complete the task. The cigar industry used a similar work system in the early twentieth century, in which employers substituted a team of three for one skilled cigar maker. Unlike the clothing industry, however, this so-called team system was common in factories that produced cheap cigars. Moreover, the team workers, mostly women, were paid by the piece, not by the day.[41]

Cutthroat competition led sweaters to increase the size of the daily tasks, probably starting in the late 1880s, when immigrants from eastern and southern Europe began to enter the industry in larger numbers, and workers were forced to speed up to an unlikely degree. Under this system, Jewish tailors were so productive that women were increasingly replaced by men working at much higher wages.[42] In Chicago, however, immigrant tailors were not as abundant as in New York and Philadelphia. In place of skilled men, Chicago sweaters trained and employed women as edge basters and even as operators, and saved the labor costs so that they could compete with their eastern counterparts. "In the shops of a lower order the task system is vigorously applied," IBLS found out in Chicago, "and the girl must accomplish a satisfactory amount of work or make room for another."[43]

Unlike in other clothing centers, therefore, a great many women were working in the Chicago sweatshops. According to the IBLS investigation, which included even large contract shops, women comprised nearly four-fifths of the 9,269 workers employed in men's clothing shops (see Table 2.2). While married women did finishing work at their homes, unmarried ones worked in the shops, where they constituted almost three-fourths of the workforce. But they suffered under a rigid gender-based division of work, which did not allow them to learn the highly skilled jobs. Skilled jobs such as trimming and pressing were practically monopolized by men, who comprised only one-fifth of the total workforce (see Table 2.3). And men apparently did the more important parts of the machine operating as well. Men's clothing workers, particularly women who were forced to accept less steady work at lower wage rates than men, suffered during the slack season; since manufacturers and large contractors did not farm out the work in order to keep their own shops busy, a sweater often reduced his payroll or left his shop idle. In the boys' jacket shop studied by IBLS, the workers lost 22.2 percent of the work days between May 1891 and May 1892. "This loss of time," the bureau stressed, "is occasioned in some measure by the illness of the operatives; in a greater measure by the failure to get continuous work."[44] Even though he secured some work in the slack season by underbidding his competitors, a sweater, either by intention or by necessity, typically cut wages. In the same boys' jacket shop, for example, the three best-paid women began working at a weekly rate of $7.25,

TABLE 2.2
The Workforce of Chicago's Men's Clothing Shops in 1892, Classified by Gender, Age, and Working Place

		Coats	*Pants*	*Vests*	*Total*
Total		4,694	2,919	1,656	9,269
Male	Men*	1,312	354	247	1,913
	Boys*	148	40	9	197
Female	Women*	23	1,468	205	1,696
	Girls*	3,211	1,057	1,195	5,463
Place	In shop	4,692	1,472	1,480	7,644
	At home	2	1,447	176	1,625

*Unfortunately, IBLS did not define these terms. Throughout its report, however, "Boys" appeared to be children in their low teens or under, while "Girls" were unmarried women.

Source: IBLS, *Seventh Biennial Report*, 419–432.

TABLE 2.3
The Workforce of Chicago's Men's Clothing Shops in 1892, Classified by Job

Job	*Sex*	*Coats*	*Pants*	*Vests*	*Total*
Operator	M	146	9	4	159
	F	1,174	955	577	2,076
Finisher	M	41	3	7	51
	F	2,026	1,525	286	3,837
Trimmer	M	394	32	55	481
	F	16	1	0	17
Presser	M	685	306	141	1,132
	F	0	1	0	1
Miscellaneous	M	194	44	49	287
	F	18	43	539	600
Total no. of employees	M	1,460	394	256	2,110
	F	3,234	2,525	1,400	7,159
No. of shops		338	122	90	550
Average no. of employees per shop		14	24	18.4	

Source: Adapted from IBLS, *Seventh Biennial Report*, 443.

which shortly went up to $7.50 and then dropped to $6.00. Other women were less fortunate. A hand sewer employed almost throughout the year first worked at $5.50 a week, but after an increase of $0.50 her rate went down to $3.75; another hand sewer worked forty-six weeks, beginning at a rate of $3.75 a week, which increased to $4.00 and then declined to $1.50.[45]

In fact, wage rates, especially those of unskilled women workers, could be easily reduced in any season, not just the slack period. Although women were employed as regular shop hands, they were the first victims of the slack season and always lived perilously close to unemployment. Because unemployed women constituted the reserve army of the clothing industry, the sweater was in a position "to dole out work in such small quantities that his employés are all eager to get as much as possible,"[46] forcing them to accept the wage rates he offered. This was particularly true of home finishers, who frequently found it hard to distinguish unemployment from underemployment. Combining housekeeping with their sewing, these women often worked for whatever they could get, and kept the wage levels in the clothing industry low. The IBLS revealed that sweatshop employees complained about the downward tendency in wages. Indeed, a female cloak maker reported that for almost the same work she received "$3 in 1890, $1.25 in 1891, and 95 cents in 1892."[47] This tendency was amply confirmed by the Congressional Committee on Manufactures. In his testimony before the CM, Abraham Bisno, a cloak maker who later became a prominent labor leader in the women's clothing industry, said that in 1891 he produced more than he had in 1885, but that he earned less.[48]

These features of the sweating system wrought a distinctive work culture in the small clothing shops. Work was usually intermittent in the sweatshops because the seasonal nature of the men's clothing industry did not allow sweaters to maintain steady work throughout the year. Even during the busy season work was often irregular at a number of small shops whose owners had failed to develop stable business relationships with manufacturers or large contractors. While the sweatshop employees were idle during the slack season (as well as sometimes in the busy season), they worked incessantly whenever there was work to be done. Their working hours extended from 5 A.M. to 10 P.M., seven days a week. Only in Jewish shops did they take Saturdays off for the Sabbath.[49]

Such a work pattern brought forth a familial atmosphere in the sweatshop. The sweater and his employees worked side by side for long hours, knew each others' families, friends, and personal concerns, and took part in each others' important events, such as weddings and funerals. While the sweater frequently loaned his employees money to tide them over in an economic pinch or to bring their family members over from their home country, they knew whether he was making money or not.[50] Claiming that he was also subject to a manufacturer's reduction in contract prices, the sweater described the manufacturer as exploiting both himself and his workers.[51] Like a family, all the members of a sweatshop shared their private lives as well as their work lives.

The familial atmosphere was possible because the boss and his hands shared common language, religion, and social customs. He recruited workers almost invariably through his network of acquaintances among his own ethnic group, so ethnic conformity between the sweater and his employees was a "rule" in Chicago, as in other clothing centers. The IBLS reported only six exceptions out of the 666 clothing shops investigated: One American and three Irish sweaters made no distinction among ethnic groups, while two Jewish shops were filled with Poles.[52] And the sweater often took in a few employees as his boarders or lodgers. Having left their families in Europe, many immigrant clothing workers made arrangements for living with sweaters, who they often found were connected to themselves either by blood or through acquaintance in the old country. And they occasionally sought a sweater's advice on personal matters, because he had come earlier to the United States and knew more about America.[53] Other sweatshop employees lived within walking distance of the workplace.[54] While the sweater located his shop in their neighborhood in order to get cheap labor, they had to be available on a short notice when he managed to secure work.

The familial environment led sweatshop employees to combine work with leisure. When workers found time to take a rest during the day, they enjoyed various forms of recreation in the workroom. They sang songs, chatted and laughed, played cards and discussed diverse issues, telling errand boys "to fetch beer."[55] Such a mixture of work and leisure in the sweatshop was vividly described in a pants maker's testimony before the CM:

> As I visited one tailor shop three weeks ago [in] the first room I came into there was a press stove; in that same room there was a bench for tailors, and, it looked to me, to lie down on and take a rest when they were too filled up with beer. I saw beer glasses and I saw food scattered around on two benches, and when I went into the next room I saw them ready to cook their meat on a stove which was for the purpose of heating irons on, and that it seemed to me that most of them were taking their meals right in that place. . . .[56]

As indicated by this testimony, there was frequently no spatial separation between work and living quarters, one of the main complaints made by investigators of the sweating system. The workers usually ate their meals at the work table or bench. In general the sweater's wife prepared meals for them, or they brought food and had it cooked on the stove that heated the iron.[57] The workers also discussed their personal concerns, became party to each others' ceremonies, and joined together in the various events that took place in immigrant settlements. In the sweatshop, therefore, fierce and ceaseless toil alternated with idleness that cultivated closeness among the workers. This intermixture of work and living, characteristic of sweatshops located in the ethnic neighborhoods, was natural to immigrant workers; in the Old World they had combined both, either in the rural field or at the village workshop.

The work culture hindered labor organizing among sweatshop workers. It did not necessarily prevent them from resorting to collective action, for it helped them build the sort of intimate personal relations that could be effectively mobilized in a strike. The workers, though they seldom struck a particular sweater, occasionally joined factory employees fighting against the manufacturers, and they helped paralyze the whole men's clothing industry during the 1910–1911 strike in Chicago. But the familial atmosphere and neighborliness that existed between the sweater and his employees not only discouraged confrontation between both sides but also limited the workers' contacts beyond their ethnic neighborhood. Working and living in the narrow boundaries of each sweatshop district and constrained by language, the workers lacked any channel of communication with other ethnic groups. "The differences of race, language and religion," observed IBLS, "prove an obstacle to the growth of organization."[58] The sweatshop employees were isolated from the mainstream of American organized labor. For example, on May 5, 1886, when hundreds of Chicago's Jewish cloak makers protested against their working conditions by marching into the downtown clothing districts, they were not even aware of the Haymarket affair, which had shocked the city the day before. It was not until after the police had forcibly driven them back to their own neighborhood that the cloak makers learned about that tragic event.[59]

Another important obstacle to organization was the fact that many of the sweatshop employees, especially unskilled ones, were not so much men's clothing workers as casual laborers. A significant number of them suffered from irregular and meager work. At the boys' jacket shop studied by IBLS, six employees out of the thirty-three men and women worked fewer than ten weeks in the one-year period and another fifteen no more than forty weeks. Moreover, these twenty-one workers were often the lowest-paid employees at the shop.[60] Such chronic underemployment at low wages drove many sweatshop employees to seek other occupations such as peddling and domestic service, especially in the slack season.

Other sweatshop employees, having learned enough to be independent and dexterous workers, sought better-paying positions in the large inside or contract shops. As the division of labor was rather simple in the small shop, an employee could be trained to do various operations. So a Czech contractor, employing twenty-six workers in his Chicago shop, claimed "that as he does not pay high wages his shop is used by employees as a training school, the employees leaving when they have learned the trade and going to the large inside shops."[61]

TOWARD THE FACTORY SYSTEM

The inside shops, willing to employ experienced hands, began to flourish in the late 1890s. As the sweating system became a dominant type of production organization in New York, Philadelphia, and to a more limited extent in other clothing centers where immigrant labor was less abundant, many manufacturers reduced the inside shop to a cutting room. But others, especially those who because of their location could not rely heavily on immigrant labor, did not. They avoided direct competition with sweaters and focused on different lines of products.

The men's ready-made clothing industry, though generally known for shoddy and ill-fitting garments, tried to produce better clothes after the Civil War. In designing garments, more and more manufacturers introduced standard sizes for men, based on the Union Army's orders for military uniforms.[62] Moreover, some began to make garments according to individual customers' measurements and taste. They established an arrangement with merchant tailors, who agreed to be paid a commission for taking orders from customers. These "special-order" or "made-to-measure" manufacturers, prospering in Chicago, achieved economies of scale by producing in volume. They made cheap clothes largely for the southern and midwestern markets.[63]

On the other hand, some large manufacturers offered fine ready-made clothes. As the country became rapidly urbanized in the late nineteenth century, city dwellers, in particular businessmen, professionals, and white-collar workers, demanded inexpensive quality clothing. To these urbanites ready-made clothing was still unattractive because it had long been identified with cheap clothes for the low-income population. Aiming at such customers, some manufacturers sought to offer quality garments after the late 1880s. When the Congressional Committee on Manufactures held its sessions in Chicago in 1892, Herman Elston, a manufacturer in the city, declared, "We are manufacturing a better class of goods than we used to," and added that the change had been "for the better in the last five years."[64] Testifying before the CM, large Chicago manufacturers repeatedly pointed out that they made a better grade of clothes for higher prices while small establishments, those of New York and Philadelphia in particular, produced a low grade of goods like "the cheapest kind of trash."[65] "[T]he better grades are in general wholly or partly made in the larger shop," the committee reported, "while the poorer grades and the finishing of the better ones are more generally made in the smaller shops or tenement-home work. . . ."[66]

It was at this point that the anti-sweatshop campaign reached its peak. On Sunday, July 29, 1888, the *Chicago Times* surprised dwellers of the city with an announcement that a series of articles planned by the paper would report "[a] dreadful, damnable reality." Under the title "Life Among the Slave Girls of Chicago," the editor declared on the front page that a personal investigation revealed working women suffering from a brutal process "whereby the marrow is ground out of the bones, the virtue out of the souls, and the souls out of the bodies. . . ."[67] Indeed, the heart-wrenching series showed that many women and children were working under wretched conditions. The articles also revealed that they were languishing under unabashed exploitation chiefly by the city's manufacturers of ready-made clothing, furnishings, cigars, boxes, and so forth. The story was written by Nell Nelson, who hid her identity as a reporter, got jobs at several shops, and gathered firsthand information about working women during her one-month study. She drew an immediate and emotional response from her readers. A few accused the working women of showing off "their finery" on weekends, or remarked that they could find a job in the country, but many expressed deep sympathy. One reader wrote a poem titled "The Sewing Girl's Lament," and another proposed to form "a society for the protection of laboring women and girls." And yet another proclaimed "opportunities for missionary work much nearer at home" than imagined.[68]

Sympathy sparked more investigations, which focused on the ready-made clothing industry because it employed women and children in large numbers. In 1891, the Chicago Trade and Labor Assembly, a federated body of local labor unions, published a pamphlet called "The New Slavery. Investigation into the Sweating System as Applied to the Manufacture of Wearing Apparel." Prepared with the help of Elizabeth Morgan, wife of socialist labor leader Thomas J. Morgan, it was not shocking or sensational, but specifically pointed out that clothing was made largely under filthy and infectious conditions in sweatshops. Noting that "[t]he conditions of the Old World are rapidly being transferred to the New" under the sweating system, the pamphlet urged the assembly to "agitate this question until the system is a thing of the past and remembered only because of its infamy."[69] The next year, the IBLS set out to study the conditions of working women in Chicago and quickly encountered the public uproar over the sweating system. In its report the IBLS described the sweating system as "a deliberate preying upon the necessities of the poor."[70]

Shortly afterward, reform-minded Chicagoans, including Florence Kelley, attacked sweatshop conditions. Kelley and her friends denounced exploitation of poverty-stricken working women and at the same time stressed the possible spread of diseases through the garments made in the sweatshop.[71] The campaign eventually resulted in the Illinois Factory Inspection Act of 1893, which was enacted with an overwhelming majority of the state legislature in favor of regulation over working conditions. This campaign was but a part of the national anti-sweatshop agitation that involved Massachusetts, New York, and Pennsylvania in the 1890s. In the midst of the agitation, the U.S. House of Representatives, noting that the sweating system had lately attracted great public attention, authorized its Committee on Manufactures to conduct a nationwide investigation in 1892. Although the committee failed to secure support for federal legislation from the House, it visited major clothing centers and held a number of public hearings, arousing much interest in sweatshop conditions.[72]

In order to cater to new demand in the midst of the campaign, therefore, many manufacturers had to dissociate themselves from the negative image of ready-made clothing. They turned their attention to national advertising. The pioneer was Hart, Schaffner and Marx—which had adopted the name when Joseph Schaffner joined the Hart brothers after their former partner Levi Abt left the firm in 1887. Having worked for seventeen years as a bookkeeper at a wholesale dry goods company, Schaffner took charge of accounting and marketing. Before long he decided to venture into national advertising, for which his partners agreed initially to appropriate $5,000. Appearing in the pages of *Harper's*, *Collier's*, *Munsey's*, and the *Saturday Evening Post*, HSM's advertisements stressed the fine quality and low prices of the company's clothes.[73] One national advertisement in 1899 declared:

> The first thing that attracts your attention about the H. S. & M. clothes is their smart, dressy appearance. You would not know them from the work of the finest merchant tailor. They are cut in the latest style, they have the right expression, they fit and keep their shape. On closer inspection you will see the fine details of workmanship, the careful tailoring, the durable quality of goods and linings. They cost only 1/3 or 1/2 the tailor's price. Thousands of good dressers are wearing them. Most men are glad to buy them when they know how good they are.[74]

After a few years of the advertising experiment, Schaffner noted with pride that it was rewarding. "Advertising increased our volume; volume has enabled us to increase our value-giving," he said, "both by lower prices and by putting more quality into the goods."[75]

Although at first other manufacturers in Chicago thought Schaffner was wasting profits and predicted his failure, they soon found advertising necessary for their own businesses. The anti-sweatshop campaign in the early 1890s focused on ready-made clothing as comprising germ-carrying garments made in disease-stricken tenement houses. In Spring 1894, for instance, when smallpox hit the city, Illinois factory inspectors, with the help of Chicago health authorities, burned up five lots of infected clothes made in the sweatshops and fumigated many others. Then the inspectors called a conference of clothing manufacturers and urged them not to send out their work to sweaters.[76] Some manufacturers saw in national advertising one way to flee this awkward situation. HSM's lead was followed by others, such as B. Kuppenheimer and Co., Alfred Decker and Cohn, Edward V. Price and Co., Scotch Woolen Mills, and Royal Tailors, all of whom strenuously advertised that their garments were manufactured in their own factories, not in the sweatshops.[77]

Many firms improved the quality of their products by substituting better material for cheap fabrics. Up until the early 1890s, low grades of ready-made clothing were made of muslin and satinet, a combination of cotton warp with a shoddy filling, while union cassimere, cassimere, and cheviot were used for the medium grades. Union cassimere was a combination of cotton warp with wool filling, and various grades of cheviot were all wool, either waste or better wool. Enterprising firms chose to use better grades of cheviots and cassimeres for their products.[78] In 1900, the pioneering HSM was again the first to announce the "guaranteed all wool" policy. Now fine garments were made of quality fabrics such as worsted, serge, "clay"—a twill weave—and tweed, in addition to better cheviot.[79]

It proved difficult to enhance such fine materials with superior workmanship, however. Although the bitter competition among contractors allowed manufacturers to enjoy lower contract prices, it frequently led contractors to neglect workmanship. They were more interested in the volume of their output, because their profits grew as volume increased. As long as a manufacturer sent out goods to be made up by a number of different contractors, workmanship was beyond his control; contractors had their own particular methods of making garments, which rendered it almost impossible for the manufacturer to get uniform quality.[80]

To produce fine garments, manufacturers needed to supervise the labor process more closely than before. Closer supervision was possible when a manufacturer brought those contractors whom he had already found reliable into his own establishment to work exclusively for himself. They were called "inside contractors." These contractors were generally independent in running their own shops, although there were variations, as some of them borrowed money, machines, and tools from the manufacturer's firm and became subject to its general shop rules and even its control over wages. In any case, the firm obtained close supervision of the production process, while not taking up the burden of managing the manufacturing end.[81]

Through such arrangements, contract shops were integrated into the inside shops. Illinois factory inspectors reported that in 1894 only five out of Chicago's thirty-five largest men's clothing manufacturers had inside shops in addition to their cutting rooms. These shops were relatively small, with the exception of Kuh, Nathan and Fischer, which employed 182 workers in one inside shop. With a combined total of 334 workers employed in their inside shops, the five manufacturers had to rely upon outside contractors, who city-wide maintained 2,196 people on their payrolls.[82] But as the American economy recovered from the depression of the 1890s and continued to prosper almost uninterrupted until the panic of 1907, the demand for better clothing expanded, accelerating the trend toward integration of outside shops. By 1900, at least seven Chicago manufacturers employed 100 or more workers in their own tailor shops. With 475 people working at HSM's alone, there were 1,651 workers in all in the inside shops.[83] A 1911 Congressional report on the men's ready-made clothing industry noted that the contract shop had been "extensively replaced by the inside shop, or by contract shops supervised by the firm," which had often relied upon more than 100 contractors to complete the work.[84]

In its internal structure, however, the enlarged inside shop was not entirely different from the small contract shop. Scholars assume that the inside shop became a factory when a manufacturer put together a number of small shops at one location and provided power and additional machines.[85] In fact, the inside shop was composed of separate production units, each the responsibility of an inside contractor. In 1916, the U.S. Commerce Department study of the men's clothing industry pointed out: "[E]ven now many large inside houses are run on the plan of the small contract shop, being simply a number of small shops assembled under one roof."[86] Although the inside shop appeared to be an integrated production unit, its managerial authority was not centralized yet, and the division of labor presumably remained almost the same as in the small contract shop. Among the 1,651 workers employed in the inside shops of the seven Chicago manufacturers, the men, supposedly skilled hands, outnumbered by two to one the women, who were almost invariably placed in unskilled jobs.[87]

The integration of small contract shops was accompanied by higher production costs. Labor costs increased in the enlarged inside shops, as skilled or experienced workers were needed more than before in order to secure good workmanship. Chicago manufacturers told the Congressional Committee on Manufactures that they offered higher piece rates to those working on better grades.[88] On the other hand, the work week in large shops was usually sixty hours at the turn of the century, much less than that in small ones, as integration made men's clothing firms bigger and more vulnerable to public scrutiny. The firms tried to get out of this dilemma by speeding up the labor process. They substituted a "bonus foreman" for the inside contractor, providing not only the working space but also all of the machinery and equipment, thus denying the contractor the elements of his independence. The bonus foreman was allowed considerable managerial authority on the shop floor so as to maintain absolute command over his workforce. Manufacturers encouraged him to drive workers by whatever means he believed were appropriate, paying him a bonus in proportion to the number of garments produced. The bonus foreman came to characterize the large inside shop, until the organized men's clothing workers pressed manufacturers to reform labor management after World War I. Because large manufacturers wanted to produce fine clothes, however, they found it difficult to quicken the labor process without depressing the quality of work.[89]

Consequently, manufacturers reorganized the inside shop by introducing the "section system." This system was in essence a form of division of labor in which the labor process was subdivided into minute operations, most of them to be carried out by unskilled but dexterous specialists. It was often called the "Boston system." In 1884, a Boston firm, Macullar, Parker, and Company, had boasted of its ready-made clothing department where the employees, specializing in rather simple tasks, attained high speed:

> In the ready-made department, specialization of labor is carefully studied, and each operative has a particular line of work, in which the greatest possible degree of proficiency is attained. A number of girls are set apart for sewing on buttons, each of them can turn out 400 firmly sewed buttons every day. Another group is devoted from morning till evening to the making of button-holes by hand; another, to linings; another, to pockets; and so on through the list.[90]

In this way, the making of a regular sack coat, which required extensive skill, was divided into 117 operations, while vest making and pants making, both less-skilled jobs, were divided into forty-five and sixty-two operations each.[91] In practice, however, some operations were merged, depending on convenience and necessity, as conceived by the firm. Only in extreme cases did a coat pass through between ninety and 100 shop hands before it was completed, while pants were assembled by about sixty workers and vests by forty to fifty. Even so, the division of labor was sophisticated, especially compared with the task system. In a sectionalized coat shop, for example, pressing was done not by one skilled worker, but by as many as nine specialists, seam and pocket pressers, armhole pressers, edge pressers, off pressers, canvas pressers, lapel and collar seam pressers, tape pressers, sleeve pressers, and under-pressers. Basting was now performed by armhole basters, wigan basters, canvas basters, first basters, second basters, and edge basters.[92] In the cutting room, spreaders laid fabrics and markers marked the top layers before cutters did their job with the cutting machines.

The section system involved reorganization of the labor process. Minutely subdivided, the process was extensively deskilled in order to be performed by poorly paid unskilled workers. Workers specializing in a rather simple operation were able to develop great speed after being trained for several weeks, and their output was higher than those working under the task system. In addition, manufacturers took pains to make goods in production flow smoothly from one section to the next; efficiency, specifically in the speed and volume of production, depended not just on the dexterity of individual workers but on organization of cooperation as well. So manufacturers carefully reorganized the whole production process, by juxtaposing, both in time and space, closely connected sections and reducing the movement of goods, accomplished by errand boys running on the shop floor, to a minimum. Subdivision invited coordination.

With the section system and subsequent reorganization of the labor process, large manufacturers such as Hart, Schaffner and Marx seized a competitive edge over the sweatshops under the task system. A study conducted in 1901 by the U.S. Industrial Commission showed that a shop employing 104 workers produced 1,650 coats in a week, completing a coat of the cheapest kind in three hours and forty-one minutes under the section system, while nineteen workers in a task shop made up three hundred coats in a week, spending fourteen more minutes on the same kind of coat. Moreover, the production cost was reduced: The sectionalized coat shop produced a coat for 55.7 cents, nearly four cents less than the task shop.[93] A New York contractor, an employer of more than one hundred people who worked on coats and overcoats under the section system, claimed, with some exaggeration, that the production cost in his shop was half that of a sweatshop, declaring, "The saving comes in utilizing highly skilled workers on the important work and employing cheaper labor for the rest."[94] In the production of better grades, especially fine clothes, large manufacturers probably enjoyed greater advantages because the work required a higher degree of skill and more time.

Such organizational innovation went hand in hand with technological developments around the turn of the century. Electrical power came into general use in the clothing shops, replacing steam power. It was an important innovation. Sewing machines powered by electricity led the way to increased speed and still higher productivity. Machines for special purposes were invented and introduced to substitute for hand techniques, including the collar pressing machine, the shoulder pressing machine, the serging machine, the collar and lapel padding machine, and the tacking machine. Other devices were developed to increase productivity by saving labor. In cutting, for example, the electric band knife made it possible to cut thirty to forty-five layers of cloth at once, whereas the earlier cutting machines could cut only fourteen to twenty layers.[95]

Technological innovations did not, however, trigger the rise of the factory system in the men's clothing industry. While steam engines had been used mainly in large shops, electric motors, whether fitted into individual machines or installed as the central power source, were available even to sweaters. Various machines for special purposes were introduced only after many men's clothing shops had already been reorganized into factories under the section system. Although the buttonhole-making machine had been in use at some inside shops and at small contract shops that specialized in that operation, other special sewing and pressing machines invented around the turn of the century were frequently ignored by leading manufacturers in the men's clothing industry. Most machines worked neither as neatly nor as reliably as experienced hands. Manufacturers of fine men's clothing preferred hand techniques to machine technology, which was extensively adopted in the production of low and medium grades. Because "the opinion prevailed that good clothes had to be handmade," noted the Commerce Department study in 1916, "many manufacturers have . . . been slow in investigating new labor-saving machines."[96] Even after World War I, this situation changed so little that Martin E. Popkin, an industrial engineer, vehemently advocated the advantages of machine tailoring.[97] The U.S. Commissioner of Labor flatly pointed out in 1904: "That which distinguishes the factory [from the small task shop] is minute division of labor, or 'section work,' as it is called in the trade."[98]

Organizational innovation led autonomous production units within the inside shop to be integrated into the factory and eventually changed the structure of the men's clothing industry. In order to adequately staff each of numerous sections, manufacturers had to maintain a large workforce. Some employed more than 500 workers under one roof, while others operated several factories, with 200 to 300 workers each. As manufacturers offering medium and low grades and even large contractors followed fine-clothing makers in adopting the organizational innovations, men's clothing establishments began to grow in size, starting in the late 1890s.[99]

In the men's clothing industry, Steven Fraser argues, the factory system grew up "especially in the period after 1905."[100] Statistics indeed show that the average size of the men's clothing establishment began to grow from 1905 on (see Table 2.4).

But the statistics do not reveal when modern factories began to be established. In addition, the table does not take into account geographical variances that allowed the growth of large factories to be offset by numerous tiny shops. Suppose that in 1900 a 200-worker factory was established in Rochester, while sixteen shops, each employing ten workers, opened in New York. Creating an average of only about twenty-one employees per establishment, this would have made no change in the average factory size throughout the country.

Contemporary observations, complementing the statistics, suggest that the factory began to develop from the late 1890s, as the American economy recovered from the impact of the 1893 depression. Rochester, Chicago, and Baltimore took the lead, later followed by Philadelphia and New York, where sweatshops mushroomed and prospered well into

TABLE 2.4
The Average Size of Men's Clothing Establishments, 1890–1914*

	No. of establishments	*Capital*	*Wage Earners*	*Average capital/ est.*	*Average wage-earners/ est.*
1890	4,867	$128,253,547	144,926	$26,352	29.8
1900	5,729	120,547,851	120,927	21,042	21.1
1905	4,504	153,177,500	137,190	34,009	30.5
1909	5,584	203,703,112	191,183	36,479	34.2
1914	4,830	224,050,401	173,747	46,387	36.0

*Except buttonhole shops

Source: U.S. Department of Commerce and Labor, Bureau of the Census, *Manufactures: 1905*, Pt. 1: *United States by Industries*, 1907, 6; U.S. Department of Commerce, Bureau of the Census, *Census of Manufactures: 1914*, vol. 2: *Reports for Selected Industries and Detail Statistics for Industries, By States*, 1919, 173–174.

the first decade of the twentieth century. In her study published in 1902, Mabel H. Willett pointed out: "This [the factory system] gained a foothold in New York six or seven years ago, and is now pushing hard the task system and the small shop."[101] And at about the same time, the U.S. Industrial Commission noted: "Quite recently what may be described as a factory system was introduced in a few establishments in New York."[102]

The industrial structure differed substantially among clothing centers; on the eve of World War I tiny shops still predominated in New York and Philadelphia, while large corporations characterized local business in Chicago, Cincinnati, Cleveland, and Rochester. Throughout the nation, however, factories directly run by manufacturing firms, whether large or small, now dominated the production of men's clothing. Although the firms still needed contractors to do the work that temporarily exceeded their own production capacity during the busy season,[103] the contract system, which had characterized the men's clothing industry a generation before, became only a minor factor. By 1914, contractors throughout the country were responsible for a mere 13.7 percent of the total value added by manufacture, though they employed nearly 29 percent of all the wage earners in the industry.[104]

WORK CULTURE IN THE FACTORY

By World War I workers faced a new environment in the men's clothing factories. The factories tended to be located beyond walking distance of most workers' residences. While many firms managed to keep their tailor shops close to immigrant settlements, others found old buildings inadequate and rented or built new ones. New buildings were usually located within the manufacturing districts so that the downtown management offices, now near the factories, could supervise the production process. In the late 1900s, for example, HSM, employing more than five thousand workers, leased a five-story building next to its thirteen-story factory at the corner of Monroe and Franklin Streets and erected two four-story buildings on the West Side of Chicago.[105] During the last decade of the nineteenth century, many small clothing shops scattered in Philadelphia's ethnic neighborhoods were replaced by large factories converging on the wholesale manufacturing area.[106] Unlike the sweatshop, the factory could be located away from immigrant settlements. Chicago's mass transit system took shape around the turn of the century, when the cable car was replaced by the electric street car and the elevated train. It connected the downtown clothing district with the North and West Sides where many Czechs, Jews, Poles, and Italians had settled. Although many could not afford the carfare, and others hesitated to go to an unfamiliar part of the city, an increasing number of men's clothing workers were forced to travel to a workplace distant and separate from their own ethnic neighborhoods.

Factories, especially those occupying new buildings, usually contained modern facilities. Although many still relied on doors and windows for ventilation, some installed suction fans, airshafts, and skylights. Large factories had washrooms, dressing rooms, and restrooms. But legacies of the sweatshop lingered. Fire escapes were frequently inadequate; wooden stairways were dark and narrow and iron steps old and "of doubtful strength"; access to the escapes was often blocked or obstructed by machines or tables. A separate lunchroom was still rare. Most workers ate their meals in the workroom, bringing lunch with them or buying from a food peddler who offered milk, coffee, fruit, cakes, cookies, and candy.[107]

Women were more conspicuous than men in the modern factory. In New York, and to a certain extent Philadelphia, where thousands of immigrant tailors continued to arrive from eastern and southern Europe until the outbreak of World War I, men had increasingly replaced women in sweatshops. But manufacturers in Chicago and Rochester employed many more women than men although the latter had once constituted the majority in the inside shops. In the two inland cities, according to a Congressional report published in 1911, the number of female employees now approached three-fifths of all the workforce in the tailor shops, with cutting rooms, stock rooms, and offices excluded. In Chicago these women were young, more than one-half of them less than twenty-one years old, while only about one-fourth of their male counterparts had not arrived at adulthood. And the women were predominantly of foreign origin, Czechs, Jews, Poles, and Italians in particular; three-fifths were foreign-born, with another one-third native-born of immigrant parentage. In this regard Chicago was also distinctive; in New York almost nine out of ten female employees were foreign-born; in Rochester more than one-half were native-born Americans.[108]

Now factory workers were placed in the industrial-capitalist context. Unlike in the sweatshop, where the relationship between an employer and his employees was sometimes subtle and frequently undefined, the owner of a large firm was almost invariably someone remote from the workers. Whether his factories were located close to his downtown office or not, the manufacturer was more often than not invisible to his employees. "The personal relation between employer and employee . . . is lost in most large factories," declared the Commerce Department study of this industry in 1916, "where the worker knows only the foreman or superintendent, and where the employer is only a name."[109] As Joseph Schaffner lamented when a small strike that had begun at one of the HSM factories in 1910 developed into a full-scale conflict between all men's clothing workers and their employers in Chicago, large manufacturers were badly informed about conditions at the factories.[110]

Lacking any channel of direct communication with their employer, workers could feel only his authority through petty bosses, foremen or forewomen who exercised comprehensive powers handed down from their predecessors. Like the inside contractor, or even the outside contractor, they held the power to hire and fire workers in their sections and to decide each employee's wage rates, as well as to administer disciplinary measures. Exercising these powers, foremen or forewomen constantly drove workers to accelerate production, and earned bonuses; each section was carefully balanced and continually readjusted to minimize overcrowding or undermanning, so that the work could flow from one section to the next according to the pace set by the management.[111] Unlike the outside contractor running a sweatshop, therefore, the bosses rarely became friendly with their section workers. Instead, they were one of the main targets of workers' protests.

Discipline was strict at the factory. As working hours in large establishments gradually declined from sixty to fifty-six a week during the first decade of the twentieth century, manufacturers exacted more labor from the workforce. The hours of entering and leaving the factory were strictly observed. A worker had to be at his or her machine or workbench at exactly eight o'clock in the morning. If late, pieceworkers were not allowed to work in the morning while those paid by the week were fined. Some manufacturers put employees' hats and coats in the dressing room and locked it to prevent them from ducking out of the factory during working hours.[112] Smoking, snacking, singing, or talking was forbidden in the factory. Pieceworkers, who could control their own output, enjoyed a limited privilege in socializing, which manufacturers later abolished so that it would not affect the work pace of those paid by the week. The foreman or forewoman could suspend unruly workers for a few days. Employees were expected to meet high standards of workmanship. When an employee made a mistake that could not be properly repaired, he or she was forced to buy the garment at its retail price.[113]

Under the section system workers lacked control over their work. In the factory, where work was steady and where the employer decided how it was to be organized, the foreman and the superintendent dominated the labor process. Petty bosses required the workers to specialize at only one fragment of the whole manufacturing process and to work at the pace that was set by management and enforced through discipline. As most of the men's clothing workers had never worked in a factory either in Europe or in America, they found it particularly distressing that there was always someone controlling their work. Some resented "interference of freedom" in the factory and chose to work in small contract shops.[114]

But most factory workers earned better wages than sweatshop employees. Factory wage rates were not comparable to those of the sweatshops, not only because factory workers did not perform the same tasks as their fellows but also because they frequently worked on different grades of garments. In the factories work was much steadier than in the contract shops; manufacturers made efforts to keep the inside shops busy even in the slack season, by maintaining a workforce smaller than they needed during the busy season. In fact, sweatshop employees frequently left after learning the trade and sought better-paying jobs in the factories.

The rise of the modern factory made manufacturers sensitive to the possibility of workers' collective action. When the family system or the sweating system dominated the men's clothing industry, manufacturers had little contact with workers because middlemen, contractors, or subcontractors were in charge of the workforce. Even if a manufacturer had a labor problem, it usually stopped short of inspiring an organized movement. But the integration of contract shops made the manufacturer not only responsible for any dispute in the inside shop, but also aware that his establishment was vulnerable to the influence of organized labor. A work stoppage in one section could disrupt the operation of the whole factory. In fact, stoppages such as "section strikes" and "shop strikes" became an epidemic in large clothing establishments in the first decade of the twentieth century.[115] Until a general strike assailed Chicago's men's clothing industry in 1910, however, petty stoppages seldom implicated the top management of the modern factories. Although subdivision of the labor process demanded an effort to integrate the segmented work, and with it managerial authority, the one lagged behind the other; foremen and forewomen still enjoyed much of their old authority on the shop floor, even though the production process had been integrated, as demanded by the section system. As long as shop floor managers succeeded in containing stoppages within their sections, the factory appeared to operate smoothly, and there appeared to be no compelling reason for top management to consolidate power. Once the lines of authority failed, however, management was confronted with a bewildering development, exacerbated by its unfamiliarity with the reality of the shop floor. This was exactly what happened in the 1910–1911 strike, which prompted manufacturers to consolidate managerial authority.

Manufacturers, aware of their vulnerability though not alarmed by it, tried to keep their employees divided. Above all, they took advantage of ethnic diversity. When they began to integrate contract shops into their factories, each of the shops was overwhelmingly dominated by one ethnic group. This apparently continued to be true while the inside contractor was in charge of his workforce. Ethnic homogeneity, however, disappeared when the inside shop was reorganized under the section system. Now the workers were assigned to various sections according to their specialties, and so they intermingled with their fellows from other ethnic groups. Unlike the sweatshop, therefore, each section of a modern clothing factory was characterized by ethnic diversity. When Jacob S. Potofsky, a Russian Jew who later became president of the Amalgamated Clothing Workers of America (ACW), was making pockets in an HSM pants shop in the first decade of this century, he worked "alongside of the Polish and Bohemian girls," while a Jewish operator sat opposite him and Italians pressed pants.[116]

Such diversity made it difficult for workers to communicate to one another, for many did not speak English. When a worker needed to talk to a neighboring worker from a different ethnic background, a third worker was often asked to translate. Foremen and forewomen encouraged ethnic prejudices among the workforce, resorting to the widespread perception that immigrants from eastern and southern Europe were inferior races. These petty bosses used pejorative titles such as "Bohunk," "Polack," "Dago," or "lousy Jew." There were ethnic cleavages among men's clothing workers, and at the workplace some of them used abusive language or gestures to denigrate each others' nationalities, a practice the ACW later endeavored to abolish by reprimanding or punishing ethnic chauvinists among their ranks. Away from the job the workers did not have the opportunity to mix with one another, for they returned to their own ethnic neighborhoods.

Manufacturers also resorted to a "divide and rule" policy, by manipulating the wage scale. In the men's clothing industry the requirements of a job were never fixed, and each job was frequently redefined according to factors such as the availability of shop hands and occasional changes in clothing styles. Wage rates were never standardized, though there appeared to be a vaguely implicit bracket within which an employer compensated for a certain type of job. The actual rates of pay were decided through individual bargaining between the foreman and each employee, as had been the case in the sweatshop. Manufacturers took advantage of a fluid wage scale and offered different wages even to employees doing the same job in the same room. "For one hundred linings," complained a B. Kuppenheimer employee during the 1910–1911 strike, "they paid one girl $1.75, and the next girl sitting from me she gets $1.50 and the third $1.25 and they never pay the same wages. . . ."[117] By favoring certain workers with higher wages, management promoted tension within the workforce.

Job hierarchies developed apparently without design, unlike, for instance, the steel industry. There, technological innovations had deskilled the labor process and made the workforce increasingly homogeneous after the early 1890s. In order to "counter the increased simplicity and homogeneity of jobs," as Katherine Stone argues, employers deliberately instituted a differentiated job structure and used it to motivate the workers.[118] Manufacturers of men's clothing, however, did not feel technology made it necessary to build up a hierarchical labor market in the factory. In introducing the section system, they had sought merely to cut down labor costs while dictating different, though variable, wage rates for each operation. When pulled together, the rates constituted a hierarchical structure of compensation and promotion. Beginning from the lowest-paying job, a worker could gradually move up to better-paying work by spending several weeks mastering an operation.

There was a definite division of labor by gender within the job hierarchy. Cutters did not admit female apprentices, and pressing required too much physical strength for a woman. Women workers were expected to confine themselves to finishing, button sewing, buttonhole making, or pocket making, while men could usually advance to better-paying jobs. Explaining the training of men's clothing workers, a Chicago foreman provided an outline of the job hierarchies in an average sectionalized coat shop around 1910 (see Table 2.5). Hierarchies varied according to the size of the factory and the level of skill required in the labor process. Thus, in a pants shop or a vest shop, which tended to be smaller and called for fewer skills than a coat shop, the list of job hierarchies was short, and so was the period of training for each job.[119]

Although the hierarchy in a men's clothing factory lacked a formal and well-defined structure, it worked as a device to prevent employees from collectively presenting a common complaint about their wage rates. The hierarchy allowed each individual to earn more by promoting himself or herself to a better-paying position. A number of workers did not seek promotion, for it usually meant "a period of reduced productivity and reduced wages" while they learned the skills necessary for the new job. They chose instead to work to achieve greater speed at their current trade. Albert Wadopian, a Russian Jew who in 1912 began working at an HSM shop, remained a lining maker until his retirement, except for the several years he spent operating his own business.[120] Some ambitious employees were determined to be "all-round" workers by learning all the operations necessary for completing a garment. Although an all-round worker received more work at better wage rates than others, it usually took two years for a beginner to become a highly

TABLE 2.5
Job Hierarchies for Female Workers in the Sectionalized Coat Shop

Stage	*Job*	*Payment*	*Training*	*Wages*
Hand worker				
1	Sleeve canvas basting	Week	3 months	$2.50–$3.00
2	Lapel padding	Piece	(taught at Stage 1)	$3.00
	Collar padding	Piece	(taught at Stage 1)	$3.00
3	Sleeve making	Piece	3 months	$5.00
4	Finishing	Piece	3 months	$7.00–$8.00
	Button sewing	Piece	1 month	$7.00–$8.00
	Buttonhole making	Piece	3 months	$6.00–$10.00
5	Collar basting	Piece	3 months	$12.00
	Collar making	Piece	3 months	$12.00
Machine operator				
1	Canvas stitching	Week/piece	3 months	$3.00–$4.00
2	Pocket facing	Piece	3 months	$4.50
	Cash pocket making	Piece	3 months	$4.50
3	Body lining making	Piece	3–6 months	$6.00–$8.00
4	Pocket making	Piece	3 months	$10.00
5	Welt pocket making	Piece	3 months	$12.00–$13.00
	Sleeve sewing	Piece	1– months	$12.00–$13.00

Source: U.S., Congress, Senate, *Report on Condition of Woman and Child Wage-Earners in the United States*, vol. 2: *Men's Ready-Made Clothing*, S. Doc. 645, 61st Cong., 2d sess., 1911, 477–479.

skilled hand. Few workers moved from the bottom to the top of a job hierarchy in a men's clothing factory. Many moved among several jobs. To them, promotion was a good opportunity to satisfy, at least in part, their desire to earn more. "[W]e have had girls make eight or ten dollars on their work," a cashier of Rosenwald and Weil, a Chicago men's clothing firm, testified in 1913 before Illinois Senate Vice Committee, "and then they will willingly stop [at a] eight or nine dollar work and start in on another position in which they can advance themselves further on. . . ." The cashier added, "A girl will deliberately stop . . . and start in on something which will promise her more money for the future."[121] Jacob S. Potofsky was also caught between the extremes. In his first job at HSM,

> I was working for $3 a week. When I got my working papers [a birth affidavit] I went back to the same shop, and I got a job for $5 a week as an errand boy. My job was to run errands, deliver bundles. . . . [A]fter I was there for several weeks, he [Potosfsky's foreman] gave me an opportunity to learn to become an operator. . . . Well, I worked on rags for a couple of weeks; and then after two weeks, I worked on piece work making pockets—hip pockets, side pockets on pants.
>
> The first week that I was on piece work I earned $7.21, which was $2.21 more than the company had paid me.[122]

Manufacturers of men's clothing could not entirely prevent workers' solidarity from growing around the turn of the century. Ironically, their failure was closely related to the organization of production that they spared no pains to keep more profitable than the sweating system. Minutely subdividing the labor process under the section system, they needed more cheap and unskilled labor than ever in order to make the new organization function successfully. Such labor could be easily found among newly arrived immigrants, from whose number the manufacturers sought to recruit their workforce. Lacking personal access to the immigrant community, however, they had to rely upon foremen and forewomen. "Often foremen were hired solely for their ability to procure help from among their countrymen," noted the U.S. Commerce Department report on the men's clothing industry in 1916, "as the large inside house had difficulty in securing sufficient employees, there being no employment agencies and newspaper advertising having proved futile."[123] In practice, petty bosses recruited immigrants through employees' networks of kin and acquaintance. A foreman usually had access only to members of his own nationality, and the most recent arrivals did not have sufficient information about available jobs to be able to connect with employers, so the workers in a shop frequently made an arrangement with their petty boss regarding additional or replacement labor. According to Albert Wadopian's recollection, they usually would ask the foreman if they might bring into the shop family members, relatives, friends, or neighbors from their home town in the old country. In some cases, they arranged jobs for countrymen who had not yet embarked for America.[124]

Pieceworkers often brought newcomers into the shop and hired them as assistants. This practice was called "inside subcontracting," because the pieceworker, although himself employed by the shop, was responsible both for the output of his assistants and for payment of their wages. It was not used extensively, outside of New York and Philadelphia, and was concentrated in the areas of pocket making, joining, busheling, and pressing.[125] When newcomers were hired as assistants, however, they were obviously connected to the pieceworker, either through kinship or through acquaintance. In this way Jacob Potofsky got his first job in this country. When he arrived in Chicago, a Russian Jew who came from the same town in the old country as Potofsky offered him work at an HSM shop, although apparently not on the firm's payroll. According to Potofsky's recollection, "He paid me $3 a week and my assignment was to write the lot numbers and to fetch the bundles for him," which allowed the man to increase his own output.[126] In ways such as these, men's clothing workers of Chicago brought social relations in the community to the workplace.

Working with others in the shop, the workers could develop their social networks. Strict discipline in the factory limited socializing on the shop floor. They could speak only a few words or exchange simple gestures among themselves. Even lunchtime was not a good opportunity for social life as the workers, particularly pieceworkers, usually had their meals at the machine or workbench to save time.[127] Yet, they made new friends in the workplace, taking advantage of the job hierarchy as well as the gender-based division of labor.[128] The section system necessarily required instruction not only of "greenhorns" trying to learn to make a stitch but also of those employees who wanted to start new jobs. While the training of workers in a pants shop or vest shop was simple and short, instruction in a coat shop took longer and demanded the close attention of both the trainer and the trainee. Under the supervision of the foreman or forewoman, the trainee was placed next to an experienced worker paid by the week, and practiced an operation until he or she became proficient. During the training period, feelings of brotherhood or sisterhood frequently developed between the two, as the experienced worker taught the learner techniques for saving time and to disguise mistakes already made.[129] In this way workers made friends with their fellows at the workplace and their networks of acquaintance became linked. In clothing centers such as Chicago, where the modern factory prevailed over the small contract shop and where immigrant workers were extensively recruited, most men's clothing workers were connected to one another, at least within their own ethnic boundaries.

Personal connections, though ethnically defined, made it possible for men's clothing workers to pursue collectively their common interests on the shop floor. Above all, they resisted exploitation by imposing their own restrictions on the competition between individuals for more earnings. In the tailor shop management set the general pace of work, chiefly according to the fastest workers' speed. But workers slowed down the fast hands by criticizing them for trying "to curry favor with the boss" and perhaps by refusing to socialize with them in the workplace. In the cutting room, on the other hand, the number of layers of cloth in one cutting was often an issue. As technological innovations, the band knife in particular, greatly increased the number of layers that could be cut at one time, cutters had to put more energy and care into their work. The United Garment Workers of America (UGW), a craft union formed in 1891 by skilled workers, chiefly German and Irish cutters, took pains to restrict either the number of layers in one cutting or the amount of a day's work. Around the turn of the century the union fixed the number of layers at thirty through collective bargaining, while in nonunion shops producing better garments it was common for a cutter to work on thirty to thirty-six layers of heavy fabric or forty to forty-five of lightweight.[130]

In their resistance to being overworked, men's clothing workers shared a long-range goal: steady employment. Although factories and large contract shops provided steadier work than sweatshops, workers in large establishments were not immune to the seasonality of the men's clothing industry. At the end of each busy season many workers were laid off for the following two or three months, while others lost wage increases they had painstakingly won at the season's beginning. To protect their earnings men's clothing workers sought to "lengthen the seasons." Although some, especially fast hands, tried to avoid layoffs by impressing their boss with their productivity, others believed that the fast hands were shortening the busy season by working fast. Most workers wanted to spread the work throughout the year. They also desired to share the work equally among themselves, especially during the slack season. As the U.S. Commissioner of Labor reported in 1904, there was "an unwritten law," which the workers were not able to enforce yet, "that when work slackens the employer shall run short time instead of laying off a part of his force."[131] The "law," promulgated by ready-made tailors, whom the UGW long neglected because of its identity as a craft union, its conservative leadership, and ethnic barriers, remained an ideal until World War I. It was brought to life by the ACW, which vigorously organized the tailors during the war years.

The demand for an equal division of work during the slack season reveals the strong solidarity that factory workers had developed by the early twentieth century. Solidarity was not incompatible with individual competition on the shop floor, which continued to characterize the workplace. According to Lottie Spitzer, an HSM employee, workers selecting bundles to sew occasionally fought with each other because some of them wanted easy or profitable ones. But competition did not necessarily prevail the workroom; Spitzer willingly let one of her fellows take a big bundle every morning.[132] After all, factory workers had complicated networks of personal connection at the workplace, which probably discouraged excessive competition among themselves.

While extended acquaintance networks helped cultivate solidarity among factory workers, their collective resentment of the strict workplace discipline fertilized the soil. Working in the modern factory, they found themselves in a new work culture. Work was not only steady but also intensified, separated from leisure. In the factories, workers were driven to exhaust themselves, and denied any recreation or socializing that might have mitigated the tedious work. Factory workers resented the discipline imposed by petty bosses who treated them like "slaves," telling them not to talk or stay too long in the restroom.[133] From their point of view, it was such discipline that made the busy season unnaturally short. Resistance to the strict discipline eventually led to the effort to "lengthen the seasons," in which they would equally share the work.

Solidarity was based on the position men's clothing workers came to occupy in industrial capitalism, as their roles as wage earners became clear in the factory. Steady employment effectively deprived work in the men's clothing industry of the casual nature that had characterized the sweatshops. A number of unskilled workers, especially those on the lowest rungs of the job ladder, hunted for other occupations during the slack season and left the men's clothing factories. In disclosing their occupation to agents of the *Lakeside Directory of Chicago* at the turn of the century, many men's clothing workers still described themselves as laborers or factory workers. But most identified themselves as tailors or tailoresses, while the skilled wanted to be called cutters, pressers, or just "mechanics" according to the trade. On the other hand, their employers did not work side by side with them and were almost never known to them. In fact, it was the employers who dictated the strict discipline they were trying to evade or resist each day. Factory discipline led men's clothing workers to see their interests as conflicting with their employer's.

The conflict was centered on the transformed labor process, over which employers failed to monopolize control. As shown in this chapter, the process was not just minutely subdivided but also carefully coordinated, which rendered it vulnerable to workers' intervention. This vulnerability was not confined to the men's clothing industry. The Ford Motor Company subdivided the labor process at Highland Park, and rearranged it in order to balance its diverse segments. Consequently, the Detroit plant turned the manufactories that comprised the company into an integrated production unit, but, finding that continuous operation of the unit could be easily interrupted by workers, instituted a well-known incentive scheme and then a notorious labor repression system as well.[134]

Vulnerability was not properly emphasized by Harry Braverman, although he offered an influential analysis of the labor process.[135] Focusing on the control that management secured by subdividing the labor process, he did not fully explore the phase during which segmented work was coordinated into a continuous flow. This coordination was equally significant in Taylorism, the basis of Braverman's theory. Frederick Taylor, already interested in the system of management in the mid-1880s, concentrated on the foremen, who enjoyed the authority to determine the procedure and method of work at each stage of the process. Taylor eventually developed the idea of functional foremanship, recommending that the foreman be divested of that wide-ranging authority and carry out instead, under the direction of a superintendent, a specific function assigned by a centralized planning department.[136] Centralized planning, however, as envisioned by Taylor, did not ensure employers exclusive control over the labor process. On this point, the historian Richard Price is convincing. Joining the debate on the labor process, he refutes the thesis that industrial capitalism really subordinated the workers to the employer. He instead conceives of real subordination, like the effort workers made to retain control over the process, as a tendency inherent in capitalism. Price suggests that in the labor process itself "a mutual and dialectical relationship exists between resistance and subordination."[137]

But the conflict of interests is not the only factor to be taken into account in the contest between the employer and the workers. Although the workplace continues to be a "contested terrain,"[138] the contest holds only within an implicit boundary; it ends as soon as a contestant renounces the relationship of employment. So the contestants make a bottom compromise to share the terrain. Furthermore, they do not come to terms under equal conditions; while affording critical leverage to an employer who can put the workforce out of employment, the relationship constrains the workers from putting the employer out of business, which is a self-destroying act. Unless the workers seek a social revolution, they are impelled to restrain themselves so that their employer might continue to be competitive and in business. Hence, the imperative of compromise.

The relationship, sustained by the imperatives of conflict and compromise at the workplace, is not independent of the larger society; each contestant resorts to any resources available, outside as well as inside the factory. While the employer mobilizes power, physical, political, or cultural, from outside, the workers try to win support from the community. This is especially the case when there is a full-scale struggle such as the 1910–1911 strike.

CHAPTER 3

The 1910–1911 Strike

Nobody expected a labor dispute to disturb Chicago's men's clothing industry in 1910. Peace had prevailed since employers had broken a strike by cutters in 1904 and then almost rooted out their union, the United Garment Workers (UGW). There had been some disputes, especially at the beginning of the busy season, but they had usually involved a limited number of workers and lasted only for a few days. Except for blacklisting a handful of union workers, employers did not concern themselves with labor relations, a realm controlled by the foremen. Unskilled workers, long divided by ethnicity and neglected by the union, never dreamed of a general strike. The 1910–1911 strike hit like a thunderstorm.

The strike, which eventually involved all the men's clothing workers in Chicago, began with a trifling trouble. It was Thursday, September 22, 1910. At Shop 5 of Hart, Schaffner and Marx, Hannah Shapiro and her fellow workers asked the foreman to raise the current wage rate. Though only eighteen years old, Shapiro, a Ukrainian Jew, was a good hand with four years' experience in the men's clothing industry. For several weeks she had worked at the rate of three and three-quarter cents for seaming a pair of pants, a quarter of a cent less than she had been paid in the previous busy season. Now the shop was again running full time and the workers wanted their old wage rate restored. Since they could seam no more than sixty pairs of pants a day, less than fifteen cents a day was at stake. But that amount was significant to them because the rate had been stagnant for years while they had had to work harder and harder. When the foreman refused, Shapiro led her fellow workers out of the shop.[1]

Although there was nothing unusual about this first walkout, it did not end up an isolated episode, as had often been the case. The next day, Shapiro and others returned to the workplace and argued in vain with the foreman and superintendents. Aware that Shapiro was the leader of the group, the bosses tried to persuade her to go back to work. But she was determined. On September 26, the following Monday, she went to the downtown HSM office and deliberately made trouble by hollering, "I want my pay." In the meantime, the work Hannah Shapiro and her fellows had left undone was given to Shops 14 and 15. But on a Wednesday, probably September 28, a man visited one of the shops and said: "Don't do that work; the people went on a strike and now you are doing that work and you know that it is scab work."[2] When the foreman threw him out of the shop, all the workers protested and, picking up their tools, quit the place. Though local newspapers ignored the walkouts for the first three weeks, news of the dispute spread by work of mouth. By October 10, about eighteen hundred HSM workers were on strike.[3]

From that point on, workers who had already quit their workplaces transformed the strike into a major event. On October 10, the HSM pants makers gathered at the West Side Auditorium, where four hundred coat and vest makers of the firm appeared and pledged to stay out, placing more than one-fourth of its eight thousand workers on strike. The strikers also decided to call out all the other HSM employees. That same day four hundred workers employed at B. Kuppenheimer and Co. quit their workplace. A week later, cutters, who had long formed a distinct group both in ethnicity and skill, walked out by the hundreds from HSM, Kuppenheimer, and other firms. By October 25, the strikers had crippled ten large firms and their number was well over sixteen thousand, more than one-third of the entire workforce in Chicago's men's clothing industry. Two days later they succeeded in forcing the UGW to call a general strike.[4] Soon the strike involved virtually all Chicago's men's clothing workers and their employers.

This strike, one of the notable "uprisings" by immigrant workers in the early twentieth century, has some distinctive features. Until the UGW called it off on February 3, the estimated forty-one thousand strikers, who had long been ethnically divided, banded together in a novel way. They did not engage in separate fights with their individual employers, but instead disregarded the lines that divided them according to their workplaces and grouped themselves into neighborhood units. Mostly immigrants concentrated in certain districts, they gathered at halls in their own neighborhoods, articulated their ideas about how to carry on the struggle, and exchanged views by sending delegations to other meeting places. The workers not only fought their employers but also asserted themselves against the leadership provided by the UGW, the Chicago Federation of Labor (CFL), and the Women's Trade Union League (WTUL). Unfamiliar with the practices of the American organized labor, they welcomed the initiative as well as the financial assistance and moral support offered by native-born leaders. When the workers disagreed with the leaders' plan of action, however, they refused to follow. In pursuing their interests, the immigrants asserted their own leadership instead of being obedient to the native-born leaders, who were out of touch with the realities of their workplaces or picket lines. Through the long and bitterly contested strike, they attempted to build up an indigenous leadership and replace outside leaders who wanted to end this struggle by making it a series of separate fights between individual firms and their employees.

These characteristics reveal themselves in the light of key questions about the strike, which still remain puzzling though the strike is now well known.[5] How did unorganized workers escalate the first trivial walkout into a general strike? Why did it happen at this particular moment? How did the workers, long divided either by ethnicity or by skills, unite and assert themselves against the native-born labor leadership? What determined the outcome of the long and bitter contest? And what did the strike leave behind?

MAKING A GENERAL STRIKE

When Hannah Shapiro led the first walkout, the UGW was not prepared to call a strike at all. The union had been organized in 1891 by skilled workers, particularly German and Irish cutters. As an affiliate of the American Federation of Labor, it soon established exclusive jurisdiction over all workers in the men's ready-made clothing industry, while custom tailors formed the Journeymen Tailors' Union of America. The UGW rapidly increased its membership to fifty thousand by 1903, and in that year succeeded in imposing upon Chicago manufacturers a closed-shop agreement, by which the employers could hire no workers but UGW members.[6]

But the manufacturers would not allow the union to control the industry. In 1903 the National Association of Clothiers had confronted the labor problem. The Association had originally been formed by manufacturers who wanted to exchange information about retailers' credit and textile production among themselves. Since frequent strikes had resulted in loss of production and the failure of timely delivery to retailers, it advised its local body in each city to establish a labor bureau "for consideration of any action upon labor questions affecting the clothing manufacturers of the city." In July 1904, Chicago manufacturers of men's ready-made clothing, who had already formed the Wholesale Clothiers' Association, established a labor bureau at the Medinah Temple building. The bureau absorbed the labor exchanges run by the Wholesale Tailors' Association, the organization of special-order firms. The next month, the Clothiers' Association repudiated the earlier agreement with the UGW by announcing that its member firms would hire anyone regardless of their union affiliation. The cutters struck in protest. Three months later, the Tailors' Association joined the ready-made firms by announcing a similar policy. The strike expanded, but failed to tie up the industry. The employers eventually defeated the UGW by starving the cutters into submission. Then Chicago's labor bureau began systematic blacklisting, controlled by Martin J. Isaacs, a lawyer responsible to both associations. With the help of two assistants, each running an office, Isaacs gathered information about many cutters' employment histories, union activity, and other items that might be interesting to employers. When a cutter applied for a job at a firm affiliated with either of the associations, he was told to get a permit from Medinah Temple, which was in fact a clearance paper. By 1910, the labor bureau had almost completely destroyed the UGW's organization in Chicago.[7]

At the same time, the UGW had made little progress in recruiting tailors. It met with limited success only in the branch that produced work clothes, where manufacturers needed the union label in order to make their garments more attractive to workers. Instead, the union concentrated its organizational efforts on cutters, mostly native-born workers of German or Irish descent, whose work was not so minutely subdivided as the tailors' under the section system. UGW members often despised immigrant workers, disparagingly calling them "Columbus tailors." When workers went on strike at a shop, UGW officers collected initiation fees from the strikers and, if the fight resulted in a labor agreement, sold union labels to the employer. But afterward the union usually took no pains to maintain the organization at the shop. Nor did the workers expect it to do so, most dropping out as soon as the strike was over.[8] Certainly, the seasonality of the industry prevented many workers from paying their dues, and language barriers discouraged the immigrants from showing up at union meetings. Above all, however, the UGW lacked the initiative to adapt itself to the changing workforce during the first decade of the twentieth century.

The union played only a small role in the making of the 1910–1911 Chicago strike. A few days after the first walkout, some women workers went to its headquarters. Robert Noren, president of District Council No. 6, a conference of the UGW locals in the Chicago area, did not have much to say to the workers, though he notified the national office of the situation. But Thomas A. Rickert, president of the UGW, thought that "it was just an over-night strike." As walkouts spread to other HSM factories, Noren asked Rickert to come to Chicago and take charge of the strike. Rickert refused. Testifying before the Illinois Senate Special Committee to Investigate the Garment Workers' Strike in January 1911, he confessed, "I didn't have any particular faith in the organization or the possibility of organizing these people."[9] When he finally arrived at Chicago in mid-October, Rickert told reporters, "The union did not precipitate this strike."[10]

The "over-night strike" had already plagued Chicago's men's clothing factories for some time. A decade of prosperity following the late 1890s had encouraged manufacturers to expand production of fine garments by offering better wages to experienced workers, while the section system enabled them to cut labor costs and increase productivity. As most large establishments instituted the system in early years of the twentieth century, however, they became involved in intense competition among themselves. The 1907 recession accelerated the competition by shrinking the market, which pressured manufacturers to cut costs. In the factories, however, experienced workers successfully resisted a reduction of wage rates by refusing to do the work and hindering the goods from flowing to the next section. Frequently, wage cuts made during the slack time had to be restored at the beginning of the busy season, and this often incurred short-lasting strikes engaging a limited number of workers, since wage rates were determined by the foreman in charge of each section. And workers' bargaining power was growing as the American economy boomed in 1909–1910.

The plague, those "section strikes" or "shop strikes" that had become endemic by the end of the first decade of the twentieth century, was germinated by efforts by manufacturers to exact more labor power from their workforce. Frustrated in their attempts to secure lower wage rates, they extended the piecework system to almost all operations except cutting. From their viewpoint, piecework was particularly desirable because finer garments needed more labor and time. They forced the workers to put in extra stitches or cut more layers of cloth for the same wage rates. Katherine Coman, a Wellesley economist who studied the strikers' grievances in November 1910, appropriately noted that there was, "in proportion to output, a reduction of wages amounting from *fifteen* to *twenty per cent*."[11] The Citizens' Strike Committee, formed by famous settlement workers, clergymen, academics, and others in order to investigate the strike, agreed on this point. After interviewing dozens of workers employed in eighteen firms, the committee declared, "There is little complaint with reference to the rates of wages paid." However, it regarded as one of the most important grievances the constant "attempts to increase the speed of the workers or the complexity of the task without a corresponding increase in pay."[12]

That grievance was indeed widespread among factory workers, who walked out before the general strike call on October 27 and stayed out to the finish. Their shared discontent crossed the lines drawn to distinguish between skills. Craftsmen joined the protest against more work without wage increases. As discussed in the preceding chapter, cutters had to spend more time and energy matching patterns to fewer yards of cloth and cutting more layers at a time. But their 1904 strike failed to bring an end to exploitation; many were replaced by Jewish apprentices, who worked faster at lower wage rates. The temporary boom in 1909–1910 improved their bargaining position, and the strike calls by unskilled workers led them to speak out. "The time consumed in extra matching owing to increased economy of cloth makes it impossible for us to get out our usual stint," declared two cutters, "and has resulted in our wages being cut as much as twenty per cent."[13]

There were other grievances, too. The modern men's clothing factory was originally an aggregate of contract shops. Once a number of the shops had been put together, the manufacturer concentrated on financing and marketing and left the factory to be run by a manager or superintendent. Although they controlled and exhorted the staff to increase the factory's output, manufacturers did not intervene in the day-to-day operation of the workrooms. As a result, the factory inherited invidious practices from the sweatshop. Foremen and forewomen, held responsible for output, endeavored to speed up the labor process by any means, including using abusive language. Petty bosses often required that workers first secure a pass from them before leaving the workroom to get a drink or go to the restroom. They ruled the workrooms like "slave drivers" or "Czars," as Jewish workers put it.[14] Factory workers also felt aggrieved at various legacies of the sweating system. Fines, called "merchandise" on the pay envelope, were imposed for losing implements such as spools and bobbins or for "even a liberal use of soap in washing hands." And when an employee fell sick, he or she was not allowed to go home, but was given "some powders—good for every ailment from an earache to a sick stomach."[15]

These grievances, though they stayed pent up during the 1909–1910 boom, made the factory workers restless. Collective action was a growing likelihood; the workers had long maintained brotherhood and sisterhood, seeking to share equally the work year round by resisting speed-up. Some had organized themselves into independent unions, but failed to reach out beyond their own work groups.[16] Most were apparently inclined toward direct action, a form of protest that had long characterized unorganized workers in Europe. Action began at HSM, the leader of innovation in the men's clothing industry and at the same time a magnet for experienced workers, who were more articulate than newcomers. Hannah Shapiro and her follows were resolved to make their walkout more than "an over-night strike," and tried to persuade others to refuse to work. In assailing the giant firm, they took advantage of its intricately organized section system, and found others ready to walk out with them. In early November 1910, when the Women's Trade Union

League, an AFL affiliate that middle-class women and social workers as well as female unionists had formed in 1903 to support organizing efforts among women workers, investigated the 1910–1911 strike, a canvas spreader told them: "When I heard about the strike I told the girls we should go down because now was the time. . . ."[17]

Soon, almost one-fourth of the HSM workforce was on strike. The firm was bewildered at the development, while, at the same time, the strikers were confused about what to do next. On October 11, workers gathered at Hod Carriers' Hall and talked about calling a general strike. But a woman named "G. Abramovitch," probably Bessie Abramovitz who already had experience in the labor movement and later married Sidney Hillman, made a plea for prudence. "Have you thought of what it means to call a general strike? Do you know what responsibilities you would burden yourselves with?" she shouted.[18] Then she proposed that each of the factories affected by the strike should be represented by a committee of two strikers, and that the committees should investigate wages and working conditions and draw up demands. In accordance with the proposal, the strike committee, then composed of Robert Noren and three other UGW officers from Chicago, framed a list of the workers' demands. The committee stressed recognition of the union above all and placed real grievances next, apparently trying to take command of the strike.[19] After sending the list to the manager of the HSM manufacturing department, therefore, the committee did not have much to do for the strikers.

Instead of waiting for a response from HSM, which did not admit to any problems at its factories, however, the strikers decided to develop their walkout into a major battle. The daily gatherings after October 10 showed the workers that they belonged to a unified group, irrespective of their workplaces. At the halls rented by District Council No. 6, the strikers, together with many of the workers who had not walked out yet, spoke out in their mother tongues or in broken English. They described their personal experiences at the factories and accused the employers and petty bosses of exploiting them. These meetings brought home to the workers that although they worked at diverse places, they shared the same resentment at the policies of their employers. Booing and hissing at the mention of HSM, Kuppenheimer, and other firms, they decided to spread the strike. They were aware that HSM was already transferring work either to other factories not affected by the strike or to contract shops.[20]

Workers who went to strikers' meetings often led the walkouts at their own workplaces without consulting either strikers or union officers. One of these was Jacob S. Potofsky, then a pocket maker at an HSM pants shop. Soon after the first trouble at Shop 5, he learned of a meeting at Hull House. While his father and brothers, also employed by the firm, stayed at home, Jacob Potofsky went to the meeting, where he saw two men from his own workroom, and heard "talk about spreading the strike from this shop [Shop 5] to all the rest of the shops." The next morning, Potofsky and the other two told the workers at their shop that they should join the strike. When the bell rang at 7:30 A.M., he urged them to gather at the center of the room. Then the foreman said to him, "Jake, what are you doing? Did I mistreat you?" "No, you've treated me very well," answered Potofsky, "but I must go. . . ."[21]

Thousands of workers walked out, following arrangements they had made with strikers. Probably, personal connections among immigrant workers facilitated such arrangements. Those who went to a strikers' meeting often planned a walkout with their acquaintances already on strike and then persuaded fellows at their workplace to quit at a designated time. As a result, a pattern emerged from the walkouts after October 10. It appeared for the first time on October 14, when, at about noon, a group of twenty-five strikers arrived at an HSM building on Polk and Forty-First Streets. At one o'clock, they blew whistles. Soon, the doors opened and seven hundred workers poured out and joined the strike.[22]

Little tin whistles became an accepted signal for prearranged walkouts, symbolizing men's clothing workers' solidarity. Robert Dvorak, a *Chicago Daily Socialist* reporter who closely observed the strike from its early days, described walkouts on October 17 as "a repetition" of the established pattern. When about one hundred strikers approached an HSM factory on Blucher and North Wood Streets, they were attacked by special policemen and private detectives. But some women managed to blow whistles. The windows were immediately opened and workers in the building shouted: "Go to it, comrades, we'll be down in a minute. Keep the doors open—they want to lock us in." The strikers "answered with a cheer" and fought to secure the exit, although beaten by the police trying to keep them from the doors. "In about five minutes," reported Dvorak, "there was a cheer from the inside and hundreds of men and women . . . dashed down the stairs to the sidewalk."[23]

The strikers often resorted to crowd action in order to call the workers out. When no advance arrangement had been made for a walkout, they urged those at work to join the strike by yelling from the street. This tactic was used particularly by cutters and trimmers, most of whom worked in the Loop. On October 17, more than four hundred cutters joined the strike. Employed at HSM, Kuppenheimer, or Hirsch, Wickwire and Co., they held a meeting of their own and then visited the strikers at Hod Carriers' Hall, "each carrying partly-opened shears above his head."[24] The next day, the cutters gathered in front of HSM's main building, at Franklin and Monroe Streets, gave "strike yells," and succeeded in calling out two hundred more. Then they went to a nearby Kuppenheimer factory and prompted one hundred fifty workers to quit the place.[25] The cutters evidently became confident of this tactic. Several days later, more than five hundred of them held a meeting at the UGW headquarters and left for the downtown clothing district, carrying shears and rules with them. The moment they arrived there, however, the police took the cutters by surprise and dispersed the crowd. "Their plan," the *Chicago Tribune* noted, "was to make stops in front of the various clothing houses in Market, Franklin, Adams and Van Buren streets and give strike yells in an effort to induce the employés still at work to join the strike movement."[26]

The brutality of the police kindled the workers' solidarity, contributing to the spreading of the strike. The police frequently assaulted the strikers as if they intended to break the strike by force, especially in the three-week period after October 10, when those already on strike were calling the others out.[27] In its official report about this strike, the WTUL noted the effects of the police brutality by giving an example:

> As one of the girls at Kuppenheimer's explained after a controversy regarding a cut of a cent for the pocketmakers, "When the foreman heard us talking about the strike he said, 'Girls, you can have your pockets and your cent back again if you'll stay.' But just then there was a big noise outside and we all rushed to the windows and there we saw the police beating the strikers—clubbing them on our account—and when we saw that we marched out."[28]

On the other hand, the strikers pressed the UGW to call a general strike in Chicago's men's clothing industry. The later walkouts between October 10 and 27 increased their ranks to around eighteen thousand, and tied up, entirely or partially, twelve large firms. However, these firms were sending work out to contractors and smaller firms, while trying to hire help from immigrant settlements. Aware that the struggle would only be prolonged unless a complete paralysis were achieved, the strikers demanded that the union issue a general strike call. But Robert Noren was evasive and Thomas Rickert would not come to Chicago. On October 26, strikers gathered at Columbia Hall and passed a motion that the union issue a call without delay, and the meeting at Hod Carriers' Hall that same day brought forth the same resolution.[29] Noren was again evasive, sloughing off the responsibility onto the UGW president, who was at odds with District Council No. 6. This time, however, Robert Dvorak confronted Noren and threatened that he would print in his newspaper a general strike call "in the name of the strikers" unless an official one was issued.[30] The next morning, Noren declared that a general strike was on.

Thousands of workers employed in contract shops and small firms immediately joined the strike. News of the walkouts spread from mouth to mouth in the ethnic neighborhoods within the clothing districts, and the strikers' activities helped the news travel. In various clothing districts strikers clashed with the police, while calling out those at work. "The southwest side, where a large number of the small contract shops are located," reported Dvorak, "was the scene of many battles."[31] Groups of strikers, without prearrangement with small-shop employees, threaded through the district. When they reached a shop, they blew whistles and held up the general strike call printed on the front page of the *Chicago Daily Socialist*. Small-shop employees almost invariably battled the police, with brooms or sticks in hand.[32] On October 28, Thomas Rickert, who had left Chicago following his short visit in the middle of the month, arrived to take charge of the situation and declared that thirty thousand workers were now on strike. On that day alone, more than ten thousand workers, mostly employees of small establishments, joined the strike.[33]

Those working at small shops, probably one-third of the forty-five thousand men's clothing workers in Chicago, were in fact ready to quit their workplaces. Many grumbled over wage cuts. Producing primarily lower grades of garments or contracting simple operations such as finishing from manufacturers, small shops relied upon the cheap labor of inexperienced hands. In such places, the workforce was recruited largely from among the Italians, the most recent immigrant group in the industry. In addition to the home work they had been doing, the Italians began replacing the Jews and Poles as shop hands from the turn of the century. Taking advantage of the constant turnover, employers cut wages or fired the eastern Europeans.[34] And small-shop employees shared the same living conditions as factory workers; in the first decade of the twentieth century, small shops were concentrated in the four districts where most of the factory workers lived.[35] In fact, the walkouts were a matter of more than passing interest to those who worked at small establishments, especially sweatshop employees; most of them wanted jobs at the factories, where personal connections were pivotal to hiring. The same connections among workers made it possible to evoke the communal tradition of collective resistance against the seigneur; when factory workers were trying to stop their work from being done at small shops, they described the manufacturers as the "clothing barons." Thus, the paralysis of the small shops was accomplished swiftly and nearly completely.

On the other hand, the general strike call did not bring forth the same response among those factory employees still at work. Many walked out on their own accord, such as roughly four hundred men and women at Edward V. Price and Co., but more were forced to quit by the strikers. Indeed, the three days from October 31 through November 2 was the most turbulent period after the first walkout. On October 31, strikers gathered at Van Buren and Halsted Streets, a point not far from the downtown clothing district. By the time they began to march toward the Loop, their ranks numbered about two thousand. But the strikers failed three times to enter the district because the police, whose entire force was held ready for strike duty, blocked the bridges leading downtown. Then the strikers stormed an HSM factory on the West Side. "Bricks and other missiles were thrown," according to the *Chicago Tribune*, "and the strikers demanded that the remaining workers walk out and join them."[36] The next day, the police arrested thirty-seven strikers for participating in "riots," which took place in front of Kuppenheimer, John J. Peklo, and other establishments. On November 2, the strikers were fiercer than ever. A. Lott and Co., a firm located on the Northwest Side, was attacked by five thousand strikers and sympathizers, some of whom "entered the building, dragged the sewing machines into the street and stoned the place."[37] The "riots" of the day left seventy-five strikers arrested, and both the police and strikers fired guns for the first time in this strike. Now more than forty-one thousand workers were on strike, and the few thousand still at work were branded as scabs.[38]

During the six-week period in which the first walkouts developed into a general strike, ethnic lines proved no obstacle to the immigrant workers' uprising. Arranging for the walkout from a workroom where several languages were spoken, factory workers managed to communicate with one another in English, even if it was often broken. Every ethnic group joined the strike in proportion to their number in the industry, leaving no particular one to be pointed to as strikebreakers. Numerically, more Czechs chose to remain at work, but the Czechs outnumbered any other group in Chicago's men's clothing factories. Jewish workers often led walkouts against their coreligionist employers, who dominated the industry but failed to win their hearts. The conduct of the strikers' meetings revealed the respect and patience the immigrant workers had for each other. On October 16, for example, a meeting at Hod Carriers' Hall attracted more than five thousand. Noren chaired and made a speech and announcements in English, but other speakers in turn addressed each of the major ethnic groups in six different languages: Bohemian, Yiddish, Russian, Polish, Italian, and Lithuanian. While one ethnic group was listening, the other strikers waited in silence until someone arose to speak in their own tongue.[39]

Throughout the six weeks, women workers were aggressive. Mostly young, particularly in their late teens, they left their jobs at marriage, and worked under tyrannical foremen. Instead of being passive and submissive to male authority, however, they usually followed their own leaders when they joined the strike.[40] Reporting a walkout at Kuppenheimer, the *Chicago Daily Socialist* pointed out that the two young women who initiated the action were "a sample of the agitators found in almost every shop of the strike-bound concerns."[41] Women also headed strikers' groups that included men, blowing whistles in front of men's clothing establishments. They often occupied the forefront of the groups in clashes with the police. In an article titled "Armed Mob Led by Girl in Fight," the *Chicago Tribune* reported that Josie Milewski, a fourteen-year-old striker, had prompted an attack on policemen at a Northwest Side factory.[42]

NATIVE-BORN STRIKE LEADERSHIP VERSUS ETHNIC WORKER SOLIDARITY

In addition to the spread of the strike, public pressure weakened the uncompromising attitude of Hart, Schaffner and Marx. At first the firm denied that the strike was taking place in its factories, claiming that the employees had no grievances about wages or working conditions. In fact, its top managers did not understand, as Joseph Schaffner later revealed to the U.S. Industrial Relations Commission,[43] why a petty problem had suddenly become an utmost concern, when the strikers had not even formulated their demands yet. When Benjamin F. Shadley, chairman of the Illinois Board of Arbitration, tried to mediate in mid-October, HSM admitted to its troubles with the employees but stressed that "the strikers made no demands and there was nothing to arbitrate."[44] By the end of October, however, it was almost completely tied up, as the strikers frustrated its attempts to send out work and hire strikebreakers from immigrant settlements. As the strike expanded its scope, local newspapers followed up daily developments. Though mostly unsympathetic to the strikers, they reported that the police handled roughly even those "aristocrat" picket lines that the WTUL had peopled with middle-class women in order to protect the strikers. Such public attention led to the formation of the Citizens' Strike Committee by twenty-five men and women of repute, including Rabbi Emil G. Hirsch, Jane Addams, and Judge Julian W. Mack, which expressed concern for the strikers' poverty and began to investigate their grievances and to consider remedies.[45] The pressure was chiefly brought to bear on HSM, the largest firm, where the strike had originated.

The expanding scope of the strike strengthened the UGW's position vis-à-vis the employers. When the strike had affected only HSM and a few other firms, Robert Noren and other Chicago officers had sought to have the union recognized, in addition to asking for wage increases and improvement of working conditions. Soon, however, no one was sure what the strikers were demanding. Thousands of them wanted "something better" but, lacking organization, they failed to formulate specific demands. The UGW, which had jurisdiction over the men's clothing industry and had admitted any strikers who paid the fifty-cent initiation fee, came to represent the strikers. Two days after the general strike was called, the union reportedly thought to advocate the "preferential shop," which would make the employers give priority in hiring, and protection against firing, to union members.[46] As the whole industry was brought to a standstill at the beginning of November, the UGW went one step farther. Thomas Rickert now pressed for the closed-shop agreement. At the same time, he made the strikers' grievances a secondary issue, probably in order to facilitate negotiations with the employers; the UGW proposed that the grievances be taken up by a committee of the employers and the union and, if it failed to settle, by arbitrators.[47] By this time about three-fourths of the strikers had joined the UGW, but Rickert did not feel that the organization was secure, because experience showed that immigrant men's clothing workers deserted the union after strikes. Now he apparently hoped to win a foothold for the UGW by instituting the closed shop.

A conference between the union and HSM began on November 4. It was made possible mainly through Jane Addams's efforts. She had a talk with Harry Hart, partial owner of the firm, who had often visited Hull House with his "social worker" wife. While Jane Addams explained why the workers walked out and how much they suffered from the strike, Harry Hart confessed that he was dismayed at her support of the strikers.[48] However, she succeeded in opening negotiations between the two sides. On the first day of the conference, the firm revealed that it was willing to increase wages and improve working conditions, but it stressed that "under no circumstances" would HSM recognize the union or accede to the demand for a closed shop. Faced with a stubborn HSM, Rickert and other union officers hinted that the UGW might withdraw the demand if the firm would allow the employees to organize shop committees to settle future grievances. While the negotiations went on, it was reported that the Citizens' Strike Committee found the strike "justified" and that an organization of the workers was necessary in the men's clothing industry. However, the UGW failed to capitalize on the report. Moreover, it was not prepared for a large-scale struggle. Strike benefits, which had been paid to only one-tenth of the strikers by the first day of the conference, had amounted to nearly $20,000 so far, a heavy drain on the union's lean treasury.[49]

The final results of the negotiations were dismal for the union. The agreement reached on November 5 provided that the strikers' grievances would be handled by a committee of three, one to be selected by HSM, another by the UGW, and a third by mutual agreement of the two. It added that the firm would not discriminate against union members. Lastly, the agreement stipulated that HSM did not recognize the union or any kind of shop organization, in addition to a pledge that the problem of open shop would not be considered as one of the grievances. The agreement was obviously an instrument of surrender. The *New York Evening Post* noted: "The promise that shop organization will not be brought up as a point of contention means a virtual defeat for the union on what . . . has been the one point on which it would insist—either a closed or a preferential shop."[50]

The HSM employees rejected the agreement. After Thomas Rickert explained it and painted it as a moral victory at a meeting of five hundred cutters, a striker retorted, "We want the closed shop and recognition of the union." When others echoed, "Yes, yes; nothing short of a closed shop," the meeting turned into an uproar with shouts of "Traitor!" "Throw him out!" and "Your agreement is rotten!" Undaunted, Rickert tried to persuade the cutters by calling their attention to the inevitable hardships if the strike continued. "Would you rather stay out and compel 40,000 men and women to stay out all winter, with hunger staring us in the face," he exclaimed, "than accept an agreement that insures us union conditions in the shops?" Rickert urged the strikers "to accept half a loaf." But the cutters drove him out of the meeting. Samuel L. Landers, an International Executive Board member of the UGW, had the same experience. After a tailors' meeting, Landers explained: "I had all I could do to get away from them. I could do nothing with them. They simply howled me and the agreement down and I had to get out."[51]

The agreement eventually brought about the downfall of the UGW's leadership among the strikers. Sidney Hillman, a rank-and-file leader in this strike, later revealed to the U.S. Industrial Relations Commission that the closed shop was "the remedy for everything" to the strikers, though most did not understand what it meant.[52] In their eyes, Thomas Rickert had "sold out" their cause. On the day the agreement was submitted to the HSM employees, strikers flocked together here and there and denounced Rickert, and that night they held two protest meetings. "The strike is not settled," claimed a speaker, continuing, "Let Rickert settle it for himself if he wants to. He has not settled it for us." He epitomized the strikers' determination, when he shouted: "Sell your needles.

Sell your shoes. Take the clothes off your back and sell them for food. But don't go back to work. You want liberty."[53] On the next two days the strikers gathered at several halls and voted to abide by the demand for the closed shop in addition to recognition of the union.[54]

Disappointed with Thomas Rickert and yet determined to win the struggle, the strikers turned to the Chicago Federation of Labor, a conference of the city's AFL affiliates that the resourceful horseshoer John Fitzpatrick had developed into a militant support group, with the help of socialists and progressive reformers, during the first decade of the twentieth century. The strikers sent a delegation to the CFL. Pointing out that the workers had lost confidence in Rickert and other UGW officers, it asked the federation to take over the leadership. August Benson of a cutters' union Local 61, UGW, professed, "I hope the federation will come forward and give us the leaders that are strong enough to handle this matter and bring the fight to a successful issue." Tobias Abrahams, another striker, appealed: "We don't know what to do. It lies with you, comrades and friends, to say what it shall be—defeat or glorious victory." A woman striker named Rose Mandelbaum pressed the federation to take part in the strike, declaring, "I hope you men won't force us to go back without the closed shop." This remark changed the atmosphere of the session; many came forward to the platform and contributed money for the strikers. The CFL instructed its executive board to intervene in the strike with full power to act.[55]

As a result, a new leadership emerged, with the strikers nominally participating. A Joint Strike Conference Board (JSCB) was formed by two representatives each from the following organizations: The CFL; the WTUL; the UGW; District Council No. 6; Strike Committee of the Ready Made Garment Workers; and Strike Committee of the Special Order Garment Workers.[56] Although Rickert and Noren took part on the board, their influence was minimal. While declaring that they were "on the job to stay," the UGW officers were not sincere in supporting the strikers. Only a few days after the board was created, ten thousand workers gathered in front of the UGW headquarters to get strike benefits. But the union did not have enough money to cash the vouchers it had issued, and simply kept its office doors closed. Finally, John Fitzpatrick, rather than either Noren or Rickert, appeared and urged the workers to go home or to their meeting places.[57] Jacob Potofsky later recollected: "A lot of people tore up slips [vouchers]. I was one of those who tore it up. We went back. It turned out that [the] United Garment Workers did not really support wholeheartedly the whole strike situation."[58] On the other hand, the JSCB members representing the strikers were probably not so much rank-and-file leaders as liaison officers between the board and the workers. Although it is not clear who they were, fragmentary evidence shows that the representatives were selected from among the cutters, a group different from the tailors both in ethnic background and in skills. Moreover, the two strike committees were most likely a temporary expedient for the purpose of negotiating with the employers; although the two branches of the industry followed different seasons, the strikers were disregarding the branch line. In any case, Fitzpatrick, chairman of the JSCB, and Margaret Drier Robins, a board member and WTUL president who had been a wealthy society lady before committing herself to labor unionism, swayed the new leadership, financing the strike and taking up a publicity campaign.

In order to prevent another disaster, the JSCB submitted an agreement proposal for ratification by the strikers before approaching the employers. Most important, the proposal insisted upon the closed shop. It also stipulated a forty-eight-hour work week for the cutters and trimmers and a fifty-four-hour week for the tailors, with a time-and-one-half rate for overtime work on weekdays and a double time rate on holidays. It further recommended that grievances should be handled first by the shop steward representing the union and, if not satisfied, should be submitted to an arbitrator agreed upon between the union and the firm.[59] Although the proposal did not specify anything but a procedure to redress their other grievances, the strikers endorsed it. Then copies of the proposed agreement were sent to all the firms affected by the strike.[60]

Nine small firms immediately signed the agreement. The general strike had brought to a standstill a number of small establishments, whose meager financial resources made them unable to endure a long struggle. By the end of October, scores of contractors had already visited the UGW headquarters and asked to see a union representative authorized to make up an agreement. More than one hundred contractors held a meeting and unanimously decided to sign up with the UGW. These contractors, in addition to dozens of small manufacturers, had already reached a settlement. With the proposed agreement offered by the JSCB, nine more firms, employing about six hundred workers in total, yielded to the strikers' demands. Now one hundred twelve firms had an agreement with their employees, who numbered eight to ten thousand in all.[61]

But the large manufacturers, employing most of the more than thirty thousand workers still on strike, ignored the JSCB's overture. Aware that the strikers were faced with hunger and the UGW had a practically empty treasury, they adopted a wait-and-see policy. Certainly the manufacturers, particularly those in the ready-made branch, were losing the major part of their business, as the busy season was already under way. Employees who had remained at work were not sufficient in number to fill even urgent orders. Some manufacturers sent work to other cities such as Milwaukee, Cincinnati, Indianapolis, and Philadelphia, but the volume was small and the work was often returned unfinished because of protests by the workers there. Others imported strikebreakers from Pittsburgh and New York, many of whom joined the strike themselves after realizing the situation.[62] However, the experience of the cutters' strike in 1904 convinced the manufacturers that they could win by starving the strikers. The Wholesale Clothiers' Association refused to discuss any settlement except an open-shop agreement, when it was approached by the Citizens' Strike Committee on behalf of the JSCB.[63]

Now relief for the strikers became a paramount factor. In this respect the CFL held the most leverage. The JSCB created a strike fund, independent of the UGW treasury. It took pains to curtail cash outlay, opening four commissary stores where strikers could get food and other necessities with a relief ticket, but found its fund falling short. As head of the CFL, Fitzpatrick immediately appealed to the affiliated labor unions for financial support. The Chicago Teachers' Federation quickly answered by deciding to assess each member twenty-five cents a week until the end of the strike. But other unions were not quick enough. Although individuals and various organizations not related to the CFL donated money, it was "only a drop in the bucket." So Fitzpatrick made another plea before the CFL in session on November 20, declaring, "The time has come when organized labor must see to it that strikes were not won because of the unanswerable argument of starvation."[64] The CFL recommended that its affiliates assess their memberships as the Chicago Teachers' Federation had. Together with the financial support offered by other labor unions across the country, the CFL's contribution amounted to $41,000, nearly three-fourths of the cash received by the strike fund.[65]

The next biggest cash contribution, more than $10,000 total, came from socialists, especially women. Emma Pischel, a socialist member of the WTUL, took part in the strike at the end of October, when the league became involved in it at the request of the UGW. As the strike grew into a major struggle, the Socialist Women's Agitation Committee and the Socialist Women's League provided more activists in the strike. Besides making speeches at many meetings, the activists were also devoted to fund raising. Soon after the strike turned into a game of endurance, these women helped the *Chicago Daily Socialist* prepare a special strike edition and made plans to sell copies on the streets. They enlisted four hundred women strikers as "newsies." With Emma Pischel in charge of the operation and Nellie G. Zeh, another socialist, covering the Loop district, the strikers sold about ten thousand copies, making more than $3,000 for the strike fund.[66] Immigrant socialists were also active in collecting money. Polish socialists, for example, resorted to house-to-house canvassing, chiefly on the Northwest Side. Led by a woman named Franceska Jankiewicz, they made $1,750.03, mostly in coins. "[I]t was touching to see collections of one hundred and fifty dollars in pennies and a thousand dollars in nickels and dimes," noted the WTUL in its official report, "telling in unmistakable language the stories of hardship and self-sacrifice typified by these gifts."[67] In fact, ethnic neighborhoods offered generous support. For instance, Jewish shopkeepers on the West Side contributed $4,000 soon after the strikers rejected the Rickert agreement, and a Polish restaurant on the Northwest Side served lunch at cost for the strikers doing picket duty.[68] Although Chicago was at the time a metropolis with a population of more than two million, the neighborhoods crowded by recent immigrants remained more like villages where the communal tradition of mutual assistance was still vigorous.

The rest of the cash contribution, more than $26,000, was raised mainly through the campaigns of the WTUL and the Citizens' Strike Committee, although they were not entirely helpful to the strikers. The leading figure in these campaigns was Margaret Drier Robins. Working with the strikers, the WTUL president became acutely aware of their deprivation. She began her fund-raising drive by declaring that the key to the strike would be "food, fuel, and milk for the babies."[69] Although her targets were primarily churches and women's clubs, Robins also moved the committee to collection: It established a milk fund for the estimated five thousand babies of the strikers' families. Unlike John Fitzpatrick, however, Robins and her co-workers publicly stressed the pitiful conditions among the strikers, often crying that contributions were inadequate or that the babies were "dying for want of milk." The workers opposed Robins's begging for charity, and the Poles at Walsh's Hall passed resolutions denouncing her campaign.[70] But she ignored them and continued to strive for public sympathy as well as contributions.[71] To the manufacturers who were waiting until hunger drove their employees back to work, the appeals made by Robins and her follows showed how desperate the strikers were.

Desperate as they became, the workers remained committed to the strike. As the employers increasingly imported strikebreakers from other cities, picketing occupied the strikers' daily activities. In order to prevent violence, the WTUL gave the pickets instructions such as, "Don't walk in groups of more than two or three," and, "Don't stand in front of the shop; walk up and down the block."[72] But the strikers often tried to break into factories manned by strikebreakers, stoned small contract shops taking work from the manufacturers, or attacked those who were on their way to or from work.

So in the latter half of November, there was another wave of "riots," in which women often led hundreds of strikers.[73]

The wave subsided when the Chicago City Council intervened in the strike. On November 28, Alderman Charles E. Merriam, apparently at the request of prominent citizens on the strikers' side, brought forward a resolution that a committee of three aldermen should be appointed and instructed to arrange a conference of the employers and the strikers. Amended to include the mayor and the city clerk as members of the committee, the resolution was unanimously adopted by the council. Mayor Frederick A. Busse, though having refused to take a hand in this strike, invited the employers for a conference. Although the two associations of Chicago's men's clothing manufacturers did not give an immediate reply, HSM accepted the invitation.[74]

The conference resulted in a new agreement. This time all three HSM bosses, Harry and Max Hart and Joseph Schaffner, accompanied by their attorney Carl Meyer, personally participated in the negotiations. They adopted a flexible attitude when the type of shop organization became the main stumbling block. The bosses agreed that the firm would not discriminate against union members, and that an arbitration committee should be established to handle grievances. But nothing more than that was won by labor representatives John Fitzpatrick, Margaret Robins, Samuel Landers of the UGW, and Edward Anderson, a striking cutter. They failed to win explicit recognition of the union. Moreover, they conceded that HSM would not have to take back strikers found guilty of violence. Burdened with the responsibility for feeding more than thirty thousand strikers, the representatives hoped that the HSM employees would accept the agreement.[75]

A tragic event portended the fate of the second agreement. A striker, Charles Lazinskas, was killed while chasing after two strikebreakers. The strikers had just resumed "riots" against the firms affiliated with either of the two manufacturers' associations, which had declined the mayor's invitation on December 1. The next day, Lazinskas and two others attacked two strikebreakers on their way home from the Royal Tailors. He was shot by a special policeman escorting the strikebreakers.[76] The tragedy was shocking enough to inflame the workers' hostility against the employers. Apparently afraid that radicals would capitalize on the mood, John Fitzpatrick urged, "Every effort must be made to have the strikers understand that the cry of 'closed shop' is a false issue. There seems to be an organized effort by some in this strike that the strike is lost unless the so-called 'closed shop' is obtained."[77] He persuaded the cutters to accept the agreement, but the tailors had a different opinion. At Hod Carriers' Hall, the largest and central meeting place, which was shared by tailors from diverse ethnic groups, the workers "groaned, hissed and hooted" at the CFL president trying to explain the agreement. After he finished, a striker exclaimed: "We just buried one of our workers, who was shot by an agent of the bosses. If we asked him whether to accept this agreement, I know the dead brother would say No!"[78] Believing that the tailors had failed to understand the agreement read in English, Fitzpatrick decided to wait until it was printed in several languages.

But the strikers appeared to be more steadfast and radical than the JSCB perceived. Fitzpatrick, Robins, and other leaders had predicted that eight to ten thousand strikers would appear at the parade that they had originally planned in order to put pressure upon the employers to accept negotiations. Although it was snowy, windy, and cold that day, December 7, at least twenty thousand, roughly two-thirds of those on strike, joined either the main procession from the Southwest Side or a contingent from the Northwest Side. The marchers revealed a radical predisposition, though the police prohibited red flags. The *Chicago Tribune* described:

> In spite of the raw, cold wind and snow, the marching strikers were enthusiastic and as the bands in the parade provided by various unions struck up the "Marseillaise" the marchers took up the refrain and sang the French revolutionary hymn in several languages. In keeping with the revolutionary music, red was the predominating color in the parade. Ribbons, sashes, and neckties of a scarlet hue were displayed by the men and women strikers along the entire line of march.[79]

The red color indicated the significant presence of radicalism among the strikers. Immigrant socialists were quite active among Chicago's men's clothing workers, both in the ethnic neighborhoods and at the workplaces. They rarely reached out beyond their own nationalities, but proved ready to help each other in multi-ethnic strikes. For example, a number of Italian socialists organized the Lavagnini Society, which, based on the West Side of the city, flourished in the 1910s. It engaged in anticlerical propaganda. On Sundays, members of the society, standing at the corners of Oakley Avenue, berated Italian churchgoers as "stupid" or "imbeciles" and told them to keep their money for their children. The society often staged dramas that preached that priests did not work but wanted money. Although faithful believers, particularly women, chose to avoid those streetcorners, they thought of the members as "all uprighteous people," not "hoodlums." Maria Valiani's husband, an HSM tailor and member of the Lavagnini Society, busied himself in the labor movement. When workers went on strike at B. Kuppenheimer and Co. at the end of World War I, he walked the picket line with his socialist friends.[80]

Jewish immigrants from eastern Europe probably supplied the men's clothing industry with more socialists than any other group. Many had been radicals before arriving in America. From the early 1880s, Jewish intellectuals had taken part in Russian radicalism, particularly in the populist movement. Frustrated by dismal failure among the peasants, many became socialists, and in 1897 they created the General Jewish Workers' League in Russia and Poland, popularly known as the Bund. Some of those who came to Chicago joined the La Salle Political Club, an organization closely related to the Socialist Labor Party of America.[81] One was Hyman Schneid, a future opposition leader in the Amalgamated Clothing Workers, who, born in a small Lithuanian town in 1889, became involved in the Bund in his early teens, with such burning idealism that he helped workers strike against his own father's tailor shop.[82] In addition, there were a number of socialists like Pearl Spencer, who were not associated with the club but who committed themselves to the labor movement. Before she married a socialist in 1909, Spencer joined a group of her fellow workers who wanted to organize their workplace. When they failed to get a charter from a national organization, probably the Journeymen Tailors' Union, the group named itself the International Ready-made Tailors, which Spencer claims became the "nucleus" of the ACW.[83]

Syndicalists, particularly the Industrial Workers of the World (IWW), also contributed to the radical sentiment among the strikers. This group, created in 1905, fiercely attacked the American Federation of Labor. Founded among craft unions, the AFL advocated its affiliates' autonomy within trade boundaries and sought labor agreements that would give them control over jobs. The policies helped the federation to grow in the midst of an economic boom around the turn of the century and to represent organized workers in the eyes of the nation. But the boom had been followed by a recession and an open-shop drive, which had weakened the AFL. Claiming that craft unionism had become an obstacle to organization of the unskilled masses, the IWW, also known as "Wobblies," preached organizing regardless of craft lines and in theory insisted upon militant strikes instead of agreements and negotiations. After Chicago's men's clothing workers rejected the UGW leadership in the 1910–1911 strike, the Wobblies attempted to take command of the struggle. William D. Haywood, a well-known revolutionary who headed the IWW, visited the city shortly after the second settlement proposal was formulated. At the Pilsen Park mass meeting on November 13, strikers demanded that Haywood make a speech in advance of Fitzpatrick and other leaders. There, the revolutionary declared that all the men's clothing workers, including those not directly engaged in the making of garments, should be out on strike.[84]

During the strike, therefore, radicals played a role more significant than simply setting the tone of the December mass parade; in addition to moral and financial support, they proposed goals and strategies to be adopted by the strikers. Socialists such as Robert Dvorak helped unorganized workers create a general strike and demand a closed-shop agreement. William Haywood and other revolutionaries urged the strikers to refuse compromising settlements and fight to the finish. Of course, the workers were not always persuaded, and many would eventually turn away from the radicals. Most were apparently unacquainted with radical tenets; many strikers regarded the closed shop as a cure for all grievances. It was probably the radicals' enthusiastic idealism rather than their revolutionary creed that engaged the strikers and guided them in a different direction from that proposed by native-born strike leaders. As "all uprighteous people," the radicals stood for something greater or more elevated than was advocated by those leaders. Like a magnifying glass, radicalism helped the strikers examine their situation and focus on their own demands.

Nevertheless, the JSCB made every effort to get the new agreement approved. When the marchers arrived at the Chicago Cubs' ballpark on the West Side, top leaders urged them to be calm and "think it over." Recognizing the unmistakable sentiment among the rank and file, the leaders postponed a referendum until the following week and undertook a "campaign of persuasion." Through speeches made at various meetings and through house-to-house visits, they assured strikers that the agreement amounted to recognition of the union. According to their argument, the "no discrimination" clause meant that HSM would not interfere with organizing activities among its employees and that shop committees could be formed by union members. Also, the leaders tried to convince the eight thousand HSM employees to return to work and contribute money for those who remained on strike. But the radicals, mostly socialists and syndicalists, insisted that the agreement yielded nothing better than an open shop and called it a "milk and water" agreement. In order to prevent the radicals from prevailing at the meetings where the vote was to be conducted, the strike leadership decided to use secret ballots.[85]

On December 14, however, the strikers again rejected the proposed agreement. They did not even put it to a vote. Only at the first polling place visited by John Fitzpatrick, Margaret Robins, and Samuel Landers did five hundred Jewish strikers cast ballots. When the leaders went to Hod Carriers' Hall, the workers refused to vote. Fitzpatrick tried to force them to take a vote by declaring that he would count abstention as a pro. Several of the workers left for Walsh's Hall on the Northwest Side. There, Poles, led by a priest called Father Lawczynski, had already defeated the agreement by an unofficial vote and, under a crucifix, pledged to stand firm for the closed shop. Hearing about the confrontation at Hod Carriers' Hall, the Poles dispatched a delegation. Bearing the priest on their shoulders, the delegates entered the hall and shouted: "Down with the agreement; we refuse to vote."[86] John Fitzpatrick and other leaders had to leave the hall, but announced that the referendum would be carried on at other places. They went to a Southwest Side hall, where Bessie Abramovitz informed them that the strikers, mostly old Jewish pants makers, would listen to them and take a vote. When Fitzpatrick began to speak there, however, delegations from Walsh's and Hod Carriers' Halls arrived and clamored, "No vote! No vote!" The leaders gave up and called a meeting of the Joint Strike Conference Board, which declared the agreement repudiated.

It was, above all, solidarity that led the strikers to reject the second agreement. They objected that it did not unequivocally recognize the union, and they resented the clause excluding those found guilty of violence, although only three were convicted. On the other hand, the strikers were aware that it was better than the first agreement because HSM had abandoned its strictly open-shop attitude and promised not to discriminate against UGW members. Besides, the new agreement clearly indicated the firm's liberal policy compared with that of the two manufacturers' associations, which had refused to meet anyone representing the strikers. And starvation and eviction were a real threat, though organized labor, neighbors, and unknown individuals had been generous. The strikers, however, were concerned about the possible consequences of their approving the agreement. While the leaders pointed out the financial contribution to be made by the returning workers, the rank-and-filers were convinced that a settlement at the largest firm alone would debilitate those remaining on strike, as other employers were exceedingly obstinate. They were not only dissatisfied with the contents of the new agreement, the *Chicago Daily Socialist* reported: "Its acceptance, they [the strikers] said, would only mean that the strikers who were not workers in the Hart [Schaffner and Marx] shops, would rush pell-mell back to work, thus destroying all of the efforts made so far by the strikers themselves."[87]

Rejection of the second agreement highlighted the class unity achieved by workers from diverse ethnic backgrounds. The unity matured, as they moved beyond their specific workplaces, and organized themselves by neighborhoods. From the start the strikers did not separate themselves into groups according to different employers. Occasionally, meetings were held by the employees of a particular firm, but those working at other places were welcome because the strikers were anxious to spread their message. Soon the lines dividing the diverse workplaces were made insignificant to the strikers. On becoming involved in the strike at the end of October, the WTUL set out to organize the campaign; the UGW was so unprepared for a major battle that it failed to secure enough space to accommodate the strikers' meetings. Although the league was at first committed only to helping women workers, Margaret Robins and her fellows had to assist all the strikers in arranging meetings and other daily activities. The WTUL divided Chicago into fifteen districts and rented one hall in each of them.[88] Since many strikers did not understand English, and since most lived in ethnic neighborhoods, the districts were carved out along the neighborhood lines, with Hod Carriers' Hall designated as the center for tailors and the UGW headquarters assigned to the cutters.[89] Together with their neighbors, the strikers themselves now organized the picketing, controlled those who strayed from the long struggle, collected ration cards, and shared the suffering. So in early December, when it was found that those still at work were largely Czech workers, residentially more dispersed than the other three major ethnic groups in the industry, the news was read at meetings of Czech strikers, who discussed various remedies.[90] Through their gatherings in these halls the rank-and-filers communicated with their leaders and with each other, as they did in rejecting the second HSM agreement. The strikers, shoulder to shoulder with their own countryfolk, were aligned against the employers as a whole. By the time the agreement was put to a referendum, the strike was already a class conflict, which led the workers to consider it in terms of a working-class strategy.

RANK-AND-FILE LEADERSHIP

The repudiation of the second HSM agreement enfeebled the leadership of John Fitzpatrick and Margaret Robins. Dismayed at the decision, both thought that the strikers did not know what was good for them. Robins and socialist members of the WTUL pressed the *Chicago Daily Socialist* to dismiss Robert Dvorak, whom they accused of having misled the strikers into believing that the majority sentiment had from the start been against the agreement.[91] Fitzpatrick and the CFL tried to make the workers reconsider by temporarily stopping strike relief and publicly admitting that the strike fund was exhausted, with little coming in. Further, the leaders announced that the UGW "had not contributed one cent" to the fund, and demanded that its books be audited by the JSCB. With the leadership drifting, the strikers became more desperate. Some resorted to violence in order to stop strikebreaking, leaving another striker, a sympathizer, and a special policeman dead. With no sign of settlement in sight, starvation and the cold drove others back to their old workplaces or to seek temporary jobs at candy factories or elsewhere. But most seemed to be prepared for the continuing fight, families moved into smaller apartments, singles arranged for living with relatives and friends. Disappointed with the leadership of the CFL and the WTUL, the strikers began to turn away from the halls, which they had packed every day.[92]

The employers, particularly HSM, ignored the JSCB as a potential party in peace negotiations. While the second agreement was pending, the two manufacturers' associations, severely criticized by Mayor Busse and Alderman Merriam, had a conference in order to discuss their own policy. The firms reportedly decided to adopt a conciliatory policy toward the strikers.[93] But the workers' rejection of the HSM agreement demonstrated that the CFL and the WTUL did not control the strikers any more than the UGW. The associations did not suggest a conference with the JSCB, while making it public that their affiliates would not discriminate against the union members and were willing to concede on the strikers' grievances. And HSM pointed out that settlement proposals so far were "useless from necessity rather than choice." It further declared that in the future the firm would negotiate directly with its striking employees.[94]

Such attitudes probably prompted the strikers to openly assert their own initiative. Toward the end of December, they wrested control of the halls from union officers. After helping the tailors at Hod Carriers' Hall turn down the second HSM agreement, for example, Sidney Hillman, though a cutter, left UGW headquarters and became chairman of the hall.[95] Soon, rank-and-file leaders called a meeting of the Czech, Polish, and Lithuanian strikers, at which they decided to frame their own proposal and present it to the employers. In addition to clauses demanding 15 percent wage increases, abolition of piecework, a fifty-hour week, and prohibition of individual bargaining, the proposal prescribed a democratic procedure for handling grievances. Instead of leaving them to be decided by an arbitration committee as in the former proposals, it stipulated: "All grievances of employes shall be presented to the representatives of the firms by the committees representing the employes of each shop where the grievances may arise. Any adjustment of such grievances must be ratified by the employes of such shops."[96]

Before the Jews and Italians endorsed the new proposal, negotiations began between the strikers and Sturm, Mayer and Co., a firm that normally employed more than five hundred workers. A busy season was approaching in the special order branch, and in the Illinois legislature, Senator James A. Henson had introduced a resolution to appoint a committee of five senators to investigate the strike. Not affiliated with either of the manufacturers' associations, Sturm, Mayer and Co. freely contacted the strikers. After several conferences, both sides arrived at a settlement quite similar to the second HSM agreement, except that the "violence" clause was dropped and the shop committee of employees was granted.[97] There was no need for a referendum because the strikers themselves had negotiated with the firm. The UGW rubber-stamped the agreement and the employees on strike returned.

Although the Sturm, Mayer and Co. settlement involved only five hundred strikers, it began to change the 1910–1911 strike from one industry-wide class conflict into many separate fights between employers and their employees. The strikers were now almost exhausted. Although the Joint Strike Conference Board resumed regular relief after Christmas, with labor unions across the country coming to its aid, the workers' suffering was often unbearable. Many left Chicago to seek employment in other cities, and a woman striker died from starvation on January 9. The strikers were waiting for the peak time to come in the special order branch, but there was a vacuum in the leadership. The rank-and-file leaders did not constitute a unified group yet. Although there was a Strikers' Executive Committee consisting primarily of cutters, it had been used chiefly as a channel of communication between the strikers and the JSCB. The strikers had yet to establish a leadership to take command of their campaign and pursue a concerted course of action between ethnic groups. It was at this moment that the Sturm, Mayer and Co. agreement was signed. Those not employed by the firm never had a chance to discuss the settlement in terms of an overall strike strategy. The striking workers of the firm returned, like water leaking through a hole in the dam of an unconsolidated leadership.

The weak rank-and-file leadership among the strikers was soon challenged by the JSCB and the UGW. Watching the Sturm, Mayer and Co. strikers return, both tried to recover their lost authority. Fitzpatrick, Robins, Rickert, and other JSCB members devised a new peace plan that was practically the same as the successful agreement, and sought separate settlements between the strikers and their employers. And Margaret Robins indirectly put pressure upon the strikers by making a "last appeal" to the public for financial support. Many exhausted strikers approved the new plan at several meetings, while the Czech workers chose to abide by the decision of the others. But the Poles at Walsh's Hall again revolted against the official leadership. Wobblies such as William Trautmann, one-time IWW secretary-treasurer, and, most likely, Irving Abrams, an English-born Jew who grew away from socialism and later became a lawyer, helped them, hoping to "revitalize the strike."[98] The Poles rejected the plan and instead drew up another proposal. This one, which included shop committees to adjust grievances, the abolition of fines and piecework, and wage increases, was on the lines of that formulated by the meeting of the Czech, Polish, and Lithuanian strikers. The Poles then visited Hod Carriers' Hall and successfully persuaded the strikers there to turn against the JSCB's plan. Other halls followed, and the opposition group claimed that eighteen thousand workers were on its side.[99]

Before the opposition proposal won consensus from the strikers, however, an agreement was reached with Hart, Schaffner and Marx. The firm had observed the settlement at Strum, Mayer and Co. It was not so anxious to build up its workforce at that moment, a slack season in the ready-made branch which was its principal market. But HSM had operated the manufacturing department relatively steadily throughout the year. Joseph Schaffner, in charge of marketing as well as of finance, perhaps saw a good opportunity to increase HSM's market share while the "association" firms remained idle. He persuaded the Hart brothers, who initially felt obliged to be in accord with the associations, though HSM was an independent firm. With full authority to act, Schaffner planned to reach a settlement with the strikers and hire two thousand more hands than its normal workforce. In addition, the strike had led him to the conclusion that "the good will of the employes is a business asset comparable to the good will of the customer."[100] As the initiator of advertising in the men's clothing industry, he probably felt bitter about the deteriorating public opinion regarding HSM. Schaffner considered the causes of the strike and discovered that the workers had no channel through which their grievances could be adjusted. The grievances, when accumulated for years, he believed, resulted in "a feeling of distrust and enmity toward their immediate superiors in position."[101] So when Thomas Rickert visited the HSM office and showed the JSCB's proposal, Joseph Schaffner found it acceptable. He met Rickert, Fitzpatrick, Robins, and H. C. Harris, a cutter and member of the Striker's Executive Committee. On January 14, Saturday, both sides easily reached an agreement that provided for no discrimination against the union members and the establishment of an arbitration committee.[102]

With the HSM agreement signed, the native-born strike leaders took the opposition movement by surprise. Instead of putting the agreement to a referendum or even reporting it at strikers' meetings, John Fitzpatrick issued a public statement after it was endorsed by the JSCB. He declared that the strike against HSM was over and urged the firm's employees on strike to go back to work as soon as the following Monday.[103] On January 15, the next day, strikers held a meeting at Hod Carriers' Hall, at which Agnes Nestor and Emmett Flood appeared, representing, respectively, the WTUL and the CFL. When Nestor finished explaining the agreement, the strikers remained silent, with only one section of the crowd applauding. As a matter of fact, the agreement did not even provide for shop committees, not to mention recognition of the union. Flood followed Nestor, only to be interrupted by some UGW officers entering the hall. Then the strikers began to clamor against the officers responsible for the HSM agreement. Italian syndicalists and other radicals belonging to the opposition group caused a turmoil in order to prevent a vote on the agreement. The uproar drove Nestor and Flood as well as the officers out of the hall. But Sidney Hillman, chairman of the meeting, stayed on the platform, together with Anzuino D. Marimpietri, an Italian tailor also serving for the hall. After a while the hall became quiet and the meeting was resumed. Hillman and Marimpietri, keenly aware of the strikers' sufferings, stressed that to accept the agreement was "the only thing to do to prevent [a] complete catastrophe."[104] Apparently there was no vote on whether to go back to work or stay out. But John Fitzpatrick had already called off the strike, which meant that the JSCB would offer no more financial aid to the HSM employees on strike. As tempers cooled, starvation compelled the workers to follow Hillman's advice.

The opposition group did not effectively cope with the move by the native-born leaders. Polish strikers at Walsh's Hall protested against the new HSM agreement. It was not ratified by Czech workers at four halls on the Southwest Side, either. However, most other halls were kept locked, as Fitzpatrick hinted in his statement that there might be no meeting until the following Monday. Then the HSM strikers began to return. Though defeated, they refused to go back individually or in haste. During the ten-day period as specified in the agreement, hundreds gathered each day and marched to their workplace, with Hillman and Marimpietri in the lead. In these days there were still opportunities for the opposition group to develop dissenting sentiments into a movement. Indeed, many strikers demanded that another parade be held. As the JSCB proved reluctant, they intended to break away from its leadership. On January 19, the dissenters planned to hold an independent meeting at which William Trautmann would be present. Out of money, they handed him the bill for hall rent, amounting to $1.50. Instead of paying it, however, Trautmann advised them to take up a collection. This drove the dissenters back to John Fitzpatrick, who "promised to give them support on condition that they remain loyal to the strike board [JSCB]."[105]

Soon the strike disintegrated. Although there were still about eighteen thousand workers on strike, the HSM settlement had turned the struggle into a collection of separate fights between workers and their employers. The UGW officers contacted B. Kuppenheimer and Co. and called a meeting of the firm's striking employees. Hirsch, Wickwire and

Co. invited a delegation of its striking workers to a conference. There was no more opposition to this self-defeating strategy. Nor were there any significant strike activities. In fact, the strike was generally thought to be over. Although union members employed at HSM paid their assessments, financial aid from the outside rapidly dwindled after their return. Some tenacious strikers occasionally attacked strikebreakers and stormed factory buildings, but thousands returned to work.[106]

In order to win a victory, therefore, the employers had only to be patient a little longer. They were under pressure: Their rival HSM had already begun full-time operation; the Illinois Senate Special Committee, after a two-week-long delay apparently due to the men's clothing firms' lobbying, was at last investigating the strike, exposing the blacklisting practices of the two manufacturers' associations. But the "association houses," including Kuppenheimer and Hirsch, Wickwire, insisted upon not entering any agreement with the UGW. With no hope for a decent settlement, Thomas Rickert called off the strike on February 3.[107]

CONSEQUENCES

The strike had important consequences. Above all, it left behind an invisible and yet potent legacy of class solidarity among Chicago's men's clothing workers. They belonged to more diverse groups than the Slavic coal miners in Pennsylvania. Like steel workers, they were deeply divided between skilled and unskilled hands. Chicago was different from the coal field or mill town, where the whole community was dependent upon one industry.[108] Yet men's clothing workers there fought a single-front battle against their employers, who had endeavored to exact more labor power by transforming the labor process and consolidating control over work. They overcame ethnic division; unlike New York's shirtwaist makers in the 1909 "Uprising of the 20,000,"[109] they did not suffer from conflicts between diverse national groups.[110] They lacked an insightful leadership that took pains to develop ethnic networks, as the IWW did in the 1912 textile strike in Lawrence, Massachusetts.[111] But Chicago's men's clothing workers mobilized throughout ethnic neighborhoods, which helped them disregard the vertical lines that divided their workplaces and achieve horizontal communication and cooperation between ethnic groups. They were eventually defeated, not just because they were badly prepared for a major contest, but because they failed to forge a consolidated rank-and-file leadership that was capable of taking advantage of interethnic cooperation and of preventing the strike from turning into a series of parallel fights.

The legacy of solidarity appeared obscure and insignificant at the end of this strike. In fact, ethnic antagonism had not entirely disappeared. Ethnic prejudices and rivalries constituted a divisive factor among Chicago's men's clothing workers even after 1911: Their local unions often had to discipline those who provoked trouble in the workroom by abusing a certain nationality; and ethnic locals competed with "international" locals for members. But the solidarity shaped by the 1910–1911 strike encouraged the workers to invoke a concerted collective action on the multi-ethnic shop floor. After the strike, stoppages became an effective weapon in which persuasion or coercion were no longer necessary in order to involve all the workers in a room. While the arbitration machinery was still in progress at HSM, for example, the firm was faced with frequent stoppages. Jacob Potofsky recalled: "We felt we had a grievance and somebody would knock with a [pair of] scissors on the table and everybody would stop. We were impatient. . . ."[112] This legacy proved so potent that the workers completely organized the city within a decade.

The 1910–1911 strike also left the workers sensitive to the relationship between the rank and file and their leaders. Throughout the fight, the strikers were so self-assertive that they often went to the brink of rebellion against the native-born strike leadership. And the outcome of the twenty-week struggle showed them how devastating a leadership estranged from the rank and file could be in a fight against the employers. Frank Rosenblum, a rank-and-file leader who distinguished himself in this strike and eventually became a prominent figure in the Amalgamated Clothing Workers, later remembered, "They [the native-born strike leaders] were completely foreign to our people. They didn't understand."[113] To the strikers, it was "They" who led the struggle into a bitter defeat. Chicago's men's clothing workers later pursued democratic procedures in their own organization, as they once had when formulating an agreement proposal.

In addition, the fight gave the workers something visible: a local union of their own. After leading the last group of HSM strikers to their workplace, Sidney Hillman said to Anzuino Marimpietri: "What now? Tomorrow you and I must go back to work or lose our jobs. What will become of these people? Who will be there to give them encouragement, to build our union? If one of us can do it, this is our opportunity."[114] When Marimpietri asked how much he needed in order to stay out and work for their union, Hillman answered that $10 a week would be enough. Marimpietri told him, "I'll go back tomorrow and give you the $10.00 each week." But Marimpietri did not have to do that. Soon HSM coat makers launched a local union chartered No. 39 of the UGW and paid enough dues to afford a salary of that amount for Sidney Hillman.[115] This local, led chiefly by young and moderate leftists, was to be the center of the labor movement among Chicago's men's clothing workers.

The strike ended as a victory on the part of the employers. This fact did not make the employers complacent, however. The new local did not concern HSM alone; the solidarity shown by the workers, as well as the tenacity with which they fought the strike, led many other employers to be more watchful than ever. Worse still, while the UGW had often turned out to be, if anything, an unreliable partner, it was now virtually discredited among the workers: The local, though affiliated with it, was in practice autonomous; and, more significant, the workers were rebelliously self-assertive. So, employers made efforts to reform labor management, which involved integration of the decentralized managerial authority on the shop floor. In these various ways, the 1910–1911 strike became a turning point in the history of Chicago's men's clothing industry.

CHAPTER 4

One Hundred Percent Organization

The eight years after the 1910–1911 strike were a period of frustration and anxiety for unionists. In 1914, the city's local unions broke with the lethargic leadership of the United Garment Workers and took the initiative in creating the ACW. The "secessionist" union, though reproached by the American Federation of Labor, soon proved viable, with two-thirds of the former UGW members supporting its devoted leaders. Moreover, the ranks of the ACW grew steadily and in 1918 reached eighty thousand nationwide, more than double the original membership. In Chicago, however, it was still confined to Hart, Schaffner and Marx. The associations not only withstood the union's repeated organization campaigns; they also defeated a strike in 1915, demolishing the footholds it had secured in independent firms early in the fight. Until the spring of 1919, ACW leaders never dreamed that Chicago could be completely organized in the foreseeable future.

But that spring, their dream came true. On May 13, 1919, seven thousand men's clothing workers held a meeting in Street Carmen's Hall, Chicago, and ratified an agreement between the Amalgamated Clothing Workers of America and thirteen leading manufacturers of the city.[1] The staunchly anti-union members of the Wholesale Clothiers' Association, led by B. Kuppenheimer and Co., Alfred Decker and Cohn, and Hirsch, Wickwire and Company, at last recognized the union and yielded to its demand that there be established a mechanism to handle grievances, like that of their rival Hart, Schaffner and Marx. At the time, the union was also negotiating with the special-order firms belonging to the Wholesale Tailors' Association and with independent firms such as Rosenwald and Weil. On May 26, workers again gathered at the hall and approved a similar agreement between the ACW and the special-order association. "This makes Chicago a 100 per cent Union city," declared Frank Rosenblum, then General Executive Board (GEB) member of the union. He added, "Every house [men's clothing firm] is now signed up with the organization. We have swept cleaner than we dreamed of."[2] Celebrating the agreements, Lazarus Marcovitz, another GEB member, recalled: "Chicago, for many years the graveyard of our hopes, the mighty fort of the employers that withstood many a gallant attack and was considered to be impregnable; Chicago, the battlefield on which our martyrs have laid down their very lives in struggles against the allied, darkest forces of capital; that city has at last been taken by our victorious army. . . ."[3]

In retrospect, the victory is not a surprise; during the period of frustration and anxiety after the 1915 strike, the ACW endeavored to assure anti-union employers of its regulatory function on the shop floor. Winning moral support from unorganized workers, the union showed the manufacturers that it could "control" the workforce. In the past, the UGW had never established a stable relationship between men's clothing firms and their employees, except in the branch producing work clothes. Immigrant tailors, distrustful of the union officers and aware of the difficulties that the section system presented in the modern factories, frequently resorted to work stoppages or walkouts in order to get wage increases or better working conditions. The ACW, however, proved that it was able to effectively prevent "section strikes" or "shop strikes." At Hart, Schaffner and Marx, union leaders had already succeeded in persuading the workers to submit their grievances to an arbitration system and assured the firm of practically uninterrupted production. Throughout the 1915 strike and wartime organization campaigns, manufacturers found that the ACW had command of their employees, both in calling them out for a fight and in sending them back to work. In the spring of 1919, the associations finally gave up the belief that no union could "control" the tailors.

The present chapter is mainly concerned with the changing relationship among employers, workers, and the union. It discusses, first of all, how a local union left behind by the 1910–1911 strike contributed to stable labor relations at HSM. It describes who led that local body and why the leaders helped launch the ACW in 1914. Then, this chapter analyzes the approach adopted by ACW leaders toward anti-union employers and unorganized workers in conducting the 1915 strike, and describes their solution for resolving ethnic rivalries within the Chicago organization. Finally, this chapter explains what impact World War I had upon the tripartite relationship already evolving in the men's clothing industry of the city.

LABOR RELATIONS STABILIZED AT HART, SCHAFFNER AND MARX

Following the 1910–1911 strike, Hart, Schaffner and Marx adopted a paternalistic approach to labor relations. The settlement plan of the strike resulted in creation of an arbitration committee, with the firm appointing its attorney Carl Meyer and the employees choosing Clarence Darrow, the socialist lawyer. Although the two failed to find a third arbitrator, they proceeded to adjust the workers' grievances. In March, the lawyers reached a decision that provided for improvements in working conditions, wage increases, time-and-a-half overtime pay, and equal division of work during the slack season. In this decision both sides also agreed to create a permanent board of arbitration. Although the strike settlement had not been devised to go that far, Joseph Schaffner believed that a channel of communication and adjustment between management and the workforce would prevent isolated grievances from accumulating to an explosive level. But he preferred to deal with the individual worker. The decision stipulated that an employee, "either by himself or by an individual fellow-worker," could present any grievance to a representative of the firm, and that, if it was not adjusted, the employee would have "the right to apply to some member of said firm for adjustment of such grievance." If the worker was not satisfied with the result, the grievance could be presented to the arbitration board.[4] In fact, the firm was afraid that a labor union dealing with it would win the employees' loyalty. In a statement prepared for the U.S. Commission on Industrial Relations (CIR) in 1914, HSM revealed: "We believed that the labor union was a competitor for the good will of the people and that both could not have this good will at the same time; we feared that the union would get the credit for anything granted to the people, thus nullifying the good effect to the Company of any concessions or benefits given to them."[5]

HSM chose only to reform its own labor management practices, and not to work with the UGW. The firm fired many of the returned workers, including those, such as Frank Rosenblum, who had been active in the strike. It barred Sidney Hillman, the only union officer representing a portion of the employees, from its factories.[6] Meanwhile, HSM established a labor department. Earl Dean Howard, an economics professor at Northwestern University who investigated the causes of the strike at Joseph Schaffner's request and advised him to seek an early settlement, headed the department. In addition to welfare work, labor manager Howard had the task of handling workers' grievances while at the same time curtailing and regulating the authority of petty bosses, whose mismanagement or personal misconduct was directly responsible for the grievances.[7]

The paternalistic scheme did not work as HSM wished. Although defeated, the workers refused to swallow what they felt was unfair practices in the workroom. They frequently resorted to stoppages or walkouts in small work units. Men's clothing workers employed in the factory had long taken advantage of the weakness inherent in the section system. Because the system, like the assembly line, depended upon a smooth flow of goods from one section to the next, a disruption at any point could bring the whole production process to a halt. Testifying before the CIR in 1914, Earl Howard recalled: "[W]hen I first came after the strike was over . . . there were little strikes, shop strikes, and section strikes, involving from a dozen to 200 men; they were almost a daily occurrence. That was one of our problems."[8]

An anti-union policy aggravated HSM's trouble. In order to prevent a labor union from taking a foothold in the workroom, HSM continued to discriminate against union men and women. Before the CIR, Sidney Hillman complained: "We found grievances had been constantly arising, and especially as this agreement [the March 1911 decision by the arbitration committee] was an open-shop agreement and most of the foremen had started a discrimination, what is usually known as a discrimination in open shops. I remember one shop had about 30 discharges in one week."[9] When workers had a grievance, therefore, they stopped working or walked out instead of resorting to the adjustment procedure. The firm took pains to make them follow the procedure, imposing disciplinary measures, especially suspension, against shop floor leaders and creating a charity and a loan fund. But HSM did not meet with much success. Jacob Potofsky, then one of the leaders at an HSM pants shop, recalled that Earl Howard

> had given me I think more than once a dismissal slip. In other words, he was executing the agreement and we had a stoppage in our shop and he came up and gave us—in accordance with the agreement provision of one hour's notice to return to work. And he turned especially to me because I was the shop chairman. He asked me to return to work and I told him I just couldn't do it unless everybody goes back to work. And he said, "You know that's a violation of the agreement and I will have to give you a suspension."
>
> I said, "You can do what you want, but I'm not going to do it." And so he gave me a suspension.[10]

In fact, there were among the workers militant socialists and syndicalists who preferred continuous confrontation to conciliation and cooperation with the firm. For example, Irving Abrams, one of the Wobblies involved in the 1910–1911 strike, eventually secured a job at HSM and settled down in Chicago. He preached syndicalist tenets not only at his workplace but on street corners, where at least once he was faced with an angry street gang.[11] "At the beginning the task [to guide the grievances into the adjustment procedure] appeared stupendous," revealed HSM in its statement to the CIR, "as grievances were highly magnified and exaggerated by frequent reiteration of the more radical leaders for the purpose of keeping the war spirit at a high temperature."

The difficulties seemed to be serious because many employees were "in opposition to the wage system, hostile to employers as a class."[12]

In order to quiet frequent uprisings in the workroom, HSM eventually gave up its anti-union attitude and chose to rely upon moderate rank-and-file leaders' influence. Having signed the 1910–1911 strike settlement plan as workers' representatives, John Fitzpatrick and Margaret Drier Robins felt obliged to make sure that both the workers and the firm lived up to it. Particularly, the Women's Trade Union League installed organizers such as Bessie Abramovitz in order to recruit new members and impress upon them the significance of labor agreements. In early 1912, when HSM tried to force a strike, apparently in order to do away with unruly unionists, Robins wrote to her husband that she had succeeded in preventing another major fight in Chicago. The WTUL president added: "We are still gripping that trade agreement [the settlement plan] like a bull dog and every day that we hang on to it it is more difficult to destroy."[13] Consequently, in the shops where union members were dominant, Robins observed, the members responded to union officers' appeal to be patient and referred their grievances to the arbitration board. HSM finally asked Hillman and Abramovitz, she wrote, "to go into the shops during the working hours and speak to the workers on the need of concerted action and the meaning of the trade agreement."[14]

The firm also elaborated the grievance-handling procedure. As workers brought up an increasing number of cases before the permanent Board of Arbitration, Clarence Darrow, occupied with other matters, was replaced by one of his partners, William O. Thompson. Although Thompson and Carl Meyer devoted themselves to hearing the grievances, they lacked technical knowledge about the men's clothing industry and could not properly handle cases of continuously changing piece rates and discharges and stoppages involving the issues of workmanship and discrimination. In April 1912, Joseph Schaffner agreed with Margaret Robins and John Fitzpatrick, both in behalf of the HSM employees, that a trade board be established subordinate to the arbitration board, with five representatives on each side and an impartial chairman selected by both sides. The new board was to handle cases presented by deputies appointed by each party and, if not satisfied with its decision, they could go to the arbitration board.[15]

In this, HSM virtually entered into a working relationship with the local unions formed by its employees. The agreement, though negotiated by Robins, Fitzpatrick, and Schaffner, was not only signed by "the Joint Board of Garment Workers," a federation of HSM employees' locals that was led by Hillman, Anzuino Marimpietri and other moderate leaders, but the workers' deputies and representatives on the trade board were all union leaders. The board functioned promptly and smoothly, with five and then only two on each side sitting on each case and decisions mostly made by the chairman. The chairman was James Mullenbach, formerly acting superintendent of Chicago United Charities, who had managed the commissary stores during the 1910–1911 strike. Pro-union, he was not a passive administrator. With Hillman and Howard, his chief deputies, trying to adjust grievances through compromises on the spot, Mullenbach called in "troublemakers" such as Jacob Potofsky and delivered a lecture which Potofsky recalled "left a lasting impression on me of the responsibility for carrying out the labor agreement and to have law and order instead of having stoppages and to have patience even when we have a grievance and a complaint—to allow the grievance process to take its course."[16] Only fourteen cases were brought up before the arbitration board during the year and a half preceding the end of 1913.

With the HSM agreement due to expire on April 1, 1913, the issue was how much power the union should enjoy, not whether it should be recognized as a collective bargaining agency. The union was still weak. Local 39, the coat makers' union, was already a giant with as many as eighteen hundred members. But Local 61, the cutters' and trimmers' union, and Locals 144 and 152, each formed by pants and vest makers, enlisted only a few hundred each. There were four or five ethnic locals admitting only specific nationalities, but they were barely surviving, each with only a few score of members paying dues. Union members constituted only about one-third of the seventy-five hundred HSM workers. The Joint Board of HSM Employees called a special meeting in conjunction with shop committees. The joint board decided to demand a union-shop agreement, which would require non-union workers to join the union after being hired. It added other demands, such as continuation of the arbitration board, establishment of a commission to adjust piece rates, a fifty-hour week, and minimum wages. It appointed Hillman and four other union leaders to a committee to negotiate with the firm. Confronting the HSM representatives, however, the committee demanded a closed shop, apparently willing to compromise if the firm insisted on an open-shop agreement. Indeed, HSM was stubborn, declaring that it would not give more than was called for by the current agreement. The joint board announced another special meeting and decided to call a strike if its demands were not granted.[17]

The firm rejected the closed shop. Above all, it was concerned that "the union was not strong enough in Chicago to furnish them [HSM] with the needed help."[18] Although trying to make production volume as even as possible throughout the year, the firm was still considerably swayed by the seasonality of the men's clothing industry. Before each busy season, it had to build up the workforce to a maximum, which a few thousand union men and women were insufficient to fill. The issue of discipline was also at stake. The quality of HSM products required fine workmanship and the section system had to be assured of a smooth flow of goods from one section to the next. A closed-shop agreement might curtail the firm's power to discipline unfit or unruly workers, by letting them allege discrimination against union members.[19]

A solution came from John E. Williams, chairman of the HSM arbitration board. For nearly two years, the board had lacked a third arbitrator to be selected by agreement between HSM and its employees. But several cases, on which the two arbitrators failed to reach a decision, needed an impartial chairman. Both sides chose John Williams, a former coal miner and enthusiastic unionist known for his skillful mediation at a mine disaster three years earlier. When negotiation between HSM and the workers became deadlocked, he talked with Hillman and hinted at the principle of the preferential shop, which gives priority in hiring and firing to union members. The principle had been articulated by Louis D. Brandeis, the future Supreme Court justice who had been involved in the 1910 New York cloak makers' strike, and it was still in an experimental stage. Hillman traveled to New York and on his return presumably gave his fellow unionists a favorable report on the preferential shop. Williams probably suggested it to Howard, too. Soon the two chief deputies agreed upon the principle, whereupon John Williams called a conference between representatives on both sides. Instead of deciding for them, he led the representatives to set aside their emotional commitment to the closed shop and recognize that the firm was mainly concerned about the labor supply, while the union was afraid of discrimination. They reached a preferential-shop agreement.[20]

The agreement, together with the augmented arbitration process, gradually developed into a system of close union-management cooperation. At first HSM was quite cautious about the preferential shop. Joseph Schaffner and his staff were fearful that it might lead to a closed shop, with the production line subject to the union's mercy. Indeed, local unions grew rapidly, as workers, with or without union cards, applied for jobs at the union office, where HSM posted a list of needed help. Eventually the firm abolished its own employment department, relying entirely on the union for labor supply.[21] Schaffner's fear proved unfounded, because the union contributed to efficient production by protecting the firm against work stoppages. And the arbitration machinery effectively resolved the differences between HSM and the workers. A system of cooperation between the firm and the union had taken root by the time the agreement was renewed in 1916. John Williams enumerated the principles underlying the system in the preamble to the new agreement:

> On the part of the employer it is the intention and expectation that this compact of peace will result in the establishment and maintenance of a high order of discipline and efficiency by the willing co-operation of union and workers rather than by the old method of surveillance and coercion. . . .
>
> On the part of the union it is the intention and expectation that this compact will, with the co-operation of the employer, operate in such a way as to maintain, strengthen, and solidify its organization, so that it may be strong enough, and efficient enough, to co-operate as contemplated in the preceding paragraph; and also that it may be strong enough to command the respect of the employer without being forced to resort to militant or unfriendly measures.[22]

At HSM, therefore, the union was assured of a secure status in return for instituting "discipline and efficiency" that guaranteed uninterrupted production in the workroom. This achievement of peaceful labor relations was a success story that applied not only to the clothing trades seized with endemic stoppages and walkouts; it was a model for American industry as a whole. In early 1914, the International Ladies' Garment Workers' Union invited Sidney Hillman to enforce the New York Protocol of Peace, which Louis Brandeis had formulated four years earlier in order to replace strikes by a judicial grievance-handling system. Later that year, the U.S. Industrial Relations Commission called upon Hillman and Howard as well as Schaffner to explain HSM's achievement. The union-management cooperation at the firm was widely and lavishly praised: George Creel, the journalist who later headed the infamous wartime propaganda agency, the Committee on Public Information, promoted HSM labor relations as "A Way to Industrial Peace" in the *Century*; in 1920 the renowned labor economist John R. Commons depicted the firm as "the republic of eight thousand people."[23]

LAUNCHING THE AMALGAMATED CLOTHING WORKERS OF AMERICA

The union-management cooperation at HSM had significant effects upon the union leadership. Reviewing its three-year experience of arbitration for the U.S. Industrial Relations Commission, the firm stressed, "Much depends upon the leaders of the workers."[24] During these years, moderates gradually prevailed within the leadership of the HSM local unions. Radical leaders, whether militant socialists or syndicalists, were essentially fighters intent on "keeping the war spirit at a high temperature," who refused to cooperate with the firm, branding arbitration as class collaboration and believing it would soon fail. Probably because they felt that an active role in the union offset their obligation to pay dues, radicals were often not in good standing, thus disqualified from running for a union post.[25] Some, such as Frank Rosenblum and Louis Taback, did take part in the HSM arbitration process as trade board representatives or deputies. But they soon softened their militancy. In its statement to the CIR, HSM pointed out: "The system [of arbitration] seems to work out a selection of the fittest candidates and trains them to become efficient leaders and executives, skilled in negotiation, in pleading and cross-examination before the judicial boards, in organizing, disciplining and leading the people."[26]

The moderate leaders were mostly Jewish ex-socialists, many of whom had taken part in the labor movement before coming to Chicago. Sidney Hillman was born in Zagare, a Lithuanian village, in 1887. After finishing his studies at a Jewish elementary school there, he went to a rabbinical seminary in Kovno, a big town with a population of 70,000, in accordance with his parents' wishes. Like many rabbinical students in those years, however, Hillman wanted to explore secular subjects forbidden in the seminary. First of all, he began to learn the Russian language from a young Jew named Michael Zacharias. Hillman was so eager to pursue the lessons that he chose to leave the seminary when its chief rabbi and then the elder Hillman tried to stop him. Zacharias helped Sidney get hired at the laboratory of Dr. Matis, a chemist who was Zacharias's uncle. Doing odd jobs there, Hillman read widely to keep abreast of Russian intellectual currents. He spent evenings mixing with socialists at Dr. Matis's house, which was in fact a local center for the Bund, the General Jewish Workers' League in Russia and Poland. Hillman became involved in the socialist labor movement and was arrested and imprisoned twice before fleeing to England in 1906. After nine months in London, he decided to leave for America, declining a business career offered by his uncle.[27]

After arriving in Chicago in 1907, Hillman appeared to estrange himself from the American or immigrant Jewish socialists. Working in a Sears, Roebuck and Co. stockroom and later at HSM as an apprentice cutter, he was absorbed in modern literature, while occasionally attending socialist lectures. Hillman did not join the ex-Bundists in Chicago or any other socialist organization, but resolved to dedicate himself to the American labor movement.[28] During the 1910–1911 strike, he acted as a moderate who, confronting the angry workers at Hod Carriers' Hall, courageously insisted upon their approving the final HSM agreement. Because Local 39 held its regular meetings at Bowen Hall of Hull House in its early years, Hillman frequented the settlement and met a number of the social reformers related to it. Jane Addams in particular advised him on various topics, including unionism. She was apparently attracted to the views held by Louis Brandeis, a leading progressive who regarded strikes as a waste that could be prevented through judicial arbitration. He believed that a preferential-shop agreement would strengthen labor unions so that they could share control over their industry with employers and become a constructive force contributing toward efficient production.[29] Addams and Brandeis, along with other progressives, had a lasting, though not always favorable, influence on Hillman's public life, as Steven Fraser shows in his acclaimed biography of the labor statesman.[30]

Before leaving for New York to carry out the Protocol of Peace in 1914, Hillman made every effort to prove that HSM locals could assure uninterrupted production by eliminating stoppages, which were chronic in the men's clothing industry. A man of impeccable integrity, consistently sensible and yet deeply compassionate, Hillman persuaded workers to be patient enough to wait for arbitration. Earl Howard, who almost daily argued and compromised with Hillman in order to make the arbitration process workable, paid tribute to the latter's role in a letter written in 1914. The HSM labor manager declared that Hillman was "largely responsible for the education of the union members to the advantages of peaceful methods of dealing. . . ." Howard also noted "the high esteem and almost veneration which the people bore toward him." When Hillman left for New York, the manager wrote, union leaders pledged themselves "to continue his policies."[31]

Other moderate leaders of less prominence were both emotionally and ideologically close to Sidney Hillman. Frank Rosenblum, born into a Russian Jewish immigrant family in 1887, was a member of the Socialist Party until 1907, a year before coming to Chicago. Though branded as a radical, he was appointed business agent of Local 144 in 1913. In temperament, however, Rosenblum was a field commander, inclined to confront opponents, give orders to his men, and drive them toward a victory. His uncompromising attitude probably made him unfit for a managerial position. After the ACW was created, Rosenblum devoted himself to organizing activities in Chicago and other midwestern clothing centers. In 1917, he opposed the vehemently pacifist tone of the union's English organ *Advance*, primarily because he believed it would put the whole organization in danger. By that time, Rosenblum was hardly a socialist, though still militant and with a strong will for power.[32] Samuel Levin was a negotiator—a formidable one so determined to advance his views that he would resort to strong-arm methods. Born in Russia in 1884, he was active in the revolutionary movement before coming to America in 1905. The 1910–1911 strike made him one of the leaders among the Jewish workers. The job as business agent of Local 61, which he took soon after the strike, gave him an opportunity to demonstrate his penetrating managerial talent. When Levin took Hillman's place as chief deputy for HSM employees in 1914, he was no longer a radical.[33] There were others without a socialist or radical past. One was Bessie Abramovitz, also a Russian Jewish immigrant, who worked closely with the Women's Trade Union League during and after the 1910–1911 strike. Anzuino D. Marimpietri, an Italian who loved to sing arias, was "a splendid lawyer" always ready to argue before the HSM arbitration board.[34] These figures were loyal to Sidney Hillman, though they often bickered among themselves, particularly Rosenblum and Levin.

Jacob Potofsky best illustrates the ideological pilgrimage made by many of the moderate leaders. He was an administrator capable of persevering through perennial contention in the organization and reconciling his own views to changing circumstances. Born in Ukraine in 1894, Potofsky came to the United States when he was eleven years old and began working at an HSM pants shop two years later. During the 1910–1911 strike, he was a rank-and-file leader barely known outside his own work gang. An active member of Local 144 after the strike, Potofsky became secretary to his shop chairman, who "didn't write very well." Soon he replaced the chairman and then was elected treasurer of the local. When Frank Rosenblum resigned as the local's business agent in 1913, Potofsky was appointed to the position because "Jake can read and write." Several weeks later, he became manager of the office shared by Locals 144 and 39. There he frequently met Sidney Hillman, and afterward he remained faithful to the magnetic leader.[35] While Potofsky showed his administrative skill in these early years, he also expressed fiery idealism based upon socialist tenets. Following a union meeting in January 1915, he deplored the business unionism that had become increasingly conspicuous in HSM locals, as union officers, who sought to assure the firm of labor supply and uninterrupted production in return for its concession of power to them, came to rule the locals. Potofsky poured out his innermost feelings on a piece of paper:

> After to-night I am disappointed. What is the use? People try to make a trade union a business. No. I don't agree. I can't agree. It is not a business to me. It was not for the last four years.
>
> From now on I shall do my work quietly and faithfully. No more will I give my opinion to my best friends. It [is of] no use. Boss rules damn it. I am sick of it. . . .
>
> Principle is also a dead word. . . . Fisher [A. N., a former Socialist Labor Party member] said, "The deputies are the managers and we have to do what they say. . . ."
>
> Some people are generous. They throw their office in your face

> anytime a word of criticism is uttered. The same people will say my organization, my office, my shop as though it is a piece of furniture they bought.
>
> Good luck to them. Watch! and you will see how they rise in society.
>
> They are honest but dry without any principle in their heart.[36]

Potofsky's socialist idealism gradually faded away in the next few years. In October 1916, he decided to leave Chicago and join Hillman at the ACW's national headquarters in New York. There Potofsky supported Hillman, who thought American participation in World War I was justified and prevailed upon Joseph Schlossberg, the union's general secretary, to stop publishing antiwar editorials in the *Advance*.[37] In September 1917, when the Bolsheviks were challenging the Russian liberal government led by Alexander Kerensky, Potofsky took another step away from socialism. He still thought the Bolshevik plan to abolish private property was "a grand idea," but, the future ACW president wrote, "I don't concur in the plan feeling that it may bring disruption to Russia and endanger its attained democracy. I have faith in Kerensky."[38] In the 1920s Potofsky was willing to declare, "I would not find anything wrong with the Capitalist System if we would have a labor union."[39] In these years he sounded exactly the same as the leaders of the American Federation of Labor. In a memorandum probably prepared for a public speech, Potofsky wrote:

> I am not denying the existence of classes and their divergent interests. . . . The problem is not the name but the approach. The mere recognition of the existence of classes is insufficient. That is precisely the trouble with our theoreticians.
>
> We must take a more practical view to the problems of life. . . .
>
> A militant union is not one that is on strike but one [that] is [on a] strike footing and turn[s to] careful negotiations [and] avoids a strike. Strike is [a] gambling weapon and should be resorted to as a last resort.[40]

Why these once radical leaders became moderates when they ascended to union office is an interesting question. And it is a significant question, which Steven Fraser fails to address in his detailed biography of Hillman. Regarding the role socialists played in the labor movement in general, the answer might shed light on the decline of socialism in early twentieth-century America. At least one thing emerges clear from a study of Chicago's men's clothing industry: Moderation was not simply encouraged by union-management cooperation but developed out of the process by which leadership evolved in the union. That process did not start from elections, in which radicals were often declared ineligible for a union post. It began on the shop floor, where union leaders had held skilled or semi-skilled jobs: Hillman was trained to be a cutter like Rosenblum and Levin, and Potofsky was a pieceworker making pockets. In other words, they occupied critical or relatively autonomous positions in the labor process, claiming a superior status on the shop floor.[41] This job hierarchy, a gender-biased structure, as shown in an earlier chapter, apparently hindered militant women leaders in the 1910–1911 strike from taking a more commanding position in the union.[42]

What is chiefly concerned here is how moderation affected the union, both in the short and the long term. Moderate as most of them were, the leaders of the HSM locals did not pursue reconciliation with the United Garment Workers' national officers. From the start, the locals were autonomous, not only in their own internal affairs but in their negotiations with the largest men's clothing firm in the United States. They grew rapidly after the preferential-shop agreement was signed up: Within three years, nine out of ten HSM employees belonged to the union. With the exception of the ethnic ones, the locals were financially stable, enjoying peaceful relations with the pro-union management, which provided union members with relatively steady work throughout the year. Unlike many UGW locals in other cities, they were able to pay the per capita tax levied by the national office. However, the HSM locals did not get anything substantial in return from the UGW headquarters. In 1913, for example, they contributed several hundred dollars to a UGW organization campaign planned for Chicago, but the campaign never proceeded beyond distributing some leaflets among workers. Above all, the 1910–1911 strike had left Chicago's men's clothing workers irrevocably distrustful of the UGW leadership.[43]

In fact, Thomas Rickert and other national officers were aghast at the growth in the number of locals formed by immigrant workers across the country. Not only in Chicago but in other cities, "Columbus tailors" increasingly joined the union in the early 1910s. In New York, an opposition group called "Brotherhood of Tailors," criticizing the reluctant Rickert regime, undertook an extensive organization campaign in 1912. Late in the year, the group called a strike, tying up the New York men's clothing industry. As he had in Chicago, Rickert made efforts to terminate the fight as soon as possible after collecting initiation fees from strikers. But the strike continued and resulted in wage raises and shorter hours, enlisting thousands of new members. Presumably, the balance of the UGW membership already opposed the work clothes makers, the basis of the regime. The officers felt their own jobs threatened. Preparing for a convention scheduled to be held in October 1914, they did their best to prevent tailors' locals from blocking their customary re-election. The officers ordered the locals to have their ledger books specially audited by the national office and in many cases to pay immediately an exorbitant amount of arrears or be disqualified from sending a delegation. Further, the office decided to hold the convention not in Rochester, New York, as originally planned, but in Nashville, Tennessee, which was difficult to reach by railroad from Chicago or New York.[44]

The Nashville convention caused tailors' locals to secede from the Rickert regime. New York locals had shared their opinions of the national office with locals in other cities, particularly Chicago. The link between the two was Sidney Hillman. Now working as chief clerk for the International Ladies' Garment Workers' Union in New York, Hillman had become acquainted with a number of Jewish labor leaders and was able to inform his Chicago fellows of the sentiments within New York UGW locals. Several weeks before the convention, Frank Rosenblum, Anzuino Marimpietri, and Hyman Schneid, a Socialist Labor Party member and leader of special-order coat makers' union Local 197, wrote to New York delegates: "We, in Chicago recognize that there is something radically wrong in the management of our international organization [the UGW], and we, desire to co-operate with delegates of New York and other cities who are of the same opinion." They further expressed their intention to challenge the regime by declaring that they wished "to accomplish the necessary changes in the personal [personnel] of our general officers, as well as constitutional changes so necessary and all important for the improvement and growth of our International Organization."[45] When Thomas Rickert refused to seat opposition delegates at Nashville because their locals had not paid the per capita tax, Rosenblum protested and led them out of the convention hall. They proceeded to hold a separate convention.[46]

The secessionists formed another UGW. Sidney Hillman was elected president, as he was a man of repute already known to New York delegates and a moderate acceptable to the American labor movement in general. The new general secretary was Joseph Schlossberg, a passionate orator affiliated with the Socialist Labor Party and a labor journalist. The secessionist group won enthusiastic support from union members in Chicago, New York, Boston, and Philadelphia, and claimed the allegiance of more than two-thirds of the UGW's sixty thousand members. Hillman tried to have his group approved by the American Federation of Labor, but Samuel Gompers, always opposed to dual unionism, did not give him a chance to present his case. In December 1914, Hillman and Schlossberg called a special convention of the secessionist group, which renamed itself the Amalgamated Clothing Workers of America.[47]

The ACW cast aside principles and practices cherished by the UGW. Disgusted with autocratic rule, the new union provided in its constitution that major issues such as constitutional amendments and election of national officers be decided by a referendum of the membership. And it chose industrial unionism, contending that the prevailing production system made organization along craft lines ineffective. Indeed, the section system instituted at the modern clothing factory had minutely subdivided the labor process and made the lines increasingly insignificant. The ACW advocated industrial unionism for an ideological reason, too. Its constitution proclaimed that the industrial union was a powerful weapon in the "constant and unceasing struggle" between the capitalist and the working class.[48]

In practice, however, the ACW already appeared to have relinquished the militant strategy advocated by many contemporary radicals. Like the United Mine Workers, an industrial union that John Mitchell had led to adopt the AFL's business-union approach around the turn of the century, the newborn union sought a labor agreement that would prescribe its relationship with the employers. In the first resolution adopted at the 1914 special convention, the union declared it would respect all existing agreements between its members and their employers, while turning down the Italian syndicalist delegates' proposition that it should not enter into any contract that provided the terms of employment for the members. Later, in the report to the second convention, the General Executive Board, the top leadership of the union, stressed that a collective bargaining agreement did not mean "the surrender of the workers' right to their employers." It was necessary, explained the GEB, in order to establish a mechanism to adjust labor disputes in a peaceable way. The board claimed: "There must be regulated relations between the employers and our organization, otherwise those relations assume the nature of spasmodic and guerrilla warfare, with all the evils accompanying it. . . . The collective bargaining agreement means the recognition of the right of the workers to a voice in industrial legislation."[49] Launched on supposedly radical principles, the ACW adopted an accommodative approach to the larger society. Within its industry, however, it aspired to a new balance of power by organizing immigrant workers, whom its nativist rival had long neglected.[50]

THE 1915 STRIKE

The ACW chose Chicago for its first organizing campaign. Certainly, New York was the largest production center, but the numerous sweatshops that teemed there presented a discouraging prospect. In Rochester, small shops were few, and large manufacturers had long worked to build up an anti-union stronghold. Baltimore ACW locals had just battled the UGW, which, in order to torment the new union, did not hesitate to cooperate with the Industrial Workers of the World. But the ACW had a reliable foothold in Chicago. From Hillman's standpoint, that foothold had to be expanded and solidified, because it was the basis of his power in the union. In early 1915, ACW leaders of the city called a meeting of officers and active members and appointed various committees in order to "feel out the tailors, and see what response we get from them."[51]

Soon, Hillman arrived in Chicago and set up the organizing staff for a systematic campaign. He appointed Frank Rosenblum as national organizer, paid by the national office, and placed him in charge of the campaign. In addition to local organizers from District Council No. 6, a heritage of the UGW, Hillman installed Hyman Schneid, a socialist leader of Local 197, in the campaign and called in several members of the Journeymen Tailors' Union, which temporarily merged with the ACW.[52] The organizers, mostly with socialist backgrounds, were assigned to each of the major ethnic groups, for example, Stephen Skala to the Czechs, Emilio Grandinetti to the Italians, and later Leo Krzycki to the Poles. And there were a number of rank-and-file members who volunteered to distribute thousands of leaflets after work. The campaign would be financed virtually completely by HSM locals, which collected $2,000 at the start and pledged to give more,[53] inasmuch as the national office was not financially strong yet.

Because of its financial weakness, the ACW sought to avoid a major struggle, focusing the campaign on bringing unorganized workers into the fold. It held a series of mass meetings, which were often overcrowded with workers. The employers immediately stopped cutting wages, and some even granted small increases. Some workers joined the union, but most did not; they were either distrustful of a labor union on account of the UGW's record or afraid of losing their jobs in a season that was not good at all. In order to attract their interest, the ACW held a parade on May Day, in which an estimated eight thousand members, almost all of them HSM employees, marched through the downtown men's clothing district. The parade created "a wonderful sentiment" among the workers and several days later those employed by the Continental Tailoring Co. went on strike, demanding reinstatement of two men discharged because of their union activities. The ACW soon called off the strike and prevented it from developing into a major battle. Three more strikes took place during this six-month campaign and also ended up isolated episodes. However, the organizers and the volunteers did routine work throughout the campaign, distributing leaflets, contacting workers employed at non-union firms, and occasionally calling shop meetings for the workers. Unorganized workers called the union "the Amalgamated," and the motto of the campaign, "I Will," circulated beyond them and later became that of Chicago. By the end of August 1915, the ACW leaders were sure that they had at least one active member at each of the men's clothing factories in Chicago.[54]

The organizing campaign forced the union to face a strike situation in September 1915. Starting in late August, the beginning of a slack season in the ready-made branch, manufacturers as usual cut wages and discharged a number of workers. Staging stoppages and walkouts, workers, particularly those employed at Hirsch, Wickwire and Co., Mayer Bros., and Scotch Woolen Mills, turned to the union and, apparently, demanded that it call a strike. At a GEB meeting held in the closing days of August, the ACW leaders agreed that sooner or later they should take a decisive measure. Things changed faster than they expected. Royal Tailors, one of the largest special-order firms, discharged some of its cutters, who immediately held a meeting and joined the ACW.[55] The union called shop meetings for the workers employed not only by the firm but by three other large companies. Observing the developments, Frank Rosenblum wrote to Hillman on September 7: "Chicago to-day appears to be on the verge of a general strike and it appears that the meeting set for the 24th [of September] is a little too far off, and that a large meeting will become necessary before that date."[56]

Hillman hurried to Chicago and urged local leaders to take a patient approach. They believed that "there is no use talking to the manufacturers before we are on strike and show them our strength."[57] They had already called mass meetings for September 14, ten days earlier than previously arranged. Hillman was aware that there was "very little possibility of getting the manufacturers to a conference" with the ACW because "[t]hey think they can defeat the union, the way they have done in the past."[58] At the meetings, which workers crowded in spite of rain that day, however, Hillman persuaded the workers to resolve that the ACW call a strike if the manufacturers did not agree to open negotiations with the union. This move was designed to win favorable public opinion in the event of a strike. In the letter sent to the employers on September 16, and printed in local newspapers, the ACW asked for a joint conference to discuss workers' demands and declared that, in case of failure to reach an agreement, "we are ready to submit any or all disputed points to an impartial board of arbitration. . . ."[59] This move was also intended to show that the union could be a partner in assuring uninterrupted production. Taking the case of the New York Protocol of Peace, the letter stressed that the ACW wanted to establish industrial peace in Chicago's men's clothing industry, "with the danger of strikes and cessations of work entirely removed."[60]

The manufacturers simply ignored the letter. The workers' demands formulated in it were moderate, compared with those of the 1910–1911 strike. Instead of the closed shop, the ACW called for a union-shop agreement; the demands also included a forty-eight-hour week, a 25 percent wage increase, equal distribution of work during the slack season, and establishment of an arbitration mechanism for future grievances.[61] In fact, almost all of the demands had already been acceded to by HSM, which was making increasing profits with the union's cooperation. Yet employers found the idea of negotiating with the union unappealing. In this, they were not simply afraid that the union would usurp their managerial prerogatives. As shown during the 1910–1911 strike, union leaders in the clothing industry had never been able to "control" immigrant workers. Experience with the UGW indicated that the leaders were often dishonest enough to take advantage of frequent stoppages, instead of enforcing a labor agreement. After contacting some employers during the 1915 strike, John Williams, chairman of the HSM arbitration board, summarized the strands of their distrust in the union:

> We [employers] regard Sidney Hillman very highly. We believe him honest, high-minded, and capable. But we don't believe he can control his people. It is notorious that union leaders in the garment trade are short-lived; they kill each other off. With Hillman dead or dethroned we should be back in the hands of the old grafting pirates, who would not enforce an agreement, who would foment shop strikes for the purpose of extorting money out of us, who would destroy the quality of our work, which has cost so much to build up, who would, in short, make life a hell to us and either drive us out of business or into insane asylums.[62]

The ACW called a strike on September 27, the last day of the ten-day period given employers to consider the union's proposal. Workers quickly responded to the call. Union members led the others in their workrooms to walk out by blowing whistles at the various "zero hours" set by the ACW. The walkout was "practically complete" on the Northwest Side, where Polish workers had already showed persistent militancy since the 1910–1911 winter, including engaging in strikes during the 1915 organizing campaign. The situation was almost the same in the downtown and West Side districts, except at Edward V. Price, a special-order firm that heavily guarded itself with special policemen, while offering wages and working conditions as good as HSM's. The exception appeared only on the Southwest Side, where many Czech workers remained at their workplaces, mostly small contract shops.[63] The next day Hillman wired Joseph Schlossberg, "Over twenty thousand people out" at most of the large manufacturers, including Kuppenheimer, Continental Tailoring, and International Tailoring.[64]

Again the ethnic community came to the aid of the strikers. Czech contractors on the Southwest Side, who belonged to the Czech Tailoring Contractors' Association, agreed to stop working in early October. Although a considerable temptation to secure steady work trapped a few into continuing, most did not want to hear "the anger and loathing of their neighbors by helping the manufacturers to subdue the workingmen," according to the Czech newspaper *Denni Hlasatel*. In fact, it was difficult "to continue working under police protection in the neighborhood of honest and peace-loving people."[65] Now almost all of the men's clothing workers in Chicago, except those employed by HSM and Edward V. Price, were out on strike. Independent manufacturers, most operating small firms with moderate financial resources, quickly opened negotiations with the ACW, and within ten days, forty-seven firms had signed union-shop agreements.[66]

However, large manufacturers, especially those affiliated with the Wholesale Clothiers' or Tailors' Association, were ready to fight. The so-called "association houses" again proved stubborn. When the Illinois Board of Arbitration contacted Martin J. Isaacs, attorney for the associations, before the strike was called, it received a cold reply. He declared that the workers had no legitimate grievances, that there would be no strike, and that there was nothing to discuss or to arbitrate. As soon as the strike began, manufacturers shipped work to other cities, New York and Rochester in particular, or gave it to Southwest Side contract shops whose employees were still at work. The association firms hired strikebreakers, too, but they were "dummies" not expected to do real work, going to various factories in order to make the firms appear busy.[67] In addition, manufacturers tried to depict the strike as a struggle between two unions, playing off the UGW against the ACW. Isaacs induced the UGW to secure labor agreements with some firms, and the *Daily Trade Record*, a paper that supported manufacturers, printed a letter that alleged, "Hillman and Schlossberg are looking for positions in the Garment Workers Union [UGW], and that is why they are making a noise as if there was actually a strike in existence."[68]

The strike turned into trench warfare, with both sides firm in their positions. The actual battles were strikers' clashes with the police, who were as brutal as five years earlier. Again, policemen were trying to break the strike as soon as it started. A few days after the strike was called, about fifteen hundred workers held two meetings, at the Hod Carriers' Hall and another nearby hall. Around five o'clock, when they were leaving, policemen, perhaps afraid of a riot on account of the sheer numbers, suddenly forced them back into the halls with clubs and brandished revolvers. It was not until three hours later that the police dismantled the barricades they erected inside Hod Carriers' Hall and released the workers. In addition, the police would not allow peaceful picketing, often blocking the streets leading to the men's clothing factories or, on other occasions, with the help of private detectives and special policemen employed by men's clothing firms, savagely beating and arresting strikers trying to picket the factories. When workers assembled by the scores or hundreds on the streets, policemen on horseback or motorcycles charged into the crowds, running over men and women.[69] Then strikers were arrested at random. On October 4 alone, for example, about one hundred workers were arrested and fifteen to twenty women strikers were pushed into a patrol wagon, whose windows they broke so as not to suffocate. In the course of this strike, the police arrested 1,971 strikers, of whom only three were convicted of any charges.[70]

Police brutality stirred up sympathy for the strikers and stimulated public efforts to bring about a settlement. As she had been five years before, Ellen Gates Starr was one of the first outsiders who came to protect the strikers by their own presence, and soon many upper-class women were on the picket line. As the brutality became a civic issue, the city council decided to investigate the subject and at the same time to appoint a special committee of five aldermen to mediate the dispute. But it did not meet success on either score. When the council ordered all permits issued to special policemen for strike duty to be withdrawn, the head of the police department refused to obey. The defiant attitude was backed by Mayor William Hale Thompson, who insisted upon noninterference in this particular strike. The special committee failed to open negotiations between the two sides, although public opinion compelled the reluctant associations to meet the five aldermen. All the committee could do was to press employers by investigating working conditions at public hearings and ordering health and other authorities to strictly regulate the shops and factories.[71]

Capitalizing on the sympathy for the strikers, Sidney Hillman succeeded in winning favorable public opinion. By early October he was already certain that there was "[v]ery little hope for real action," though the city council had become involved in the fight. Hillman believed "the struggle with the association[s] will come down to a test of endurance."[72] With the help of a public relations agent hired by the ACW, Hillman repeatedly proclaimed that the union was willing and ready to submit its demands to arbitration. While the city council was investigating police brutality, the ACW held a parade in the downtown men's clothing district. At least seven thousand workers marched through the streets, with messages such as "THE BOSSES HAVE STRONG UNIONS BUT REFUSE TO RECOGNIZE OUR UNION" inscribed on their banners. The parade helped to keep enthusiasm alive in the ranks and at the same time stimulated public opinion supporting arbitration. Another parade was held with Mother Jones in the lead, when public hearings revealed that women workers often earned less than $10 a week under unsanitary conditions. Soon Jane Addams, Harold L. Ickes, and other notable men and women formed the Citizens' Committee for Arbitration in the Clothing Industry, and most of the local newspapers published editorials in favor of arbitration.[73]

By the end of October, however, union leaders were concerned about their financial situation. Public opinion, though favorable, did not bring much money into the ACW strike fund. There were individuals donating and organized efforts taking up collections, but the total amount available to tide them through the end of the strike was only about $20,000, less than one-sixth of the strike fund. Other unions contributed only $2,573, as Samuel Gompers practically locked up union treasuries to punish the "outlawed" ACW. Hillman appealed to the Chicago Federation of Labor and the Women's Trade Union League, asking the officers to help him as individuals. Sympathetic as they were to the strikers, the officers would not risk enraging the powerful Gompers. Thus, the strike had to be financed chiefly by the ACW members themselves. Assessments upon the membership and donations from the national office and from HSM locals, in addition to normal income, approached $99,000, and accounted for more than five-sixths of the strike fund.[74] But the fund was insufficient to sustain about twenty thousand workers still on strike. On October 28, Frank Rosenblum wrote to Joseph Schlossberg that "our only danger" lay in running out of money. He explained, "Our expenses are increasing, while our income is decreasing each week."[75]

The strike came down to a stalemate. On October 26, a strikebreaker shot and killed a striker and antagonism against the employers ran high among the workers, but Hillman and Chicago ACW leaders failed to capitalize on the sentiment, except in appeals for money to Schlossberg and the New York locals.[76] While most of the independent manufacturers signed an agreement with the ACW by early November, the association firms appeared deaf and mute and made no significant move. The citizens' committee published and distributed a pamphlet titled "Why Not Arbitrate?" but the employers did not respond to it. The Illinois arbitration board persistently attempted to mediate the dispute, but the firms, after repeatedly ignoring the board, finally sent a curt answer: "Your proffered services are declined, with thanks."[77] They sent their work, though there was not much of it, chiefly to New York contractors, which the union failed to stop. Again, they were waiting for the strikers to come back because of hunger.

In early December, ACW leaders decided to call off the strike. The union did not have enough money to feed the strikers and their families, though many conceded their strike benefits to needier fellows. A number of them, probably about four thousand, had already crossed the picket line and returned to the old workplaces or had found jobs somewhere else. Unlike the UGW officers during the 1910–1911 strike, Hillman and other leaders chose to confront the strikers with the acknowledgment of defeat. At a mass meeting called on December 12, 1915, he asked the workers to approve the decision. Three thousand men and women wept and accepted it.[78]

The 1915 strike was the first systematic fight by Chicago's men's clothing workers. The *Survey* noted that "orderliness" was one of the contrasts to the 1910–1911 strike: The workers walked out promptly according to the leaders' order and held meetings "in an orderly manner," whereas they had been an unorganized "mob" five years earlier.[79] John Williams described the strikers as "a well drilled, thoroughly officered army." He explained: "Previous strikes [in the garment industry] have been spontaneous uprisings of an aggrieved and infuriated populace, ruled by the mob spirit. . . . The present strike was planned with a coolness and thoroughness comparable to that of the general staff in Germany."[80]

The orderliness was partly due to the way the strikers were organized. At the beginning of the strike the leaders established three district headquarters: Troy Hall on the Southwest Side; the Jewish Educational Alliance on the Northwest Side; and Hod Carriers' Hall, covering the West Side and the Loop, as the central meeting place. At each hall union officers chaired the meetings and directed shop chairmen, who represented the men and women working at each factory and took charge of picketing and relief as well. So the strikers mobilized according to workplace, not along ethnic neighborhood lines, as they had five years before.[81] The union did not rely upon the rank-and-file initiative formed among immigrant workers living in the neighborhoods, a salient feature in the 1910–1911 strike, which prevented John Fitzpatrick and Margaret Robins as well as Thomas Rickert from taking effective command of the workers.

The orderliness also reflected the fact that ACW leaders were in command of the strikers. The 1915 organizing campaign had already shown the leaders how deep-rooted the workers' distrust was in regard to the labor union: Organizers painfully realized that "the unpleasant memories" of the UGW were "[a]gainst us at the present in the campaign."[82] Therefore, the ACW sincerely formulated workers' grievances in its demands, wholeheartedly supported their survival throughout the strike, and courageously admitted its defeat. After the strike, the *New Republic* pointed out that "preparedness for the next strike is the the question of the hour in the Chicago clothing trades."[83]

The orderliness was above all based on the worker solidarity that had been developing since the 1910–1911 strike. This was evident from the start. In early October, when many contract shops were still working on the Southwest Side, Czech workers refused to do the work sent from a strikebound factory. Some were members of the UGW and well aware that its rival ACW was conducting the strike, but they were not bothered by the rivalry. "As soon as you learn that our shop has accepted scab work, let us know, and we shall stop work immediately and join you," the Czechs said to the strikers. The *Denni Hlasatel* explained: "Many of them had taken part in the 1910[–1911] strike and know how it would feel if somebody should break the strike and counteract the efforts of the strikers."[84] Throughout the 1915 strike, therefore, Chicago's men's clothing workers saw and felt their solidarity. Even though the strike ended in defeat, the workers knew how thoroughly they were united. Agnes Kazmar, a Polish tailoress employed at a contract shop during the fight, remembers: "I guess they [the strikers] figured it was a lost cause at that time, but it helped a lot because it put an idea into people's head. And they figured if they had something to gain, it would be worth while."[85]

The solidarity was rooted in working-class consciousness. Men's clothing workers obviously felt "the identity of their interests as between themselves, and as against other men whose interests are different from (and usually opposed to) theirs."[86] Some of the workers, imbued with socialism, syndicalism, and other radical ideas, defined their interests in a clearcut language of class. Talking about Jewish social life in early twentieth century, Pearl Spencer, a Ukrainian Jew employed at a Chicago men's clothing shop after coming to America in 1907, recalled: "The upper class looked down upon them [immigrant workers], they exploited them, they take the profits over. But they were only immigrants, common peasants from villages, that couldn't read or write."[87]

For others such as Maria Valiani, class consciousness was tinged with popular religion. Explaining the ACW organizing activities at B. Kuppenheimer and Co. in the 1910s, Valiani pointed out, "People started to understand that we must be united against the millionaires." The reason was "because the millionaire is out to get all they can." She continued: "If he's got one million, he wants two million. And the poor people, they have to stick together if they want to . . . live halfway decent. . . . If you're a wage earner, you'll never be a millionaire."[88] Maria Valiani described the conflicting interests in accordance with her religious faith: "Jesus said . . . [y]ou shall never enter in the kingdom of heaven . . . because if you're rich, that means you didn't pay your subjects enough to live on. . . . And that's why they're suffering."[89] Apparently, she interpreted the Christian doctrine in terms of that popular mentality that traditionally differentiates "us" from "them."[90]

Although class solidarity did not wipe out ethnic rivalry, as indicated by the internal strife that soon swamped the Chicago ACW organization, it nonetheless made the 1915 strike significant. Though defeated, workers found themselves united, with the ACW on their side. There were more frustrations to overcome until Chicago was completely organized in 1919. But manufacturers had already begun to suspect that the union could control the workforce. The suspicion was in fact created by workers, who expressed solid support for the ACW. And they would continue to do so for years to come.

REORGANIZATION AND ETHNICITY

The 1915 strike left in its wake a change within the Chicago ACW organization. The fight brought in more than ten thousand new members, who were assigned to the existing locals, except No. 39, already a big one with about twenty-five hundred members. As a result, four coat makers' unions were greatly expanded: Local 197 won about seven thousand members, mostly Jews and Italians; Local 38 twenty-three hundred Poles; Local 6 more than twelve hundred Czechs; and Local 269 hundreds of Lithuanians. These locals needed a conference to coordinate their activities. District Council No. 6, which the ACW tried to reactivate during the 1915 organizing campaign, was a paper organization without a secure source of income. The HSM locals had their own joint board but the new members were not working at that firm. In March 1916, a new Chicago Joint Board (CJB) replaced the council, composed of delegates from all the locals in the city and ordained to direct their organizing activities and coordinate their possible differences. It was more than just a conference, and had the authority to levy a per capita tax on the membership and to elect its officers, particularly business manager, by a referendum.[91]

Soon, however, divisions emerged within the CJB. New members dropped out in greater numbers than expected; independent firms that had signed an agreement with the union discriminated against ACW members as soon as the 1915 strike ended in defeat. In the spring of 1916, while cutters were on strike, the CJB appeared to function smoothly. When the cutters' strike turned into another defeat chiefly because of cutting done in other cities, the locals that were losing members began to complain. Four locals, Nos. 39, 61, 144, and 152, retained the core of their membership, HSM employees. But the other four were hardly self-sustaining, comprising only twelve hundred members altogether, roughly one-tenth of the peak membership reached several months earlier. The CJB was financially in bad shape because of the reduced membership and could not engage in an organizing campaign to make up, even partially, for the loss. The four small locals, led by Hyman Schneid and Louis Taback of Local 197, attacked CJB business manager Samuel Levin and secretary-treasurer Jacob Potofsky, both of whom resigned from their positions. The ACW General Executive Board intervened. At its session in October 1916, the board, believing that the small locals needed financial assistance, decided to provide regular aid until they could secure enough members to be self-sustaining.[92]

This internal strife involved ethnic problems. Out of the four small locals complaining about the CJB, three were so-called "nationality locals" formed by Czechs, Poles, and Lithuanians, and the other one, Local 197, was composed chiefly of Jews and Italians. Hyman Schneid and his followers often demanded that the coat makers be divided up among the ethnic locals, with a Jewish and an Italian one to be created. But the mainstream within the ACW leadership was squarely opposed to the idea, believing that, as Potofsky put it, "the very existence of the organization was being threatened."[93] ACW leaders were certainly afraid of ethnic division, taking pains to eliminate or at least suppress ethnic prejudices, which employers had long encouraged and taken advantage of in order to prevent workers from resorting to collective action.

More important, mainstream leaders believed the union's organizational form had to match the workplace structure. Organization along ethnic lines was impractical in carrying out collective bargaining and arbitration. At HSM, for example, the labor agreement and the arbitration mechanism were based upon an existing form of work organization, the section system. The section was the basic unit in day-to-day transactions between the union and the firm, such as changes in jobs and wage rates. Because a section was composed of workers with diverse ethnic backgrounds, it was impossible or even suicidal for an ethnic local to agree on, for example, increasing wage rates for one nationality alone. As Potofsky pointed out in regard to the internal strife, "[T]he people who were in charge of Hart Schaffner & Marx situation could not afford to sub-divide the organization."[94] That was why HSM locals were formed and grew along trade lines, such as coat making or pants making; immigrant workers, though unable to understand English, chose to remain in the trade locals, leaving ethnic ones always struggling hard to survive.

To the ACW leaders, however, the ethnic local was not a temporary expedient eventually to be thrown away. Although it proved awkward and sometimes obstructive to the union's daily business, they needed the local because it provided potent leverage, particularly with organizers who specialized in single ethnic groups. At the start of the 1915 organizing campaign in Chicago, for example, the leaders enlisted several organizers, particularly Stephen Skala and Emilio Grandinetti. Mostly Jews, the leaders had very limited access to the workers belonging to other ethnic groups. On the other hand, an organizer could easily approach such a group when he or she was familiar with its language, culture, and personal connections. And the organizer usually constituted a link between the leadership and the rank and file, both representing to the top leaders his or her countryfolk and persuading them to listen to the leaders. When the national office decided to offer financial aid to Chicago locals, therefore, it was designed above all to retain ethnic organizers. Moreover, many immigrant workers took pride in having their own ethnic local. Soon after the internal strife subsided, Italians of Local 39 petitioned for a charter and an organizer. They accused the local's Jewish officers of "incapacity and racial hatred." The fact was that the Italians, having once formed Local 270, were now the only major ethnic group without an independent local in Chicago. The petition declared: "The Italians wanted not to be deprived of a right known and given to other nationalities, especially when you mind that the size of the Italian Branch [of Local 39] was far superior to some other Local."[95] As Frank Rosenblum felt, the matter was perhaps "stirred up by Grandinetti who is seeking to get his job back as organizer."[96] But Rosenblum later admitted, "We must have Bohemian, Polish, Italian, and Jewish organizers at all times, to have one without the other creates discontent which must be avoided."[97]

The final solution to the internal strife came from an organizational reform of the Chicago Joint Board. In early 1917, when the CJB started an organizing drive, it was again faced with complaints by Local 197 and the three ethnic locals. As the campaign did not bring in many members and as the national office, occupied with urgent matters in other cities, did not provide the promised financial aid, these four locals tried to take members away from Local 39 and vice versa. The General Executive Board, meeting at Chicago in February, held a conference with representatives of local unions in the city and decided to abolish Local 197 and transfer its members to Local 39. Later, Local 39 absorbed the Czech and Polish locals, according to the policy adopted at the 1918 convention, which recommended one local union for all workers engaging in the same trade at each men's clothing center. On the other hand, in September 1917, the ACW decided to permanently place the organizers of the four small locals and an Italian organizer—it was Grandinetti—on the payroll of the national office. The ethnic locals were restored after Chicago was completely organized in 1919, and prospered in the 1920s, each with three to five thousand members; only the Lithuanians, a small group in the men's clothing industry, had around one thousand.[98] The ACW preserved the leverage and pride offered by the ethnic local.

The long controversy within the Chicago ACW organization shows that the fate of ethnic locals depended mainly on the form of work organization and the advantages and frictions involved in the locals. Recently, Steven Fraser has argued that the locals were abolished as part of an ethnic integration policy pursued by the ACW leadership. He points out that ethnic conflict in the ACW, particularly between the Jews and the Italians, was rooted in divergent cultural heritages and ideological orientations. According to Fraser, the conflict was eventually replaced by ethnic cooperation under the leadership seeking "cultural transformation" among the membership.[99]

In fact, the conflict was often complicated by ideological differences irrespective of ethnic lines. For example, when Joseph Schlossberg wrote impassioned antiwar editorials in the *Advance*, he found the dissenters headed by his own countrymen, Hillman and Frank Rosenblum.[100] Socialists, together with syndicalists, were generally opposed to or doubtful of the idea of arbitration cherished by the ACW mainstream. It was these radicals and the workers following them, not just Italian syndicalists, that ACW leaders tried to convert by preaching "contractual obligation, economic self-interest, and the parliamentary practices of union and national politics." As Hillman, Bessie Abramovitz, and others did at HSM, the leaders strove to prevent work stoppages and to guide grievances into the arbitration process. ACW educational programs in the 1920s, which Fraser regards as an important part of the efforts toward "cultural transformation," consisted chiefly of music, as well as labor movement and political issues, rather than subjects intended to promote ethnic integration.[101]

WARTIME EXPANSION

Soon after the internal strife ended, American participation in World War I intensified labor-capital tension in the men's clothing industry. It initially slowed production of civilian clothing, as prices soared and consumers chose to forgo new clothes, and led employers to impose lower wages and longer hours on workers. However, the United States government ordered millions of military uniforms for American soldiers fighting in Europe. At first uniform orders were placed with manufacturers in New York and other eastern cities, who had them made by non-union labor, especially women and children working under sweatshop conditions, using the pretext of producing war munitions and threatening workers who complained with arrest and imprisonment. As orders placed by the government were undermining working conditions throughout the men's clothing industry, workers fought back. The war had stemmed the influx of European immigrants, the most important source of the clothing workforce, and the general labor shortage, due to vigorous wartime production, put the workers in a better position to bargain with their employers. As inflation prompted the workers to demand higher wages, labor disputes plagued the industry. As in several other industries, strikes or worker slowdowns frequently disrupted production of uniforms.[102]

Trying to take control of the increasingly unruly workers, the ACW called the Wilson administration's attention to the inferior labor standards that were being applied to military contract work. Hillman discussed the situation with Florence Kelley, former chief Factory Inspector of Illinois and now president of the National Consumers' League, who delivered a protest to the war secretary, Newton D. Baker. Soon, Hillman met with the secretary's assistants, Walter Lippman, a former editor of the *New Republic*, and Felix Frankfurter, a future Supreme Court justice. In August 1917, Baker adopted the two men's advice that a Board of Control and Labor Standards for Army Clothing be established in order to enforce an eight-hour day, a minimum wage scale, sanitary inspection, and, above all, collective bargaining in the manufacture of military uniforms.[103]

It took several months for the War Department to effect the proclaimed intent. In fact, the Wilson administration had not formulated its wartime labor policy yet. It was not until the spring of 1918 that the federal government established the National War Labor Board, with equal representation of employers and employees, in addition to the public. The board recognized workers' rights to organize, collectively bargain, and demand wage standards set by labor unions. Certainly it condemned strikes, the ultimate weapon in workers' hands, and was inclined to preserve the prewar status quo in labor relations, restraining unions from recruiting new members by coercive means. But its guidelines were in general favorable enough to encourage organized labor to pursue expansion of the membership during the war years, whereas, in the past, the federal government had never allowed the unions a voice in making the national labor policy, and had almost invariably intervened in industrial disputes to the detriment of the workers.[104] Under the new guidelines, William Z. Ripley, a Harvard economist appointed Administrator of Labor Standards in Army Clothing, aimed to ensure the smooth and fast production of the uniforms. His policy was clearly enunciated when Wanamaker and Brown, a Philadelphia firm, locked out its employees, accusing the ACW of obstructing production. Ripley immediately directed the firm to meet with union representatives, pointing out that the workers were already ACW members. Under the administrator's threat to cancel the uniform contract, the firm promised to comply with union employment conditions.[105]

Anxious to share in the wartime expansion, the ACW decided "to make a test in Chicago by using the authorities that helped so much in the Eastern uniform situation."[106] A recession in the latter half of 1917 led manufacturers in the city to reduce the workforce and lower wage rates. The union again engaged in an organizing drive, but failed to attract many of the unorganized workers, as employers reduced production of civilian clothing.[107] Only at John Hall, one of the firms doing the military work, did the ACW succeed in recruiting a great number of the employees. In early June 1918, John Hall discharged several workers who were union members. Hillman arrived in Chicago and filed a complaint with the War Department, while asking Potofsky to "assure on my behalf Dr. Ripley that I will do all in my power to prevent strikes on uniforms in the market [Chicago], and also that the local officers here are desirous to co-operate with his office."[108] But the firm continued to dismiss union members and even locked out the whole workforce for a while. In August, William Ripley finally intervened and ordered the firm to reinstate the discharged workers, recommending that it adjust all grievances in conference with the ACW.[109]

Until the end of 1918, when the U.S. government halted uniform orders following the armistice in Europe, the ACW made every effort to drive a wedge into Chicago's stubbornly anti-union associations of men's clothing manufacturers. As soon as the John Hall case was settled, the union became involved in a dispute at Alfred Decker and Cohn, another large association firm making military uniforms. When a worker who had been discharged for asking for a wage increase came to the Chicago Joint Board, it called a shop meeting for the firm's employees. Only forty, out of about fifteen hundred, appeared but they appointed a committee to submit grievances to the management. The workers selected for the committee were promptly discharged, whereupon the union filed a complaint with the War Department, while continuing to organize most of the workers. In early September they went on strike, demanding wage increases and recognition of the shop committees, which the ACW had under its complete control. Eventually, William Ripley himself took up the case and made Alfred Decker and Cohn accept the union demands. The union did not always succeed in organizing workers making uniforms, however. Scotch Woolen Mills, another large association firm, chose to give up its contract with the federal government rather than deal with the ACW. Through an organizing drive that was timed to take advantage of the government's support, however, the union succeeded in making an inroad both into the associations and at the same time into independent firms such as Rosenwald and Weil.[110]

From the viewpoint of manufacturers, especially of the association members, the ACW unmistakably proved its command over workers. As a matter of fact, employers were fearful of the union's influence upon their workforce. When the 1915 strike ended, they noted that the workers were not disappointed with the union at all, even though it had obviously been defeated. Although most of their employees soon dropped out of the membership, in the spring of 1916, when the union was negotiating with HSM for a wage increase, the association firms quickly announced a 10 percent raise of their own so that the ACW would not take advantage of the issue for an organizing drive. Exactly the same thing happened one year later, and again in 1918. In fact, many manufacturers felt that some kind of workers' organization was necessary in order to prevent frequent work stoppages and walkouts. During the 1917 organizing campaign, for example, B. Kuppenheimer and Co. became so tired of endless troubles in the workroom that the head foreman of the firm cried, "For God's sake, do not stop work in the shop." He further urged: "If the wages are not enough or if you have some other grievances, select a committee and send it to the firm. I assure you that the matter will be promptly adjusted."[111] Now, with the federal government supporting the right to organize, the union not only won a foothold in some of the firms, but also showed that it had the power to call out the employees or send them back to work.

The ACW demonstrated its command of the workers even in those shops where most of the workforce did not officially belong to it. In the earliest days of 1919, HSM agreed with the union that working hours be reduced from forty-eight to forty-four a week. Soon New York's manufacturers followed the lead and even Chicago's special-order firms' association did the same by the end of January. But the Wholesale Clothiers' Association, consisting of ready-made manufacturers, declared that they would not effect the forty-four hour week until April 28. Angry at the delay, the workers employed at a Kuppenheimer factory on the Southwest Side walked out. Samuel Levin, now a member of the ACW General Executive Board and manager of the Chicago Joint Board, arrived at the scene and urged them to return to work the next day and leave the factory not at 5:15 P.M. but at 4:30 P.M., quitting time on the forty-four-hour-week schedule. The workers not only followed his advice; they attended a shop meeting called by the union. The association quickly announced that the reduced hours were in effect.[112]

A show of strength on the ACW's part, however, drove the association firms to abandon their anti-union policy. In February 1919, the union planned an intensive organizing campaign for Chicago. By that time it already had a firm hold on New York's men's clothing industry, though contract shops there were still beyond its control, and had secured even Rochester, the well-known open-shop fortress. Now the Chicago Joint Board created a committee of twenty-six organizers, headed by Frank Rosenblum. The organizers began the campaign by calling mass meetings, at which Joseph Schlossberg made fiery speeches. Then Sidney Hillman arrived in Chicago and addressed six thousand workers at a gathering at Street Carmen's Hall. There, the workers adopted a resolution in favor of a strike against all the anti-union men's clothing manufacturers of the city. At the March 1919 GEB meeting, however, Hillman fixed on the strategy "not to involve the whole [men's] clothing industry in a general strike but to tie up individual houses [that is, firms]."[113]

The strategy turned out to be quite effective. In fact, the industrial situation was favorable to it. While there were no more uniforms being made by the end of 1918, manufacturers found an upsurge in civilian clothing orders, as World War I, after having drained hundreds of thousands of consumers from the American market in the previous two years, was finally sending them home. Now men's clothing firms, whether in the ready-made or special-order branch, had to build up their workforce to a maximum. On the other hand, the war had continuously pushed up living costs, which led workers to demand wage increases again in the spring of 1919. The organizing campaign soon revealed how vulnerable the manufacturers were to workers' collective action at this particular point. B. Kuppenheimer and Co., one of the campaign's targets from the start, let its fifteen hundred workers go on strike by discharging a committee of them for demanding higher wages. In three weeks, the firm agreed to take back all the strikers and have shop committees organized, though it refused to recognize the union. In addition, Kuppenheimer agreed "to pay the strikers for all the time they have been out," obviously in order not to lose any of their employees to other manufacturers.[114]

There were a number of separate short strikes throughout March and April that ended up as workers' victories. Workers who were members of the ACW were active in the campaign. By mid-March they had distributed fifty thousand leaflets preaching unionism. "Floating cutters" effectively took advantage of the hectic industrial situation. Many secured jobs at non-union firms, agitated unorganized workers, and were discharged with a week's wage; the next day they went to another firm and did the same thing. Manufacturers made concession after concession, raising wages and promising job security, sickness and other benefits, and profit sharing. By the end of April, however, most of their employees had been organized by the ACW, and many independent firms had signed agreements with the union.[115]

The association firms finally surrendered in May 1919, thanks to a critical break in their ranks, which was brought about by the ACW's campaign strategy. In late April, the ACW forced the issue of union recognition on Alfred Decker and Cohn and Kuppenheimer, who, having recently undergone strikes that completely tied up their establishments in the midst of an exceptionally busy season, were apparently tired of fighting. Alfred Decker and Cohn quickly agreed to recognize the shop committee and to bargain collectively with its employees, although without accepting the ACW as their representative. On the other hand, Kuppenheimer contacted Jacob Abt, president of the Wholesale Clothiers' Association, and declared: "We are through; we are going to sign an agreement with the union."[116] Although he had led the association members in defeating the 1915 strike, Abt answered this time that an association-wide agreement would be better. The association opened negotiations with Hillman, Rosenblum, and Levin, and assented to a proposal providing the preferential shop, equal division of work during the slack season, and establishment of an arbitration mechanism identical to that of HSM. On May 13, Hillman announced the terms at Carmen's Hall, where seven thousand workers cheered the victory. Thirteen days later, workers approved a similar agreement with the Wholesale Tailors' Association, which always stood with the other body as far as labor relations were concerned.[117]

Soon, the ACW proclaimed that the organization of the men's clothing workers in Chicago was complete. A few independent firms such as Sears, Roebuck belatedly came to terms with the union. Even those contract shops scattered on the outskirts of the city, difficult to organize but always dependent upon the manufacturers, came under its control. Because the agreements signed in these months were on the preferential-shop basis, most workers soon joined the union. By the fall of 1919 the membership had expanded to thirty thousand, two out of every three men's clothing workers in Chicago. Even the overalls workers, whose employers had an agreement with the UGW, threw away their old membership cards and joined the ACW.[118]

The ACW's triumph in Chicago was part of the remarkable growth that American organized labor achieved during the war years. With workers in New York, Rochester, and other cities following its banner in 1919, the union saw its membership jump from 38,000 in 1915 to 177,000 in 1920. During the same period the number of organized workers in the United States increased from about two and a half to more than five million. Moreover, most of the new recruits were immigrants engaged in meat packing, textiles, construction, steel, and several other industries. Although conservative unionists had long regarded them as bad material for organizing, immigrants staged militant strikes and joined unions, taking advantage of the extensive labor shortage, vigorous industrial activity, and encouraging national labor policies of the war years.[119]

As part of the overall union expansion, the ACW organizing campaign in Chicago had distinctive characteristics compared with others, particularly in the meat-packing and steel industries. In both of those industries, which had increasingly applied mass-production techniques starting in the last decades of the nineteenth century, craft unions, though once powerful, had been prostrate for at least a decade before World War I. During the war, they sought to expand their footholds, prompted by workers' unrest as well as by the favorable conditions. Diverse unions holding partial jurisdiction over the industries launched a joint campaign. A dozen craft unions created a Stockyards Labor Council in 1917, pooling their organizing staff and making financial contributions to the new body; the next year, no fewer than two dozen established a National Committee for Organizing Iron and Steel Workers in a similar way. The committee met with dismal failure, not only because it could not get any help from Washington in starting a campaign as the armistice in Europe approached; it chose national confrontation with the resourceful steel makers, even though by the end of 1918 the participating unions had contributed only $6,300 to the campaign for a half-million workers. The Stockyards Labor Council was cautious, though not as cautious as the ACW, which separately pressured individual manufacturers of Chicago by paralyzing their factories at a time when they were intensely competing for larger market shares in the postwar years. By contrast, the council concentrated on the largest meat packers in the city as a group, hindering them in their competition with packers in other production centers, and enlisted at least thirty thousand workers in 1918.[120]

More than campaign strategy distinguished the ACW; its leaders envisioned a different function to be performed by unionism. The AFL affiliates in the meat-packing and steel industries had never been dependable partners to the employers, nor had they enjoyed support from the majority of the workforce. The principal unions, the Amalgamated Meat Cutters and Butcher Workmen and the Amalgamated Association of Iron, Steel, and Tin Workers, were craft organizations that had once been powerful enough to disrupt production and to dictate employment terms for the skilled workers. Wartime conditions led the unions to engage in comprehensive organizing drives and to achieve success in the meat-packing industry. With the unskilled workers in their fold, from the employers' viewpoint, the unions would have had the production process at their mercy. In fact, however, the unions had never been in command of the workforce, owing to the chasms that divided their English-speaking members from the unskilled immigrants and black workers. When the employers challenged the Amalgamated Meat Cutters and Butcher Workmen during the postwar recession, the union, already weakened by jurisdictional fights as well as divided along ethnic, racial, and skill lines, again fell apart after a disastrous strike in 1921–1922.

On the other hand, the ACW, in winning moral support from unorganized workers, endeavored to prove that it was able to "control" the workforce, and to assure employers of uninterrupted production. Its vision belonged to the mechanism that regulates excessive business competition in labor-intensive industries, a function that Colin Gordon has stressed in his important study of the New Deal. Unionism achieved this function when employers, concerned about labor costs and an unwieldy workforce, were furnished with no better alternative, and when workers, constrained by the uncertain conditions of wage working and a skewed relationship of power, sought to improve their position within the capitalist system.[121] Contrary in part to Gordon's argument, however, "established union strength" was not a factor that contributed to regulatory unionism in Chicago's men's clothing industry; it was before the ACW took a firm hold that Sidney Hillman and other union leaders emphasized such a function. As indicated by their approach to the 1915 strike and wartime campaigns, they took pains to organize the workforce by persuading anti-union employers of the benefits of unionization. This explains in part why the ACW not only expanded its Chicago membership without a major struggle, but retained a stable organization there through the recession.

Strategy and vision helped to completely organize Chicago. It was class solidarity, however, that enabled ACW leaders to prove their control over the Chicago workforce. In the 1915 strike, men's clothing workers of the city demonstrated unity based on class consciousness. This unity was compatible with ethnicity; it overshadowed virulent antagonism among ethnic groups while leaving room for perennial rivalries, which the leaders effectively shaped into a multi-ethnic alliance against the employers. When the employers were most vulnerable owing to the wartime boom, the ACW was able to harvest the fruits of unity.

Harvesting is one thing, but preserving is another. This is especially true of the workers, whom experience had taught to be sensitive to the interrelationship between the leaders and the rank and file. Cultivating is yet another; worker solidarity is not an immovable tree but a changing current dependent on experience at the workplace and in the community as well.

CHAPTER 5

The Amalgamated Establishment

"The vanguard of the American labor movement was in convention," wrote renowned journalist William L. Chenery for the *Survey*, referring to the fourth biennial convention of the Amalgamated Clothing Workers held at Boston in May 1920. Chenery noted that the union had succeeded in organizing about 175,000 workers, nine-tenths of the whole men's clothing workforce, in less than six years since its creation. Through the years, it had lifted them from "the bottom of the economic ladder," roughly doubling their wages and reducing weekly working hours from fifty-two to forty-four, and put judicial process in place of the autocratic power of the bosses in the workroom. Now, Chenery stressed, the ACW planned to do more. At the convention, it resolved to experiment with cooperatives and banks, work for unemployment insurance, and promote efficiency in production. Reporting on the convention for the *Nation*, Mary Heaton Vorse agreed with Chenery. She found "the spirit of practical idealism and democracy at work" and dubbed the ACW as "the vanguard of labor unions both in its past achievements and in the future programs."[1]

To contemporary observers, especially those disappointed with Samuel Gompers's pure and simple unionism, the ACW was an inspiring departure from the American Federation of Labor. The AFL was in retreat after World War I; the great steel strike of 1919 constituted a massive defeat for organized labor, and, as political leaders stressed return to "normalcy" and conservative courts supported the status quo ante, employers across the country preached the "American Plan" to dislodge the closed shop.[2] On the other hand, the ACW, an "outlawed" organization that Gompers would not pardon for challenging the United Garment Workers, appeared ready to confront the challenges of the times. The union had successfully organized on the principle of industrial unionism, abandoning the old craft lines. It had contributed as much as $100,000 for the striking steel workers and put money and organizers as well into the 1919 Lawrence, Massachusetts, textile workers' strike. The ACW was attempting to federate all the unions in the clothing and textile industries. Moreover, the union now welcomed innovative programs. Sidney Hillman declared that the ACW was willing to apply the scientific-management theory in cooperation with employers, though the AFL condemned it as a threat to unionism. Some observers, such as the famous economist George Soule, believed that the trend represented by the ACW signified the birth of "new unionism" in the United States.[3]

In the late 1920s, however, the ACW, its Chicago organization in particular, did not present a particularly striking contrast to the AFL. In *A Theory of the Labor Movement*, published in 1928, labor economist Selig Perlman argued that this apparently radical union had, "in practice, turned its efforts not to fighting capitalism in its industry, but to securing a thorough-going job control," suggesting that Hillman and his colleagues were following in the wake of Gompers's business unionism as it had been devised four decades earlier.[4] Similarities were evident in Chicago. The ACW regarded the city as a laboratory, where it experimented with employment exchange and unemployment insurance and sought inspiration regarding ways to raise labor productivity. It aspired to a role that craft unions filled in iron, coal mining, and other industries; these unions enjoyed "their dual status as supplier of managerial services and skilled labor."[5] The ACW organization in Chicago was also a model for other local bodies elsewhere, both in its cooperation with management and in its financial stability. Above all, the Chicago Joint Board owed its pioneering and exemplary status to the fact that the city remained completely organized throughout the 1920s. Such a secure position enabled the union to gain solid control over jobs and to consolidate bureaucratic rule over the rank and file. Moreover, the joint board had the power to ward off communist attempts to capture the organization and stop grass-roots opposition to the union leadership, which resulted in languishing democracy. Although it still preached industrial unionism, the Chicago ACW organization had become an AFL-type business union.

This ironic turnaround is the main topic of the present chapter. This chapter begins with an analysis of the union bureaucracy, which the Chicago Joint Board established to ensure labor supply to employers and to provide unemployment insurance for workers. It also discusses the impact that labor-management cooperation, particularly the efforts to introduce production standards on the shop floor, had on the relationship between the CJB leaders and the union ranks. It then describes how the bureaucracy threatened union democracy. Finally, this chapter debates, in a broad context, the basis of business unionism in the perspective of workplace.

UNION BUREAUCRACY

When the men's clothing firms of Chicago signed up with the ACW in 1919, the union's organization in the city needed to be readjusted.

Because the agreements provided for a preferential shop, most workers soon joined the union, and membership expanded from six thousand in early 1919 to thirty thousand by the fall that year. Besides the existing locals, the old ethnic ones were restored and two more were created for clothing examiners, fabric spongers, and bushelmen who repaired defective garments. Soon, women workers, concerned about their underrepresentation in the ACW leadership as well as gender-related issues at the workplace, formed their own local, which never thrived in the 1920s; although the ACW paid tribute to their cause by appointing a female member to its General Executive Board, the local was essentially at odds with the others, which were primarily concerned with job issues and ethnic needs.[6] Except the new ones, all the locals now had sufficient members to pay for their business agents and organizers. Complete organization of Chicago, however, required the union to make industry-wide decisions, as most of the manufacturers in the city, having dissolved the two employers' associations, formed the Industrial Federation of Clothing Manufacturers and demanded such decisions. So the CJB, as the federation of the ACW locals in the city, came to take charge of day-to-day business with the employers, putting all the business agents on its payroll.[7]

Assignment of new responsibilities led to a financial rearrangement. The CJB had levied a per capita tax upon the members, but the income from the tax was scarcely sufficient to make it a powerful body. Now, with about thirty business agents on its payroll, the CJB needed much more money. The union decided that all dues should go directly into the CJB treasury, with only a portion then distributed to the affiliated locals. The CJB took most of the dues. When the dues were $2 a month, for example, it kept ninety-two cents and allocated only 5.5 cents to the locals, apportioning the rest to the national office and for special purposes.[8]

As a result, the Chicago ACW organization became highly centralized. The local unions were deprived of the power to negotiate with employers, as the CJB controlled the business agents. They were independent only in internal activities affecting their own members. They sent delegates to the CJB, who elected a president, a board of directors, and other unpaid officers, but the delegates did not appoint the paid staffs, who negotiated with the employers. The business agents were elected by the rank and file. Out of the thirty-three agents now needed, the manager in command of the CJB staffs and two business agents at large were chosen by a referendum of the entire Chicago membership; the rest, each of whom worked only within a particular trade, were elected by the members employed in that trade, after careful screening by the CJB leadership. Consequently, the staffs, and the manager in particular, were independent of the unpaid CJB officers as well as the delegates. In fact, they enjoyed more power and prestige than the others.[9]

The CJB grew into a powerful bureaucracy, chiefly owing to the policy of cooperation with management, which, first of all, involved labor supply. The 1919 agreements stipulated that the firms apply to the ACW for workers before trying to hire help from the streets and that the union send qualified workers within forty-eight hours. So the CJB established an employment department and opened three offices, one each on the West, the Southwest, and the Northwest Sides.

But the offices did not function smoothly, although the union, having worked with HSM, had experience in this field. While the number of unemployed workers swelled during the slack season, the offices did not exchange information with each other and failed to reduce the volume of unemployment as effectively as possible. Unemployed workers frequented all three branches because of the placement method that was yet to be developed. Inside the office, they pushed their way toward a two-square-foot window in the partition, which kept them from overrunning the desks. Those strong or lucky enough to reach the window were "accustomed to exchange compliments and insults with the employment clerk," finding jobs available for themselves or not. Moreover, employers were often dissatisfied with job applicants provided by the union. Because Chicago produced various grades of garments from the finest through the medium, it was not easy to fill specific positions with adequate hands. Some employers valued workmanship than anything else, while others preferred speed. As a result, a number of job applicants were dismissed after the trial period of two weeks specified in the agreements.[10]

The CJB gradually realized that it ought to reorganize the employment offices. As a postwar depression hit the men's clothing industry in the latter half of 1920, unemployed members grew in number and burdened the already inadequate placement system with additional work. In July 1921, at a point when the ready-made season was in full swing and the special-order season slack, the CJB devised a plan to transfer temporarily jobless members from the latter branch to the former or vice versa according to seasonal changes. It seemed "a scientific distribution of the workers to meet the needs of the industry, make the best use of the man-power in the market, eliminate waste and provide for more continuous employment for our members."[11] Indeed, the plan turned out to be effective among the cutters, who numbered only a little more than three thousand. As pointed out by the CJB manager Samuel Levin, however, some tailors were afraid that "their usual earnings would suffer because the work is in a different branch of the industry."[12] Many presumably failed to be transferred because the CJB employment offices did not pool requisitions and job applications. A year later the union studied the offices to find the source of the problem. The results showed that "a properly organized employment office" could reduce both the volume of joblessness and the friction involved in transfer.[13]

In July 1922, the CJB commissioned Bryce M. Stewart to reorganize the employment department. He had been working on the employment exchange program run by the Canadian Department of Labor. Stewart immediately replaced the three offices with a central employment exchange office at the CJB headquarters, where the employers sent all their requisitions. And he introduced a filing system to keep detailed information about jobless members. The office gave the unemployed serial numbers when they registered and then notified them of available jobs in their turn. The new system turned out to be quite effective in providing the employers with needed hands.[14] Several months after Stewart reorganized the employment department, the labor manager of Alfred Decker and Cohn remarked: "The exchange [the CJB employment office] is able to familiarize itself with the quality of help required in our plant and weed out such workers as are not adapted to our [production] processes. The present classification of help with regard to skill, experience and general adaptability to the operations of a particular factory is a big advance."[15]

The new office put the employment exchange in order and at the same time gave many union members their first encounter with the fledgling CJB bureaucracy. It had a large waiting space with rows of chairs that were never overcrowded because jobless workers, once registered, did not have to report every day. And the reformed system successfully eliminated an old, mischievous practice, by preventing workers from applying to more than one branch office at once and picking a favorite out of different jobs in hand. Above all, an applicant had to secure a statement from the business agent in charge of his or her workplace, which declared the the applicant had quit "under proper circumstances." As far as employment was concerned, Chicago's men's clothing workers were under the ACW's control.[16]

However, the CJB could not completely control the jobs available in Chicago's men's clothing industry. Unemployed workers did not necessarily register at the employment exchange office. "After long experience in the men's clothing industry," noted its director Bryce Stewart, "they have come to think of the constantly recurring periods of unemployment as inevitable, and some have deliberately forborne to register in slack times in order that the few vacancies occurring might be available for less fortunate members."[17] As a result, the office often failed to fill some of the requisitions, although needed hands were on streets.

Another program of the union-management cooperation, unemployment insurance, greatly strengthened the CJB's job control. Toward the end of World War I, Sidney Hillman began to think about insurance, which British labor, a source of his inspiration, had enjoyed since the early 1910s. Since the chronic seasonality of the men's clothing industry drove roughly half of the maximum workforce out of work for two to three months each year, a device to protect against the evils of enforced idleness was more acutely needed than in most other industries. For Hillman, it was the employers' responsibility to protect the workers from unemployment because they failed to offer their employees a chance to work and earn a living all the year round. Beginning in early 1919, he publicly called for out-of-work benefits. Apparently in order to develop an unemployment insurance plan, he appointed Leo Wolman, a Johns Hopkins economist, as director of the union's research department, at Felix Frankfurter's recommendation.[18]

It was not an easy task for the ACW to get unemployment insurance put on the negotiating table with employers. Soon after its 1920 Boston convention, the union asked for an out-of-work benefit plan in Baltimore and then in Chicago. However, unemployment insurance was alien to the employers, who declared the issue out of the question, pointing to the adverse industrial situation. The men's clothing industry was indeed being pulled into the postwar depression in the latter half of 1920. The following spring the union even had to accept a 10 percent wage cut in Chicago and to battle employers in New York and other eastern cities who wanted to break its grip while curtailing production. The depression continued into 1922 and put the ACW on the defensive. In the spring of that year, when the agreements signed in 1919 were to be renewed in Chicago, the employers demanded a 25 percent reduction in wage rates and unrestricted managerial prerogatives, especially in discipline and the adoption of new production techniques. The union eventually agreed to a 10 percent wage cut but in return won the concession that it could ask for an increase in wage rates and raise the issue of unemployment insurance on the anniversary of the renewed agreement.[19]

Soon, the ACW found a good opportunity to institute the insurance in Chicago. In late 1922, the industry began to recover from the postwar depression and it appeared ready to prosper in the foreseeable future. In December, HSM again took the lead by agreeing to establish an unemployment fund, with contributions from both the firm and the employees. Several weeks later, Sidney Hillman and then Leo Wolman arrived in the city and formulated the union's demands, which included a wage increase and "creation of an unemployment fund by contributions from the employers." Employers, particularly those affiliated with the Industrial Federation of Clothing Manufacturers, refused. But both sides agreed to have the issue of wage increases decided by a Special Board of Arbitration, which granted a 10 percent raise as demanded by the union.[20] The decision opened a way to unemployment insurance. The ACW "decided to take 3 per cent of the 11 [*sic*] per cent and put that in an unemployment fund and say that one-half of it came from the employers and the other half from the employees," Leo Wolman recalled a few years later.[21] The independent firms, including the contractors, soon reached a similar agreement with the ACW.

From the employers' viewpoint, the union's unemployment insurance proposal was not as objectionable as it appeared at first glance. It would not put a heavy burden on them because their contributions were to be taken from the wage raise. In principle they had to contribute 1.5 percent of the payroll, which, together with their employees' contribution at the same rate, would be deposited in a fund. A future raise in wage rates would certainly mean additional costs on top of an already swollen payroll, which might place the employers at a disadvantage in competing with manufacturers in the other men's clothing centers. On the other hand, out-of-work benefits would reduce a high labor turnover in the industry. Because production fluctuated wildly, many workers quit their workplace in slack times and employers had difficulty in building up a maximum workforce at the beginnings of the busy seasons. Men's clothing firms were especially concerned about retaining experienced workers, since it took several weeks to train a "greenhorn." When the unemployment insurance plan was put into effect, Bryce Stewart, one of the principal figures who formulated it, anticipated that "the management will have the advantage of more versatile workers, well equipped to meet emergency conditions."[22]

The ACW's proposal was based on the idea of unemployment prevention. A number of American social scientists and reformers had made a strenuous and continuous effort to develop an unemployment insurance plan that could prevent or at least reduce joblessness.[23] The American Association for Labor Legislation in particular, a progressive reform group formed in 1906, took the initiative in the effort. John R. Commons, one of its leading figures, believed that financial incentive devices would encourage employers to reduce social ills at the workplace. By 1914, such belief was developed into a concrete program, which became the basis of the ACW unemployment insurance proposal written by Leo Wolman. And John Commons, chairman of the special arbitration board that awarded a 10 percent wage increase in 1923, helped Wolman and others to work out the Chicago unemployment insurance plan in detail.[24]

As a result, the Chicago plan created a peculiar form of social insurance. It provided that each manufacturer have a separate account in the unemployment fund and maintain the balance of the account above a certain level. As unemployed workers drew benefits from the account, a firm had to offer them steady work in order to prevent its account from being drained below the specified level. Moreover, those employers who succeeded in reducing unemployment were allowed to discontinue their contributions once their accounts reached an amount that could pay the maximum benefits for two years. This scheme did not allow all the contributions to be pooled in one fund so that the insured could share the risk according to the fundamental principle of insurance. Certainly, the principle was not entirely ignored; the contractors would have their own and their employees' contributions pooled in one fund. But the three largest firms, HSM, Kuppenheimer, and Alfred Decker and Cohn, would have access to an independent fund, and the other manufacturers were supposed to deposit their contributions in one general fund while keeping separate accounts therein.[25] The Chicago unemployment insurance plan was essentially an aggregate of independent company programs.

Chiefly because the Chicago plan would constitute a separate and limited financial resource for most firms, it provided inadequate benefits for the unemployed—40 percent of full-time earnings, with $20 a week the maximum, paid for no more than five weeks in any one year. Consequently, the workers were entitled to only two weeks' wages, while many were laid off for more than ten weeks in a year. A few years after the plan was inaugurated, the small benefit was cut down to 30 percent of the earnings with the maximum of $15 a week. A protracted depression in the mid-1920s quickly drained a number of separate accounts in the manufacturers' fund and put other funds in danger.[26]

The ACW took part in the administration of the unemployment insurance funds. The Chicago plan established five boards of trustees, each to control one of the five funds and make administrative rules in regard to contributions and benefits. In practice, the boards appeared to be almost one and the same body; John Commons chaired them all and the trustees representing the ACW were the same people on each of them; only the employers' representatives were different. The trustees had once considered that each of the Chicago firms should manage its own program. As this would result in complications and as some firms refused to be burdened with insurance work, however, the boards created one office to administer all the funds.[27] The administration of the funds involved the CJB employment exchange office. Schedule A, which defined terms and conditions of benefits, stipulated that an employee, when jobless, promptly register with the office and that his or her unemployment be considered to begin on the date of registration. In order to remain eligible for the benefits, the workers had to accept any job offered by the exchange, because the plan counted only involuntary unemployment due to lack of work. The schedule specified that an employee "who declines to accept suitable employment" be disentitled to benefits.[28] The unemployment insurance office secured information about each worker's joblessness from the CJB employment exchange, in addition to the payroll reports from the firms.

Now the CJB, Bryce Stewart believed, was able to "match demand and supply [of labor] more promptly and efficiently."[29] Indeed the CJB's job control became so effective that in a few years the union could transfer between the two branches of the industry not only the cutters but also the tailors. In the mid-1920s, when Chicago firms were coping with a long recession, the union apparently satisfied their meager demand for workers. In the fall of 1927, however, the employers saw the tide turning and advertised jobs in newspapers, while the CJB often failed to supply needed hands. Now the union again resorted to the old transfer scheme that had been applied to the cutters early in the decade. This time the scheme was both extensive and coercive. When the CJB employment exchange office had no more jobless workers on its registration list, it called on business agents to send in tailors as well as cutters who they believed were available for transfer. The workers, if unwilling to move, could refuse only at the risk of losing unemployment benefits.[30]

Job control gave the CJB a formidable disciplinary power over union members. Owing to the preferential-shop agreement, the ACW had more than forty thousand members in Chicago by the fall of 1921, almost all the men's clothing workers of the city. Now the CJB, with its employment exchange complemented by the unemployment insurance plan, became virtually the sole authority to distribute jobs. In other words, the union had the power to deprive workers of their jobs and of their livelihood by expelling them from the membership. Indeed, expelled members often appealed for reinstatement, crying that their livelihood was in danger.[31] Moreover, the CJB could remove workers from their jobs and keep them unemployed as long as it wanted by placing their names on the bottom of its employment exchange list. In fact, the union frequently disciplined unruly members by threatening to take them off their jobs. For example, when a trimmer at Hirsch Wickwire refused to pay $25, which the union assessed as a penalty for quarreling in the workroom, union officials told him that he would be removed from his job if he did not pay the amount. The trimmer apparently paid up.[32]

Unemployment insurance helped the CJB gain financial stability, too. It began paying in May 1924, five months later than originally planned, as the depression that began late in the previous year resulted in insufficient funds. The union handled the benefit checks. They were assigned to business agents, who called a shop or local meeting and handed the checks over to the workers. Those not attached to a specific firm, particularly temporary cutters working here or there, received their checks from the CJB employment exchange office.[33] As stipulated in the unemployment insurance agreements, the CJB claimed, "Every member in order to receive any benefit must be in good standing. . . ."[34] The scheme forced the members to pay their dues and assessments. In January 1925, for example, two unemployed cutters asked the Executive Board of Local 61, cutters' and trimmers' union, why the local office was withholding their benefit checks. The board told each of them "to make arrangements to take something out of each check to be applied on the payment of his indebtedness to the organization."[35] Soon the local adopted a rule that a member, if in arrears in the payment of dues, should pay a specified amount out of the benefit checks.[36] The CJB stayed financially stable even during the protracted recession in the mid-1920s.

On the other hand, the ACW paid a price for job control and financial strength. Its unemployment insurance, along with its banks, housing projects, and other welfare programs, did not make the ACW a "good union," as Lizabeth Cohen suggests in her richly detailed study of Chicago's working-class life in the interwar period. Stressing that the faith workers had in "moral capitalism" was "born out of the promise of employers' welfarism in the twenties," she argues that welfare capitalism compelled unions to launch their own programs in order to compete with employers.[37] In the men's clothing industry, however, unemployment insurance, the most important welfare program in the 1920s, was not initiated by the employers but by the ACW, which drew its inspiration from British labor. Moreover, it seems likely that the insurance did not help lead workers to the idea of holding either the employers or the union responsible for their own welfare. Many members and even some officers thought the amount of the benefits was insufficient and preferred to have the 3 percent contributions returned to their weekly pay envelopes, regarding the benefit as part of their wage. And because the ACW played a major role in the administration of the insurance, discontent with benefits was leveled at the union. The amount varied not only because it depended on each worker's average wage, period of unemployment, and other factors but because many small firms reduced it when they did not have enough money in their funds.[38] As a result, there was confusion, suspicion, and ill feeling among the workers with regard to the CJB's handling of the insurance. A cutter alleged that union officers forged his name on a check and appropriated his unemployment benefit. A trimmer, when told that the amount of his benefit check would be applied to his obligations to the union, snatched the check from the hands of an ACW officer and destroyed it.[39]

Furthermore, workers protested against the powerful union bureaucracy. They felt aggrieved particularly by business agents, who confirmed a worker's eligibility for benefits by making a statement that he or she was involuntarily out of work, and who held back the check when a union member was not in good standing. A pants maker named Louis Kirshenbaum, finding his benefit less than expected, criticized the method of distributing the checks. Claiming that a lot of workers received more than their share, he wrote to the ACW organ *Advance* that "the present system of distributing insurance has a tendency to bring about corruption. . . ." It turned out that Kirshenbaum received less because he was out of town for a while and was not available for employment. Certainly, however, the pants-maker had a point when he argued: "The distribution of the insurance lies mainly in the hands of the Business Agents. . . . Standardizing the insurance, like dues and assessments, would immediately deprive the Business Agents of their present power."[40]

UNION-MANAGEMENT COOPERATION

The ACW prepared for a new era following the war. When the union proclaimed that it had completely organized Chicago's men's clothing industry, it did not intend to impose arbitrary rule on the production line. The agreements signed by the union in 1919 stressed its responsibility for efficient production, as had the preamble to the 1916 Hart, Schaffner and Marx agreement. They stipulated that "there should be no deterioration or reduction in efficiency, output and quality of workmanship on the part of the workers; and the Board of Arbitration and Trade Board, as well as the officers and members of the Union, are responsible for the maintenance of efficiency. . . ."[41] Sidney Hillman confirmed the spirit of the agreements in words reminiscent of his earlier efforts at HSM. "The new agreement brings an era not only of new power but of new responsibilities," said the ACW president, "and our organization will see to it that the workers bear these responsibilities." Hillman added: "We will show that not only can we fight hard but that we can also do constructive work when given the opportunity."[42]

With formidable disciplinary power over the rank-and-file members, therefore, the ACW leaders attempted to assure efficient production. As soon as the union laid a firm hold on the men's clothing industry at the end of the 1910s, it involved itself in the issue of how much labor a worker ought to perform. Men's clothing workers, when organized, intended to put an end to exploitative practices in the workroom.

In New York and several other production centers, where sweatshops proved stubborn, they abolished piecework. They regarded it as successor to the notorious task system that had long driven them to exhaustion by making a team of tailors complete an increasing amount of work. The workers replaced it with the "week-work system," a method of compensation by which a worker earned the weekly wage for the hours employed, not for the amount of work done. Soon many firms, especially those in New York, accused their employees of lying down on the job. They demanded reinstitution of piecework and resolved to risk a fight, particularly when the men's clothing industry was caught in the postwar depression.[43]

Sidney Hillman sought a solution to the issue before it embroiled the ACW in a major strike. At the 1918 convention New York delegates proposed that the week-work system be established across the country. Hillman did not give his answer, advocating "home rule" instead of a national policy. However, week work implied a restriction of output, the very reverse of his constructive approach to the industry. The leader was convinced that the union was responsible for efficient production, as provided by its labor agreements. In Chicago, most of the work was done at piece rates that were frequently revised through arbitration. Production was smooth, but there were definitely evils in piecework; many workers complained that it was a self-driving device that exhausted them and shortened the busy season. A logical alternative was week work based on standards of production. Under this system, the workers engaged in an operation were regularly classified into several groups according to their individual output, and all those belonging to the same group received the same weekly wage.[44]

Production standards involved a fundamental issue of employment relations, for they compelled a choice between the contradictory imperatives of conflict and compromise, which all workers have to make with regard to compensation for labor power. The introduction of standards was an approach to the issue, but not its solution. If production goals were set high, workers would have to work hard to join the group they wanted, and if low, employers would not accept the new system. And wage scales had to be determined for the standards; low rates linked with high standards would only bring forth a revised version of the task system. Therefore, production standards presented the familiar issue in a different form that had to be resolved through bargaining between capital and labor.

But Sidney Hillman had a sincere faith in science as well as arbitration. He believed that fair production standards could be set by applying the time and motion study, an integral part of scientific management. During the last years of the nineteenth century, Frederick W.

Taylor had claimed that employers could achieve efficient production through centralized planning of the production process, systematic analysis of each operation, supervision of worker performance, and incentive payment. When Taylor tried to popularize his ideas with his "Principles of Scientific Management," published in 1911, the theory, symbolized by the stopwatch, drew firm opposition from organized workers. Samuel Gompers and other AFL leaders believed that it would facilitate speed-up and undermine craft unionism by displacing skilled workers.[45] However, while organized labor in general was uncompromisingly distrustful of scientific management, Hillman had "no quarrel" with it. He was aware that even experts "find it difficult, if not impossible, to retain scientific accuracy and impartiality under pressure of employers whose interests they serve." So the ACW leader proposed to employ scientific management practitioners "to study the problems of work, from a broad point of view, considering the health of the worker, the permanent interests of the industry, the effect of inadequate tools and machines upon the workers and so on."[46] He actually did so for Henry Sonneborn, a Baltimore men's clothing firm. In cooperation with representatives of the firm, the union's experts established a normal speed by studying every motion involved in each of about one hundred fifty operations. They determined a maximum and a minimum performance speed and classified the workers. When a new pocket-making technique was introduced, however, the firm claimed that it enabled an employee working at the normal speed to make one hundred pockets a day, while the workers contended they could turn out only about seventy. The ACW took the case to arbitration.[47]

The opposition within the ACW feared that production standards would establish an easy way to exploit labor power inasmuch as they were to be fixed jointly by the union leaders and the employers. When Sidney Hillman placed a proposal endorsing standards before the 1920 Boston convention, opponents, particularly socialist delegates from New York, claimed that it would lead to "a return to slavery." They believed that employers, in collaboration with the ACW leaders, would raise the standards. Some argued that the depressed situation in New York was due to employers' mismanagement, not to the lack of standards. Others worried about possible dissension among the rank and file, as the membership was definitely divided between an opportunity to earn more and the need to preserve workers' health and solidarity.[48] The opponents doubted the motives behind the proposal. A delegate from Montreal bluntly expressed skepticism, when he asked: "The general board [the ACW General Executive Board] came to Montreal and insisted on putting certain production standards into our agreement. What have they got to do with production? Are they doing the boss's work?"[49]

Supporters of the proposal stressed in the main that the standards would be under the control of the union, stating that, for example, "the standards would be made by the workers themselves," or "the Amalgamated would see to it that the standard was not too severe." One of these was general secretary Joseph Schlossberg, the so-called "conscience" of the ACW. He urged New York delegates, the strongest opponents of production standards, to escape from "the shadow of the dead past," pointing out that "we speak of standards under the direction and jurisdiction and with the approval of our organization."[50] His point appeared especially significant in the immediate postwar years, when workers' control, as well as industrial unionism, was believed to be an essential ingredient for achieving socialism, as in the newborn Soviet Union.

Sidney Hillman chose to follow the imperative of compromise, rather than conflict, when he finally spoke out forcibly. He declared, "I believe that what is understood by week work is the privilege of the individual to lay down on the job if he so desires," and warned that that privilege would involve the ACW in exhausting battles and eventually destroy the men's clothing industry. Praising the proposal as "a middle ground between piece and week work," he urged the convention to "legislate for our organization as a whole and at the same time adopt a program that will help the industry."[51] The ensuing vote on production standards gave Hillman a victory, but it also revealed dissension on the issue; the tally was 178 for and 88 against.

As indicated by the debate, the week-work system with production standards was intended to increase labor productivity by applying the union's power. ACW leaders were aware that employers needed it for exactly that purpose. In March 1920, Frank Rosenblum, a GEB member in charge of organizing activities in midwestern cities, wrote to Hillman: "The situation in Cleveland is a good deal like the situations in other places, in as much as the employers expect the organization [ACW] to do what they failed to do all these years without the organization, to establish standards and systems in their shops, and they want this done overnight."[52] The leaders believed that employers paying by the week were suffering from low productivity in comparison with those taking advantage of piecework, and were losing their competitive edge. Week work, if allowed to continue, would damage the ACW, as the employers were expected either to risk a battle or to go out of business. In spite of the official recommendation that production standards replace both of the existing work systems, therefore, the ACW leadership apparently intended to impose the standards upon the week workers.

In practice, the union took pains to establish production standards where the week-work system was in effect, while leaving piecework virtually untouched. Regarding a labor dispute in Cincinnati in September 1920, Sidney Hillman remarked that he could have settled it more quickly by proposing piecework. In a letter to Rosenblum, he wrote: "All this evidence tends to confirm my contention that the need in this situation is for the establishment of standards of production as soon as possible—before the matter becomes a real issue."[53] It did become "a real issue" in New York. In the summer of that year, workers of the city refused Hillman's proposal to institute standards, accusing him of "class collaboration." In October, when the existing labor agreements were due to expire soon, employers faced with the postwar depression demanded piecework and strict discipline over the workforce. The uncompromising attitude on both sides led to a six-month-long lockout, which forced the workers to accept production standards.[54]

In Chicago, standards were introduced in the cutting rooms, while almost all of the tailors did piecework. Because cutting was still a highly skilled job and a process crucial to the quality of garments, the cutters were paid by the week so that speed would not undermine workmanship or harm fabrics, the most expensive item among materials. Some employers had already tried group standards in the cutting room. But James H. Tufts, a professor at the University of Chicago who chaired the Cutters' Commission, an adjunct to the HSM arbitration system, revealed that workers did not produce up to the standards, particularly during the slack season. While slow workers were never expected to reach the standards, he pointed out, "many of the faster men have felt that they should not cut more than this standard of average, in order to offset the deficiency of their fellows when they were paid only or little more than the minimum wages."[55] In April 1921, when New York firms were fighting against the week-work system, Chicago's manufacturers asked their arbitration board to establish enforceable production standards in the cutting and trimming rooms. James Tufts, now chairman of the board, ruled that every four weeks the cutters be grouped into five classes: A for those who produced 115 percent or more of the average output; B for those who produced 105 percent or more but less than 115 percent; and so on. Tufts also fixed the amount of wages for each class.

However, production standards were instituted only little by little. Because any change in models and styles affected time and motion involved in cutting, it was difficult and impractical to set a single standard for all the different sorts of garments produced by a firm. And small manufacturers employing only a few cutters did not appear to be interested in establishing standards, which would require them to spend additional money and time. HSM again took the lead. In early May 1921, the firm opened negotiations with the ACW, which became deadlocked because each side proposed very different standards. Four months later, James Mullenbach, chairman of the HSM trade board, finally suggested a middle ground and both sides accepted it, though complaining respectively that it was either too liberal or too harsh. The next year, the firm established another set of standards for trimmers, who cut trimmings to accompany the basic fabric of a garment. Other large firms introduced HSM's standards, with some adjustments.[56]

Cutters and trimmers resisted introduction of production standards. In the spring of 1923, B. Kuppenheimer and Co. instituted a set of standards on overcoats. Soon, "it was found," reported Sidney Rissman, business manager of the cutters' and trimmers' union Local 61, "that out of the one hundred and twenty-five men cutting overcoats none of the men were earning the money they were paid." In the shops where standards were installed, therefore, there were a number of stoppages, which cutters and trimmers claimed were justified despite union leaders' reprimands. The workers apparently resorted to soldiering, too; they deliberately slowed down the work pace when their employers attempted to institute standards. In June, Sidney Rissman urged that "when standards were introduced in any shop our members must at least show that they are making an honest effort to produce the requirements of the standards."[57]

Once a set of standards was established, workers wanted compensation for the extra labor they put in to meet the standards. When they believed a wage raise was inadequate, cutters and trimmers protested to union leaders rather than to employers. In February 1923, when the ACW began to weigh the demands to be presented to Chicago firms several weeks later, workers emphatically contended that a substantial wage increase be included. Having suffered two 10 percent wage cuts in the previous two years, they urged the leaders "not to misinterpret the sentiment of the rank and file." And they specifically pointed out that "at the present time the cutters and trimmers are receiving less than a living wage for services requiring more than ordinary skill to perform." When the union announced a 10 percent wage increase along with the plan to establish unemployment insurance at a special meeting of Local 61, many made "a joke of the meeting by booing our International and Local officers."[58]

However, production standards gradually became an established feature of the cutting and trimming rooms. A number of workers tried to benefit from the standards, as arbitration occasionally raised the wage scale to guarantee the cutters and trimmers against pecuniary loss. Some fast hands tried to produce and earn more, since the wage rates were differentiated roughly in proportion to individual output. And slow workers wanted access to the minimum wages, which seemed to be higher than those they had been receiving. "A group of low-paid trimmers" of HSM appeared at an executive board meeting of Local 61, held in September 1922, and asked why standards had not been installed yet in the trimming room, saying "they are unable to earn anything even resembling a living wage."[59]

Above all, the economic depression compelled the cutters and trimmers to accept production standards. Chicago's men's clothing firms did not fare well in the mid-1920s; in the fall of 1923, only one year after the postwar recession ended, another depression began. This time, it was chiefly due to a change in consumers' tastes. After World War I, Americans began to prefer lower-priced garments, while spending increasing amounts on passenger cars, radios, and other modern conveniences. While fine men's suits priced at more than $50 became a drug on the market, those priced at less than half that were popular, and expensive boys' suits were replaced by sweaters and separate pants. The change troubled manufacturers of quality garments, who had been dominant in Chicago since the turn of the century. A number of firms went into liquidation, and those remaining in business curtailed production. Some closed down their old shops and opened new ones in the South Side black neighborhoods or moved to smaller cities where white but still cheap and unorganized labor was available.[60] Consequently, unemployment and layoffs weakened workers' resistance to production standards.

Employers raised production standards little by little. They instituted the revised standards through separate negotiations with the ACW, claiming that they, producing diverse models and styles, needed different sets of standards. Some firms, hit seriously by the depression, asked the union to increase the normal speed, the basis of classification, and set the standards higher than those at other firms. The ACW often made concessions in order to keep the firms in business. Then the other firms demanded the same or corresponding concessions, which the union granted in spite of workers' protests.[61]

Production standards led to a conflict over an old practice that restricted output in the cutting room. The cutters had long insisted on handling fabrics of only one kind in each cut. Diverse fabrics mixed in one cut required more time and energy than one fabric piled at the same height; the workers had to match one with another in laying them on the cutting table, and fabrics had different textures, with some easier to cut than others. In fact, the cutters created work for themselves by cutting different fabrics separately when it was possible to work on them in a single cut. Firms producing low or medium grades of garments had their cutters working on mixed fabrics, but manufacturers of quality clothes never succeeded in doing so, chiefly because the old practice assured them of fine workmanship. As they began to produce cheaper garments demanded by consumers in mid-1920s, however, these manufacturers also wanted to cut mixed fabrics, under production standards.

In January 1925, the practice became a stormy issue in Chicago's Local 61. Planning to produce cheap clothes, HSM asked for Sidney Hillman's permission to cut mixed fabrics. When the local's business manager, Sidney Rissman, announced at a meeting that Hillman proposed that the union should agree to the request, the workers vehemently opposed the proposal. Above all, they were afraid a chain reaction would be triggered by a concession. "To grant the request of the firm of Hart, Schaffner & Marx," they claimed "would only be an invitation to the other firms in this market to request permission to introduce the cutting of mixed fabrics into their cutting rooms." Members of the local even hinted that the proposal might lead to a revolt against the union leadership. The "consensus" at the meeting was that "even if our Business Manager should agree with the firm of Hart, Schaffner & Marx and our International President, we are against it [the cutting of mixed fabrics] and will go to the limit to prevent its introduction in the market."[62]

Only two days after the meeting, however, Rissman reported to the executive board of Local 61 that Hillman had agreed to HSM's request. The board declared that the members would not cut mixed fabrics until Hillman explained why he allowed the firm "to enter this opening wedge."[63] At the same time, it decided to cash in all the bonds and securities held by the local, in anticipation of a battle. When the firm told cutters to work on mixed fabrics, they refused. Soon, Hillman arrived in Chicago and declared that he had allowed the cutting of mixed fabrics only at HSM and that the arbitration mechanism would never have the power to extend it to other manufacturers. Several weeks later, when the manufacturers opened negotiations with the ACW to renew labor agreements, they demanded its permission to cut mixed fabrics. The union apparently refused, but before long it began to allow one firm after another to remove the old restricting practice.[64]

The ACW endeavored to raise labor productivity beyond the cutting and trimming rooms. In the spring of 1924, the union proposed a series of reforms to Chicago's employers. As an alternative to another wage reduction, the ACW pledged to help those struggling against the depression to cut production costs. It encouraged them to produce cheaper garments and urged ready-made firms to venture into special-order lines and vice versa, so that the firms could take full advantage of their production facilities, inasmuch as the two branches had alternating seasonal cycles. The proposed changes required a reorganization of the labor process. The union took up the job of eliminating unessential operations and merging simple ones in the tailor shops. In the cutting rooms it subdivided the process and made the cutters work according to an instruction ticket instead of their own calculations for cutting. The ACW even cut wage rates in the reorganized workrooms, assuming that an increased volume of work would compensate for the lower rates. These innovations introduced by the union increased productivity; for example, in 1926, when Chicago began to recover from the depression, HSM dismissed 150 cutters, nearly half of its cutting force, offering $50,000 to be distributed among the discharged workers. The innovations, known as the X construction plan, were soon applied to other production lines than those that manufactured cheaper garments.[65] As a result, however, workers had to exert themselves to prevent their earnings from dropping.

Therefore, a number of Chicago's men's clothing workers felt sour about the ACW. They expressed their discontent indirectly by attacking the arbitration process. The arbitration board cut wage rates twice during the postwar depression, drawing angry protest from the workers.[66] After production standards were introduced, the trade board often involved itself in classification of cutters and trimmers and readjustment of the standards, and in many cases made decisions unfavorable to the workers. The board no longer appeared impartial. In late 1924, when Local 61 was formulating its own demands for the ACW leaders to consider in negotiations with the employers the following spring, its members recommended that the trade board be abolished or disempowered. About ten weeks later cutters and trimmers again hammered the arbitration mechanism. Discussing Sidney Hillman's proposal to cut mixed fabrics at HSM, they asserted, "It is about time for us to wake up and limit the power of the Trade Board and the Board of Arbitration."[67]

Workers also occasionally censured the ACW leadership. In 1926, for example, Otto F. Deckelmeir, an HSM cutter, was called before the executive board of Local 61 because he had said, "to hell with the Union [ACW], and to hell with the Board of Directors of the Union." Although Deckelmeir explained that some of his fellows had stirred him up by improperly criticizing him, the board fined him $50, one week's wage for a cutter.[68] In September 1925, vest makers at Alfred Decker and Cohn, who found their wages reduced under the X construction plan, reprimanded the leadership. At a meeting, they adopted a resolution protesting to Sidney Hillman and the CJB manager Samuel Levin "against this reduction and the negotiation of further reductions without consulting the people."[69] Four weeks later, Hyman Schneid, now a socialist leader of Local 39, introduced a resolution denouncing the plan at a coat makers' meeting. Pointing out that the innovations initiated by the ACW did not bring in enough additional work to compensate for wage cuts, his resolution demanded that "in the negotiations with the manufacturers our representatives shall not grant anything that will tend to lower our standards."[70] Although Jacob Potofsky felt that "[t]here is no one in Chicago or around here [New York] that needs to apologize for past negotiations with employers,"[71] the Schneid resolution clearly expressed the reproachful sentiment among the rank and file.

OPPOSITION CRIPPLED

Workers' discontent with the ACW leadership, which peaked in the mid-1920s, did not develop into an organized opposition movement. Above all, the ranks had benefited much from the union, which had secured them against arbitrary domination and excessive exploitation by employers and helped them enjoy a better, although not improving during that particular period, standard of living. Moreover, they were faced with adverse circumstances. The economic outlook was gloomy; the men's clothing industry was in the grip of a chronic depression, which appeared particularly serious in Chicago. The political atmosphere was unfavorable; the progressive impulse, stalled during World War I, had been replaced by a prevailing conservative outlook. And radical groups, rearranged as the far Left formed an independent party in the early 1920s, often fought one another. Partly because of their infighting, opposition groups within the union failed to capitalize upon the negative sentiments. By the time Hyman Schneid drew up his resolution denouncing the X construction plan, the ACW was deeply involved in the Left-Right conflict.

After forming the Workers' Party in 1921, American communists plotted to capture organized labor. They were led by William Z. Foster, a former leader of the Industrial Workers of the World. As early as in 1911, when the IWW still abided by the idea of building a new revolutionary labor movement, Foster had advocated a strategy to take over established labor unions by "boring from within." Soon he left the IWW and tested the strategy among railroad workers and in the great steel strike of 1919. The next year, Foster launched the Trade Union Educational League [TUEL], a body formed to carry out his cherished design, which became the "industrial arm" of the communist party. In the clothing industry, the league aimed first at the International Ladies' Garment Workers' Union and tried to organize a caucus by combining with opposition groups within it. A virulent struggle ensued in New York ILGWU locals, which threatened the national organization, as the New York rank and file comprised mainstay of the union. In 1923, the ILGWU expelled the communists and began to quell the Left-Right conflict.[72]

The ACW also encountered a political struggle in its New York locals during the early 1920s. During the 1920–1921 lockout, communists contended that Sidney Hillman and other "treacherous leaders" should be deposed on account of "their advocacy of peace and negotiation with employers."[73] But it was not until the summer of 1922 that ACW leaders became concerned about the factional strife. At the GEB meeting held in August, Frank Rosenblum pointed out that "New York is permeated with small politics," and proposed to "go all the way to make a peaceful settlement." Hillman deplored that the national office was being dragged into a struggle brought about by outsiders, and asked Joseph Schlossberg, editor of the *Advance*, "not to put anything in the paper that would bring us in a quarrel."[74] Only two months later, however, when the New York Joint Board held an election of its officers, open contention for power arose. In this metropolis, militant socialists won support from the ranks disappointed with the union-management cooperation, particularly regarding the introduction of production standards. Two locals, ruled by the Left, protested against the election and threatened to withdrew from the ACW if a new election was not called. Soon, fifteen business agents resigned and Hillman had to take a hand by appointing two of his men as assistant managers of the joint board.[75]

The conflict continued, but the ACW leadership stayed on the line until the summer of 1924. From the start, it had been wary of politics. Although there had been attempts to have the union commit to the Socialist Party in the 1910s, Sidney Hillman had steered clear of any official endorsement. In the next decade, however, he became increasingly interested in political power, probably because he was frustrated by the unfriendly attitudes of Woodrow Wilson's successors. In 1922, the ACW participated in a Conference for Progressive Political Action (CPPA), which a number of labor organizations and socialist leaders sought to build into a pressure group. The next year, the union sent observers to the Farmer-Labor Party convention, to probe the prospect for a viable labor party in the United States. The socialists within the ACW had often persuaded the union to support newspapers and politicians they preferred, for instance, Eugene V. Debs when he ran for the U.S. presidency in 1920, and to send its blessings to Soviet Russia. Hillman, apparently trying not to alienate them, often accepted socialist proposals, and he took the initiative in organizing a Russian-American Industrial Corporation, which raised $300,000 and invested it in a Russian clothing production project. In October 1921, Hillman even received a letter of thanks from Lenin for his aid to Soviet Russia. Indeed, the Workers' Party never publicly attacked the ACW.[76]

But the issue of a third party put the communists at odds with the union. In order to win a broad support in the 1924 presidential election, they chose to organize a united front of all radicals and liberals. The communists worked through the Farmer-Labor Party, which was going to nominate U.S. Senator Robert M. La Follette for president at its June convention. A number of socialists and labor leaders, who helped launch the third-party movement, also approved of concerted action but did not want the communists to dominate the convention. Suddenly, however, the communists abandoned their united front policy, following Moscow's direction. This turnaround prompted socialists and labor leaders to participate in the CPPA, whose nomination La Follette accepted. Sidney Hillman sent ACW representatives both to the Farmer-Labor Party and to the CPPA. In fact, he sought a labor party with a footing as broad as possible. A labor leader brought up in the progressive reform movement, he chose to commit the ACW to the CPPA, hoping eventually to transform it into a party. At the August 1924 GEB meeting, Hillman declared: "To eliminate ourselves [from the CPPA] means to line up with Foster and [Benjamin] Gitlow [of the Workers' Party]. Our business is to get closer and closer with the rest of the labor movement."[77]

Soon the Left-Right conflict was in full swing within the ACW. The communists, ousted from the ILGWU and now "betrayed" by the ACW, attacked at various points. At the 1924 ACW convention, two delegations from a New York local contended for seating; one had been sent by the right wing and the other by the TUEL-led opposition. Hillman placed the matter before the convention, which admitted the former after a three-hour debate. Then Rochester was entangled in an open quarrel complicated by Italian syndicalists, who had long been critical of the ACW leadership. There, the union suspended several members and nullified an election, apparently in order to remove left-wing officers. However, the political strife was getting worse in New York, the largest clothing center, which, with more than one-third of the ACW membership, had naturally attracted the communists' attention. In August 1924, they held a mass meeting at which Benjamin Gitlow, a major figure in the Worker's Party, accused the ACW leaders of corruption and class collaboration. Bitter charges and counterattacks plagued the New York Joint Board, which consequently became too enfeebled financially as well as morally to hold its ground against employers. At last, in January 1925, Sidney Hillman announced that the union would no longer tolerate disruption, and soon afterward suspended three officers.[78]

But the ACW was not in danger. Although the New York Joint Board was the largest in terms of membership, it had never held a tight grip on the numerous small shops in the city, and had failed to secure financial stability. On the other hand, the CJB, containing more than one-fourth of the ACW membership and enjoying a stable status in finance and in relations with the employers, was the main force of the union. Unlike the ILGWU, whose main force in New York was almost wrecked by strife, the ACW was still strong.[79]

The CJB effectively contained the Left-Right conflict. Certainly Chicago was not immune at all to the political strife. Several weeks after Hillman took drastic steps in New York in February 1925, the same leaflets issued by communists there appeared in Chicago. CJB manager Samuel Levin suspended twelve members who had distributed the leaflets and removed them from their jobs, whereupon the communists called a meeting at Temple Hall to discuss the policies of the ACW and the suspension of the members. On March 23, the day the meeting was to be held, the manager, who was also invited to address the meeting, arrived at the hall accompanied by thousands of loyal members who had been mobilized by the CJB. The communists refused to open the place, so Levin rented Street Carmen's Hall, close to Temple, and held a meeting. There, about twenty-five hundred workers adopted a resolution supporting the ACW leadership "without a dissenting vote."[80] The communists took the next and also the final offensive in Chicago at the election in December 1925. A communist named Nathan Green ran for the CJB managership, denouncing "Wage Cuts in the Form of Readjustments" and demanding "Reinstatement of Members Expelled Because of Difference of Opinion." But the result was disappointing for the Left: Green won 1,390 votes, while Levin secured 13,276, more than 45 percent of the whole Chicago membership.[81]

The Left-Right conflict in Chicago proved trivial partly because the communists failed to cooperate with other opposition groups. In 1922, Philip Aronberg, a communist member of Local 39, took over from Hyman Schneid as the leader of the opposition within the Chicago ACW organization. Late in the year, Aronberg challenged Samuel Levin in the election for CJB manager. It was hardly a contest, although the communist won 4,358 votes, more than one-fourth of the support attracted by Levin, which were probably delivered by various opposition groups. By abandoning the united front policy in 1924, however, the communists apparently alienated themselves from the socialists and the syndicalists, and no longer spearheaded the opposition in Chicago. Thus, in spite of widespread discontent with union officers regarding unemployment insurance, production standards, and reorganization of the labor process, Nathan Green's campaign in 1925 ended up a fiasco.[82]

Moreover, the Chicago ACW organization had long resorted to repressive measures in order to weaken the leftist opposition. Watching Chicago's men's clothing workers being organized in 1919, Sidney Hillman became concerned about their radical disposition. He wrote to Joseph Schlossberg: "There is a feeling prevailing in the rank and file that we, the Amalgamated, stand for what the I.W.W. stand[s] for. If this is permitted to go on, we will soon have a real crisis in our organization."[83] One way to prevent such a crisis was "weeding out the disrupters and getting some discipline in the ranks," as Frank Rosenblum asserted in 1920 while trying to make Cleveland's workers accept a labor agreement proposed by himself.[84] Indeed, some were expelled. In 1921, the union kicked out two communist members of Local 39 on the charge of spying on union activities in order to inform the U.S. government. Others were deprived of their positions. The next year, for example, the business agent in charge of HSM Factory C transferred a communist shop chairman from his section and appointed another man to his place.[85] Or the union assessed fines. Peter Garafolo, a shop chairman and member of the Italian local No. 270, collected funds for William Foster, the presidential candidate of the Workers' Party, in the fall of 1924. His business agent first tried to unseat him from his position. After failing because of workers' opposition, the agent charged that Garafolo had appropriated CJB funds, and succeeded in having him fined $25, in addition to $47 in restitution.[86]

Union officers used heavy-handed tactics in meetings. When workers appeared not to accept a union proposal, the officers often forced an open vote on them. For example, the Lithuanian local No. 269 protested that in 1919, when the CJB proposed to increase the monthly dues from eighty cents to $1.25, officers compelled members to approve the proposal "by simply uttering 'Aye,' or rising to their feet, which is not [a] democratic way of solving the problems at all."[87] And union officers occasionally deprived the opposition of the opportunity to present dissent. In 1922, Philip Aronberg and other communists of Local 39 demanded that the CJB investigate the way the local's officers conducted meetings. The communists accused the officers of "denying members expression of their views" by arbitrarily adjourning meetings before they could raise an objection to the decisions of the chair. The left wing further charged the officers with "[e]ndangering the lives of the membership by closing down meeting[s], turning out the lights and causing chairs to be hurled amongst the membership inflicting bodily injuries upon members assembled."[88]

The union's examination of nominees for election was probably the most devastating of the measures used against the opposition. In its protest against union officers' conduct of meetings, Local 269 pointed out: "The [Chicago] Joint Board has willed to introduce the new rules, which give the Administration the right to scrutinize the biography of a candidate for any office as far back as eleven years of his life and to either accept or reject him on the ground of the results thereof (which means the granting [of an] autocratical power to [the] Administration). . . ."[89] The rules, the particulars of which are not available, were adopted, and the CJB Board of Directors examined nominees "so that the best interests of the organization may not be impaired," as claimed by a CJB officer.[90] Since a GEB member of Chicago presided over the examining sessions, assisted by directors who obviously belonged to the union's mainstream, examinations were most likely a device to disqualify opposition candidates. Indeed, the CJB officer who had boasted of the rules wrote in the *Advance*: "Members who want to be active on behalf of the best interests of the organization, are always welcome in the organization midst—and, by the same token, let it be known, are others deterred."[91] In these ways, the Chicago ACW organization prevented the Left-Right conflict from developing into a major storm.

In the process, however, the CJB practically crushed legitimate criticism of the union's mainstream. The conflict involved a controversy over freedom of expression. The ACW leaders made sure that the official organs did not report on the political strife, afraid that the news would aggravate the conflict. Except for Hillman's occasional reproaches on the factional fight, therefore, the *Advance* rarely published anything revealing about the ongoing conflict. Above all, the communists, who needed publicity about their struggle, criticized the policy. A worker declared that "our official organ . . . owes it to the membership to keep them well posted on all matters concerning the Organization. . . ." Another, asserting that "it is radicals who always preach freedom of speech and the right to express one's opinion," demanded that the paper publish critical letters from the members.[92] As soon as advocacy of free expression led to attacks on major policies of the ACW and union officers' arbitrary attitudes,[93] the *Advance* stopped publishing such letters.

With the communist opposition waning within the ACW, public criticism of the union leadership virtually stopped. In May 1926, after the union had successfully subdued the Left-Right conflict, freedom of expression became an issue at its convention. Four resolutions were introduced demanding that the leadership "provide adequate means . . . for ample expression of differences of opinion and groupings." Delegates, particularly Hyman Schneid of Local 39, argued that the *Advance*'s editorial policy kept in the dark not only factionalism but also legitimate criticism. And others demanded that members expelled "for political reasons" be reinstated, arguing that expulsion was "a method of suppressing opposition and differences of views inside the organization." Except for censuring the top leaders' support for the La Follette candidacy, however, the opposition went no farther.[94] Delegates from Toronto introduced a resolution condemning the ACW leadership, in which they contended that it "has followed the class collaboration policies of the American Federation of Labor by collaborating with the clothing employers in increasing efficiency of production, reduction of production costs through minimum standards of production and piece work, reduction of working forces and reduction of wages through so-called readjustments. . . ."[95] When Sidney Hillman placed the resolution before the convention, with the resolutions committee's comment that it was "unjust in its criticism," there was neither discussion nor one vote in favor of it.

In Chicago, where the union officers had a firm hold over the rank and file, they hardly tolerated criticism. In March 1928, for example, about fifty members of Local 61, all out of work, had a meeting. The men's clothing industry of the city had already recovered from the depression that had struck in the middle of the decade, but at that point there were many workers seasonally unemployed. When a business agent of the local, having distributed jobs, announced that there were no more available, the fifty who did not get any assembled on the spot and voiced their discontent. Five of them were called before their local's executive board on charges of "organizing and conducting an unauthorized meeting of the unemployed members of Local 61, and making statements detrimental to the organization." The board removed one from the employment exchange registration for a while and warned the others of suspension from the union.[96] Officers were not strict only about collective action. In 1928, Local 39 fined a coat maker $50 for asserting that "the Union was run as a bosses union, the Unemployment Insurance Office was mismanaged, the Union denied the members the right to vote, etc." The worker appealed to the CJB, but it sustained the local's decision, finding him stubborn in his views.[97]

BUSINESS UNIONISM

Chicago's employers tested the strength of the ACW only once throughout the 1920s. In 1925, International Tailoring and J. L. Taylor, both controlled by the same management, demanded a wage cut, pending negotiations to renew their agreements with the ACW. When the union rejected their demands, the two firms attempted to run their factories on an open-shop basis and the workers walked out in a strike that also affected the firm's affiliates in New York. With other employers closely watching the course of this fight, both sides mobilized their resources. The firms resorted to a sweeping injunction in New York and apparently encouraged the police to raid the CJB office. The New York Joint Board assembled a picket line of ten thousand workers at one point, and the CJB had its treasury heavily drained. The strike ended in complete victory for the ACW.[98] In Chicago, other factors threatened the union.

Some employers moved their facilities to the South Side or to other cities free of the grip of the ACW; recovery from the depression of the mid-twenties resulted in the establishment of new firms, which were run as open shops. However, the organizing campaigns in the last two years of the 1920s led the CJB to reclaim complete control over the men's clothing industry of the city.[99]

Throughout the twenties, therefore, the ACW remained firmly established in Chicago's men's clothing industry, although, like many other unions, it underwent an extensive and abrupt membership decline. By 1925, the CJB had lost practically one-fourth of the forty thousand members it had represented at the beginning of the decade, while nationwide the ACW experienced more than fifty thousand dropouts in the same period.[100] The American organized labor movement in general, having achieved a remarkable expansion during World War I, shrank from about five million members in 1920 to fewer than three and a half million nine years later. For many unions the twenties were "lean years," as Irving Bernstein has put it. With a number of factors, such as nativist sentiment and unfriendly courts, militating against unionism, employers took the offensive, applying various stratagems against labor organizations, from the open-shop drive to welfare capitalism.[101] In Chicago, however, the ACW did not have to contend with anti-union policies. While a handful of employers across the country were experimenting with programs to attain efficient production with unions' cooperation, which the new AFL president William Green endorsed in 1925,[102] Chicago's men's clothing firms were already running their shops under just such programs. With new patterns of consumption and competition from non-union shops taking away a significant portion of their market share, which primarily accounted for the CJB membership loss, the firms chose to work with the union instead of going back to the pre-union era with its endemic strikes. Although some challenged or escaped from the ACW, most relied upon its power to secure labor supply and to raise productivity.

The ACW showcased its establishment in Chicago by building a home of its own. In March 1927, Sidney Hillman turned the first spadeful of soil in a ceremony that initiated a million-dollar building project at the corner of Ashland Boulevard and Van Buren Street. Named the Amalgamated Center, the building, completed in fourteen months, had a large auditorium, a gymnasium with bowling alleys, a library, and even a dental clinic in addition to spacious offices. The CJB announced its May Day plan, which included dedication of the center, to be followed by a mass meeting and a concert for thirty-five thousand men's clothing workers. Under the heading "Quiet May Day Here Is Forecast," the *Chicago Daily News* reported on April 30 that the celebrations planned by the ACW and other organizations signified "that no violence or disturbance will demand the attention of authorities as in former years, when police surveillance was ordered to protect government buildings against outbreaks."[103]

The Amalgamated Center was a symbol of the fact that the ACW's establishment in Chicago was a business union based upon labor-management cooperation, not upon militant socialism. The employers no longer resorted to arbitrary discharges and fines in order to maintain discipline on the shop floor, and they did not have to be concerned about building up and then cutting back their workforce. With its control over the jobs available in Chicago's men's clothing industry, the ACW supplied them with needed workers and put its members to work through a formidable disciplinary power. The ACW was acutely aware that it had grown strong enough to establish "law and order in the shop" by winning a portion of the managerial authority from the employers. Reviewing the growth of the ACW in Chicago in 1922, Leo Wolman and his associates appropriately pointed out:

> It [the ACW] has become an indispensable ally of management in the task of securing the willing co-operation of the workers in the industry, that has superseded the enforced co-operation under the old régime of fear and hate. And along with its enlarging responsibilities for the discipline of the shop, the union has acquired corresponding rights and privileges, that have, in turn, contributed to its growth both in number and in solidarity, and made of it a powerful force working toward self-government in the industry.[104]

Indeed, the ACW was "a powerful force." Representing organized men's clothing workers, the union claimed a power that employers had to respect in making decisions about wages, hours, work rules, and working conditions. Yet the union was not exactly "working toward self-government in the industry," but instead was turning itself into a junior partner at the sacrifice of union democracy. In Chicago, where the successful union-management cooperation had enabled the ACW to obtain a solid job control, the officers exercised forcible authority over the ranks. There, the authority appeared akin to that of the employers. Particularly to those workers who were not in conformity with the ACW's policies, it was a substitute for the coercion of the non-union era. When rank-and-file members were dissatisfied with policies, especially regarding production standards and reorganization of the labor process, they frequently resorted to work stoppages despite the union officers' reproaches. But even these members rarely challenged the authority, only occasionally expressing their discontent. And workers failed to develop an organized opposition, as the left wing of the union engaged in an exhausting factional struggle. In fact, the ACW barely tolerated an opposition movement in Chicago, employing various repressive measures that proved effective chiefly because of the union's formidable disciplinary power. Finally, it set aside democratic procedures through which the ranks could properly express their will and check the leadership. While cooperation with management assured the ACW of a secure place in the landscape of Chicago's men's clothing industry, therefore, the power it gained through its policies helped the union hold down rank-and-file initiatives, which the workers had shown during the 1910–1911 strike.

Next, the ACW turned to business unionism, like the craft organizations of the late nineteenth century or the industrial ones in the mid-twentieth century.[105] Contemplating business unionism in the post–World War II years, David Brody has argued that it was collective bargaining that blockaded possibilities for transforming the balance of power in the industrial landscape. Organized labor, particularly the Congress of Industrial Organizations, aimed at structural change in the existing balance when the war ended, but the contracts it secured from management soon harnessed the upsurging movement. Labor leaders retreated from political action and gave priority to wages and income security, rather than to issues of control, at the bargaining table; employers, establishing the workplace rule of law based on contractual relationships with unions, succeeded in containing rank-and-file activism on the shop floor. According to Brody, therefore, "[t]he contractual logic" was a critical factor in the trend toward business unionism in postwar America.[106] He has further suggested that organized labor had respected this logic since the mid-1930s, which eventually resulted in "workplace contractualism." Trying to show that it is not a system contingent on mid-twentieth-century industrial pluralism, he asserts, "The proximate causes as I have explored them compel us to see workplace contractualism as determined by the contemporary [from the mid-1930s onward] mass-production and legal-political regimes."[107]

The same trend seems to have been working in the ACW in the 1920s. This, however, was not a parallel development; it was an essential part of the complex process which had begun in the Progressive era. In order to understand this, unionism must be placed in a larger context. The type of unionism that Sidney Hillman preached in the ACW followed a formula developed by Louis Brandeis and endorsed by John Commons, as shown in Chapter 4. Along with many others who tried to confront the swelling "labor problem" around the turn of the century, these leading progressives found a solution in collective bargaining. Believing that industrial conflict is avoidable given the organic mutuality of interests between employers and employees, they intended to establish the rule of law at the workplace by instituting the collective contract and arbitration process, a judicial process through which the two parties could resolve strife in a peaceful way. This scheme required the union to be incorporated into a legal entity so that it could enter into a contract. The scheme further demanded that the union be a responsible party with substantial authority to channel rank-and-file activism into the mechanism. The first condition became a de jure reality in New Deal collective bargaining policies, particularly the Wagner Act of 1935, which were shaped according to the progressive prescription, as Melvyn Dubofsky has pointed out in his recent book.[108] The second condition was provided by the National War Labor Board, which, faced with a tide of wildcat strikes during World War II, adopted an elaborate system of grievance procedures that had originally developed in the clothing industry, and imposed its doctrine of union responsibility that helped labor leaders discipline the dissenting ranks.[109] The Taft-Hartley Act of 1947, the legal framework that stipulated the relationship between labor, capital, and the state in postwar America, did not discard but retained, with restraints clamped down on organized labor, the New Deal labor relations system, as Christopher Tomlins has recently claimed in his important book.[110]

Moreover, in the case of the ACW at least, "workplace contractualism" seemed to be rooted in something that underlay the union-management contract. It came from the imperative of compromise at the workplace. As shown in the preceding chapter, the union took pains to prove that it had control over men's clothing workers in the latter half of the 1910s, when it still did not have a contract with most employers in Chicago. In fact, the ACW endeavored to bring the employers to the bargaining table by demonstrating its command of the workforce, as they remained not simply fearful of organized labor but mindful of the irresponsible United Garment Workers. No doubt, even in the earliest years of the union business unionism lurked within its agreement with HSM, which distressed young Jacob Potofsky, and which gained a remarkable momentum after World War I. The ACW's prewar organizing strategy reveals that it sought compromise with management, although it assumed a militant posture. This contradiction, dictated by the imperatives of conflict and compromise at the workplace, set the union leaders at odds with each other. Although they usually presented a united front while engaged in an organizing campaign, they recognized their division more clearly once the campaign was over. While radicals intended to keep "the war spirit at a high temperature," moderates meant to keep the truce alive. The union contract in this situation favored the latter, for it was an instrument of compromise, which by definition curtails, though never annuls, room for conflict. The instrument represented the imperative of compromise, which, while it redirected many radicals to moderation, as shown in Chapter 4, and enabled moderates to cripple other hawks through the Left-Right struggle, drove the ACW leadership into business unionism.

In a final analysis, "workplace contractualism" was also dependent upon changing social relationships in the community. Certainly, the protracted depression in the industry, along with the unfavorable political landscape and social atmosphere, compelled union leaders to follow the imperative of compromise. On the other hand, rank-and-file members did not pursue a policy of confrontation either, nor did they assert themselves against the increasingly estranged leadership, as they had done in the 1910–1911 strike. Despite isolated protests, they appeared to be acquiescent. Their diffident posture, which made it difficult for the leaders to mobilize the rank and file and resort to the imperative of conflict at the workplace, was in fact part of a larger cultural change in the community. This change is discussed more thoroughly in the next chapter.

CHAPTER 6

The Union in the Cash Nexus

In the mid-1920s, when the ACW became less of a militant and supposedly radical organization and more of a business union under a bureaucratic leadership, the rank and file appeared to lose interest in union activities. In Chicago, where in the previous decade men's clothing workers had been so self-assertive and rebellious against the established authority that Joseph Schlossberg had praised the city as "the Bunker Hill of the Amalgamated,"[1] they seemed rather passive in the latter half of the twenties. They often ignored local union meetings or Chicago Joint Board staff elections. As a matter of fact, low attendance was less an occasional phenomenon than a recurrent problem. In this period, it seemed to be a chronic disease. Union meetings in the organization were plagued by low attendance. In order to keep rank-and-file activism alive, the CJB had launched a program of educational meetings that were combined with concerts. In the mid-twenties, however, it was evident that even this program had become prey to rank-and-file indifference.

ACW members' withdrawn and indifferent attitude toward their organization appears to have resulted partly from structural factors. The reduced volume of production in Chicago had a depressing impact upon the numbers of men's clothing workers there, forcing roughly one-third of them to leave the trade by the mid-twenties. The leadership of the ACW, the CJB in particular, was increasingly conservative and obstinate after the Left-Right conflict and became estranged from the rank and file. And the social atmosphere of the decade, which President Calvin Coolidge summed up when he declared, "The business of America is business," was unfavorable to the labor movement.[2] Moreover, there were greater constraints. Selig Perlman stressed "the enormous strength of private property in America" and "the inadequacy of the political instrument," by which he meant that in America the state was inherently weak as an instrument of economic reform and that the political party system offered a bleak prospect for labor politics.[3] William Forbath and other social scientists have recently corroborated this argument, showing that among the branches of government the judiciary has proven to be the strongest buttress of the existing economic order.[4] Labor historians have also noted the constitutional and political constraints on the development of the American labor movement.[5]

These factors, though evidently significant, only constitute the circumstances that faced Chicago's men's clothing workers; they do not explain why a change took place in the workers' attitude toward the ACW. Under the circumstances, there were certain courses of action available, including a challenge to the union leadership. This issue demands scrutiny. Observing in the 1920s that the ACW was turning toward business unionism, Perlman argued that the trend was dictated by "job and wage consciousness" as well as prescribed by structural constraints. Many scholars, particularly new labor historians in the last generation, have attacked this assertion, showing working-class presence.[6] But American workers did not subscribe to class politics, at least until the New Deal established a class-based coalition, as Richard Oestreicher has recently argued in his attempt to synthesize findings by new labor historians and new political historians.[7] Yet Perlman's view does not appear convincing. He took pains to show that "job and wage consciousness" originated from the group psychology that he thought wage earners shared in a world of limited opportunity. Perlman abstracted the psychology of the medieval guild, in which he believed the members shared the scarce opportunities for trade and formed a communal tradition that was later handed down to the modern trade union.[8] This view ignores cultural changes experienced by modern workers, including those that men's clothing workers in Chicago experienced in the 1920s.

In order to understand the change in the rank-and-file attitude toward the ACW, then, questions remain: How did union members interpret their circumstances? What did they think of themselves? What kind of relationships did they form among themselves? What choices did they have in connection with the union? The preceding chapter has already explored these questions, but in the perspective of workplace. This chapter will put them in the context of community, the other sphere of the workers' lives.

THE UNION COPING WITH URBAN DISPERSION

The urban space of Chicago was largely reorganized during the second and third decades of the twentieth century. As slums and congestion, crime and corruption, poverty and disorder in American metropolises had channeled the deep apprehensions of the nation into the urban reform movement of the last years of the nineteenth century, reformers who believed in the influence of the environment upon regeneration and progress made efforts to improve the physical landscape of the city. Daniel Burnham, though not a consistent progressive, carried out such a reformist idea in his Chicago Plan of 1909. An architect and urban planner who helped shape the City Beautiful Movement, he was inspired by Baron Georges Haussmann's ambitious project for Paris. Burnham proposed to rebuild a Chicago in which all Chicagoans, including working people in particular, would be relieved of moral malaise and take part in material prosperity.[9]

Congestion was a major target of Burnham's plan. The congested districts were not simply a hotbed of poverty, vice, and disorder; they were also a social impediment to securing the industrious labor force essential to prosperity. He stressed that "good workmanship requires a great deal of comfort on the part of the workers in their homes and their surroundings, and ample opportunity for that rest and recreation without which all work becomes drudgery." More importantly, congestion was a physical barrier to the development of an urban infrastructure, which was particularly indispensable to Chicago because the city was a preeminent center of industry and transportation. On the one hand, therefore, Burnham gave attention "to the betterment of commercial facilities; to methods of transportation for persons and for goods; to removing the obstacles which prevent or obstruct circulation; and to the increase of convenience."[10] On the other, he offered a remedy for the slums. Referring to the neighborhood of Halsted Street and Chicago Avenue and, in general, to the slums of the inner city, Burnham emphasized:

> The electrification of railways within the city, which cannot be long delayed, will serve to change radically for the better the dirty conditions in this neighborhood; but the slum conditions will remain. The remedy is the same as has been resorted to the world over: first, the cutting of broad thoroughfares through the unwholesome district; and, secondly, the establishment and remorseless enforcement of sanitary regulations which shall insure adequate air-space for the dwellers in crowded areas, and absolute cleanliness in the street, on the sidewalks, and even within the buildings.[11]

Therefore, Burnham's plan was to affect the notoriously congested districts from which men's clothing workers had been drawn. The Chicago Plan Commission, which Mayor Fred Busse appointed in November 1909 to oversee future development of the city, adopted Burnham's proposals as its own guidelines. In the following two decades the commission took pains to mobilize public support for the plan and to have more significant projects implemented (see Map 1.1). Huge railroad facilities emerged along Canal Street, one block west of the south branch of the Chicago River: The Chicago and North Western Railway terminal, already under construction when Burnham devised the plan, was completed in 1911; two freight terminals were added before World War I ended; and Union Station opened its doors to passengers in 1925. Major arteries were cut: Twelfth Street (Roosevelt Road), widened in 1912 from sixty-six to 108 feet along two miles between Wabash and Ashland, afforded effective east-west passage leading to the Loop; north and south through roads appeared, with Ashland, Robey (later Damen), and Western broadened and opened where they were closed; and in 1924, Ogden Avenue became a diagonal thoroughfare offering a direct connection between the West and North Sides.[12]

These changes in urban space, in addition to the land fill on the long lakeshore, the development of Michigan Avenue and Wacker Drive, and others, involved relocation of a large number, perhaps tens of thousands, of Chicagoans. Property owners, especially wealthy businessmen associated with the influential Commercial Club, which promoted Burnham's proposals and provided the Chicago Plan Commission with financial and other support, stressed a tremendous boost in property values and a substantial raise in city revenues.[13] On the other hand, tenants had to move either because their apartments were demolished or because rents went up along with property values. This is not to say that those improvements according to the 1909 plan were the single most important factor in Chicago's population movement in that period, for there is no denying that Chicagoans living in the crowded neighborhoods had been moving into better houses even before the plan began to be executed. The point is that the imposed reorganization of urban space provided an effective impetus for the movement.

In the two decades following the 1909 plan, therefore, ethnic groups, long trapped in the congested districts of the city and most significantly represented in its men's clothing industry, moved into new settlements.[14] Czechs, who had arrived in America and entered the industry earlier than other new immigrant groups, had already begun their gradual but continuous westward movement before the plan was implemented. In 1914, there were more than 102,000 Czechs, born either in Europe or in America, living in Chicago. Although each and every ward of the city had a certain number of them, "Czech California," expanded to the west and now called Lawndale, attracted nearly fifty thousand, while Pilsen, the old Czech district on the Southwest Side, retained twenty thousand. Some, particularly property owners, were determined to remain in Lawndale, putting up an organized resistance to the influx of other nationalities, but many abandoned the district and resettled in Cicero, a suburb next to Lawndale and only six miles away from the Loop. By 1920, there were more than fifteen thousand Czechs living in the town, constituting the largest ethnic group, which set the tone for the area with an evolving array of institutions such as the Sokol gymnasium, the Free Thought school, and the mutual aid society.[15]

East European Jews of the Near West Side ghetto also moved westward. Unlike the Czechs, they leaped three to five miles into North Lawndale, primarily because of the Chicago Plan. In the first half of the 1910s, railroad tracks and a freight terminal moved into the eastern end of the ghetto, and a number of factories encroached on the contiguous area west of Halsted. Most Jews left the well-known neighborhood of Jefferson and Maxwell Streets, and were replaced by Italians and other new arrivals. An elementary school there, in which Jewish children had comprised 95 per cent of the pupils at the turn of the century, found the same percentage represented by Italians in 1916. Many of the Jews fled to the Northwest Side, but the majority resettled in North Lawndale, as the Twelfth Street car line extended its service to Crawford Avenue (later Pulaski Road). By the end of World War I, there were estimatedly 100,000 Jews living in Lawndale, slightly less than half of the entire Jewish population of 225,000 in Chicago. Hence, in 1927, the Jewish People's Institute, their most important community center, once called the Chicago Hebrew Institute, abandoned its West Side building and moved into a spacious house at the heart of the Lawndale district.[16]

Poles on the Northwest Side moved along Milwaukee Avenue after the streetcar line was extended to Lawrence Avenue and electrified in 1905–1906. Their movement was gradual—from West Town to Logan Square to Avondale—but still conspicuous, particularly after World War I. By the end of the war, they had already formed a distinct Polish neighborhood between Diversey and Addison, and most belonged to either of the two Roman Catholic churches, St. Wenceslaus and St. Hyacinth. More Poles resettled in this local community, called Avondale, in the following decade, replacing Germans and Scandinavians who had moved there less than a generation before. In 1930, Poles were the largest ethnic group, constituting more than one-fourth of the population of 48,000 there.[17]

South Italians, latecomers who up until the war had established themselves on the periphery of the Jewish ghetto on the Near West Side and the Polish enclave on the Near North Side, closely followed the two groups. While increasingly scattered all over the city, they moved chiefly westward and northward. On the West Side, they fled the vicinity of Hull House and flocked to the neighborhood of Halsted and Marshfield. There were more than thirteen thousand Italians, over one-fifth of the population of sixty thousand in 1920, living in the area. In the following decade, they moved farther west, especially around Harrison Street between Western and Robey. The Italian perimeter on the Near North

Side began to disintegrate after the late 1910s, as its population gravitated toward "Little Italy" in the neighborhood of Wells and Halsted Streets between Division and North.[18]

Men's clothing workers were ready to participate in the urban migrations. Above all, they had more choices in residence. Mostly new arrivals from eastern and southern Europe, they had usually lived close to their workplaces, typically the small contract shops that relied upon abundant cheap labor easily employed or dismissed depending on a widely fluctuating volume of business. Beginning in the last years of the nineteenth century, however, Chicago's manufacturers rapidly expanded their workforce and regularized the volume of production as much as possible, endeavoring to take full advantage of their investment in large modern factories. By the 1910–1911 strike the factories had been increasingly concentrated in the Loop, which did not lure many residents but provided convenient transportation. Certainly, many workers wanted to stay close to their workplaces. Anna Miles, a Polish tailoress working at a Hart, Schaffner and Marx shop when the strike came, recollects that her real complaint was the ten-hour work day, because she had to walk about a mile on her way home. "There were streetcars you could take," she adds, "but [al]most everyone walked."[19]

By the late 1910s, however, most men's clothing workers of Chicago could afford to patronize the expanding mass transportation system and were able to move away from the factories that continued to converge on the Loop. They were earning more than before. It is difficult to figure out from wage rates how much money they made on average, because many worked on piece rates and were idle for several weeks during the slack season, and because manufacturers offered better wages than contractors. And yet other evidence indicates higher earnings following the U.S. entry into World War I, in April 1917. They worked much longer hours, though not at higher rates. As a result, the ACW found it hard to get unorganized workers interested in the union. Frank Rosenblum, who was in charge of the CJB organization campaign at that point, was keenly aware of the situation. "The reason it is difficult to get immediate results in Chicago," he explained to Sidney Hillman, "is because the tailors here have never made as much money as they do now, and have never been treated as well."[20] After the ACW completely organized the city in 1919, wages were increased considerably following a decision of the arbitration board by which those who earned thirty dollars or less a week, the worst-paid group, received a 20 percent raise.[21] Even if these workers had been idle for twelve weeks a year, their annual earnings would have approached the $1,500 level, a point that sociologist Ernest Burgess, estimating the annual subsistence budget for a "standard" family of five at $850, designated as the well-off category in his survey on Chicago's working-class families in 1919.[22] There were recessions and wage cuts in the following decade. Still, the wages seemed to be high enough to drive many firms out of the city while attracting workers. Morris Ginsburg, a coat maker who worked at a small shop before the war and became an active unionist afterward, remembers: "When I got back in the tailoring line, the money wasn't too bad. So, I stuck to it."[23]

Moreover, most men's clothing workers appeared willing to move into a better environment. They were younger than those engaged in other trades. According to a survey the CJB prepared for the arbitration board at the end of 1919, in a large firm employing approximately two thousand workers four-fifths of the workforce were under forty years of age, and in another the same percentage of its roughly 3,700 workers were under thirty-five. Women, who composed an increasing majority of the workforce in Chicago but who very often left the industry upon marriage, represented the fresh blood of second-generation immigrants. The men, many of whom were called "old-timers" after the war, were more often than not young and had small families. The CJB found out in its 1921 study of their family status that married workers constituted only 57 percent of the membership and that most, seven out of ten, had no or one to two children. "Because of the very large percentage of young people in the industry and the comparatively small number of so-called standard families," concluded the CJB in its 1919 survey, "the cost of living is obviously not equally so important a matter as it is in many industries in which older people with larger families are in the majority."[24]

In the twenties, therefore, men's clothing workers found their homes dispersed throughout metropolitan Chicago. The residential pattern is clearly indicated by a map that in 1937 Robert J. Myers took pains to make in his doctoral thesis on the industry (see Map 6.1).

The residential patterns, which the ACW, by securing wage increases, had helped its members create from the mid-teens on, ironically presented problems to union activities. The immediate impact of the dispersion over greater space was the fact that because of geographical distance Chicago's men's clothing workers found it increasingly burdensome to take part in union activities. This became obvious as early as the late 1910s. In order to attend a local union meeting, which was usually held at eight o'clock in the evening, the workers had to make an additional journey after work. Hence, locals were considerate in locating their headquarters in the neighborhoods that held the majority of membership; although cutters and trimmers, still constituting a distinct group based on skill, had their own office next to their workplace in the Loop, coat makers and pants makers, the majority of whom were Jew-

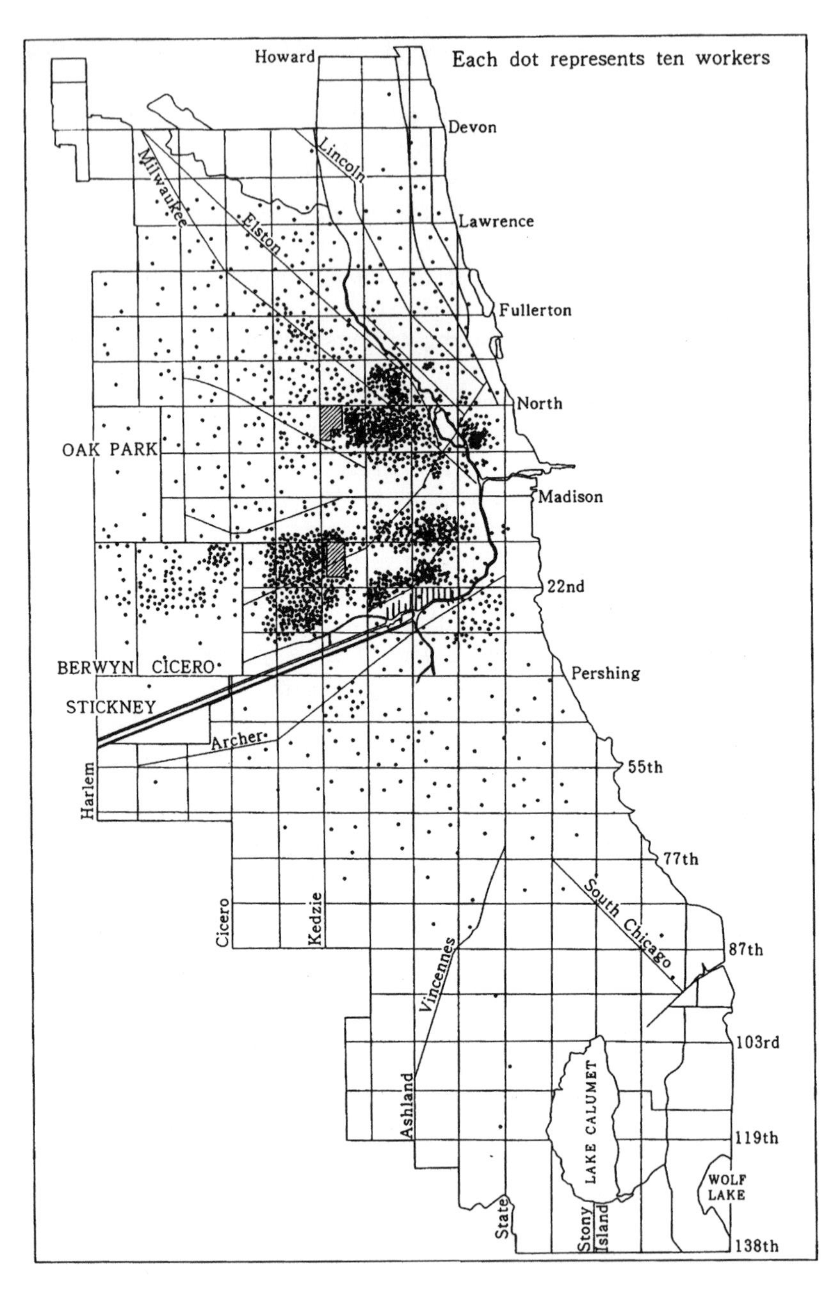

MAP 6.1

Residences of 19,500 Chicago Members of the Amalgamated Clothing Workers, 1923–1924. Adapted from Robert J. Myers, "The Economic Aspects of the Production of Men's Clothing" (unpublished Ph.D. thesis, University of Chicago, 1937). Courtesy of the Chicago and Central States Joint Board, UNITE.

ish, met at the Near West Side headquarters; and the predominantly Swedish and Polish vest makers' union held regular meetings in the vicinity of Milwaukee and North Avenues.[25] Yet it was undeniable that the burden of making the journey was to a certain extent discouraging. In late 1917, when the ACW was in the middle of an organizing drive to capitalize on the wartime boom in the men's clothing industry, the CJB was concerned about how to create an atmosphere of rank-and-file activism sufficiently strong to prevail over that burden. A. N. Fisher, a Socialist Labor Party member who as a CJB officer wrote a report on the meetings of the shop chairmen that was published in the ACW organ *Advance*, frankly and unmistakably acknowledged:

> There are several suggestions under consideration [about] how to make our members interested in the local meetings. This question requires a carefully worked out plan on account of the great territory of the city of Chicago. Our members are scattered over a great area and it takes some of them forty five minutes to an hour's ride to attend the local meeting.[26]

The CJB leaders searched for a solution. In the late 1910s, when the Chicago organization was engaged in a campaign against the anti-union employers, they counted on rank-and-file militancy, but they were not entirely complacent about it. Once the industry had been completely organized, they found the question articulated by Fisher peculiarly annoying. Control of the city awarded the leaders potentially enormous power over the union members, based on job control. But their power was ultimately dependent upon the ranks behaving forcefully enough to intimidate the employers. Now that the battle had turned into a truce, albeit an unstable one because of employers' skepticism and everyday skirmishes on the shop floor, as well as business fluctuations and nation-wide competition, the leaders needed a loyal and active but at least ostensibly less militant membership. Their solution was education. In May 1920, the ACW General Executive Board decided to recommend to the coming convention that a national educational department be established "to enhance the spiritual developments of our membership." It stressed that education was "a work of vital importance," admitting that it had neglected the field chiefly because "the organization was in the past extremely busy with various economic problems that were before us."[27]

Soon, the CJB expanded the educational work with which it had already begun experimenting in the 1919–1920 winter. Modeled on educational undertakings initiated by local unions, the Chicago organization launched its own program of educational meetings combined with concerts. The following year, it confidently announced that "our efforts were so successful, and the requests from our members for such activities were so numerous, that we were obliged to continue and even extend our program for this season."[28]

Now, for the five-month-long season from November 1920 through March 1921, it offered eight lectures. Topics centered around the labor movement, with speakers who ranged from the political center, represented by Frank P. Walsh, former chairman of the U.S. Industrial Relations Commission, to the far Left, embodied by William Z. Foster, the leading organizer of the 1919 steel strike, who later headed the American Communist Party.[29] Apparently in order to lure workers toward the educational meetings, the CJB offered a concert preceding each meeting, which was usually performed by the Chicago Symphony Orchestra. The music provided by the orchestra consisted by and large of traditional folk songs and popular classical pieces, particularly those written by nationalist composers such as Anton Dvorák. The result was remarkable. After the first two concerts in the 1920–1921 season, recording secretary Maurice C. Fisch reported to Potofsky, "Our second concert was fully as successful as the first, which is in itself great progress."[30]

Furthermore, CJB leaders were careful to take into account the burden of making the journey, and to address rank-and-file social needs in the ethnic neighborhoods. The leaders were acutely aware how difficult it was to attract members to union activities. Instituting the educational program in November 1920, the CJB also established an evening school and offered classes in grammar, advanced English, and the labor movement. M. C. Fisch promised Potofsky that the CJB was going "to make a great effort to make this affair a success," pointing out: "Of course this is the hardest undertaking as it is rather hard to get people together after work, and participate in evening-school classes."[31] So CJB leaders carefully planned the educational meetings. They decided that in addition to the six concerts each season at the Ashland Auditorium, which covered the Jewish and Italian members on the West Side, two should be held at Sokol Chicago Hall on the Southwest Side and two more at Wick Park or Schoenhofen's Hall on the Northwest Side. They also decided to hold the concerts at eight P.M. on Friday, the evening workers liked to spend relaxing in anticipation of the weekend that followed the half holiday included in the forty-four-hour week. The leaders arranged the meetings "so as to enable our members and families to enjoy the activities of our organization close to their homes."[32] As a matter of fact, it was only natural for CJB leaders to consider the social needs of the ethnic communities to which the members belonged; the 1910–1911 strike had proven that ethnicity, long regarded as an explosive feature of the workplace, could provide powerful leverage for mobilization in the community, and the leaders had since made efforts to promote ethnic cooperation and harmony, though not integration.

The educational program devised with great care helped the CJB almost conquer geographical dispersion and bind its members to the ACW, but it was deceptive. They did come to educational meetings, possibly in thousands. Their response was so ardent that the CJB had to offer sixteen meetings in the 1922–1923 season and fifteen in the following winter. In retrospect, however, the response indicates rank-and-file desire for cultural and social activities as much as interest in the labor movement. Firstly, the preference for music was so obvious that the CJB Educational Committee presented a "Musicale instead of an educational meeting" on two occasions out of the sixteen in the 1922–1923 winter and announced four entirely musical programs out of the fifteen meetings in the following year.

Secondly, members came to the concert-lectures with their families, including children, as suggested by the committee. One of the results that did not please the CJB was that children tended to disturb the educational meetings. Another was that during the meetings many members wandered around, either to take care of their children or to socialize. So the committee advised in its 1921–1922 season handout, "Members who have their children with them, are kindly requested to keep them from disturbing the meeting." In addition, it asked the audience "to remain seated to the end of this program." In the following seasons, the committee continued to print this advice, adding specifically, "Walking around disturbs the meeting."[33]

By the 1924–1925 winter it had become clear that the CJB's educational work was in trouble. Leaders of the organization chose to make a few changes for the coming season, apparently in order to replace festivity with sobriety. They cut the number of educational meetings down to ten, abolishing all of the musical programs except one. While geographically apportioning the meetings as they had done before in order to cultivate ethnic harmony, the leaders decided to move the concert-lectures to Sunday afternoons at 2:30 P.M., except for those on the Northwest Side, which were to take place on Wednesday evenings; possibly they hoped for temperate behavior in anticipation of the following work day. Moreover, they chose to rely on their internal resources for the lectures; the CJB stopped inviting speakers of national reputation, in particular prominent radicals, and instead substituted ACW officers and staff, incumbent or former, although it was willing on one occasion to give an opportunity to a U.S. senator from Minnesota to talk about the Farmer-Labor Party.[34]

These changes were most likely the prelude to the CJB's abandonment, rather than refurbishment, of the educational work. They might have helped the Chicago leadership redirect the concert-lecture program toward cultivation of rank-and-file loyalty and activism. From the members' viewpoint, however, they made the programs less inviting. Again, there is no way to learn how the ranks felt about the changes, but there is some indirect evidence. The educational programs that some locals reinstituted in the fall of 1926 and continued in the following season were focused on different topics from those chosen by the CJB; while the joint board gradually narrowed down the scope of topics to trade union issues, particularly the ACW itself, locals preferred broad political questions, such as the ideals of democracy, human rights, and feminism, which they invited outside speakers to discuss, taking into consideration their members' interests.[35] Besides, the CJB appeared less enthusiastic about its own educational program in the 1924–1925 winter. Reshuffling the program, it announced neither the speaker nor the topic for two of the meetings, something which had never occurred in the previous seasons. Apparently, therefore, many members no longer cared to take part in the program.

They did not seem to care much about other union activities, either. For example, in the staff election that the Chicago Joint Board held in the first winter after the city was completely organized in 1919, three out of every five members cast their vote. CJB recording secretary M. C. Fisch wrote in a letter to Jacob Potofsky of the ACW national headquarters that the election was indeed "a very hot one."[36] The voting rate fluctuated until the 1925 election in which communist candidate Nathan Green challenged the powerful CJB manager, Samuel Levin. In the remaining elections of the decade, however, only half of the Chicago members cast their votes.[37]

The CJB sealed the fate of its own educational work: It did not offer any concert-lectures in the 1925–1926 winter, although four years later it restored classes in economics and English, which were taken by no more than a few members. There were good reasons. The ACW had just fought an important battle in Chicago as well as in New York, to prove that it was strong enough to pass the employers' test and powerful enough to keep its membership in line, and its treasury was low on cash, partly because of the battle and partly because of the shrinking membership. Most significantly, however, Chicago ACW members had compelled the CJB to drop the program by turning educational meetings into cultural and social events and then neglecting the meetings. The rank and file twisted and foiled the purpose of the program, which was at the very least to foster such commitment that workers would be willing to make the burdensome journey after work in order to participate in union activities.

Certainly, local unions made efforts to involve their members. These unions were concerned about diminishing rank-and-file interest. Cutters of Local 61 proclaimed at a shop meeting held in April 1926, "The question of enforcing the by-laws on the attendance of meetings was voiced by several brothers and the body unanimously agreed that the fine of one dollar should again be enforced. . . ."[38] On the other hand, locals resumed their own educational programs. When the CJB gave up the initiative in this field, however, only some unions, such as the coat makers, pants makers, or vest makers, were big and rich enough to finance their own undertakings. Even their scattered efforts had stopped by early 1928.[39]

The CJB's abandonment of the educational program was a trivial event that received scant attention from the ACW membership, but it was, in fact, a grave moment in the history of the labor movement in Chicago's men's clothing industry before the Great Depression. The movement had been born and grew up at the crossroads of the workplace and the ethnic community. Now the CJB, frustrated in one sense and complacent in another, was going to walk down a single road; there was no more effort to tap ethnic resources, except by the languishing ethnic locals; instead, the union relied increasingly on job control. The union did continue to meet the social needs of the membership, as indicated by the bowling lanes in the basement of the Amalgamated Center and the annual balls given by the CJB and the locals, but it no longer reached out to the ethnic communities. As a matter of fact, the quiet decision made by the CJB was closely connected to the spatial and cultural changes taking place in the communities to which rank-and-file members belonged. Once these communities have been explored, therefore, the full meaning of that decision is revealed.

CULTURAL IMPLICATIONS OF THE URBAN MIGRATION

By the time the CJB decided to abandon its educational program, Chicago's cultural landscape had been significantly changing in two aspects. In the summer of 1919, a race riot spread out of the Black Belt toward the Loop and the West Side, which left thirty-eight people dead and 537 injured after a two-week-long period of chaos. This had a lasting impact on the local population and the whole nation as well; it led Chicagoans to an increasingly rigid form of residential and social segregation and to a concealed and yet acute level of racial consciousness.[40] In particular, men's clothing workers of the city, who on the West Side saw their neighborhoods encroached on by African Americans, considered themselves as existing above the bottom step of the racial hierarchy.[41] In the late 1920s, when a number of runaway shops appeared on the South Side, ACW members were losing their jobs to those poorly paid African Americans. At this level, they shared a terrain much enriched by rapidly elaborating mass culture. As Lizabeth Cohen has masterfully shown in her *Making a New Deal*, workers in Chicago increasingly enjoyed mass-oriented movies and radio programs in addition to mass-produced commodities available at chain stores, while still retaining their ethnic perspectives and patronizing their neighborhood stores.[42] Compared with the pre–World War I years, not with the Great Depression era, however, ethnic institutions were evidently less vigorous.

During the 1920s, urban dispersal of immigrant workers as well as ethnic middle-class families provoked significant cultural changes. Above all, ethnic institutions dwindled, as Czechs, Jews, and Poles found their new neighborhoods less densely populated by their own countryfolk. To be sure, the old neighborhoods had been mixed, but the numbers and density of the predominant nationality had made a difference. By 1920, Czechs had become the largest ethnic group in Cicero, but since they comprised only a little more than one-third of its whole population, they had to share the town with a number of other nationalities, especially the Poles, who constituted one-sixth and ranked second. In 1930, Jews were the unrivaled ethnic leaders in North Lawndale, but claimed only one-fourth of the population there, amid a variety of numerically smaller groups. The Poles of Avondale, more than one-fourth of the district's population, found themselves mixed with Germans, Swedes, Norwegians, and others.[43]

Such sparseness relative to the earlier settlements made uninviting claims on ethnic social life. Even though certain blocks teemed with members of a particular ethnic group and their institutions such as community centers, churches, synagogues, parochial schools, and so forth, concerns rose over the dilution of national identity. Czechs, Jews, and Poles complained about "a foreign element" making inroads on their zone. While antisemitic Poles did not like to see Jewish stores on Milwaukee Avenue taking away Polish business, Jews were troubled in turn by the Italians entering their Douglas Park neighborhood.[44] On the other hand, ethnic leaders felt distressed by inward, rather than outward trends, and worried that their countryfolk were growing indifferent toward their nationality. This was not a new concern, as they had long worked to promote education in the mother tongue and observance of the national religion, which they believed to be a critical element in defining and preserving a sense of nationality. Now, however, their fears took on a sinister new object, complicated by the material advances they and their countrymen enjoyed in the New World.

For the urban migrations seemed to detach many people from the old ethnic institutions. Cicero's Czechs established a Free Thought school named after T. G. Masaryk at the beginning of the 1922–1923 academic year, only to find the classrooms for the first and second grades left empty. Although many Czechs posed "as active members in our [F]ree [T]hought organization," school officers deplored that there were "all the unfavorable and often troublesome conditions which the patronat [board of directors] must often face, conditions which are really ascribable to the indifference of our people, an indifference which may be noticed among all our lodges, clubs, and societies."[45] Orthodox Jews felt disgruntled at people who, having left the West Side, began to "free themselves from their Jewish duties and Jewish obligations." "Not only do they not pay any attention to the Jewish education of their children," a reporter criticized, referring particularly to residents of the well-off North Side, "but they get out of touch with Jewish life as well, and the more modern and fashionable among them, even join Reform Temple. . . ."[46]

Detachment from ethnic institutions inevitably reflected the Americanization process, which led new immigrants, inbetween peoples in the hierarchy of races, to become indifferent to blackness but anxious to identify with whiteness.[47] Certainly, many believed that their former nationalities were compatible with Americanism. When the war in Europe caused the American public to be concerned about immigrants' patriotism during the mid-1910s, some Czechs, for example, asserted that the Czech people could adopt American traits without losing their national characteristics. "The much abused hyphen is not a sign of cleavage," argued a Czech editor, "but a sign of unity."[48] However, other immigrants suffered from tensions between their old nationality and Americanism, which appeared to increase in the new settlements. A Polish woman expressed her agony in a letter to a weekly newspaper published by the Polish National Church, writing that she and her family used to live in the vicinity of the church so that they could attend all services there. "But one day something came upon me," she recollected in early 1929, "and I persuaded my husband to withdraw our savings from the parish bank and to buy a pretty little house in a new neighborhood." Shortly after they moved, the writer came "to feel lonely among all the strange neighbors," Dutch, Scotch, and Italian people, and realized that "my new home, although it was much prettier than the old one, was impractical." It was so far from the church that her children could not attend the parochial school. Furthermore, she felt "heartbroken" at finding that her two daughters had married, without her knowledge, a Dutch and an Italian man. Hence, her husband grieved, saying, "If we had lived in a Polish parish our children would have attended Polish affairs and joined various lodges, and in that way they would have found Polish husbands for themselves."[49]

But acculturation did not necessarily draw mobile immigrants into the American working class, just as the urban migrations, though facilitating their Americanization, did not promote working-class solidarity. Instead, physical migration appeared to promise them social mobility. The new settlements where Chicago's men's clothing workers moved in the 1910s and '20s offered a much better environment than the old. Some settlements, originally developed for middle-class families and shortly after confronted by massive social changes, retained their old characteristics, even as they became distinctly working-class districts, increasingly sought out by workers of diverse trades and from various nationalities. Others emerged as new, secure working-class communities. These characteristics did not pass unnoticed by new residents.

Cicero is a case in point. Originally part of a wetlands called Mud Lake, the town was already a middle-class suburb at the beginning of the twentieth century, with approximately three thousand residents living in detached brick houses. The following two decades saw a number of working-class families move in along with a score of large factories such as the huge Western Electric Hawthorne plant. By the Great Depression, the plant employed 38,000 workers, more than one-third of whom constituted a predominant portion of Cicero's population of 75,000. According to a *Chicago Tribune* report on the town, residents were aware that "the community has no centering of great wealth; it is in the hands of the mass of toilers."[50] Yet it was a "new" and "modern" environment, much different from earlier Czech settlements. A story about Czechs in metropolitan Chicago, published in 1946 when Cicero had been built up for more than a decade, stated:

> Suburbs like Cicero and Berwyn, offering opportunities for real homes, open spaces, gardens and a healthy community life, have attracted these native sons of the newcomers of yesterday, who were eager to get as far away from the tenement memories of their pioneer fathers as they could. Today these regions are beauty spots, gleaming with new brick and stucco dwellings, wholly detached or of the two-family type—a symbol suggesting that the Czechoslovak in America has arrived.[51]

In addition to better houses and a beautiful landscape, Cicero maintained miles of paved streets where stores displayed "all the contrivances of the modern era," in other words, "everything from electric washing machines to talkies." The *Tribune* report compared the town to "a nineteen-year-old youth looking only in the future—alert, up-to-the-minute, confident." And it characterized the Czechs, along with other major ethnic groups there, as "a people eager that their children have greater advantages than they have known."[52]

Lawndale in the twenties was not such a "new" or "modern" district as Cicero, and yet it proved to be a remarkably improved environment for Jewish immigrants and their children. Beginning in the 1870s, land developers invested in the boggy prairie that was then part of the town, and built substantial brick houses for the middle class. Soon, well-to-do immigrants arrived. While wealthy Czechs settled to the south, naming their zone after California because it looked as beautiful as they believed the state was, and then moved west toward Cicero, successful Jews moved north, bringing a social club formed by businessmen, doctors, and judges.[53] Lawndale also drew working-class immigrants and large factories such as McCormick Works. Workers settled in multi-family houses, which became predominant between 1895 and 1914, a period in which Lawndale saw more than 3,700 such units built. However, the units were not cramped tenements; they were more often than not two-story, two-family houses or modern apartment buildings with fewer than ten units. Such structures continued to characterize Lawndale until the Great Depression, when the district began rapidly to deteriorate.[54] Furthermore, they appeared to be "fine houses with lawns in the front yard and gardens growing between buildings," as a reporter, having taken a stroll through the locality in Spring 1919, described the area in the Jewish socialist newspaper *Forward*. The writer stressed, "I recognize this is a Jewish neighborhood only because of the butcher shops, synagogues, and the Jewish music. . . ."[55] Thus, Lawndale was in sharp contrast with the "ghetto." "It would be unjust to designate this district as a 'Jewish Ghetto,'" declared another reporter, who praised it "as the most beautiful and well situated Jewish district in the whole world. . . ." This *Daily Jewish Courier* reporter continued:

> The expanding Jewish Lawndale district is of a different character entirely. It is beautiful and free. The entire district is covered with grass and trees. The Jews walk about proudly, appreciating the blessings of America. . . .
>
> This Jewish district is young, but from day to day it is developing. Various Jewish institutions are being built there; and whenever we pass by the magnificent Douglas Boulevard our hearts soar with pride to witness among the beautiful homes, the large synagogue, and we can hardly refrain from crying "How well-off we Jews are by having such a good and comfortable dwelling place in the second largest city of America![56]

Avondale in the twenties was a well-established working-class district. It had been the independent town of Jefferson, chiefly a farming community tied to the Chicago market, until the last decade of the nineteenth century, when the city annexed it and provided it with streetcar service, in addition to water lines and sewers, in place of the condemned

Milwaukee toll road. Avondale and neighboring Logan Square lured German and Scandinavian immigrants as well as manufacturing interests such as the Lyon and Healy piano and organ factory. As a result, Avondale underwent a long building boom in the construction first of single-family houses and then of two-family structures, which slowed down during World War I and then picked up again. By the onset of the Great Depression, these two types of dwelling dominated the district, constituting more than four-fifths of its buildings. In addition, these structures more often accommodated home owners than in other parts of the city; in 1930, the proportion of home ownership in Avondale was 37 percent, while in Lawndale it was no more than 25 percent.[57] Just before the war, a Polish resident thought it only natural for Poles to move to Avondale. "It is not at all surprising that our people are leaving the overcrowded and smelly neighborhoods and are moving en masse into our district," he wrote, "in which one can breathe clean, healthful air." As a matter of fact, this resident was delighted at the ameliorating surroundings there: "Rows of nice homes which have been built and are continuing to be built, and the streets which have been asphalted only a few months ago in our neighborhood, have greatly improved the appearance, healthfulness, and growth of our parish."[58] Several years later, a Polish journalist agreed, referring particularly to home ownership: "During the war many of our brothers living in other settlements accumulated little fortunes with which they decided to buy nice homes. As their old settlements were rather too old and well filled, they came to Avondale and with the accumulated money have built nice homes."[59]

With the exception of the Italians, the majority of whom were also mobile and yet trapped in deteriorating districts, spatial movement meant social mobility. As indicated by contemporary observers, the noticeably better environment in the new settlements represented the material advances immigrants had made in America. Workers living there might have continued to think of themselves as such, much as their offspring did more than a generation later.[60] In the twenties, however, they apparently appreciated being able to ascend one or two notches up the social ladder, and they willingly showed it by moving to better neighborhoods.[61]

This suggests a reality different from what Olivier Zunz has argued in his detailed analysis of the changing social landscape in Detroit. A new economic order established by the automobile industry and war production in the 1910s, he shows, brought to the city a spatial image delineated more by class than by ethnicity, as its space was reorganized in accordance with social stratification. But that spatial surface did not exactly represent the social subsoil, which Zunz did not explore, arguing, "Social stratification preceded class consciousness in Detroit."[62] Although this spatial image also characterized Chicago, ethnic workers moving into the new settlements did not find its social structure rigid. In the 1920s at least, the urban migrations seemed to assure them of future progress, instead of fixing or lowering their place in American society, which appeared to happen during the Great Depression.

Moreover, movement also implicated a third change, the growth of economic individualism, another reason the mobile workers failed to embrace working-class solidarity. Like detachment from ethnic institutions, the rising individualist ethos was linked to the larger Americanization process. Immigrants were aware that ethnic institutions were in trouble in the new settlements after World War I; their churches and parochial schools managed on diminishing human and financial resources; their nationalist organizations strove against declining support in sentiment as well as in material; and their stores stretched to attract patronage from beyond the ethnic boundary. Faced with such deteriorating conditions, immigrants rearranged by degrees their relations with each other, the accumulated consequence of which was not clearly understood by their contemporaries, whether immigrants or hosts. In retrospect, however, a subtle permutation of social relations took place in the ethnic community, where communalism gave way to individualism. This cultural change was in fact tangibly happening in the mutual aid society, a window that opens onto the larger process of accommodation to the world of commodities.

INDIVIDUALISM IN THE ETHNIC COMMUNITY

As discussed in the first chapter of this book, the mutual aid society represented the process by which immigrants adapted to the world of commodities. A pecuniary translation of the communal tradition lingering over eastern and southern Europe, it helped them familiarize themselves with the cash nexus, or social relationships mediated through money; in order to provide mutual assistance against the economic insecurity attached to wage working, its members sought to offer one another a helping hand, represented of necessity by a certain amount of money. As a social medium, however, money was a scarce resource, which soon led the members to replace familial care based on communal personal interdependence with reciprocal concern delimited by economic individualism. This process of becoming familiar with the medium of the market and with the cash nexus had not been completed when mutual aid societies adopted the principle of balancing benefit against contribution. In fact, the need to maintain the balance not only promoted the process, but, by instigating recurrent episodes of dispute over benefit payments, kept it going. While the process in general proceeded on such an ordinary route of everyday life and over such a long span of time that immigrants seldom articulated their feelings or thoughts about it, those episodes presumably helped form a current at the bottom of their consciousness that continued to flow during the later history of the mutual aid society.

The society, in order to remain solvent and survive, had to always be on the move, chiefly because it was founded upon an increasingly defective principle of finance. If a society started with a certain number of members and then closed its doors, it would soon be forced to charge ever-greater assessments as death took away one member after another. In order to prevent that, it had to keep the doors open and, hopefully, to expand its membership continuously and boundlessly, which would lead to a shrinking pecuniary burden on each of the swelling number of members. In time, however, this self-aggrandizing momentum would encounter the inevitable boundary of the population, that is, a limited organizational base. As long as the base had continued to expand, mutual aid societies appeared to be promising. Once it stopped expanding, the societies became locked in deadly competition. Then, they turned to a fascinating but self-defeating solution, lowering dues and fees while raising benefits for prospective members.

This was evident as early as 1910. A Jewish society called the Slutsker Aid Verein announced that it was offering a four-hundred-dollar death benefit in addition to a five-dollar sickness benefit for six weeks and a no-interest loan fund. "You receive all this for merely 50 cents monthly dues," advertised the society. The Order of the Western Star, a Chicago-based Jewish fraternity, strove to convince prospects that sixty-cent monthly dues would guarantee a disability benefit of five hundred dollars as well as a death benefit of the same amount, along with fifty dollars for funeral expenses. The order had in fact a deficit of $2,500,000, an average of $150 for each of its members. Numerous societies, large or small, went bankrupt. The Jewish *Courier* argued that there was no hope for improvement in mutual aid societies as long as they resorted to "a wildcat scheme." The daily stressed, "It is the system—the basic condition of the lodge system—which is rotten."[63] The Polish *Dziennik Zwiazkowy* agreed:

> There are numerous insurance societies—even in Chicago—which, in their competitive zeal, endeavored to outdo each other . . . by lowering premiums for members and promising many things. Finally . . . all of them failed. They would not carry the risks that they had placed upon their shoulders. Thousands of members by being

> greedy for lower monthly rates lost their insurance, and some were even deprived of the opportunity to insure themselves elsewhere because of their age.[64]

In addition, frequent embezzlement made matters worse. The urge to self-aggrandizement led to large-scale fraternal orders, where the leadership, secretaries and treasurers in particular, practically enjoyed a free hand in management. While small societies relied on amateurs who helped the fellow members handle meager sums of money, large orders employed professionals with business skills to operate huge funds. But the orders usually lacked appropriate control over management. As a result, they often lost enormous amounts. The Polish Roman Catholic Union found out in 1910 that some ninety thousand dollars was missing, and soon suspended its treasurer.[65] Less than two years later, when the secretary of the Western Star discovered that the treasurer was more than five thousand dollars short in his accounts, the secretary kindly loaned him that amount, which turned out to be the order's money, not a personal loan. One year later, the Workmen's Circle revealed that its secretary was responsible for a shortage of several thousand dollars in its funds. These incidents instigated the *Courier* to cry, "There is practically no one Jewish order of national repute and devoted to insurance, from which the 'big officials' did not commit theft."[66]

These troubles compelled a number of mutual aid societies to initiate significant reforms that would draw them closer to being life insurance companies. While small societies ensnared in suicidal competition went bankrupt in those years, large ones took pains to avoid the quicksand and find a path to a financially sound basis. Many states recommended such a path. In 1911, state insurance commissioners met in Mobile, Alabama, and drew up legislation to require a reserve fund, higher dues, and regular auditing, including as well a ban on societies with fewer than five hundred members. As an increasing number of states enacted these regulations in the following years, mutual aid societies, small and large, made efforts to prevent their passage, accusing life insurance companies of lobbying to give arbitrary power to the state insurance commissioners.[67] As a matter of fact, many societies were well aware that in order to remain solvent they needed to maintain a reserve, as the Czecho-Slavonic Benevolent Society (C.S.P.S.) had already begun to do at the turn of the century.[68] So one new Jewish society called the People's Order promised to adopt the modern insurance system as well as democratic control over management, and another, the Jewish National Workers' Alliance, decided to install "the most modern and secure insurance system, which is known as the 'American Experience Table' [of Mortality], based on a legal reserve of four per cent."[69]

On the other hand, mutual aid societies had to be careful to keep their disbursements under control, thereby reminding their members of the role that money, the medium of the market, plays in social relationships. Because death benefits were the major disbursement, the societies often refused to pay if there seemed to be a good reason for default. In the early 1910s, as a result, there were a number of lawsuits reported in various newspapers. Such lawsuits apparently awoke readers to the distance between brotherly bonds and balanced detachment, as opposed to the tension between familial care and limited concern. This was what the Czech newspaper *Denni Hlasatel* stressed in an article published in November 1914. Referring to frequent reports of such lawsuits, it drew a line between native-born American societies and Czech. Although there were some cases where a society, American or Czech, might not pay on account of a member's own actions, the newspaper argued, American societies acted "very much like some insurance companies which always look around for a reason to refuse the payment, and very frequently succeed." According to the article, however, Czech societies always considered the principles of brotherhood, knowing that "the money goes to a widow who may have to raise several children. . . ." The newspaper emphasized: "American societies are conducted strictly along hard business lines, and when there is a chance of refusing the payment of a death benefit, all brotherly feelings and principles cease."[70]

The contrast did not seem to be as striking as *Denni Hlasatel* claimed. It was true that American societies were usually larger and more businesslike than ethnic ones. But it was also true that in operation ethnic societies were obliged to emulate their American counterparts. This was exactly the point made in a Jewish *Courier* article. The newspaper reported that an order called B'rith Abraham, at its convention held in May 1913, had rejected a resolution that an elderly member who was no longer able to pay his dues should have the dues advanced by his lodge and afterward deducted from his benefit. As a matter of fact, the resolution apparently reflected an issue that existed in many societies, since a number of first-generation immigrants from eastern and southern Europe had already retired by this time. To those immigrants, its repudiation meant they had to resign from their society, usually with no claim to their benefits, while to the remaining members it meant more secure funds. "If true brotherly spirit would prevail among the lodge brothers," bemoaned the *Courier*, "such a thing would never occur." The tone of the report might have been colored by the fact that B'rith Abraham was a German Jewish order, to which the Orthodox Jewish newspaper was not always impartial. Yet the newspaper still had a point, when it contrasted brotherly bonds with balanced detachment by adding: "Let us hope that in the near future our lodges shall be more saturated with the spirit of brotherhood, which is the basis of our fraternal organizations. In the mean time they are all the same . . . dollar organizations."[71]

More than anything, World War I drove mutual aid societies to act like American fraternal orders and even like life insurance companies. Initially, the war only aggravated the conflict between brotherhood and detachment. It did so especially in the Czech orders and in nationalistic Polish ones such as the Polish National Alliance. The war presented an unprecedented problem, the combined burden of lost dues and high casualties. While Czech and Polish nationalists encouraged young compatriots to enlist as Old World nationals and serve the cause of independence, their mutual aid societies had to calculate the increase in the financial burden occasioned by the war and reckon who should assume how much of that burden. Firstly, the societies were faced with loss of the monthly dues that the enlisted men were unable to pay, though they retained their memberships. When the U.S. Government inquired about their policy in November 1917, the C.S.P.S. answered, "These members enjoy the same rights and privileges as all others." The society explained that although it had no special bylaws covering soldiers or sailors, many of its lodges made "voluntary contributions for the benefit of enlisted men." Soon, however, the C.S.P.S. was in agony. In January of the following year, the society had more than three hundred members in the armed forces and expected the number to increase to four hundred by the end of the month. Who should pay on their behalf? It would be unjust for "[t]he old people who have been members for a long time" to do so. Although the society was ready to pay death benefits for soldiers and sailors killed in action, it pleaded, "More cannot be demanded of us." In fact, it could not avoid raising its dues.[72] But that was a decision made through an agonizing conflict between brotherly bonds and balanced detachment.

Secondly, other societies had yet to decide how to pay the expected rise in the number of death benefit payments. The Order of the Czech-American Foresters discussed this question at its annual convention, held in January 1918. It admitted that the order had to provide for its sixty members in the battlefield, as the United States took care of only wounded, not deceased, men, but it also felt obliged to protect its main assets. So the order proposed to create a special fund for the enlisted members. This society took pains to keep the cost down by spreading disbursements from the fund over time, instead of making the customary lump sum payment. "In order to be properly prepared for serious losses in some cases," according to a newspaper report of the order's convention, "it will be advisable not to pay out full amounts of death benefits, but to make payments in installments distributed over several years."[73] So high casualties on the front forced many societies at home to confront the old tension between needs and resources.

Eventually, however, the war forced mutual aid societies to transform themselves. It posed a threat to their very survival, by raising a breakwater against the massive waves of immigration, which was reinforced, though not completely, by legislative action in the first half of the 1920s. Most of the societies suffered a decrease in membership.[74] On the one hand, they apparently made efforts to keep disbursements under tighter control, which inevitably exacerbated the old tension.[75] On the other, they pressed for reforms, which had been introduced in prewar years. While the small societies languished under conditions of severe restraint, large ones strove for solvency by building up bigger reserves and securing higher revenues. Most large societies stocked their reserve funds from monthly dues and initiation fees, and abandoned assessment once and for all. This was what the Czech-American Foresters did in 1921, as the Czecho-Slavonic Fraternal Benevolent Society already had seven years before.[76]

Accordingly, additional revenues for the reserve had to come from higher dues. Now large societies were able to insist on the necessity of raising dues, by citing as an adversary the huge and vigorous life insurance company offering expensive but secure benefits, not the petty and languorous society. While small societies tried to stick to fifty or sixty cents as their monthly dues, augmented by irregular but increasingly frequent assessments, large societies simply raised their dues; in August 1919, the Workmen's Circle announced that a new list of rates for the $500 benefit required an eighteen-year-old member to pay $5.20 a year and a forty-year-old $11.40, and five months later the C.S.P.S. unveiled its new rates for the $1,000 benefit, which required that members in these categories should pay $14.16 and $30.72 each.[77] These new rates reflected the high inflation that followed the start of World War I. As the Czech society had argued in raising its dues two years before, however, it had decided to do so "after examination of figures which showed that the amount paid in was not sufficient to take care of all cases of death."[78] Furthermore, the new rates were still lower than those of a regular life insurance company. The society stressed, "No one would say that these rates are too high, in fact, they are much smaller, comparing them with the rates of life insurance companies."[79]

But large mutual aid societies, in other words, fraternal orders with between thousands and hundreds of thousands of members, had in fact become cooperative life insurance companies. Indeed, the Jewish *Courier* introduced the Jewish National Workers' Alliance as "a cooperative insurance organization," explaining that the order was issuing "fifteen- and twenty-year policies which offer the same privileges as those of an insurance company."[80] As indicated by the *Courier*, fraternal orders were in fact selling a commodity of protection against economic insecurity. In 1920, when Czech Free Thought societies tried to work out a plan to unite with one another, they proclaimed, "Each member [of the existing societies] will have the right to select a new policy best suited to his purpose—either a straight life policy, an endowment policy, or one which includes an old-age pension."[81] By the early 1930s, Italian societies, which started later than and followed the steps of Czech and other ethnic societies, issued certificates guaranteeing all benefits.[82]

As commodities, such policies or certificates individualized the membership and linked individual members to the fraternity, instead of uniting one member with another. Now each member contributed to his or her own account and derived benefits from it, without much regard to the other members. The members still shared their risks; when a member died only a few years after joining a society, he or she could receive a full benefit, greater than the amount of contribution. But that was less due to the fact that the member joined a fraternity than that he or she had bought an insurance policy. Indeed, the Czech-American Foresters discussed, at its convention held in 1921, what to do about such a member. Although the order had paid the full benefit, the Chief Forester reported, "We believe that a continuation of this policy would be unjust to older members who have been paying for years." Acknowledging that many societies did not pay in full unless a member had contributed for five years, he recommended an eclectic plan, in an effort to balance benefit against contribution on the individual basis: "[B]ut we think that the payment of half of it [the full benefit] at the death of a member who has been with us two years, and half of it two years after death would be no hardship on anybody."[83] Balanced detachment, instead of brotherly bonds, prevailed in the fraternity.

Mutual aid societies had come to resemble life insurance companies so much that following the war they made efforts to differentiate themselves by appealing to nationalism. As a matter of fact, there was a significant difference between the societies and regular life insurance companies; where the latter aimed to make profits for its stockholders, the societies were cooperatives working for the benefit of their own membership. This difference proved to be insignificant, however, to the ethnic community. For the societies had shed much of the communal function that they had once assumed. Certainly, they continued to offer moral and financial support for national causes, such as parochial schools and nationalist movements.[84] "This refutes the contention frequently voiced that the Czech aid societies are nothing but insurance companies, and, therefore, not very different from the American mutual aid societies," wrote the Czech newspaper *Denni Hlasatel* in early 1917.

"Insurance is, of course, the essence of membership, even in our societies," it quickly added. But it stressed in the end: "To be a member of our societies, means not only ownership of a security, but the performance of a duty toward our people as well."[85]

But there was considerable pressure against such a nationalist posture, which seems to have increased through the 1920s. In the earlier years of the Great Depression, therefore, the Polish National Alliance felt compelled to protest that "there is being promulgated by our enemies a third theory, namely, that Polish insurance and benevolent associations should also discard their nationalistic tendencies and, following the example of American insurance associations, mind their insurance and humanitarian business only." This protest apparently did not weigh much, however, as the order tried to deny the fact that Polish societies had undergone a metamorphosis. It simply insisted that Poles had formed the societies "for preserving the national language and national traditions," and had introduced the insurance scheme only "as a necessary cement."[86] In fact the scheme did not bind but fractured, in that it not only individualized the membership of mutual aid societies but also, by diversifying their vested interests, prevented them from realizing long-desired unification into a single giant order.[87]

The efforts to differentiate themselves from life insurance companies were part and parcel of an attempt by the mutual aid societies to redefine their idea of nationality. As indicated by the Polish National Alliance, they had long taken pains to cultivate national identity in a strange world. The societies had regarded the mother tongue as the critical element determining national consciousness, and its use was required in their meetings. In order to survive competition with the insurance companies as well as with each other, however, they had to reach beyond the boundary of language. In the early twenties, when the tide of immigration had already subsided against the breakwater raised by World War I, the societies were anxious to maintain or, hopefully, expand their membership. They were well aware that their self-aggrandizing momentum, though having been effective within the language boundary, was losing its thrust.

Consequently, while some societies, such as the Czecho-Slavonic Union and the Workmen's Circle, tried to enlist children or even older people over forty,[88] most apparently concentrated on the younger generation, which was expected to contribute for a long time and claim benefits only in the distant future. There were problems involved in a campaign to attract this generation. Mostly American-born, these young people often did not speak the mother tongue of the first generation. Some societies, such as the Czech Sisterhood, would not permit the use of English, which they were afraid might put an end to their national identity. But many others felt it more important to lure youth and created English-speaking lodges.[89] Besides, the generation that grew up in America was less firmly attached to its parents' homeland and less prone to seek the Old World ties that had attracted the first generation toward the mutual aid society. The Jewish *Courier* complained that young Jews of Chicago knew nothing beyond the city, and lamented, "Youth does not possess any *Landmanshaftliche* traditions."[90] And yet Jewish societies endeavored to recruit young members. In general, mutual aid societies extended their idea of nationality beyond the language and traditions of the motherland.

On the other hand, the need to expand led the societies to stress the role of money within the fraternity. In order to lure the younger generation, they adopted new approaches. During World War I, some, especially Czech societies, installed special organizers to carry out their membership campaigns. The organizers visited diverse places and helped found new lodges and enlarge smaller ones. Some of the Czech societies benefited from this practice, but others tried and then abandoned it, chiefly on account of the balance sheet; the organizers could work more effectively in an open field not limited to a specific nationality, such as that occupied by American fraternal orders.[91] At any rate, these societies were already acting like the life insurance companies, which had long been employing insurance agents. Other societies, again Czech ones in particular, employed incentives to encourage their members to enlist compatriots. The Czech-American Union held a contest and awarded cash prizes for those who introduced the most members, and the Czech-American Foresters offered a reward of one dollar for each new member acquired, and considered a proposition that the reward be raised to one dollar and fifty cents.[92] Cash rewards were designed to tap the resource of social networks retained by the members but they also had the effect of introducing the medium of the market into those networks.

Although money did not altogether replace the medium of the field in the ethnic fraternity, it did take on an increasingly significant role and apparently helped revise conventional norms. There were many cases in which a society assisted its less fortunate members above and beyond its own requirements, and they presented a good opportunity to boast of brotherly spirit. When a Chicago lodge of the Czech-American Union took up a collection, in addition to paying benefits, for one of its members who became disabled in 1918, the Czech *Denni Hlasatel* reported the matter, stressing: "An important difference between a brotherhood and an insurance company lies in the fact that the latter, when called on, will perform no more than its stipulated duty, while the former will do more."[93] It is paradoxical, however, that the report emphasized that brotherly bonds were still alive in comparison, not with the small mutual aid society, but with the modern insurance company, an embodiment of balanced detachment, which fraternal orders had chosen to revile as their enemy. Likewise, many members now felt it necessary to revise their traditional rituals. The Czech-American Foresters, for instance, decided not to read all the proposals to change their rites, afraid that it would take up too much time, at their convention held in 1918. There was instead a lively discussion. Some insisted that their traditional rituals still fascinated a number of people. Referring to physical injuries occasionally happening during these ceremonies, others called the rituals "antediluvian" and demanded more modern and democratic rites.[94] There were a variety of factors affecting the call for revision. An important one was the fact that the old rites appeared not simply outdated but inconsonant with the modernized structure and businesslike style of the order, now a cooperative life insurance company.

The readjustment of conventional norms, the development of balanced detachment in particular, indicates that the cash nexus had now permeated the mutual aid society. This is evident when the society of the 1920s is contrasted with that of the 1870s. A translation of communal mutual assistance, the old society was a tool with which immigrants coming to the world of commodities protected themselves from economic insecurity and uncongenial surroundings. It was a form of traditional personal interdependence, which they recreated to provide a measure of familial care that could meet many of their economic and social needs, as communities had done in Europe. That tool was, so to speak, a cane made of steel, which a member in misfortune would have found reliable even after death. Soon, however, money, the essentially scarce medium of exchange in the world of commodities, forced the society to restrict such care and instead proffer limited concern. There was a brotherly bond in the society, but it was now a bamboo cane, reliable only under less stress and lasting not as long as a steel one. Furthermore, the bond weakened as provision against economic insecurity became commodified, in the form of insurance policies, and individualized, in the adoption of isolated transactions of selling and buying between the society and each member. By the 1920s, the society had become a cane made of split bamboo, which was a bundle tied with the medium of the market. Now balanced detachment, instead of familial care, swayed the social relations within the society.

Eventually, commodification in the societies, along with businesslike practices associated with it, compelled members to conceive of the fraternity in terms of the cash nexus. The conception was not novel; it had originated from the necessity of balancing benefit against contribution, and continued to develop as recurrent disputes over benefit payments reminded immigrants that the nexus extended into the brotherhood. So it had long flowed like a current in their minds. Yet commodification had a decisive influence on the current, which forced members to reconcile themselves to the social detachment implicated in that context. For them, the mutual aid society was no longer a binding institution based on communal personal interdependence. It was now an epitome of economic individualism.

This transformation, coupled with the urban migrations around World War I, loosened the grip of the mutual aid society. Urban dispersion apparently restrained a number of members from being active in their societies. Although there were attempts to organize societies in the new settlements,[95] and although many societies moved their offices along with the relocated community centers, the increased physical space in the less thickly populated ethnic community was not encouraging to their efforts. This might have enhanced a thirst for social congeniality and the appeal of brotherly bonds as well, and encouraged members to be active. The societies, however, were unable to respond, because the cash nexus had already turned them into "dollar organizations" and driven individual interests to eclipse brotherly spirit. Perhaps this situation prompted the Czech *Denni Hlasatel* to voice its concern about the waning interest in fraternal activities among the membership after the mid-1910s. In an editorial published at the end of 1917, it pointed out, "Leaders of our [fraternal] organizations are complaining that members show insufficient interest even when the time comes to elect their officers." The newspaper contrasted this with the fact that previously such occasions lured large numbers of members. "Recent years have presented a different picture," it observed. The newspaper added, "Some of the annual meetings have not had enough members to constitute a quorum."[96] Although the *Denni Hlasatel* blamed lazy officers alone, the waning interest resulted chiefly from the metamorphosis of mutual aid societies and from urban dispersion as well.

This conceptual change was representative of the cultural transformation that took place in the ethnic community. The mutual aid society, a center of social life in the community, is here assumed to be, as it were, a window through which to look into immigration and acculturation as a collective process; immigrants shared, to a certain extent, the transforming experiences that its members underwent in the fraternity. The immigrants initially tried to recreate the community they had known in Europe, only to establish a different kind of community, a voluntary and open-ended association with no enforcing power. The cash nexus, along with American values such as personal freedom and self-reliance, impelled them to free themselves from the binding ties based on communalism. They felt less and less obligated to the enfeebled power of the ethnic community, which was further attenuated by the urban dispersion of its constituency. Moreover, the cash nexus appeared to deeply penetrate the new settlements, a better environment that, with pride, many immigrants felt showed off their material advance in America. For, while the environment symbolized successful accommodation to the American world of commodities, their advance had better familiarized these immigrants with the nexus than their less fortunate compatriots. In the ethnic community of the twenties, therefore, the constituency, mediated with money more than ever before, gave evident assent to economic individualism, though it was not completely dissuaded from communalism.

There was organized resistance to the economic individualism that was transforming the ethnic community. It was led by immigrant socialists, who hoped to displace the principles of private property and the free market and preached nationalization and industrial unionism. Baptized with working-class internationalism, they made efforts to reach beyond the ethnic boundaries that had long divided themselves into a number of language sections. Not just because they chiefly focused on the workplace but also because they barely comprehended the changes taking place in the community, however, they were fated more to become victims than to reinforce their resistance.

The socialists working in the ethnic neighborhoods, with the exception of the Italians, followed the center of the community moving into new settlements, and established branches there. By early 1919, Jewish socialists belonging to the Socialist Party of America had already launched a Douglas Park branch in Lawndale, and two years later Czechs formed a socialist club for their countryfolk living in Cicero and other western suburbs of Chicago.[97] Polish socialists also moved northwest along Milwaukee Avenue. In the meantime, Chicago's socialists were involved in worldwide internal conflicts. The right wing expelled militant radicals and reorganized itself, while the far Left launched the Communist Party. The larger conflict crippled the local movement, bringing to a standstill ethnic socialism, Jewish in particular.[98] After the split, socialists resumed their normal activities, such as election campaigns and open lectures, in addition to mass meetings in protest against repressive political acts such as the imprisonment of Nicola Sacco and Bartolomeo Vanzetti in 1921.[99]

Local socialists, however, failed to secure a firm foothold in the ethnic community. Certainly, there were well attended mass meetings; more than three thousand men and women crowded Carmen's Hall, where in February 1923 Eugene V. Debs appeared to support the well-known lawyer William A. Cunnea for the mayorship of Chicago. And there were new members enrolled in the socialist movement.[100] But these events were isolated occurrences, not a sustained trend. In fact, the movement was unmistakably on the decline. After the mid-twenties, particularly the 1924 presidential election, there were no important socialist activities in the city.[101] Why this happened is a significant question, worthy of a separate study.

What is important here is not simply the fact that socialists failed to keep the field, but that few ethnic workers committed themselves to socialism. There is no direct evidence to indicate how the workers, men's clothing workers in particular, responded to local socialist activities. There are some clues, however. Some workers who had already absorbed radical tenets in Europe drifted away from the socialist movement, as ACW leaders did in the 1910s. Morris Ginsburg, for instance, who in Russia had once been imprisoned for distributing socialist literature, no longer committed himself to the movement after arriving at Chicago in 1908. "I couldn't get involved in the Socialist Party in the U.S. as much as I wanted to," he recollects, "because my time was limited." Ginsburg adds, "I worked 12 hours a day for $3.00 a week."[102] Most were simply not very interested in socialism. Jack Mitchell, a Russian Jew who had stayed in England and learned socialist doctrine from his father before getting a job at a Chicago's men's clothing firm in 1921, remembers how the majority of workers thought about socialism. While Mitchell and his friends paid attention to developments in Russia after the October Revolution, according to his memory, "We found that the Russian experiment was not really of great interest to the average worker." Mitchell states further, "We felt that a dictatorship of any kind was not what we had in mind as a philosophy for our [union] members."[103]

While some workers actively disapproved of socialism, often regarding it as a Jewish movement, most simply remained aloof from socialist politics. Chicago's men's clothing workers were aware how much they owed to radicals in the 1910–1911 strike and in the ensuing organizing drives, and they appreciated the contribution made by socialists. They probably felt that their own union was more or less oriented toward socialism, as noted by Lottie Spitzer, a socialist ACW member who was quite active in the teens and twenties. Although she never knew who belonged to the Socialist Party, according to her recollection many supported Debs and read the *Forward*, a Jewish socialist newspaper. Yet Spitzer was obviously conscious of workers' aloofness. Whenever an election came up in the early twenties, she would call on friends and neighbors and busy herself with "handling out leaflets and standing on the corner talking to people." On such occasions Spitzer emphasized that socialists were fighting for workers, a point that presupposes that the radicals did not belong among the working people. She recollects:

> When I talked to the people I would persuade them to vote for the socialist ticket. I would tell them this man is fighting for us. If we lose this man we are going to lose a lot. We had to see that this man got into office—he's working for the working people. That's what I kept telling people.[104]

The workers' aloofness, grafted onto the traditional popular mentality differentiating "us" from "them" as discussed in an earlier chapter, was associated with the cash nexus. When Lottie Spitzer stressed that the socialist was "fighting for us," she often encountered a skewed conception of socialism in that context. Seeking votes in the ethnic community, Spitzer took pains to prevail on her neighbors to shed such a conception. "Some people asked me if they'd get paid for it [voting for the socialist ticket]," she recollects. So she answered that "the Socialist Party didn't have any money to pay—they didn't buy votes, we bought hearts—we wanted support to come from the heart—the vote should come from the heart."[105] Of course, the conception was a product of urban political corruption around the turn of the century. Equally significant, however, is the fact that it appeared against a backdrop of the complex identity and social relationships that immigrants had formed in the ethnic community.

As immigrants, ethnic workers found themselves implicated in politics both in the Old World and the New, which also opened a door to political disengagement. Whatever had impelled them to leave Europe, immigrants obviously felt strongly tied to their old country. This was especially the case in earlier years of settlement, as suggested by the riot that the Russian Revolution of 1905 caused among Chicago Jewry, or by the loyalty that a number of Polish American socialists showed toward their homeland party.[106] The emotional tie, though weakening over time, led immigrants to formulate the notion that they remained part of the old nation, for instance, "the American branch of the Czech nation."[107] As the Zionist movement developed in America, such a notion, to a certain extent, pervaded the Jewish community, too.

On the other hand, ethnic workers were more often than not politically accommodative in more than one sense. Trying to explain why American workers did not vote along class lines, Richard Oestreicher has argued that immigrants and their children held "the desire to adapt to existing power in ways that would facilitate, rather than threaten, their priorities of family integrity, economic well-being and cultural defense."[108] Such a predisposition not only impeded their ability to mobilize for radical changes; it was often a bar to their joining the American polity, as shown by their frequent disregard for naturalization and citizenship. For many ethnic workers, priorities lay in economic interests rather than in political influence and social status in America.

No doubt, the priorities were not fixed but changing, as the workers secured a stake in the American political and social landscape. To those immigrants who continued to make a living as wage earners, however, economic interests apparently remained their primary concern, keeping them out of American politics. As long as they identified themselves as immigrants, that concern often turned out to be a double-edged sword against political commitment. When Czech nationalists criticized that materialism restrained their American compatriots from contributing as generously as they would have expected, for example, the *Denni Hlasatel* protested: "Whatever the ideals may be of those people who reproach us, we did not come to America with the thought of founding a new Bohemia, but to assure ourselves a decent living."[109] Therefore, priorities placed on economic interests in America opened the way for ethnic workers to stay disengaged from politics on either side of the Atlantic Ocean.

As long as political disengagement, instead of commitment, remained characteristic of the identity that ethnic workers held for themselves, it helped them understand American politics in terms of the cash nexus, as Lottie Spitzer learned. True, in the twenties a number of them filled out citizenship papers and their leaders aspired to political power, as in the case of the ACW leadership partaking in third-party politics. But that did not always ensure their active participation in the American polity. Most workers, not merely alienated from American politics but also more detached from one another in the postwar years, remained aloof from socialism. Immigrant socialists were unable to commit them to a collective project for the radical transformation of the United States. Furthermore, the socialists no longer appeared capable of mobilizing the community for the cause of the labor movement. They had lost their foothold there, although they would reclaim it during the Great Depression, when communalism was further weakened but common misery led ethnic workers into confrontation with employers. By that time, however, most of the workers supported New Deal liberalism. What is concerned here is the fact that during the twenties radicalism declined in the ethnic neighborhoods. Radical politics was victimized by the profound changes that took place in the attitude of immigrant workers, who were relying less on the communal tradition than on the individualist ethos in comprehending social relationships.

Their attitude was not entirely new. When the ACW endeavored to organize workers by taking advantage of wartime circumstances, Sidney Hillman became concerned over apparently radical militancy in the rank and file. Chicago leaders had a different opinion: Frank Rosenblum believed that tailors were not much interested in the union because they received more money and better treatment than ever before, and Samuel

Levin had a similar and poignant view. Anxious to recruit workers at John Hall, which the leaders thought of as a test case, Levin closely observed their attitude toward the ACW. In early July 1918, he reported to Hillman that "from all informations I find the people [there] lost spirit for the Union as the people are fluctuated." Levin quickly added, "[T]hose that are still working are telling us that without getting an increase [of wages] they don't see the benefit of a union." In the postscript to the letter, the CJB manager admitted that he lately found the spirit still high, but pointed out that the ACW needed to take care of the wage demand. Levin stated, "Though they expect an increase immediately, but I have changed my mind in regard to the spirit."[110]

Such an attitude, now encouraged by the economic individualism that pervaded the physically dispersed working-class neighborhoods, had mixed effects. To a certain extent it promoted rank-and-file loyalty to the ACW; economic individualism did not preclude collective action, as long as people could expect to benefit from acting together. Established as "a powerful force" in Chicago's men's clothing industry, the union did protect its members from abusive industrial practices and helped improve their living standard. They moved into better houses and apparently bought more consumer goods, enjoying the material advances they made. Indeed, there were many workers loyal to the union leadership; in 1925, Samuel Levin stormed a meeting called by communists with about twenty-five hundred members, and won support from almost half of the Chicago membership when radicals mounted a challenge in the CJB staff elections. In the adverse economic and political circumstances of the day, the union probably offered more benefits than drawbacks.

But rank-and-file loyalty was also constrained by economic individualism. Seen in that light, the ACW did not appear as attractive from the mid-twenties on. Now failing to deliver the goods, the union cooperated with management and told its members to work harder for the same rewards. There was newly instituted unemployment insurance, but many workers believed the benefits were simply part of the wages that the union withheld from their pay. Discontent ran high in the mid-twenties, but did not lead to the rebellious self-assertion that Chicago's men's clothing workers had shown in the 1910–1911 strike. Radicals, stricken by political infighting and frustrated at workers' aloofness, failed to consolidate the opposition within the ACW. On the other hand, ACW leaders found the Chicago membership not just shrinking, but increasingly indifferent toward the union. Indifference was in part due to the generation gap; younger members, constituting probably the majority in the mid-twenties, did not share the pains "old-timers" had taken to build up the organization. There was also a cultural change involved in the rank-and-file attitude. The educational work abandoned by the CJB indicates that the ranks were less interested in broad political topics than in cultural and social activities. Some locals took pains to reactivate the work, but, with limited resources and short-lived programs, could not stem the tide or awaken the majority of the membership to the cause except regarding bread-and-butter issues.

This narrow perspective, cross-fertilized by the decline of radicalism, had a more devastating impact. Radicalism never predominated over the workers, but it did inspire them. As revealed in the 1910–1911 strike, radicalism functioned like a magnifying glass that, bringing their own demands into focus, guided them to take a different direction from the native-born strike leaders. Sidney Hillman had a social vision as well as personal charm, and commanded respect from rank-and-filers up to the early 1920s. As a moderate, however, he steered his union toward the American Federation of Labor, as socialism declined both at the workplace and in the community. By the mid-twenties, there remained no inspiring group of radicals available to the workers. In the perspective characterized by individualism, the ACW was hardly something greater or higher than an economic institution. Its Chicago membership, whose self-assertive solidarity had been in part based on communalism and inspired by radicalism, was fragmented.

For ACW leaders, their leverage was now curtailed. The ethnic working-class community was no longer the same resource it had been in prewar years. It had once provided interwoven social networks that were elaborated at the workplace and often could be counted on when a contest took place between immigrant workers and their employers. And it had once given support, moral and material, strong and wide, to its constituents involved in major battles against their employers. But now, characterized less by communalism than by individualism, it lost its binding power upon the constituency and became ineffective in mobilizing on workplace issues. The dynamic relationship between community mobilization and labor organization no longer obtained.

In order to sustain the vulnerable position of the ACW vis-à-vis the employers, therefore, its leaders needed an authority, stronger than ever before, over the rank and file. Concentrating on the workplace, they made efforts to consolidate their authority by fortifying bureaucracy and crippling opposition within the union. They also stressed cooperation with management, as Hillman had already preached at the 1920 ACW convention, because their authority was chiefly dependent on job control. This organization, now well established on Chicago's industrial landscape, became just another business union with a shrinking membership.

That retreat into the establishment, after all, was basically determined by the complex of undercurrents that the men's clothing workers of Chicago formulated both in the spheres of production and of consumption. With the communal tradition giving place to the individualist ethos in the community, the imperative of conflict yielded to that of compromise at the workplace. For, communal personal interdependence finally yielded to social detachment in the community as well as at the workplace, making it less feasible to mobilize ethnic neighborhoods in the contest against the employers. The complex of undercurrents constituted by those four tendencies was at last stabilized, though it would look fluid during the Great Depression.

CONCLUSION

This study analyzes why the American labor movement was in retreat during the 1920s. Concentrating on the ACW and in particular its Chicago organization, I have discussed why the union, faced with a shrinking and lukewarm membership, turned to business unionism, which was seemingly inconsistent with its earlier progressive posture. I have tried to provide answers not only by investigating the political, economic, and social circumstances besetting Chicago's men's clothing workers, but also by probing the internal dynamics created by the workers and their organization.

These internal dynamics turned out to be as critical a factor as structural constraints, affecting the ACW from its origins. While the ACW strove for a place in a staunchly anti-union industry, its rank and file showed rebellious self-assertiveness rooted in both the workplace and the ethnic community, which helped to completely organize Chicago by the end of the 1910s. ACW leaders, mostly moderates recruited from higher levels of a gender-biased job hierarchy and aspiring for a new balance of power in the industry, secured control over jobs. They consolidated their power within the union by taking advantage of job control. And yet the leaders were faced with profound changes in the community. Men's clothing workers, increasingly scattered all over the city, took an active part in American culture, in particular consumerism as well as racialism. These changes enfeebled the community and compelled workers to narrow their perspective to economic individualism. The transformation was in part a consequence of their own success. They had secured a collective voice, with the ACW protecting against arbitrary rule by their employers, which allowed them to enjoy their material advances. And yet that transformation weakened worker solidarity so much that in time they could hardly assert themselves against either the union leaders or the employers. To a certain extent, therefore, the leaders became at once bureaucratic and accommodative as they responded to the increasingly withdrawn membership, the ultimate basis of their power vis-à-vis the management. In a sense, the ACW retreated into the establishment.

These dynamics were not entirely a product of the adverse circumstances that besieged the union during the 1920s, nor an expression of some ingrained psychology often ascribed to American workers in general. No doubt the ACW found itself constrained by chronic recessions and unfriendly political trends, not to mention the courts, which upheld the existing order. But these constraints do not explain the changing social relationships among its Chicago members. The union members showed something quite close to "job and wage consciousness," but not from the start; such psychology became distinct and significant only from the mid-twenties on. The dynamic is, rather, related to "workplace contractualism," an institutional logic that harnesses rank-and-file militancy. And yet it was less imposed upon the workplace by the union and the management than derived from the community in which the members lived.

In Chicago, men's clothing workers went through, over a span of just two generations, the long—often taking several centuries—process in which the corporate community disintegrated and lost its material basis, the feudal relations of property and control. For the workers, immigration represented above all a movement from the margins of capitalism into the center. Their movement amplified the process of their acculturation that had already begun in Europe; the United States was a full-fledged capitalist society pervaded by individualism and liberalism. Furthermore, their experience represents an interesting irony of history. What put them on the move was mainly, on the one hand, emancipation and population pressures, and, on the other, American capitalism, which from the late nineteenth century introduced the system of mass production, endeavoring to secure unskilled labor essential to the minutely subdivided labor process. This pulling factor led the immigrants to identity as wage earners, an identity also based on the racial hierarchy, and to worker solidarity. It also allowed them to recreate the communal tradition, which proved to be a powerful resource in the contest against the employer. But at the same time it quietly and yet quickly destroyed the tradition. Mass production turned out commodities on an overwhelming scale, soon pushing American society into the stage of mass consumption. This accelerated the process of commodification to such a degree that the ethnic community became encamped in the cash nexus and enfeebled in the twenties. The community was no longer able to mobilize itself on behalf of its constituents when they battled their employers. Besides, the process undermined the labor movement from within, leading ethnic workers to interpret their inside relations on the shop floor in terms of economic individualism. The workers underwent a cultural change that appeared dramatic, as the urban landscape and in particular residential patterns once helped them turn to the old tradition but soon exposed them to those destructive forces.

All told, then, this study stresses the significance of communalism in the labor movement. Today's organized labor represents the achievements American workers have made in the last century. In contrast to its marginal position of a century ago, it is now established as a junior partner in American industry that can influence decisions when working conditions are the issue. It still retains a distinct political voice, which cannot be as readily dismissed as it was a few generations ago, having significantly adjusted the inequalities of power in America. However, these achievements have also been constrained by a tendency that, by focusing on the shop floor, neglected the community. This is true even of the ACW, a union that took as much pain to reach beyond the workplace as any other union in modern American history; its leaders as well as rank-and-filers vaguely perceived the changes taking place in the community. It is in the community that the forces inherent in capitalism, especially when reinforced by mass production and mass consumption, have turned out to be devastating to worker solidarity and eventually to the labor movement itself. Now is the time to look beyond the workplace.

APPENDIX

The Spatial Context of History

Characteristically, historians stress context, but it is almost invariably the temporal context, not the spatial, that commands our attention. The spatial context is often presumed to make no significant difference in the course of history. This presumption, though apparently reinforced through academic specialization from the late nineteenth century, basically derives from the Enlightenment project. For the project was founded on a belief in progress, a temporal ideal ingrained in the Western intellectual tradition, which suggests Man's dominance over nature. The ideal includes the conquest of space, in particular the space that the Europeans "discovered" through oceanic voyages in the fifteenth century, as a challenging natural environment. Developing in accordance with this project, the natural sciences have resorted to abstraction in treating space, usually by conceptually separating it from the context. They have preached a conception of space as an unlimited, shapeless void without substance. Defined in these terms, space lacks dynamism and a causative power. This conception has pervaded the social sciences and history as well, resulting in "the subordination of space in social theory."[1]

Space, if ever taken into account, appears to be no more than a container, an environment in which history unfolds itself. This is true of the *Annales* school, seemingly the most geographically conscious historians in our period. Fernand Braudel, who is well known to have strongly advocated "total history," divides history into three levels, *longue durée*, groups and groupings, and events, and assigns the first part of his masterpiece *The Mediterranean* to the first level, a history of "man in his relationship to the environment." He pays particular attention to geography, believing, "It helps us to rediscover the slow unfolding of structural realities, to see things in the perspective of the very long term."[2] As Bernard Bailyn notes in his incisive review of the book, however, Braudel fails to integrate the three levels into "a comprehension of the organic totality of Mediterranean life," leaving the spatial dimension of the history of groups and groupings and of events yet to be explored.[3] This is why in the preface to the second edition of *The Mediterranean* Braudel modifies his approach and retreats from "the dialectic of space and time (geography and history) which was the original justification of the book."[4]

Fortunately, a number of geographers have recently developed a new perspective on space, which I believe will help probe the spatial dimension of history. Geography has long been isolated from history and social sciences as well. Even historical geography, a field that is conventionally believed to be a bridge, has also failed to promote interdisciplinary cooperation; it has been "focused upon *landscapes* transformed by man rather than upon *man* as an agent of landscape change."[5] Since the late 1960s, however, when dissenting geographers asked themselves if their academic practices had any social relevance and then embraced critical social theory, Marxism in particular, they have explored the relationship between the social process and the spatial form.

They found a pathbreaker in Henri Lefebvre, the independent French Marxist who argued that capitalism survives by extending itself in space. "[C]apitalism has found itself able to attenuate (if not resolve) its internal contradictions for a century," declared Lefebvre, "*by occupying space, by producing a space.*" Here he referred not to natural but social space. Unlike the sociological world Georg Simmel meant by the same terminology,[6] social space has become "a commodity that is bought and sold, chopped up into lots and parcels." There, capitalism dominates everyday life and reproduces its own social relations. "Reproduction (of the relations of production, not just the means of production) is located not simply in *society as a whole*," argued Lefebvre, "but *in space as a whole.*"[7] As a matter of fact, it is a defying task, far beyond my concern here, to examine the vast and elusive domain of his thought. The point is that Lefebvre called attention to the problematical relationship between society and space and asserted an idea of space as a social construct.

This idea is shared by Manuel Castells, the French sociologist who once had considerable influence on dissenting geographers by introducing structural Marxism into urban studies, particularly consumption in the city. On the other hand, he accuses Lefebvre of humanism in pushing the idea so far that space appears to be the work of man's free creation. This accusation is certainly based on his Althusserian disregard of human agency. The point Castells wants to emphasize is that space is specified by the link between social structure and social relations. Space is to him "a social form that derives its meaning from the social processes that are expressed through it."[8] So Castells proposes that space be interpreted in terms of the social process.

David Harvey, leading the new trend in geography since the early 1970s, has painstakingly elaborated such ideas from the perspective of

Marxist political economy. His work as a whole starts from the concept of social space. Pointing out that there are various conceptions of space, he declares, "The problem of the proper conceptualization of space is resolved through human practice with respect to it." Harvey refuses the conception held by modern physics. Instead, probing how space is related with society, he argues, "Spatial forms are . . . seen not as inanimate objects within which the social process unfolds, but as things which 'contain' social processes in the same manner that social processes *are* spatial."[9]

He eventually developed this argument into the "urbanization of capital" thesis. Harvey believes that under capitalism, capital exploits surplus value in the primary circuit, that is, within the production process of the commodity. Here it tends to be overaccumulated relative to the investment opportunities and to be devaluated unless the excess capital is eliminated from circulation. Therefore, according to his theory, the state often intervenes in the flow of capital and leads overaccumulated capital into the secondary circuit, in other words, into the construction of the physical infrastructure helpful to promote both production and consumption. The investment results in the so-called built environment, such as transport networks, factories, offices, houses, schools, and parks, which form a totality of urban landscapes. The tertiary and last circuit of capital, investment in science and technology to develop the productive forces and social expenditures related to reproduction of labor power, is not directly involved in the built environment.

In understanding the built environment that the capitalist society creates "in its own image," the conflict between capital and labor is particularly significant. There are two factions of capital chiefly involved in the process of creating urban space, one seeking to appropriate rent, such as landlords and financial institutions that invest in real property, and the other seeking to make a profit by building physical structures. Labor is in conflict with these factions of capital; labor "uses the built environment as a means of consumption and as a means for its own reproduction." Moreover, capital in general intervenes in the struggle around the built environment, which is not just an outlet for surplus capital but provides leverage over labor, such as home ownership, costs of living, consumption, and work discipline. To Harvey, therefore, urban space is an integral part of the social process constituted by capitalism. He claims that "all aspects of production and use of the built environment are brought within the orbit of the circulation of capital."[10]

Harvey's thesis, whose richness cannot be reduced to a rough summary such as this, calls for theoretical discussion because it contains controversial notions, such as the overaccumulation and devaluation of capital. More important, it needs to be sufficiently examined in the light of historical evidence, since his arguments are derived more from Marx's writings than from empirical research. Nevertheless, Harvey provides an interesting perspective for historians working on urban space, in that he calls attention to the dynamic process of spatial transformation. It is such a perspective that the editors of *Radical History Review* emphasize in the 1979 special issue on "the spatial dimension of history." Pointing out that a fully elaborated spatial category is absent in the work of Braudel or any other historians and that Marxist geographers work at too abstract a level to be much interested in concrete processes of spatial transformation, they advocate "a complex view of spatial relations as the outcome of intense struggle and negotiation among groups over the appropriation and use of social resources."[11] And it is such a perspective that Roy Rosenzweig adopts in his fine study of working-class recreational patterns, including leisure activity on the contested terrain of parks and playground, in Worcester, Massachusetts.[12]

Elizabeth Blackmar has also adopted such a perspective, with a subtle but significant implication, in her important study of New York City's housing market. In the midst of a geographic abundance of land, Blackmar explains, colonial Manhattan proprietors created artificial scarcity by forming social monopolies of landownership, while by the end of the eighteenth century an increasing number of workers detached from their employing householder resorted to tenant housing. The housing market thus created gave propertied New Yorkers the power to command rents, through which they turned lower Manhattan into a business district while carving out "respectable" neighborhoods for their own residence. These geographical changes brought about social displacement, forcing independent artisans to give up their control of real property, the basis of patriarchal authority to organize economic activities and appropriate the dependents' labor in their household.[13] In this sense, Blackmar implicitly suggests that space, involved in the social process, has an impact upon social changes.

I believe this suggestion implies a spatial perspective on the social process, which is latent in Harvey's thesis, though he seems to be reluctant to make it explicit. If space is not merely a social construct but also part and parcel of the social process, it might, in turn, affect the process. In fact, Jon Amsden has cautiously explored this perspective in his essay published in the *Radical History Review* special issue. He stresses the significance of the spatial dimension in historical analysis by taking an example from an antiracist rally that took place in Los Angeles on a Saturday in June 1979. Local activists marched through the city center to attract the attention of people who on Saturdays usually filled a street leading to *La Placita*, a historic plaza with a bandstand. As soon as the demonstrators had passed the crowd, intending to hold a meeting at a different square located considerably away from the plaza, however, the march broke down. It attracted no one from *La Placita*, and most marchers turned less enthusiastic about the square, whose space the city had organized in ways unfavorable to a rally. Amsden argues that this event provides "startling confirmation for the idea that the built environment can at times profoundly influence both individual and collective human behavior." But he does not push the idea farther. Amsden only makes a cautious and yet vague call for "the 'spatial imagination': the ability and propensity to understand society as it is arranged geographically as well as in the way that it may change through time."[14]

The spatial perspective is implied in John Merriman's *The Margins of City Life*. In this study of French urban periphery in the first half of the nineteenth century, he shows how spatial marginality contributed to social differentiation between the bourgeoisie and the proletariat and eventually to the political process leading to the Second Empire. In the faubourgs of Reims, for instance, one of the diverse urban peripheries dealt with in this book, woolens workers mobilized around such factors as the concentration of work, the impact of mechanization, the organization of social life, and the influence of utopian socialism and republicanism. "But," stresses Merriman, "the spatial concomitants of large-scale industrialization and urban growth also contributed to the social and political conflict that followed the revolution of 1848." For, the workers, condemned to live in the margins of the city because of their economic role, built up neighborhood solidarities and a sense of exclusion from the urban center, which he argues "played a major, perhaps even determining, part" in their mobilization. The political challenge based upon "self-identification and solidarities that were both social and spatial" and the effort of the elites to extend their dominance to the periphery, therefore, appear to constitute a major theme of French history in and even beyond this period.[15]

Merriman does not explicitly discuss the spatial perspective, however. Since the book is primarily concerned with the concept of marginality, which he regards as both social and spatial, his interest in space is contained within the margins of the nineteenth-century French city. Throughout the book, therefore, Merriman does not attempt to explore the space beyond or elaborate the concept of space or its relationship with society. To those trying to understand, in general, how history is intertwined with geography, he leaves a basic question unanswered: What is the space that affects the social process?

This question does not seem to be valid to those still preoccupied with the legacies of the Enlightenment project. British sociologist John Urry, for example, in his essay examining the relationship between space and society, acknowledges that it is necessary to explore the spatial as well as temporal relations between social entities. Yet he insists it is a categorical mistake to think of space and society as interacting. The reason, he emphasizes, is that unlike society space is not a substance.[16] This is certainly true of Euclidean space, a conception that understands space to be void in contrast with structure. We are indeed so thoroughly accustomed to the old notion that the word *space* instantly calls up a geometrical model in our mind. The reality is not that abstract, however. Space is also irreducibly concrete. In fact, it is so pervasively intimate to our everyday life that we do not very often give heed to a banal truism that it has a material basis, land. As such, it is an object to be owned and used; above all, it is a condition of production and reproduction. And as such, it is a substance around which social relations, including property relations, are shaped. Space, that is, social space in the Lefebvrian sense, inextricably interleaves social relations; it is not merely a container but rather a medium.

It is this conception that some geographers take pains to integrate into social theory. Derek Gregory, a leading philosopher of geography, finds in theories of structuration "a return to the concrete which marks a major renaissance of the interconnections between social relations and spatial structures as a central focus for scientific inquiry."[17] I do not share his belief. Although theorists of structuration, especially Anthony Giddens, to whom Gregory pays particular attention, regard both time and space as essential to the constitution of social systems, they do not seem to subscribe to the conception of space as a medium. Giddens points out that time and space are more than mere environments of action. Yet he treats them as such when analyzing individual action in the framework of time-geography. As a matter of fact, his theory centers around the notion of the duality of structure, a problematic of interaction between the individual and the social system, neither between individuals nor between collectivities. In such a theory, there is no place for the space mediating social relations. Finally, beginning with a premise that "the search for a theory of social change . . . is a doomed one," Giddens does not seem to be interested enough to explore the historical dimension of social change.[18] So it would be next to impossible to coordinate his theory of structuration with a historical approach to changing social relations. Likewise, space appears to be no more than a container in Nigel Thrift's preliminary exploration of the implications the structurationist school has for his effort to develop a Marxist theory of determination of social action.[19]

Edward Soja has also endeavored to combine space with social theory, asserting "a third interpretive geography, one which recognizes spatiality as simultaneously . . . a social product (or outcome) and a shaping force (or medium) in social life." He formulates the two-way flow between society and space as a "socio-spatial dialectic," and tries to develop it into a historical and geographical materialism. The dialectic is based on spatiality, a specific concept that designates not space per se but a spatial structure created by society. Spatiality cannot be separated from or reduced to physical and/or psychological spaces, argues Soja. Together with temporality, space becomes the structure defining "how social action and relationship (including class relations) are materially constituted, made concrete." He finds this process of constitution/concretization a problematic that will help introduce a spatial dimension to dialectical materialism.[20]

The "socio-spatial dialectic" deserves scrutiny. For Soja, the spatial is social. He regards spatiality as a substance in the sense that it is simultaneously a social product and a social medium.[21] Perhaps he emphasizes this point, partly intent on introducing the geographical dimension to historical materialism and partly wary of spatial fetishism, a tendency to reify the social into space and divert away attention from class struggle.[22] In so doing, however, Soja seems to forget that space always retains its physical attribute as a context of human life. This inherent contextuality coexists and intertwines with the substantiality that space acquires when integrated into the social process, whether in the form of a commodity or not. Exclusive focus on one of the two attributes leads to a miscomprehension of space. For instance, Peter Saunders stresses contextuality in his survey of urban sociology, concluding with an unconvincing call to separate the social from the spatial and go back to nonspatial social sciences.[23] On the other hand, Soja sacrifices contextuality for the sake of substantiality, though the former is latent in his own notion of spatiality. He is indeed so one-sidedly interested in developing a theory of space that he does not even seem to wonder if it is ever possible to theorize the particularities that characterize space as a context.[24] Presumably, the one-sidedness leads Soja to neglect empirical research to support his "socio-spatial dialectic," which he has forged chiefly through philosophical speculation.

In my opinion, then, it is necessary to empirically explore the idea of space as a social medium. Such an exploration will, on the other hand, help to broaden our understanding of history. Where Braudel, treating space as a container, has failed to integrate geography with history, that idea introduces substantiality and helps to see how social space in the Lefebvrian sense interleaves and mediates social relations. At the same time, the idea does not deny contextuality and helps to see how space, through its physical attribute, enables and constrains social interaction. In these respects, space appears to constitute the other context of history, as the temporal one is significant in that it is believed to make a difference in the course and the meaning of an event or current. It is in this sense that I pay attention to the spatial context.

This brings me back to the spatial perspective discussed earlier. In order to properly explore the spatial context, it is certainly necessary to probe how space helps people form distinct social relations and mobilize themselves. The spatial perspective indeed demands an effort to keep in mind not only how social relations affect spatial structures but how the relations are expressed in the structures, as Olivier Zunz attempts in his study on Detroit around the turn of the century.[25] More important, that perspective requires an attempt to comprehend how people experience space; social relations are after all based on a totality of lived experience, which includes the way they feel and interpret the built environment, as Yi-Fu Tuan shows in his book *Space and Place*.[26]

NOTES

Citations are shortened even at first appearance, except for public documents and private publications; the sources are given in full in the bibliography.

ABBREVIATIONS

ACW Papers	Amalgamated Clothing Workers of America Papers, 1910–1975, Labor-Management Documentation Center, Catherwood Library, Cornell University
CCSJB Papers	Papers of the Chicago and Central States Joint Board, the Amalgamated Clothing and Textile Workers' Union, Chicago Historical Society
CJB Papers	Papers of the Chicago Joint Board, the Amalgamated Clothing Workers of America, Chicago Historical Society
CPA	Oral History Archives of Chicago Polonia, Chicago Historical Society
HSM Papers	Papers of Hart, Schaffner and Marx, Hartmarx Corporation
ICP	Italians in Chicago Oral History Project, University of Illinois at Chicago Library
ILHP	Oral History Project in Immigration and Labor History, Downtown Library, Roosevelt University
JEPP	John E. Philbin Oral History Project, CCSJB Papers, Chicago Historical Society (I failed to track down this material in my last visit to Chicago Historical Society in August 2000, and have left intact its incomplete citations in the following notes)
NYTP	Interviews Conducted by N. N. Gold for the Oral History Research Office of Columbia University in 1963 and 1964, New York Times Oral History Program: Columbia University Collection (microfilm ed.), Widener Library, Harvard University
Press Survey	Chicago Foreign Language Press Survey (microfilm ed.), Chicago Historical Society
WTUL Papers	Papers of the Women's Trade Union League and Its Principal Leaders (microfilm ed.), Schlesinger Library, Radcliffe College

CHAPTER 1. THE ETHNIC COMMUNITY IN THE WORLD OF COMMODITIES

1. U.S. Congress, Senate, *Report on Condition of Woman and Child Wage-Earners in the United States* (hereafter *Woman and Child Wage-Earners*), vol. 2: *Men's Ready-Made Clothing*, S. Doc. 645, 61st Cong., 2d sess., 1911, 13–14.

2. Ibid., 45–46.

3. U.S. Department of Commerce and Labor, Bureau of the Census, *Census of Manufactures: 1914*, vol. 2: *Reports for Selected Industries and Detail Statistics for Industries. By States* (1919), 173–174.

4. *Woman and Child Wage-Earners*, II: 53–57.

5. U.S. Immigration Commission, *Reports*, vol. 11: *Immigrants in Industries: Pt. 5, Silk Goods Manufacturing and Dyeing—Pt. 6, Clothing Manufacturing—Pt. 7, Collar, Cuff, and Shirt Manufacturing*, S. Doc. 633, 61st Cong., 2d sess., 1911, 431–433.

6. Ibid., 286–288.

7. Maria Czarnecka, interview by Einar Hanson, CPA, box 2 side 1, 1, 5.

8. Frank Catrambone, interview by Mary Piraino, ICP, box 3 folder 17, 1, 3–5.

9. U.S. Immigration Commission, *Reports*, vol. 26: *Immigrants in Cities*, S. Doc. 338, 61st Cong., 2d sess., 1911, 125–129.

10. Zofia Kowalczyk, interview by James Young, CPA, box 3 side 1, 1, 5–6; side 3, 1; and side 4, 2–3.

11. Eugene Pomorski, interview by James Young, CPA, box 6 side 1, 1–2; and side 3, 5–6.

12. Kuznets, "Immigration of Russian Jews."

13. Pearl Spencer, interview by Elizabeth Balanoff, ILHP, book 26, 1, 4, 7, 9–10. For Jewish women's work experience in clothing trades, particularly in dressmaking, see Glenn, *Daughters of the Shtetl*, 18–30.

14. Berend and Ránki, *Economic Development in East-Central Europe*, 2–7; Woolf, *History of Italy*, 19–25, 275–283. The quotation is from Berend and Ránki, *Economic Development in East-Central Europe*, 3.

15. Blum, "European Village"; "Internal Structure and Polity."

16. Blum, "Internal Structure and Polity," 546–547.

In fundamentals, I do not agree with many historians about the concept of community. A number of social historians define it in terms of locality and/or of personal relationship, and portray its decline chiefly as a consequence of urbanization and modernization (see, for example, Frisch, *Town into City*; Dawley, *Class and Community*; Pacyga, *Polish Immigrants*). In an effort to synthesize a diversity of studies, Thomas Bender suggests in *Community and Social Change* that the nineteenth century saw American society bifurcated into the gemeinschaft and the gesellschaft, not the one submitting to the other. The suggestion is based on his conception of community as a distinctive network of close personal relations; the network is indeed compatible with an impersonal association of individuals seeking common interests. This conception guides Bender to refute the view of those historians who repeatedly find the community disintegrating in the period subject to their attention. But it also directs him to ignore the material basis of community, a peculiar set of relations of property and control that I mention in the text. Truncating the basis, Bender insists the community was not decaying in colonial New England, where specialists find that it was (see, for example, Greven, *Four Generations*; Lockridge, *New England Town*). From my perspective, the community was alive and yet on the decline, because the tradition of collective control survived the principle of private property already established there.

The issue has been a major concern in sociology since Ferdinand Tönnies defined gemeinschaft as opposed to gesellschaft in the late nineteenth century. He derived these terms from his observation of social life in the family and in the city; he inferred the gemeinschaft from the former, blurring a line to be drawn between the community and the family and suggesting the decline of community to be connected with the rise of city. Tönnies was aware that the declining community was part of larger social transformation, particularly capitalist development (see his *Community and Society* , 42–43, 57–62, 64 ff.). But he was mainly interested in the universal theory of social life and human nature, not in the specific forms in which his concepts appeared in history. After Tönnies, there was a tradition formed in social sciences, especially in sociology, that conceives of the city as the center of gesellschaft, with all its negative implications for intimate social life, and as the predator of gemeinschaft (Simmel, "Metropolis and Mental Life," *Sociology of Georg Simmel*, 409–424; Park et al., *City*; Wirth, "Urbanism as a Way of Life"). This tradition has continued to seek the prototype of gemeinschaft in the family. There are variations, which, following Tönnies's conceptualization, have failed to formulate a proper concept of community on its own material basis (Nisbet, *Quest for Community*; Janowitz, *Community Press in an Urban Setting*; Suttles, *Social Construction of Communities*).

Historians, who like Bender are often more interested in conceptual tools to borrow from social sciences than theoretical implications of their findings, have also failed to shed the defective framework that analogizes communal life to the family. Recently, however, some have paid attention to the basis of community, reconsidering the concept in historical perspective. See Calhoun, "Community" and "History, Anthropology and the Study of Communities"; Smith, "'Modernization' and the Corporate Medieval Village Community"; Theibault, "Community and *Herrschaft*." See also Macfarlane, "History, Anthropology and the Study of Communities."

17. Blum, *End of the Old Order*, 383–393; Pounds, *Historical Geography*, 197–223.

18. Berend and Ránki, *Economic Development in East-Central Europe*, 18–19; Kieniewicz, *Polish Peasantry*, 180–182, 203–205, 221–226; Pilch, "Migrations of the Galician Populace"; Stankiewicz, "Emigration from the Kingdom of Poland"; Woolf, *History of Italy*, 275–283.

19. Trebilcock, *Industrialization of the Continental Powers*, chs. 4–5, 205–384; Rudolph, *Banking and Industrialization in Austria-Hungary*, 40–63; Berend and Ránki, *Economic Development in East-Central Europe*, 132; Kieniewicz, *Polish Peasantry*, 190–192; Woolf, *History of Italy*, 275–283; and Mack Smith, *Modern Sicily*, 469–473.

20. Gabaccia, *Militants and Migrants*, 8–11. The quotation is from 10.

21. Davies, *God's Playground*, II: 185–192; Wandycz, *Lands of Partitioned Poland*, 197–201. For social life in the Polish village, see Pacyga, *Polish Immigrants*, 111–125.

22. Pounds, *Historical Geography*, 223–227.

23. Balch, *Slavic Fellow Citizens*, 39–42. The quotation is from 39.

24. Bell, *Fate and Honor*, 127.

25. Ibid.

26. Banfield, *Moral Basis*, 85.

27. Ibid., 7–10. Recently Virginia Yans-McLaughlin has accepted this view. See her *Family and Community*, 61–62, 109.

28. Bell, *Fate and Honor*, 73. See also Gabaccia, "Neither Padrone Slaves nor Primitive Rebels" and *From Sicily to Elizabeth Street*, 4–5; Briggs, *Italian Passage*, 15–16.

29. Gierke, *Community*, 96–104, 124–133, 241–243; Blum, "European Village." See also Bloch, *Feudal Society*; Duby, *European Economy*; Herlihy, *Medieval Households*.

30. Blum, "European Village," 164–166. See also Davis, *Society and Culture*, ch. 4, 97–123; Thompson, *Customs in Common*, especially ch. 8, 467–538.

31. Weinryb, *Jews of Poland*, 71–78.

32. Baron, *Russian Jew*, 21–25, 35–38; Levitats, *Jewish Community*, 25–40.

33. Levitats, *Jewish Community*, 18–19, 105–121; Baron, *Russian Jew*, 52–56, 67–70, 135–145; Rischin, *Promised City*, 37–38.

34. Zborowski and Herzog, *Life Is With People*, pt. 3, chs. 1–2, 191–238; Sorin, *Time for Building*, 12–25.

35. Kuznets, "Immigration of Russian Jews," 116–117; Mendelsohn, *Class Struggle in the Pale*, chs. 1, 3 and 5, 1–26, 45–62, 82–115; Rischin, *Promised City*, 24.

36. Mayer and Wade, *Chicago*, chs. 3–4, 117–282; Pacyga, "Chicago's Ethnic Neighborhoods." For social geography of Chicago in the late nineteenth century, see also Einhorn, *Property Rules*; Jaher, *Urban Establishment*, ch. 5, 453–575; Keating, *Building Chicago*; McCarthy, *Noblesse Oblige*; Sennett, *Families against the City*.

37. Philpott, *Slum and the Ghetto*, 22–41, 66–69, 130–139.

38. McCarthy, "Bohemians in Chicago," 15–24; Horak, "Czechs in Chicago," 22–29; Auten, "Sweating System."

39. Wirth, *Ghetto*, chs. 9–12, 153–261; Mazur, "Jewish Chicago"; Cutler, "Jews of Chicago"; Auten, "Sweating System," 611–612.

40. Kantowicz, *Polish-American Politics*, 14–22 and "Polish Chicago"; Auten, "Sweating System," 612–613. See also Pacyga, *Polish Immigrants*, 126–157.

41. Nelli, *Italians in Chicago*, 22–40; Candeloro, "Chicago's Italians"; Auten, "Sweating System," 607.

42. Spencer, interview, 21–22.

43. Quoted from Horak, "Czechs in Chicago," 56–57.

44. Bertha Adamik, interview by Nancy Skiersch, CPA, box 1 side 1, 1–2; side 4, 26–27.

45. Alfred Fantozzi, interview by Anthony Mansueto, ICP, box 12 folder 75, 13.

46. For the racial context of national consciousness developing among immigrant groups, see the rapidly expanding literature on whiteness. Particularly relevant to my conception are the following: Eric Arnesen, "Up from Exclusion"; Barrett and Roediger, "Inbetween Peoples"; Glickman, "'American Standard of Living'"; Ignatiev, *How the Irish Became White*; Jacobson, *Whiteness of a Different Color*; Orsi, "Religious Boundaries"; Roediger, *Wages of Whiteness* and *Abolition of Whiteness*; Towers, "Projecting Whiteness." See also Conzen et al., "Invention of Ethnicity"; Gans, "Comment"; Sollors, ed., *Invention of Ethnicity.*

47. *Daily Jewish Courier*, 14 Feb. 1922, Press Survey, reel 32. See also ibid., 18 Jan. 1924, Press Survey, reel 38.

48. Ibid., 6 Oct. 1920, Press Survey, reel 38. See also ibid., 13 Jan. 1920, Press Survey, reel 38.

49. Ibid., 7 Mar. 1923, Press Survey, reel 38.

50. In addition to Yans-McLaughlin, *Family and Community*; Briggs, *Italian Passage*; Gabaccia, *From Sicily to Elizabeth Street*, see Barton, *Peasants and Strangers*; Kessner, *Golden Door*; Ewen, *Immigrant Women*; Smith, *Family Connections*; Nugent, *Crossings*. For insightful reviews of immigration historiography, see Higham, "Process to Structure"; Matthews, "Paradigm Changes"; Morawska, "Sociology and Historiography of Immigration."

51. Bodnar, *Transplanted*, 115. See ibid., especially ch. 1, 1–56.

52. Rodgers, "Tradition"; Morawska, *For Bread with Butter*, especially chs. 1, 2, and 4, 22–78, 112–156.

53. Russell A. Kazal has rightly stressed that in conceiving assimilation historians ought to pay attention to the host society. See Kazal, "Revisiting Assimilation."

54. Samuel, *Theatres of Memory*, vol. 1: *Past and Present*, especially 3–47, 288–312, 429–477. See also Hobsbawm and Ranger, eds., *Invention of Tradition.*

55. While this term is borrowed from Immanuel Wallerstein, the center and the margin of capitalism are here used as a geographical concept, not as an economic one like his core or periphery. For Wallerstein's terms, see his *Modern World-System I*, 15–16, 100–103, 116–117, 347–357.

56. Wolf, *People Without History*, 353.

57. Braudel, *Civilization and Capitalism*, vol. 1 *Structure of Everyday Life.*

58. Reddy, *Rise of Market Culture.*

59. Ryan, *Cradle of the Middle Class*. The quotation is from 234.

60. For Sicily, see Gabaccia, *Militants and Migrants*, 20–25.

61. *Dziennik Chicagoski*, 22 July 1892, Press Survey, reel 49.

62. *Daily Jewish Courier*, 23 Dec. 1918, Press Survey, reel 32.

63. Lynd and Lynd, *Middletown*, 21, 45, 49, 52, 80–84, 153–178. See also Fox, "Epitaph for Middletown."

64. In addition to the studies cited in note 34, see *Daily Jewish Courier*, 4 May 1913, 20 Mar. 1914, Press Survey, reel 36.

65. I borrow the term cash nexus from Marx, though his English translators usually prefer "the money relationship" as Ben Fowkes does in *Capital*, I: 1025.

66. Smith, *Family Connections*, 132–143.

67. Jacub Horak, "Foreign Benefit Societies in Chicago," Illinois, Health Insurance Commission, *Report*, 1919, 523–531.

68. *Narod Polski*, 22 Oct. 1913, Press Survey, reel 55; Capek, *Czechs in America*, 254; Robinson, "Helping Each Other!"; Wytrwal, *America's Polish Heritage*, 156–157.

69. Schiavo, *Italians in Chicago*, 57. Humbert S. Nelli, discussing the number of Chicago's Italian mutual aid societies around World War I, believes an estimate of 160 groups to be "more reasonable" (see *Italians in Chicago*, 173). Except that the estimate was made by an officer of the *Unione Siciliana*, an Italian fraternal order, however, Nelli gives no conclusive evidence about the number. In fact, the number was rapidly changing especially during the period, with many societies created, disbanded, or consolidated with others.

70. *La Tribuna Italiana*, 20 Nov. 1907; *L'Italia*, 16 Feb. 1913, both in Press Survey, reel 30. See also Clawson, *Constructing Brotherhood*, ch. 3, 87–110.

71. *Denni Hlasatel*, 20 June 1911, 4 Sept. 1911, Press Survey, reel 5. See also ibid., 27 May 1912, Press Survey, reel 5.

72. *Dziennik Chicagoski*, 12 Nov. 1892, Press Survey, reel 54.

73. *Dziennik Zwiazkowy*, 23 Oct. 1910, reel 54; *Daily World*, 29 July 1918, reel 38, both in Press Survey. See also *Dziennik Zwiazkowy*, 12 Jan. 1918, Press Survey, reel 54.

74. *Daily Jewish Courier*, 4 May 1913, 20 Mar. 1914, Press Survey, reel 36.

75. Italo-American National Union *Bulletin*, Mar. 1927, Press Survey, reel 30.

76. *Dziennik Zwiazkowy*, 1 Feb. 1908, Press Survey, reel 55.

77. Horak, "Czechs in Chicago," 72; *Dziennik Chicagoski*, 17 Aug. 1896, Press Survey, reel 54; *L'Italia*, 15 Mar. 1913, Press Survey, reel 30. See also *Dziennik Zwiazkowy*, 30 Sept. 1910, Press Survey, reel 49.

78. *Dziennik Chicagoski*, 10 June 1891, 11 June 1891, 2 Aug. 1892, 5 Aug. 1892, 19 Aug. 1892, 23 Aug. 1892, 18 Sept. 1892, 19 Sept. 1892, 12 Oct. 1892, 21 May 1895, 29 Nov. 1895, 4 Jan. 1897, 25 May 1908, reel 54; *L'Italia*, 3–4 July 1897, reel 30, all in Press Survey.

79. *Sunday Jewish Courier*, 2 Apr. 1922; *Daily Jewish Courier*, 7 May 1922, both in Press Survey, reel 36.

80. *Dziennik Chicagoski*, 22 July 1896, reel 54; *L'Italia*, 17 Mar. 1894, reel 30, both in Press Survey.

81. Schiavo, *Italians in Chicago*, 55.

82. Horak, "Foreign Benefit Societies," 526.

83. Horak, "Czechs in Chicago," 65–66.

84. Vecoli, "*Contadini* in Chicago."

85. Handlin, *Uprooted*, 173–174.

86. Thomas and Znaniecki, *Polish Peasantry*, II: 263.

87. Handlin, *Uprooted*, 173–174.

88. Bodnar, *Transplanted*, 120–130. See also Bodnar, "Ethnic Fraternal Benefit Associations."

89. *Dziennik Zwiazkowy*, 5 Dec. 1910, Press Survey, reel 54.

90. McCarthy, "Bohemians in Chicago," 41.

91. Adamik, interview, side 4, 26.

92. *Denni Hlasatel*, 7 July 1918, Press Survey, reel 5.

93. *Narod Polski*, 15 Jan. 1913, Press Survey, reel 49.

94. Horak, "Foreign Benefit Societies," 527–529.

95. Ibid., 526–527.

96. See Table 18 in Ernest W. Burgess, "A Study of Wage-Earning Families in Chicago," Illinois, Health Insurance Commission, *Report*, 1919, 228.

97. *Denni Hlasatel*, 23 Mar. 1914, reel 5; *Daily Jewish Courier*, 2 Dec. 1914, reel 36, both in Press Survey.

98. *Denni Hlasatel*, 23 Mar. 1914, Press Survey, reel 5.

99. Ibid.

100. *Svornost*, 25 Oct. 1883, Press Survey, reel 5.

101. *Denni Hlasatel*, 23 Mar. 1914, Press Survey, reel 5.

102. Stalson, *Marketing Life Insurance*, 816–817.

103. Quoted from Keller, *Life Insurance Enterprise*, 71.

104. Maria Valiani, interview by Anthony Mansueto, ICP, box 13 folder 81, 30–31.

105. *Sunday Jewish Courier*, 2 Apr. 1922, Press Survey, reel 36.

106. Ibid.

107. *Denni Hlasatel*, 23 Mar. 1914, Press Survey, reel 5.

108. *Dziennik Zwiazkowy*, 7 Dec. 1910, Press Survey, reel 54.

109. Ben Shloime, "The History of B'nai Moishe," *B'nai Moishe Alexandrovsky Benevolent Aid Society, 1909–1934* (no publication data), 11–13.

110. Katznelson, *City Trenches*.

CHAPTER 2. FROM THE SWEATSHOP TO THE FACTORY

1. For an overall view of the men's clothing industry, see Fraser, "Combined and Uneven Development"; Cobrin, *Men's Clothing Industry*; Seidman, *Needle Trades*, chs. 1–3, 3–78. For the early development, see Willett, *Women in the Clothing Trade*; Pope, *Clothing Industry*; and Nystrom, *Economics of Fashion*.

2. Illinois, Bureau of Labor Statistics, *Seventh Biennial Report*, 1893 (hereafter IBLS, *Seventh Biennial Report*), 358.

3. U.S. Congress, House, *Report of the Committee on Manufactures on the Sweating System*, H. Rept. 2309, 52d Cong., 2d sess., 1893 (hereafter *Report on the Sweating System*), VI.

4. Nelson, *Managers and Workers*, 36–38.

5. *Woman and Child Wage-Earners*, II: 504–505. For a broad overview of nineteenth-century Chicago, see Cronon, *Nature's Metropolis*.

6. Abraham Hart, "The 50 Years of Hart Schaffner & Marx" (1937), no pages, HSM Papers; Hart, *Pleasure Is Mine*, 117–119.

7. Andreas, *History of Chicago*, III: 722.

8. Pierce, *History of Chicago*, III: 172–173.

9. *Woman and Child Wage-Earners*, II: 487.

10. Stansell, *City of Women*, 105–119; Browning, "Clothing and Furnishing Trade."

11. Mayer and Wade, *Chicago*, 54.

12. *Woman and Child Wage-Earners*, II: 486–487. For the family system in Philadelphia, see Passero, "Ethnicity in the Men's Ready-Made Clothing Industry," 139–141, 254–255.

13. Pope, *Clothing Industry*, 18–19.

14. Hounshell, *American System to Mass Production*, 89.

15. *Woman and Child Wage-Earners*, II: 416.

16. Pierce, *History of Chicago*, III: 173.

17. *Woman and Child Wage-Earners*, II: 486, 489–490.

18. IBLS, *Seventh Biennial Report*, 368.

19. Wilentz, *Chants Democratic*, 108–124.

20. IBLS, *Seventh Biennial Report*, 362–363, 403. David Montgomery claims that manufacturers had already applied that form of division of labor in the inside shop before the 1880s and that contractors furthered the trend during the decade (*Fall of the House of Labor*, 116–123). This was true in the production of work clothes, which required fewer complicated skills than any other men's outer garments. But the making of suits, overcoats, and topcoats was a highly skilled job, barely divided up in the inside shop before the decade. In 1896, for example, Henry White, general secretary of the United Garment Workers, noted: "[C]heap clothing is generally manufactured on a large scale so that the work can be systematically divided into many divisions . . . but the well-made garments require the long, continuous, and careful work that the workers at home or in small shops can give" (Henry White, "The Sweating System," U.S. Department of Labor, *Bulletin*, no. 4 [May 1896], H. Doc. 33, pt. 4, 54th Cong., 1st sess., 1896, 360–379. The quotation is from 364).

21. White, "Sweating System," 369–370; *Report on the Sweating System*, 74–75, 93–94.

22. U.S. Department of the Interior, Census Office, *Report on the Manufactures of the United States at the Tenth Census (June 1, 1880): General Statistics*, 1883, 392; U.S. Department of the Interior, Census Office, *Report on Manufacturing Industries in the United States at the Eleventh Census: 1890*, Pt. 2: *Statistics of Cities*, 1895, 134–137.

23. Cobrin, *Men's Clothing Industry*, 56.

24. *Report on the Sweating System*, 74–75, 79–83.

25. IBLS, *Seventh Biennial Report*, 366–368.

26. *Report on the Sweating System*, VI. The relationship between contractors and subcontractors is described on the basis of the arguments that Steven Fraser formulates in explaining the unequal but symbiotic relationship between manufacturers and contractors. See his "Combined and Uneven Development."

27. IBLS, *Seventh Biennial Report*, 380–382.

28. Ibid., 367.

29. Ibid., 361–362.

30. Ibid., 371–372, 376–378.
31. Mayer and Wade, *Chicago*, 152–154.
32. *Report on the Sweating System*, VI.
33. Ibid., 71–72; IBLS, *Seventh Biennial Report*, 419–432.
34. IBLS, *Seventh Biennial Report*, 364.
35. U.S. Industrial Commission, *Reports*, vol. 15: *Immigration and Education*, 1901 (hereafter *Immigration and Education*), 321.
36. IBLS, *Seventh Biennial Report*, 365.
37. Ibid., 363, 366, 376.
38. Ibid., 374.
39. Ibid., 383–385.
40. The term *concentrator* is used to distinguish sweatshop workers doing relatively skilled jobs from unskilled or semi-skilled specialists working in the factory. In the sweatshop where the division of labor was simple, most workers retained or acquired considerable artisanal skill because each of them had to perform several operations, including some that required a high degree of technical knowledge and dexterity. On the other hand, factory operatives specialized in only one operation among between forty and more than one hundred. They did not need to be skilled, as the labor process was minutely subdivided in the factory from the 1890s.
41. Cooper, *Once a Cigar Maker*, 11, 169, 225–228.
42. *Immigration and Education*, 345–348.
43. IBLS, *Seventh Biennial Report*, 393. A study by the U.S. Labor Commissioner incorrectly noted that "[t]he task system has always been confined to New York. . . ." See U.S. Congress, House, *Eleventh Special Report of the Commissioner of Labor: Regulation and Restriction of Output*, H. Doc. 734, 58th Cong., 2d sess., 1904 (hereafter *Regulation and Restriction of Output*), 548.
44. IBLS, *Seventh Biennial Report*, 386.
45. Ibid., 384.
46. Ibid., 388.
47. Ibid., 395.
48. *Report on the Sweating System*, 92–93. See also IBLS, *Seventh Biennial Report*, ix–x, 68–70, 86–87.
49. IBLS, *Seventh Biennial Report*, 393.
50. Rischin, *Promised City*, 182–183; Glenn, *Daughters of the Shtetl*, 133–138.
51. IBLS, *Seventh Biennial Report*, 366.
52. Ibid., 381. For ethnic conformity in Philadelphia's sweatshops, see Passero, "Ethnicity in the Men's Ready-Made Clothing Industry," 190–192.
53. Glenn, *Daughters of the Shtetl*, 134–135.
54. Compiling smallpox cases found in Chicago's sweatshop districts in 1894, Illinois factory inspectors stressed: "In considering the juxtaposition of the cases and the shops, it should be borne in mind that the employees ordinarily live on the same premises, or next door, or in the same block, and always within walking distance. . . ." (Illinois, Factory Inspectors, *First Special Report on Small-Pox in the Tenement House Sweat-Shops of Chicago*, 1894 [hereafter *Special Report on Small-Pox*], 43). For the neighborhood location of clothing shops

in Philadelphia, see Passero, "Ethnicity in the Men's Ready-Made Clothing Industry," 193–195.

55. IBLS, *Seventh Biennial Report*, 373; *Report on the Sweating System*, 91; and Glenn, *Daughters of the Shtetl*, 134–135.

56. *Report on the Sweating System*, 90.

57. Ibid., 220–221.

58. IBLS, *Seventh Biennial Report*, 398.

59. Carsel, *Chicago Ladies' Garment Workers' Union*, xix–xx, 19–21.

60. IBLS, *Seventh Biennial Report*, 384–386.

61. *Woman and Child Wage-Earners*, II: 431.

62. Cobrin, *Men's Clothing Industry*, 46.

63. Myers, "Production of Men's Clothing," 22–23; Cobrin, *Men's Clothing Industry*, 152–153.

64. *Report on the Sweating System*, 85. For the urban middle classes in the late nineteenth century, see Blumin, *Emergence of the Middle Class*, ch. 8, 285–297.

65. *Report on the Sweating System*, 82–83, 85–87.

66. Ibid., XX.

67. *Chicago Times*, 29 July 1888, 1.

68. Ibid., 4 August 1888, 2; 5 August 1888, 17.

69. Chicago Trade and Labor Assembly, "The New Slavery. Investigation into the Sweating System as Applied to the Manufacture of Wearing Apparel" (Chicago: Detwiler, 1891), Thomas J. Morgan Papers.

70. IBLS, *Seventh Biennial Report*, 358.

71. For Kelley's role in the campaign, see Waugh, "Florence Kelley."

72. *Report on the Sweating System*, III–IV, 261–266.

73. Hart, "50 Years"; (Hartmarx), "The Hartmarx and Hart Schaffner & Marx Centennial Celebration" (1987), no pages; Max A. Hart, interview by author.

74. Photocopied in (Hartmarx), "Centennial Celebration."

75. Ibid.

76. *Special Report on Small-Pox*, 8.

77. Myers, "Production of Men's Clothing," 24; *Woman and Child Wage-Earners*, II: 509–510.

78. *Report on the Sweating System*, 9–10.

79. (Hartmarx), "Centennial Celebration."

80. *Woman and Child Wage-Earners*, II: 418.

81. Ibid., 419. For inside contracting in other major industries, see Englander, "Inside Contract System."

82. Illinois, Factory Inspectors, *Second Annual Report*, 1895, 48–52.

83. Illinois, Factory Inspectors, *Eighth Annual Report*, 1901, 57 ff.

84. *Woman and Child Wage-Earners*, II: 418.

85. For example, see Fraser, "Combined and Uneven Development," 537–539. David Montgomery claims that workers' pressures for wage increases and their opposition to contracting contributed to the development of the factory system in the clothing industry (*Fall of the House of Labor*, 120–123). There is substantial evidence that workers demanded that the manufacturers should

establish and directly run their own factories. But it is still dubious whether manufacturers actually took the demand into consideration in establishing the modern clothing factory. And at the end of the busy season they almost always wiped out the wage increases they had been forced to give at its beginning.

86. U.S. Department of Commerce, Bureau of Foreign and Domestic Commerce, *The Men's Factory-Made Clothing Industry: Report on the Cost of Production of Men's Factory-Made Clothing in the United States*, Miscellaneous Series no. 34, 1916 (hereafter *Men's Factory-Made Clothing Industry*), 19.

87. While the women numbered only 502 and the children fifty-one, there were 1,098 men in the inside shops of the seven firms (Ederheimer, Stein and Co.; Hart, Schaffner and Marx; Kohn Bros.; Kuh, Nathan and Fischer; B. Kuppenheimer and Co.; Royal Tailors; and Strouss, Eisendrath and Co.). See Illinois, Factory Inspectors, *Eighth Annual Report*, 1901, 57 ff.

88. *Report on the Sweating System*, 84–85.

89. *Regulation and Restriction of Output*, 543, 548.

90. *Macullar, Parker and Company*, 21.

91. Popkin, *Manufacture of Men's Clothing*, 249–274.

92. *Woman and Child Wage-Earners*, II: 445–476.

93. *Immigration and Education*, 348–351.

94. *Woman and Child Wage-Earners*, II: 426.

95. Ibid., 494, 510; *Regulation and Restriction of Output*, 537–538.

96. *Men's Factory-Made Clothing Industry*, 180.

97. Popkin, *Manufacture of Men's Clothing*, 394–399.

98. *Regulation and Restriction of Output*, 547.

99. Ibid., 177.

100. Fraser, "Combined and Uneven Development," 537.

101. Willett, *Women in the Clothing Trade*, 39.

102. *Immigration and Education*, 348.

103. Fraser, "Combined and Uneven Development," especially 528–541.

104. *Census of Manufactures: 1914*, II: 174.

105. *Chicago Examiner*, 16 May 1908; *Chicago Tribune*, 13 August 1909, both in newspaper scrapbooks, HSM Papers.

106. Passero, "Ethnicity in the Men's Ready-Made Clothing Industry," 193–198.

107. *Woman and Child Wage-Earners*, II: 321–343. For immigrant workers' experience of modernity at the clothing factory, see Glenn, *Daughters of the Shtetl*, especially 137–139.

108. *Woman and Child Wage-Earners*, II: 18–19, 33–43.

109. *Men's Factory-Made Clothing Industry*, 161.

110. Joseph Schaffner, testimony, U.S. Commission on Industrial Relations, *Final Report and Testimony*, 11 vols., S. Doc. 415, 64th Cong., 1st sess., 1916 (hereafter Industrial Relations Commission, *Final Report*), I: 564–566.

111. *Men's Factory-Made Clothing Industry*, 166.

112. IBLS, *Seventh Biennial Report*, 393.

113. For work discipline at the clothing factory in general, see Glenn, *Daughters of the Shtetl*, 151–153.

114. *Woman and Child Wage-Earners*, II: 439–440.

115. Earl Dean Howard, testimony, Industrial Relations Commission, *Final Report*, I: 571–574, 592–594.

116. Jacob S. Potofsky, "The Reminiscences of *Jacob Samuel Potofsky*," NYTP, Pt. 2, No. 151, 23.

117. Women's Trade Union League of Chicago, "Statement on the Strike of the 35,000 Unorganized Garment Workers of Chicago," (1910) (hereafter "Statement"), WTUL Papers, reel 9.

118. Stone, "Origins of Job Structures."

119. *Woman and Child Wage-Earners*, II: 480.

120. Albert Wadopian, interview by author; *Woman and Child Wage-Earners*, II: 477, 479.

121. Illinois, General Assembly, Senate, *Report of the Illinois Senate Vice Committee*, 49th General Assembly, 1913, 417.

122. Potofsky, "Reminiscences," 22.

123. *Men's Factory-Made Clothing Industry*, 19.

124. Wadopian, interview.

125. *Woman and Child Wage-Earners*, II: 462. See also Glenn, *Daughters of the Shtetl*, 105–106.

126. Potofsky, "Reminiscences," 20.

127. Glenn, *Daughters of the Shtetl*, 150–154.

128. Ibid., 143–148. See also Argersinger, *Making the Amalgamated*, 86–90.

129. *Woman and Child Wage-Earners*, II: 476–480. See also Glenn, *Daughters of the Shtetl*, 151.

130. *Regulation and Restriction of Output*, 538–539, 549.

131. Ibid., 549.

132. Glenn, *Daughters of the Shtetl*, 150.

133. Ibid., 266–267.

134. Meyer, *Five Dollar Day*, 9–36.

135. Braverman, *Labor and Monopoly Capital.*

136. Taylor, *Scientific Management*, 94–109; Nelson, *Taylor and the Rise of Scientific Management*, 38–41, 76–85; Montgomery, *Fall of the House of Labor*, 221–225.

137. Price, "Labour Process and Labour History." The quotation is from 62. See also his "Conflict and Co-operation" and "Theories of Labour Process Transformation." Cf. Joyce, "Labour, Capital and Compromise" and "Languages of Reciprocity and Conflict."

138. Edwards, *Contested Terrain.*

CHAPTER 3. THE 1910–1911 STRIKE

1. Anna (Hannah) Shapiro, testimony, Illinois, General Assembly, Senate, Special Committee to Investigate the Garment Workers' Strike, Proceedings, 3 vols., 47th General Assembly, 1911, Illinois State Archives, Springfield, Illinois (hereafter Proceedings), II: 242–272. Cf. Sive-Tomashefsky, "Identifying a Lost Leader."

2. Proceedings, II: 252.

3. *Chicago Daily Socialist*, 10 Oct. 1910, 11 Oct. 1910. Cf. Robert Dvorak, "The Fighting Garment Workers," *International Socialist Review* 11, 7 (Jan. 1911): 385–393.

4. *Chicago Daily Socialist*, 24 Oct. 1910, 25 Oct. 1910, 27 Oct. 1910.

5. In addition to the essay cited in note 1, see Buhle, "Socialist Women and the 'Girl Strikers'"; Weiler, "Walkout"; Fraser, *Labor Will Rule*, ch. 3, 40–76.

6. Stonewell, "Journeymen Tailors' Union"; Myers, "Policing of Labor Disputes," 654–656.

7. Cobrin, *Men's Clothing Industry*, 88; Myers, "Policing of Labor Disputes," 656–657; Thomas A. Rickert, testimony, Proceedings, III: 25–32, 1–41 (pagination inconsistent). The Illinois Senate Special Committee devoted its attention almost exclusively to blacklisting. See especially testimony by George H. Alexander, Martin J. Isaacs, and Henry B. Tobias, all in Proceedings.

8. Seidman, *Needle Trades*, 82–90; Zaretz, *Amalgamated Clothing Workers*, 77–85. For recent discussions about union nativism, see Asher, "Union Nativism"; Barrett and Roediger, "Inbetween Peoples."

9. Proceedings, III: 25 of the second section.

10. *Chicago Tribune*, 14 Oct. 1910.

11. "Statement," 3. (Italics in the text) See also ibid., 6–8, 11–12, 16; Robert Dvorak, "The Chicago Garment Workers," *International Socialist Review* 11, 6 (Dec. 1910): 353–359.

12. *Chicago Tribune*, 6 Nov. 1910. See also *Survey*, 19 Nov. 1910, 273–275.

13. "Statement," 19.

14. Dvorak, "Chicago Garment Workers," 355; *Chicago Daily Socialist*, 25 Oct. 1910.

15. "Statement," 3–4, 13; Dvorak, "Chicago Garment Workers," 356.

16. Spencer, interview, 26–27.

17. "Statement," 11–12.

18. *Chicago Daily Socialist*, 12 Oct. 1910.

19. See strikers' demands printed in ibid., 21 Oct. 1910.

20. For example, see ibid., 12 Oct. 1910, 20 Oct. 1910, 22 Oct. 1910.

21. The quotations are from Potofsky, "Reminiscences," 24–26.

22. *Chicago Daily Socialist*, 17 Oct. 1910.

23. Ibid., 19 Oct. 1910; *Chicago Tribune*, 18 Oct. 1910.

24. *Chicago Daily Socialist*, 19 Oct. 1910.

25. *Chicago Tribune*, 19 Oct. 1910.

26. Ibid., 26 Oct. 1910.

27. Myers, "Policing of Labor Disputes," 701–725.

28. Women's Trade Union League of Chicago, "Official Report of the Strike Committee. Chicago Garment Workers' Strike, October 29, 1910–February 18, 1911," WTUL Papers, reel 131 (hereafter "Official Report"), 9.

29. *Chicago Daily Socialist*, 24 Oct. 1910, 25 Oct. 1910, 27 Oct. 1910.

30. Robert Dvorak, "The Garment Workers' Strike Lost: Who Was To Blame?" *International Socialist Review* 11, 9 (Mar. 1911): 550–556.

31. *Chicago Daily Socialist*, 28 Oct. 1910.

32. Ibid., 18 Oct. 1910, 19 Oct. 1910, 27 Oct. 1910; *Chicago Tribune*, 25 Oct. 1910.

33. *Chicago Daily Socialist*, 29 Oct. 1910.

34. "Statement," 14.

35. See pp. 23–25 in the text. See also Myers, "Production of Men's Clothing," 219.

36. *Chicago Tribune*, 1 Nov. 1910.

37. Ibid., 3 Nov. 1910.

38. *Chicago Daily Socialist*, 2 Nov. 1910.

39. *Chicago Tribune*, 17 Oct. 1910.

40. Jo Ann Argersinger has also stressed the conspicuous role played by women garment workers in the 1913 Baltimore strike (*Making the Amalgamated*, 36–39).

Susan Glenn has called attention to the ambitious attitude that Jewish women showed while working at clothing shops (*Daughters of the Shtetl*, 122–131). For the negative effects that marriage and the male-dominated work environment may have had upon women's participation in the labor movement, see Tentler, *Wage-Earning Women*. See also critical views articulated in Kessler-Harris, *Out to Work*, especially 151–171; Benson, *Counter Cultures*.

41. *Chicago Daily Socialist*, 25 Oct. 1910.

42. *Chicago Tribune*, 3 Nov. 1910. See also ibid., 2 Nov. 1910.

43. Schaffner, testimony, Industrial Relations Commission, *Final Report*, I: 564–566.

44. *Chicago Tribune*, 19 Oct. 1910.

45. Ibid., 31 Oct. 1910, 2 Nov. 1910.

46. Ibid., 29 Oct. 1910.

47. Ibid., 3 Nov. 1910.

48. Hart, *Pleasure Is Mine*, 146–147.

49. *Chicago Tribune*, 5 Nov. 1910.

50. *New York Evening Post*, 5 Nov. 1910, newspaper scraps in Jane Addams Papers, reel 53.

51. The quotations are from *Chicago Tribune*, 6 Nov. 1910, pt. 1, 1.

52. Sidney Hillman, testimony, Industrial Relations Commission, *Final Report*, I: 566–571.

53. Unidentified newspaper scrap dated 6 Nov. 1910, Addams Papers, reel 53.

54. *Chicago Tribune*, 7 Nov. 1910, 8 Nov. 1910.

55. All quotations are from ibid., 7 Nov. 1910.

56. *Clothing Workers of Chicago*, 34; "Official Report," 12.

57. *Chicago Tribune*, 12 Nov. 1910.

58. Potofsky, "Reminiscences," 27. See also "Official Report," 13–14.

59. "Official Report," 12–13.

60. *Chicago Tribune*, 10 Nov. 1910.

61. *Chicago Daily Socialist*, 29 Oct. 1910, 31 Oct. 1910, 2 Nov. 1910, 12 Nov. 1910; *Chicago Tribune*, 11 Nov. 1910.

62. *Chicago Daily Socialist*, 2 Nov. 1910, 7 Nov. 1910, 11 Nov. 1910, 19 Nov. 1910, 23 Dec. 1910.

63. *Chicago Tribune*, 15 Nov. 1910.

64. The quotations are from ibid., 21 Nov. 1910.

65. "Official Report," 14–17, 41.

66. Ibid., 30; *Chicago Daily Socialist*, 15 Nov. 1910; Dvorak, "Fighting Garment Workers," 388.

67. "Official Report," 30. See also *Chicago Daily Socialist*, 31 Oct. 1910, 3 Nov. 1910; *Chicago Tribune*, 16 Nov. 1910.

68. "Official Report," 17–18, 20; *Chicago Daily Socialist*, 31 Oct. 1910, 10 Nov. 1910, 14 Dec. 1910, 20 Dec. 1910, 9 Jan. 1911; Dvorak, "Fighting Garment Workers," 387; *Chicago Tribune*, 15 Nov. 1910. See also Glenn, *Daughters of the Shtetl*, 197–206. For neigborhood support to strikers in nineteenth-century cities, see Gutman, *Work, Culture, and Society*, ch. 5, 234–260.

69. *Chicago Tribune*, 14 Nov. 1910. For Robins and her role in this strike, see Payne, *Reform, Labor, and Feminism*, especially 86–91.

70. Dvorak, "Garment Workers' Strike Lost," 556.

71. *Chicago Tribune*, 16 Nov. 1910, 28 Nov. 1910, 29 Nov. 1910, 11 Dec. 1910, pt. 1, 7, 12 Dec. 1910, 4 Jan. 1911, 6 Jan. 1911, 7 Jan. 1911; *Chicago Daily Socialist*, 11 Jan. 1911. Collette A. Hyman examines various aspects of the WTUL activities related to this strike in "Labor Organizing and Female Institution-Building." But she neglects to examine how the strikers felt about the activities, especially fund raising and handling of the second agreement. For a comprehensive description of the league's organizing activities in the clothing industry, see McCreesh, *Women in the Campaign*. For internal developments of the WTUL, see Dye, *As Equals and As Sisters*.

72. "Official Report," 11.

73. *Chicago Tribune*, 18 Nov. 1910, 19 Nov. 1910, 20 Nov. 1910, pt. 1, 5, 26 Nov. 1910, 27 Nov. 1910, pt. 1, 7.

74. Ibid., 29 Nov. 1910, 30 Nov. 1910; "Official Report," 21.

75. *Chicago Tribune*, 1 Dec. 1910, 2 Dec. 1910, 4 Dec. 1910, pt. 1, 1; "Official Report," 21–22.

76. *Chicago Tribune*, 3 Dec. 1910.

77. Ibid., 5 Dec. 1910.

78. *Chicago Daily Socialist*, 6 Dec. 1910.

79. *Chicago Tribune*, 8 Dec. 1910.

80. Valiani, interview, 36–42, 44–48, 56; Alfred Fantozzi, interview by Anthony Mansueto, ICP, box 12 folder 75, 15–20.

81. Levin, *Jewish Socialist Movements*, chs. 1–4, 16–20, 3–62, 250–341; Bregstone, *Chicago and Its Jews*, 59–62; Carsel, *Chicago Ladies' Garment Workers' Union*, 22–35; Glenn, *Daughters of the Shtetl*, 177–186.

82. Hyman Schneid Fiftieth Anniversary Labor Celebration Committee, "We Greet Hyman Schneid," Chicago Joint Board Secretary Files, CJB Papers.

83. Spencer, interview, 26–27.

84. Dvorak, "Garment Workers' Strike Lost," 553. See also Melvyn Dubofsky's exhaustive study of the IWW, *We Shall Be All*.

85. *Chicago Tribune*, 9 Dec. 1910, 11 Dec. 1910, pt. 1, 7; *Chicago Daily Socialist*, 12 Dec. 1910.

86. *Chicago Tribune*, 14 Dec. 1910, 15 Dec. 1910; *Chicago Daily Socialist*, 15 Dec. 1910, 16 Dec. 1910; Nestor, *Women's Labor Leader*, 126–128.

87. *Chicago Daily Socialist*, 16 Dec. 1910. See also *Clothing Workers of Chicago*, 43.

88. *Chicago Daily Socialist*, 31 Oct. 1910.

89. Through newspaper articles the following are identified as the meeting places: Apollo Hall, 12th St. and Blue Island Ave.; Casino Hall, 12th and Union Sts.; Columbia Hall; Hod Carriers' Hall, Harrison and Green Sts.; Kriezek's Hall, Homan Ave. and 25th St.; Metropolitan Hall, Jefferson and O'Brien Sts.; Musicians' Hall, 164 E. Washington St.; National Hall, Center Ave. and 18th St.; Sokol Chicago; UGW headquarters, 275 La Salle St.; Walsh's Hall, Noble and Emma Sts.; West Side Auditorium; Young People's Socialist League Hall, 180 E. Washington St.

90. *Chicago Daily Socialist*, 3 Dec. 1910.

91. Dvorak, "Garment Workers' Strike Lost," 552; Nestor, *Women's Labor Leader*, 127. Mari Jo Buhle sketches various activities by socialist women in her "Socialist Women and the 'Girl Strikers,'" but fails to mention that those affiliated with the WTUL were not always in accord with the workers.

92. *Chicago Tribune*, 16 Dec. 1910, 18 Dec. 1910, pt. 1, 6, 19 Dec. 1910, 21 Dec. 1910, 24 Dec. 1910, 25 Dec. 1910, pt. 1, 3, 28 Dec. 1910, 4 Jan. 1911, 7 Jan. 1911; *Chicago Daily Socialist*, 20 Dec. 1910, 23 Dec. 1910; "Official Report," 20; Dvorak, "Garment Workers' Strike Lost," 556.

93. *Chicago Tribune*, 7 Dec. 1910, 9 Dec. 1910, 10 Dec. 1910; *Survey*, 10 Dec. 1910, 413–416, 17 Dec. 1910, 442–443.

94. *Chicago Tribune*, 20 Dec. 1910.

95. Potofsky, "Reminiscences," 30; *Chicago Tribune*, 31 Dec. 1910; Soule, *Hillman*, 23–25.

96. Dvorak, "Garment Workers' Strike Lost," 554.

97. *Chicago Tribune*, 5 Jan. 1911, 6 Jan. 1911, 8 Jan. 1911, pt. 1, 7.

98. Irving Abrams, interview by Frank Ninkovich, ILHP, book 17, 1–3.

99. *Chicago Tribune*, 11 Jan. 1911, 12 Jan. 1911, 14 Jan. 1911; *Chicago Daily Socialist*, 11 Jan. 1911, 12 Jan. 1911, 13 Jan. 1911; "Official Report," 31–32.

100. *Joseph Schaffner*, 89.

101. Schaffner, testimony, Industrial Relations Commission, *Final Report*, I: 564–566. See also Hart, *Pleasure Is Mine*, 140–143.

102. *Chicago Tribune*, 15 Jan. 1911, pt. 1, 1–2; "Official Report," 32.

103. *Chicago Tribune*, 15 Jan. 1911, pt. 1, 1.

104. Marimpietri, *From These Beginnings*, 14. See also *Chicago Daily Socialist*, 16 Jan. 1911; Dvorak, "Garment Workers' Strike Lost," 554; Nestor, *Women's Labor Leader*, 128–129.

105. *Chicago Tribune*, 19 Jan. 1911.

106. Ibid., 22 Jan. 1911, pt. 1, 7, 25 Jan. 1911, 29 Jan. 1911, pt. 1, 6; *Chicago Daily Socialist*, 31 Jan. 1911.

107. *Chicago Tribune*, 20 Jan. 1911, 21 Jan. 1911, 23 Jan. 1911, 24 Jan. 1911, 27 Jan. 1911, 28 Jan. 1911, 3 Feb. 1911, 4 Feb. 1911.

108. Greene, *Slavic Community on Strike*; Brody, *Steelworkers in America* and *Labor in Crisis*.

109. Tax, *Rising of the Women*, ch. 8, 205–240; Dubofsky, *When Work-*

ers Organize, 42–58; Schofield, "Uprising of the 20,000"; Waldinger, "Another Look at the International Ladies' Garment Workers' Union."

110. It is often assumed that ethnic conflicts affected the course of the 1910–1911 strike. Steven Fraser has recently argued that "[i]ndeed, at the very height of the HSM strike a committee of Italian workers . . . issued 'A Call for Action,' denouncing the pending arbitration agreement with the company, which had been worked out by the mainly Jewish leadership of the strike" ("*Landslayt* and *Paesani*," 280). Although it is not clear whether Fraser refers to the second or third HSM agreement, neither were "worked out by the mainly Jewish leadership of the strike." Such an assumption leads Rebecca Sive-Tomashefsky to write that "ethnic and factional rivalries" prolonged the strike ("Identifying a Lost Leader," 936). But both fail to show evidence to substantiate the assumption.

111. Tax, *Rising of the Women*, ch. 9, 241–275; Dubofsky, *We Shall Be All*, 227–254; Cameron, "Bread and Roses Revisited."

112. Potofsky, "Reminiscences," 44.

113. Quoted in Myers, "Policing of Labor Disputes," 690.

114. Marimpietri, *From These Beginnings*, 14–15.

115. *Chicago Daily Socialist*, 6 Feb. 1911; "Extracts of Minutes of Local 39, January 29, 1911 through March 17, 1914," Anthology of Historical Documents, ACW Papers, box 40 folder 7.

CHAPTER 4. ONE HUNDRED PERCENT ORGANIZATION

1. *Chicago Herald & Examiner*, 14 May 1919, newspaper scrap in ACW Papers, box 322, Red Books, I: 171.

2. *Advance*, 30 May 1919.

3. Ibid.

4. The Decision of the Arbitrators in the Matter of the Arbitration between Hart, Schaffner and Marx and their Employees, "Arrangements for Adjusting Relations between Hart, Schaffner and Marx and their Employees Represented by the Joint Board of Garment Workers" (1914), ACW Papers, box 215 folder 16 (hereafter "Arrangements"), 4–6. The quotation is from 6.

5. The Experience of Hart, Schaffner and Marx with Collective Bargaining, "The Hart Schaffner & Marx Labor Agreement: Industrial Law in the Clothing Industry" (1920), ACW Papers, box 215 folder 16 (hereafter Experience), 64–70. The quotation is from 68.

6. Marimpietri, *From These Beginnings*, 15.

7. Howard, "Cooperation in the Clothing Industry." See also Howard to William Z. Ripley, 25 Jan. 1919, Papers of William Z. Ripley, box 2 folder 1919.

8. Howard, testimony, Industrial Relations Commission, *Final Report*, I: 571–574, 592–594. The quotation is from 571.

9. Ibid., I: 568.

10. Potofsky, "Reminiscences," 96.

11. Abrams, interview, 5–7.

12. Experience, 65.

13. Margaret Robins to Raymond Robins, 9 Mar. 1912, WTUL Papers, reel 53. See also Women's Trade Union League of Chicago, *Biennial Report 1911–1913*, WTUL Papers, reel 131, 10–11; Payne, *Reform, Labor, and Feminism*, 92–95.

14. (Margaret Drier Robins), "Some of the Results of the Hart, Schaffner & Marx Agreement," WTUL Papers, reel 12.

15. Agreement Creating Committee to Establish Trade Board and to Formulate Rules for its Guidance; Report of Committee Establishing Trade Board with Rules of Procedure, both in "Arrangements," 7–14.

16. Potofsky, "Reminiscences," 97.

17. Ibid., 47–48; Minutes of the Joint Board of Hart, Schaffner & Marx Employees, ACW Papers, box 40 folder 9, 5 Feb. 1913, 8 Mar. 1913. See also Josephson, *Hillman*, 74–79.

18. Quoted from Josephson, *Hillman*, 77.

19. John E. Williams to Mark Cresap, 27 July 1913, ACW Papers, box 38 folder 9.

20. Soule, *Hillman*, 42–45; Josephson, *Hillman*, 76–77.

21. Williams to Cresap, 27 July 1913, ACW Papers, box 38 folder 9; Jacob Potofsky, interview by Elizabeth Balanoff, ILHP, book 4, 16.

22. "The Hart Schaffner & Marx Labor Agreement" (1916), ACW Papers, box 215 folder 16, 1–2.

23. Creel, "A Way to Industrial Peace," *Century* (July 1915): 433–440; Commons, "The Labor Court," *Independent*, 5 June 1920, both in ACW Papers, box 322, Red Books, I: 29–32, 42–43.

24. Experience, 68.

25. Potofsky, interview, 12; Potofsky, "Reminiscences," 91–92; Josephson, *Hillman*, 77–78.

26. Experience, 68.

27. Josephson, *Hillman*, 22–37.

28. Ibid., 38–41.

29. Louis D. Brandeis, "Purpose of the Protocol," in *Out of the Sweatshop*, ed. Stein, 121–123. See also Josephson, *Hillman*, 67–71.

30. Fraser, *Labor Will Rule*.

31. Earl D. Howard to Anne Morgan, 2 Mar. 1914, ACW Papers, box 38 folder 9.

32. Frank Rosenblum, interview by Elizabeth Balanoff, ILHP, book 4; Sol Brandzel, interview by author; Biography of Frank Rosenblum, ACW Papers, box 243 folder 6.

33. Samuel Levin to Gladys Dickson, 5 Sept. 1946, ACW Papers, box 242 folder 17; John E. Williams, "(The Immigrant in Industry)," in *John E. Williams: An Appreciation with Selections from His Writings*, ed. Jacob S. Potofsky (Chicago: Chicago Joint Board, Amalgamated Clothing Workers of America, no date), ACW Papers, box 38 folder 16, 45–48.

34. *New York Times*, 24 Dec. 1970, 24; "Anzuino D. Marimpietri Biographical Data," ACW Papers, box 242 folder 18.

35. The quotations are from Potofsky, "Reminiscences," 34–40.

36. Potofsky's memorandum dated 29 Jan. 1915, ACW Papers, box 172 folder 2 (punctuation added).

37. Potofsky, "What a Difference" (no date), ACW Papers, box 172 folder 2; Potofsky, "Reminiscences," 112–113; *Documentary History*, 1916–1918, 10–11, 163–165.

38. Potofsky's memorandum dated 22 Sept. 1917, ACW Papers, box 172 folder 2.

39. Potofsky's memorandum with no date, ACW Papers, box 172 folder 5.

40. Potofsky, "Class Struggle" (no date), ACW Papers, box 172 folder 4.

41. Soffer, "Trade Union Development."

42. For a general discussion, see Kessler-Harris, "Where Are the Organized Women Workers?"

43. John E. Williams, "The Fancies of Fabius," *Streator (Illinois) Independent-Times*, 5 Feb. 1916; Industrial Relations Commission, *Final Report*, I: 571.

44. The Case of the United Garment Workers of America, reprinted in *Documentary History*, 1914–1916, 33–40; Zaretz, *Amalgamated Clothing Workers*, 85–90, 93–96; Josephson, *Hillman*, 90–92; Soule, *Hillman*, 62–64; Schlossberg, *Rise of the Clothing Workers*, 26–27.

45. Chicago Delegates Conference to New York Delegates Convention Conference, 1 Sept. 1914, ACW Papers, box 322, Red Books, I: 104.

46. Soule, *Hillman*, 64–66; *Documentary History*, 1914–1916, 7–8.

47. Marimpietri to Joseph Schlossberg, 22 Oct. 1914, box 13 folder 15; Potofsky to Sidney Hillman, 31 Oct. 1914, box 21 folder 14; Edward Anderson to Schlossberg, 9 Nov. 1914, box 8 folder 12; Marimpietri to Isidor Kantrowitz, 11 Nov. 1914, box 38 folder 9; Marimpietri to Hillman, box 3 folder 42; Frank Rosenblum to Schlossberg, 18 Nov. 1914, box 15 folder 9; Levin to Schlossberg, 18 Nov. 1914, box 12 folder 14; Joseph Cillo to Schlossberg, 20 Nov. 1914, box 9 folder 28; Bessie Abramovitz to Hillman, 20 Nov. 1914, box 1 folder 2, all in ACW Papers. See also *Documentary History*, 1914–1916, 43–44.

48. The Constitution of the Amalgamated Clothing Workers of America, ACW Papers, box 208 folder 4.

49. "Report of the GEB," *Documentary History*, 1914–1916, 127–191. The quotations are from 140.

50. For a general discussion, see Asher, "Union Nativism."

51. Marimpietri to Schlossberg, 25 Feb. 1915, ACW Papers, box 13 folder 15. See also Marimpietri to Schlossberg, 15 Feb. 1915, box 13 folder 15; Hillman to Eugene J. Brais, 12 Mar. 1915, box 36 folder 24, both in ACW Papers.

52. The Journeymen Tailors' Union soon broke away from the ACW, not only under the pressure of the antisecessionist Samuel Gompers but also because of jurisdictional disagreements in the special-order branch. See Eugene J. Brais Correspondence, particularly letters sent to and received from Thomas Sweeney, ACW Papers, boxes 36 and 37.

53. Hillman to Brais, 5 Mar. 1915, 8 Mar. 1915, 16 Mar. 1915, 24 Mar. 1915, box 36 folder 24; Rosenblum to Brais, 9 Mar. 1915, box 36 folder 49; Brais to Hillman, 10 Mar. 1915, 22 Mar. 1915, box 1 folder 31; Stephen Skala, "Story of the Great Organizing Campaign in Chicago, 1915–1919" (undated manuscript, which is printed in the *Advance* in May to June 1922), box 38

folder 12 (hereafter Skala, "Story"), 4–5, all in ACW Papers.

54. Abramovitz to Hillman, 13 Apr. 1915, box 1 folder 2; Levin to Hillman, 6 May 1915, box 3 folder 25; Marimpietri to Hillman, 28 Apr. 1915, 11 May 1915, 6 July 1915, 31 July 1915, box 3 folder 42; Rosenblum to Hillman, 9 Apr. 1915, 13 Apr. 1915, 14 Apr. 1915, 15 Apr. 1915, 20 Apr. 1915, 23 Apr. 1915, 26 Apr. 1915, 3 May 1915, 7 May 1915, 4 June 1915, 10 June 1915, 17 June 1915,7 July 1915, 21 July 1915, 29 July 1915, 3 Aug. 1915, box 5 folder 6; Potofsky to Schlossberg, 5 July 1915, box 14 folder 25; Potofsky to Hillman, 13 Apr. 1915, 3 May 1915, box 21 folder 14; Rosenblum to Potofsky, 9 Aug. 1915, box 23 folder 5; Hillman to Brais, 17 Mar. 1915, 18 Mar. 1915, 24 Mar. 1915, box 36 folder 24; A. S. Glasman to Brais, 27 Mar. 1915, box 36 folder 21; Rosenblum to Brais, 24 Mar. 1915, 8 Apr. 1915, 15 Apr. 1915, Apr. 1915 with no date, 15 May 1915, 27 May 1915, box 36 folder 49; memorandum dated 13 May 1915, box 271 folder 3; Skala, "Story," 5, all in ACW Papers. See also *Chicago Daily Journal*, 1 May 1915; *Chicago Daily News*, 1 May 1915, both in ACW Papers, box 322, Red Books, I: 27.

55. Minutes of GEB Meetings, 27–29 Aug. 1915, box 164 folder 3; Potofsky to Schlossberg, 2 Sept. 1915, box 14 folder 25, both in ACW Papers.

56. Rosenblum to Hillman, 7 Sept. 1915, ACW Papers, box 5 folder 6.

57. Hillman to Schlossberg, 14 Sept. 1915, ACW Papers, box 5 folder 20.

58. Hillman to Schlossberg, 15 Sept. 1915, ACW Papers, box 5 folder 20.

59. Hillman et al. (to Chicago's manufacturers), 16 Sept. 1915, ACW Papers, box 5 folder 7.

60. Ibid.

61. Ibid.

62. Williams, "The Fancies of Fabius," *Streator (Illinois) Independent-Times*, 20 Nov. 1915, ACW Papers, box 322, Red Books, I: 139.

63. Skala, "Story," 10–12; Josephson, *Hillman*, 123.

64. Hillman to Schlossberg, 28 Sept. 1915, ACW Papers, box 11 folder 5.

65. *Denni Hlasatel*, 6 Oct. 1915, Press Survey, reel 1.

66. Circular letter, 6 Oct. 1915, ACW Papers, box 12 folder 20.

67. Hillman to Schlossberg, 29 Sept. 1915, box 11 folder 5; Schlossberg to Hillman, 30 Sept. 1915, box 11 folder 5; Schlossberg to Hillman, 1 Oct. 1915, 4 Oct. 1915, box 5 folder 21, all in ACW Papers. See also Myers, "Policing of Labor Disputes," 790–793.

68. *Daily Trade Record*, 4 Oct. 1915 (typewritten copy), ACW Papers, box 38 folder 13.

69. Chicago, City Council, Committee on Schools, Fire, Police and Civil Service, Proceedings of Investigation of Alleged Police Brutality During Garment Workers' Strike, 1915, ACW Papers, box 39 folders 3 and 4. See especially testimony of Ellen Gates Starr, Sam Guyer (Geier), Herman Isovitch (Hyman Isovitz), Edward Schinder, and Harry Waxman, ibid., 134–160, 391–412, 445–452.

70. Potofsky to Schlossberg, 4 Oct. 1915, ACW Papers, box 14 folder 25; Myers, "Policing of Labor Disputes," 837–840.

71. *Documentary History*, 1914–1916, 146–147; Myers, "Policing of Labor Disputes," 796–798.

72. Both quotations are from Hillman to Schlossberg, 4 Oct. 1915, ACW Papers, box 11 folder 5.

73. Citizens' Committee for Arbitration in the Clothing Industry, "Why Not Arbitrate? What the Leading Chicago Newspapers Say of the Clothing Strike" (1915), box 293 folder 20; Hillman to Schlossberg, 22 Oct. 1915, 24 Oct. 1915, box 11 folder 5; undated memorandum, box 38 folder 13; Amalgamated Clothing Workers of America, Strike Bulletin (no date), box 322, Red Books, I: 135, all in ACW Papers. See also *Documentary History*, 1914–1916, 147, 151.

74. Jacob S. Potofsky and M. A. Glatt, "Financial Report of Chicago Clothing Workers' General Strike. 1915–1916," ACW Papers, box 38 folder 13, 19; Mary Anderson and Olive Sullivan to Margaret Drier Robins, 18 Nov. 1915, WTUL Papers, reel 23.

75. Rosenblum to Schlossberg, 28 Oct. 1915, ACW Papers, box 15 folder 9.

76. Hillman to Schlossberg, 6 Nov. 1915, box 5 folder 21; Marimpietri to Schlossberg, 29 Oct. 1915, box 13 folder 15, both in ACW Papers.

77. Quoted in Myers, "Policing of Labor Disputes," 790. See also Hillman's correspondence with the Illinois Board of Arbitration dated 12 Nov. 1915, ACW Papers, box 38 folder 14.

78. Josephson, *Hillman*, 130–132; Potofsky, "Reminiscences," 102. I do not agree with Steven Fraser, who argues that the strike was "rightly considered a victory" (*Labor Will Rule*, 101).

79. *Survey*, 16 Oct. 1915, ACW Papers, box 38 folder 14.

80. *Streator (Illinois) Independent-Times*, 20 Nov. 1915, ACW Papers, Red Books, box 322, I: 139.

81. Ibid.; Skala, "Story," 10–12.

82. Glasman to Brais, 27 Mar. 1915, ACW Papers, box 36 folder 21; Skala, "Story," 5.

83. *New Republic*, 1 Jan. 1916, ACW Papers, box 322, Red Books, I: 147–148.

84. *Denni Hlasatel*, 9 Oct. 1915, Press Survey, reel 1.

85. Agnes Kazmar, interview, JEPP.

86. Thompson, *Making of the English Working Class*, 9. See also other works by Thompson: "Eighteenth-Century English Society"; *Poverty of Theory*; *Customs in Common*.

For critiques on Thompson's concept of class, see Anderson, *Arguments Within English Marxism*; Johnson, "Thompson, Genovese, and Socialist-Humanist History"; "Culture and the Historians"; and "Three Problematics." For discussions in defense of Thompson's position, see Wood, "Politics of Theory and the Concept of Class"; McLennan, "Thompson and the Discipline of Historical Context."

For a feminist critique of Thompson's conception, see Scott, *Gender and the Politics of History*, especially ch. 4, 68–90. See also Stansell, *City of Women*; Blewett, *Men, Women, and Work*.

87. Spencer, interview, 14.

88. Valiani, interview, 50–51.

89. Ibid., 52.

90. Ginzburg, *Cheese and the Worms*, especially 16. See also Ossowski, *Class Structure*. For an insightful discussion about how class consciousness is related to popular religion, see Gramsci, *Selections from the Prison Notebooks*, 180–183, 419–421.

91. Rosenblum to Hillman, 21 Jan. 1916, box 5 folder 7; Potofsky to Schlossberg, 25 Jan. 1916, 27 Jan. 1916, 20 Mar. 1916, 31 Mar. 1916, box 14 folder 26, all in ACW Papers.

92. Potofsky to Schlossberg, 11 Sept. 1916, 24 Sept. 1916, box 14 folder 26; Rosenblum to Hillman, 27 June 1916, box 5 folder 7; Rosenblum to Schlossberg, 6 Sept. 1916, box 15 folder 10; Levin to Hillman, 7 July 1916, box 3 folder 25; Potofsky to all Chicago local unions, 6 Oct. 1916, box 38 folder 10; Potofsky to GEB, 6 Oct. 1916, box 167 folder 6; Hyman Schneid et al. to GEB, 6 Oct. 1916, box 167 folder 6; Minutes of GEB Meetings, 9–14 Oct. 1916, box 164 folder 4a, all in ACW Papers.

93. Potofsky to GEB, 6 Oct. 1916, ACW Papers, box 167 folder 7.

94. Ibid.

95. E. Galti et al. to Schlossberg, 14 Dec. 1916, ACW Papers, box 38 folder 9.

96. Rosenblum to Schlossberg, 26 Dec. 1916, ACW Papers, box 15 folder 10.

97. Rosenblum to Schlossberg, 16 Mar. 1917, ACW Papers, box 15 folder 11.

98. Rosenblum to Schlossberg, 22 Jan. 1917, 23 Jan. 1917, 12 Mar. 1917, box 15 folder 11; Rosenblum to Schlossberg, 4 Apr. 1917, box 15 folder 12; Rosenblum to Hillman, 30 Mar. 1917, box 5 folder 7; Marimpietri to Schlossberg, 15 Sept. 1917, box 13 folder 15; Minutes of GEB Meetings, 15–20 Feb. 1917, box 164 folder 5; Minutes of GEB Meetings, 16–19 Aug. 1917, box 164 folder 6, all in ACW Papers; *Advance*, 27 Apr. 1917, 29 June 1917, 6 July 1917, 13 July 1917, 21 Sept. 1917, 19 July 1918. For ethnic rivalry and leverage as well in the Baltimore ACW organization, see Argersinger, *Making the Amalgamated*, 69–73.

99. Fraser, "*Landslayt* and *Paesani*."

100. Hillman to Schlossberg, 14 May 1917, box 11 folder 7; Rosenblum to Potofsky, 2 June 1917, box 25 folder 4; Schlossberg to Rosenblum, 15 June 1917, box 15 folder 12, all in ACW Papers. See also Potofsky, "Reminiscences," 112.

101. See, for example, *Documentary History*, 1918–1920, 181–192; ibid., 1920–1922, 245–266.

102. Gormly, "Trade Agreements"; Bing, *War-Time Strikes*, 59–60.

103. "Standards of Labor in the Manufacture of Army Clothing in the United States," *Monthly Labor Review* 5, 4 (Oct. 1917): 30–33. See also *Documentary History*, 1916–1918, 133–134; Potofsky, "Reminiscences," 104–105.

104. Bing, *War-Time Strikes*, 116–125, 151–175; Conner, *National War Labor Board*, especially chs. 2–3 and 7–8, 18–49, 108–141.

105. Soule, *Hillman*, 85–89; Josephson, *Hillman*, 169–170. See also Hillman to Walter Lippman, 5 July 1917, box 7 folder 4; Hillman to Newton D. Baker, 16 Oct. 1917, box 7 folder 4, both in ACW Papers.

106. Levin to Hillman, 6 June 1918, ACW Papers, box 3 folder 25.

107. Levin to Schlossberg, 30 Nov. 1917, box 12 folder 14; Levin to Hill-

man, 5 Jan. 1918, box 3 folder 25; Rosenblum to Potofsky, 24 Dec. 1917, box 15 folder 14; Skala to Potofsky, 17 Jan. 1918, box 26 folder 28, all in ACW Papers. See also *Advance*, 23 Nov. 1917, 30 Nov. 1917, 14 Dec. 1917, 4 Jan. 1918, 11 Jan. 1918, 1 Feb. 1918, 15 Feb. 1918, 1 Mar. 1918, 22 Mar. 1918, 17 May 1918, 31 May 1918, 14 June 1918, 21 June 1918, 28 June 1918.

108. Hillman to Potofsky, 21 June 1918, ACW Papers, box 21 folder 15.

109. Levin to Hillman, 6 June 1918, 29 July 1918, box 3 folder 25; Hillman to Potofsky, 17 June 1918, box 21 folder 15; Levin to Potofsky, 9 Aug. 1918, box 22 folder 32, all in ACW Papers. See also *Advance*, 28 June 1918, 16 Aug. 1918.

110. Levin to Hillman, 3 July 1918, 14 Aug. 1918, 9 Sept. 1918, 11 Sept. 1918, 21 Sept. 1918, 23 Sept. 1918, 13 Oct. 1918, 15 Oct. 1918, 21 Oct. 1918, 24 Oct. 1918, 31 Oct. 1918, box 3 folder 25; William Z. Ripley to Alfred Decker and Cohn, 24 Sept. 1918, box 4 folder 47; Employees of Alfred Decker and Cohn to the firm, 4 Sept. 1918, box 6 folder 42; Levin to Schlossberg, 17 Aug. 1918, 4 Sept. 1918, 2 Nov. 1918, box 12 folder 14; Hillman to Schlossberg, 30 Sept. 1918, box 21 folder 15; Hillman to Potofsky, 1 Oct. 1918, box 21 folder 15; Potofsky to Hyman Isovitz, 22 July 1918, box 21 folder 28; Potofsky to Levin, 13 Sept. 1918, box 22 folder 32; Skala to Potofsky, 30 July 1918, box 26 folder 28, all in ACW Papers. See also *Advance*, 5 July 1918, 12 July 1918, 2 Aug. 1918, 16 Aug. 1918, 23 Aug. 1918, 20 Sept. 1918, 27 Sept. 1918, 4 Oct. 1918, 18 Oct. 1918, 25 Oct. 1918, 1 Nov. 1918, 8 Nov. 1918, 15 Nov. 1918, 29 Nov. 1918.

111. *Advance*, 13 July 1917. See also Rosenblum to Schlossberg, 8 June 1917, box 15 folder 12; Marimpietri to Schlossberg, 22 Apr. 1918, box 13 folder 15, both in ACW Papers; *Documentary History*, 1916–1918, 119–121; *Advance*, 26 Apr. 1918, 10 May 1918.

112. *Advance*, 10 Jan. 1918, 24 Jan. 1919, 7 Feb. 1919; *Documentary History*, 1918–1920, 120–121.

113. Skala, "Story," 30. See also *Advance*, 21 Feb. 1919, 14 Mar. 1919, 28 Mar. 1919; *Documentary History*, 1918–1920, 123–124.

114. *Advance*, 21 Mar. 1919, 4 Apr. 1919.

115. Ibid., 4 Apr. 1919, 11 Apr. 1919, 2 May 1919; Alfred Decker and Cohn to employees, 25 Apr. 1919, ACW Papers, box 38 folder 11; *Daily News Record*, 6 May 1919, newspaper scrap in ACW Papers, box 322, Red Books, I: 170; Josephson, *Hillman*, 185–186.

116. Quoted in Josephson, *Hillman*, 186.

117. *Advance*, 25 Apr. 1919, 2 May 1919, 9 May 1919, 16 May 1919, 23 May 1919, 30 May 1919.

118. Ibid., 6 June 1919, 20 June 1919, 1 Aug. 1919.

119. *Documentary History*, 1920–1922, ii–iii; Montgomery, *Fall of the House of Labor*, 332 ff. For the wartime labor policy of the Wilson Administration, see also Kennedy, *Over Here*, 266 ff.; Dubofsky, "Abortive Reform"; Brody, *Workers in Industrial America*, ch. 1, 3–47.

120. Brody, *Labor in Crisis* and *Butcher Workmen*; Barrett, *Work and Community in the Jungle*. See also Helpern, *Down on the Killing Floor*.

121. Gordon, *New Deals*, ch. 3, 87–127. The quotation is from 93.

CHAPTER 5. THE AMALGAMATED ESTABLISHMENT

1. Chenery, "The Vanguard of Labor," *Survey*, 22 May 1920; Vorse, "The Amalgamated Clothing Workers in Session," *Nation*, 22 May 1920, both in ACW Papers, box 322, Red Books, I: 273–277.

2. Montgomery, *Workers' Control*, ch. 3, 48–90.

3. Budish and Soule, *New Unionism in the Clothing Industry*. See especially ch. 7, 156–204. "New unionism," as used by Budish and Soule, implies a progressive and accommodationist approach to the existing American society. David Montgomery uses the term in a different sense, referring in particular to the militant and radical movement of the 1910s. See his *Workers' Control*, ch. 4, 91–112.

4. Perlman, *Theory*, 233, 278.

5. Soffer, "Trade Union Development," 141.

6. Minutes of Executive Board Meetings of Local 275, 8 Aug. 1927, 23 Aug. 1927, 30 Aug. 1927, 12 Nov. 1928, CJB Papers. See also Glenn, *Daughters of the Shtetl*, 231–234, 236; Argersinger, *Making the Amalgamated*, 95–120. For broad discussions of feminism in the labor movement, see Kessler-Harris, "Where Are the Organized Women Workers?"; Dublin, *Women at Work*; Levine, *Labor's True Woman*; Gabin, *Feminism in the Labor Movement*.

7. *Advance*, 24 Oct. 1919.

8. *Documentary History*, 1920–1922, 136; Minutes of GEB Meetings, 2–6 Sept. 1919, ACW Papers, box 164 folder 9.

9. *Advance*, 24 Oct. 1919.

10. Ibid., 27 Oct. 1922, 3 Nov. 1922; Binder, "More Government," *Survey*, 15 Sept. 1923, scraps in ACW Papers, box 322, Red Books, II: 289–290; *Documentary History*, 1922–1924, 86–87.

11. *Advance*, 22 July 1921.

12. Ibid.

13. Ibid., 7 July 1922. See also ibid., 13 Oct. 1922.

14. Bryce M. Stewart, "The Chicago Employment Exchange," *Documentary History*, 1922–1924, xxv–xxviii; *Advance*, 7 July 1922, 27 Oct. 1922, 3 Nov. 1922; *Documentary History*, 1924–1926, 28.

15. Binder, "More Government."

16. Ibid.

17. Bryce M. Stewart, "Unemployment Insurance Agreement," *Documentary History*, 1922–1924, xxviii–xxxiii. The quotation is from xxxii.

18. Nelson, *Unemployment Insurance*, 82–84; Josephson, *Hillman*, 197; Soule, *Hillman*, 104–105; Myers, "Production of Men's Clothing," 156–158.

19. *Advance*, 18 June 1920, 23 July 1920, 1 Apr. 1921, 22 Apr. 1921, 24 Feb. 1922, 7 Apr. 1922.

20. Ibid., 2 Feb. 1923, 9 Mar. 1923, 16 Mar. 1923, 13 Apr. 1923, 18 May 1923, 25 May 1923, 1 June 1923; Millis, "Unemployment Insurance"; Nelson, *Unemployment Insurance*, 85.

21. Leo Wolman, "Value of the Unemployment Insurance Scheme in the Clothing Industry," New York, Department of Labor, *Eighth Industrial Conference*, 1924, 137–144. The quotation is from 142.

22. Stewart, "Unemployment Insurance Agreement," xxxiii.

23. Nelson, *Unemployment Insurance*, 10–16.

24. Leo Wolman, "A Proposal for an Unemployment Fund in the Men's Clothing Industry," Amalgamated Educational Pamphlet no. 5 (New York: Amalgamated Clothing Workers, 1922), ACW Papers, box 287 folder 1922; Robert W. Bruère, "Cementing the Broken Year," *Survey*, April 1925, scraps in ACW Papers, box 322, Red Books, III: 89–92.

25. Stewart, "Plan of Unemployment Insurance."

26. Ibid., 471–472; "Agreement between Clothing Manufacturers of Chicago and Amalgamated Clothing Workers of America Establishing an Unemployment Insurance Fund" (1923), ACW Papers, box 40 folder 2 (hereafter "Agreement"); *Documentary History*, 1926–1928, 230.

27. Rights and Duties of the Board of Trustees under the Unemployment Insurance Agreement Entered into Between the Union and the Clothing Manufacturers of Chicago, John R. Commons Papers, reel 7 frames 768–770; Minutes of Meetings of Board of Trustees, B. Kuppenheimer and Co., Inc. Unemployment Insurance Fund, 21 Jan. 1924, Commons Papers, reel 7 frame 789; Stewart, "Plan of Unemployment Insurance," 472, and "Unemployment Insurance Agreement," xxix.

28. "Agreement," 10; Minutes of Meeting of Trustees of Unemployment Funds (Established by the Chicago Industrial Federation of Clothing Manufacturers and the Amalgamated Clothing Workers), 18 Apr. 1924, Commons Papers, reel, 7 frames 800–802. See also contractors' unemployment insurance agreement with the ACW as well as HSM's in Commons Papers, reel 8 frames 52–73.

29. Stewart, "Unemployment Insurance Agreement," xxxii–xxxiii.

30. *Advance*, 16 Sept. 1927, 10 Feb. 1928.

31. For example, see Nathan S. Klein to Schlossberg, 27 Nov. 1921, CJB Secretary Files, CJB Papers. For the Chicago ACW membership in 1921, see a report on the CJB enclosed in Maurice C. Fisch to Leo Wolman, 23 Sept. 1921, ACW Papers, box 38 folder 12.

32. Minutes of the Executive Board Meetings, Local 61, Amalgamated Clothing Workers of America, August 8, 1922–December 27, 1932, CJB Papers, 15 July 1924, 10 Feb. 1925. See also ibid., 25 Oct. 1927, 29 Nov. 1927.

33. Stewart, "Plan of Unemployment Insurance," 477; *Documentary History*, 1924–1926, 143; *Advance*, 1 Aug. 1924.

34. *Advance*, 2 Sept. 1927. See also ibid., 27 May 1927.

35. Minutes of the Executive Board Meetings, Local 61, CJB Papers, 20 Jan. 1925. See also ibid., 17 Feb. 1925, 24 Feb. 1925, 12 June 1928.

36. Ibid., 19 May 1925.

37. Cohen, *Making a New Deal*, especially 209–210. For a broader discussion of welfare capitalism in the United States, see Brody, *Workers in Industrial America*, ch. 2, 48–81; Brandes, *American Welfare Capitalism*; Gitelman, "Welfare Capitalism Reconsidered."

38. *Advance*, 5 June 1925, 27 May 1927, 2 Sept. 1927, 16 Nov. 1928.

39. Minutes of the Executive Board Meetings, Local 61, CJB Papers, 27 Apr. 1926, 13 Sept. 1927. See also ibid., 11 June 1929, 25 June 1929.

40. The quotations are from *Advance*, 19 June 1925. See also ibid., 26 June 1925.

41. Ibid., 18 July 1919.

42. Ibid., 23 May 1919. For Hillman's accommodationist approach, see Fraser, "Dress Rehearsal for the New Deal."

43. Josephson, *Hillman*, 224–225.

44. Louis Levine, "Sidney Hillman Explains How Clothing Workers Plan to Standardize Production on the Basis of a True Measurement of Human Efficiency," *World*, 11 July 1920, scraps in ACW Papers, box 322, Red Books, I: 325–327; Soule, *Hillman*, 136–140.

45. Montgomery, *Fall of the House of Labor*, ch. 5, 214–256; Nadworny, *Scientific Management and the Unions*, chs. 4–5, 48–86.

46. The quotations are from Levine, "Sidney Hillman Explains," 327.

47. Ibid., 326–327. Steven Fraser describes Hillman's approach to scientific management from an ideological perspective. See his "Dress Rehearsal for the New Deal," 218–223.

48. *Documentary History*, 1918–1920, 343–350. Steven Fraser discusses production standards in terms of radical politics in "Dress Rehearsal for the New Deal," especially 233–235.

49. Chenery, "Vanguard of Labor," 274.

50. *Documentary History*, 1918–1920, 343–350. The quotations are from 345, 346, 349.

51. The quotations are from ibid., 350–351.

52. Rosenblum to Hillman, 22 Mar. 1920, ACW Papers, box 5 folder 7.

53. Hillman to Rosenblum, 1 Sept. 1920, ACW Papers, box 5 folder 7.

54. Josephson, *Hillman*, 224–241.

55. Board of Arbitration for the Agreements between the Amalgamated Clothing Workers and the Chicago Clothing Manufacturers, Decision of April 14, 1921, ACW Papers, box 38 folder 16. For HSM's efforts to establish production standards before the above decision was made, see Howard to James H. Tufts, 6 Oct. 1919, box 1 folder 14; James H. Tufts, Status of the investigation for improving efficiency in the Trimming Room (1919?), box 2 folder 2, both in Papers of Hart, Schaffner and Marx Labor Agreement.

56. *Advance*, 16 Sept. 1921, 10 Nov. 1922.

57. Minutes of the Membership Meetings, Local 61, Amalgamated Clothing Workers of America, December 5, 1922–May 2, 1939, CJB Papers, 5 June 1923.

58. Ibid., 6 Feb. 1923, 3 Apr. 1923, 11 May 1923, 5 June 1923. The quotations are from 6 Feb. 1923 and 5 June 1923.

59. Minutes of the Executive Board Meetings, Local 61, CJB Papers, 12 Sept. 1922.

60. Myers, "Production of Men's Clothing," 17–19, 29–30, 33–34, 37–38.

61. Minutes of the Membership Meetings, Local 61, 5 Feb. 1924, 7 Apr. 1925, 5 Jan. 1926, 2 Feb. 1926, 1 Nov. 1927, 7 May 1929; Minutes of the Executive Board Meetings, Local 61, 27 Nov. 1923, 8 July 1924, 16 June 1925, 11 Aug. 1925, 22 Sept. 1925, 13 Oct. 1925, 6 Jan. 1926, 25 Jan. 1926, 18 Oct. 1927, 29 Jan. 1929, 14 May 1929, 13 Aug. 1929, 20 Aug. 1929, both in CJB Papers.

62. Minutes of the Membership Meetings, Local 61, CJB Papers, 6 Jan. 1925.

63. Minutes of the Executive Board Meetings, Local 61, CJB Papers, 8 Jan. 1925, 20 Jan. 1925.

64. Ibid., 25 Jan. 1926, 17 May 1927, 10 Jan. 1928, 11 Dec. 1928; *Advance*, 27 Mar. 1925, 8 May 1925.

65. Thomas W. Holland, "The X Plan in the Clothing Trade," unidentified booklet in ACW Papers, box 322, Red Books, IV: 124; *Documentary History*, 1924–1926, 12–13, 100–102.

66. *Advance*, 22 Apr. 1921, 20 May 1921, 7 Apr. 1922.

67. Minutes of the Membership Meetings, Local 61, CJB Papers, 6 Jan. 1925. See also Minutes of the Executive Board Meetings, Local 61, CJB Papers, 25 Oct. 1924.

68. Minutes of the Executive Board Meetings, Local 61, CJB Papers, 6 July 1926, 17 Aug. 1926.

69. Workers of Alfred Decker and Cohn Vest Shop to Hillman, 25 Sept. 1925, ACW Papers, box 4 folder 37.

70. Memorandum by Schneid, 27 Oct. 1925, ACW Papers, box 38 folder 12.

71. Potofsky to Isovitz, 1 Nov. 1925, ACW Papers, box 21 folder 28.

72. Draper, *American Communism*, ch. 9, 215–233; Weinstein, *Decline of Socialism*, ch. 6, 258–271; Dubofsky, *We Shall Be All*, 222–225; Barrett, "Boring from Within and Without"; Sylvia Kopald and Ben M. Selekman, "The Epic of the Needle Trades," *Menorah Journal*, April 1930, 303–314.

73. Tailors' Committee of the Amalgamated Clothing Workers, "Our Struggle Must Be Won!" *Workers' Challenge*, 5 Feb. 1921, newspaper clippings in ACW Papers, box 208 folder 3.

74. Minutes of the GEB Meetings, 10–12 Aug. 1922, ACW Papers, box 164 folder 19.

75. Notes in Minutes of the GEB Meetings, 4–6 Jan. 1923, box 164 folder 20; 14–20 June 1923, box 164 folder 21, both in ACW Papers; Fraser, "Dress Rehearsal for the New Deal," 233–235.

76. Minutes of the GEB Meetings, 6–20 May 1924, ACW Papers, box 164 folder 23; *Documentary History*, 1916–1918, 167, 208–210; ibid., 1918–1920, 243, 259, 304–305, 339–340; ibid., 1920–1922, 396; ibid., 1922–1924, 184, 365; "Russia and the Amalgamated," *Nation*, 14 June 1922; Letter by V. Ulyanov (Lenin) to President Hillman, ACW Papers, box 322, Red Books, II: 8; Kopald and Selekman, "Epic," 311–312. See also Fraser, "'New Unionism' and the 'New Economic Policy.'"

77. Minutes of the GEB Meetings, 31 July-3 Aug. 1924, ACW Papers, box 164 folder 24. See also "G. E. B. Statement on La Follette and Wheeler Campaign of 1924," *Documentary History*, 1924–1926, 399–402; Draper, *American Communism*, chs. 2 and 5, 29–51, 96–126; Weinstein, *Decline of Socialism*, chs. 7 and 8, 272–323.

78. *New York New Leader*, 17 May 1924, newspaper clippings in ACW Papers, box 322, Red Books, III: 283; Benjamin Stolberg, "The Collapse of the Needle Trades," *Nation*, 11 May 1927, 524–525; *Advance*, 5 Dec. 1924; Min-

utes of the GEB Meetings, 10–13 Nov. 1924, ACW Papers, box 164 folder 25; ibid., 9–14 Feb. 1925, ACW Papers, box 165 folder 1.

79. Kopald and Selekman, "Epic," 311.

80. *Advance*, 27 Mar. 1925, 3 Apr. 1925, 17 Apr. 1925; Leo Wolman, "The Truth about the Meeting in Chicago on Monday Night, March 23, 1925," ACW Papers, box 172 folder 7.

81. *Advance*, 11 Dec. 1925, 18 Dec. 1925, 1 Jan. 1926; Report of the Chicago Joint Board staff election, December 1925, CJB Secretary Files, CJB Papers. The quotations are from Nathan Green's platform found in the files.

82. *Advance*, 22 Dec. 1922, 29 Dec. 1922; Report of the Chicago Joint Board staff election, December 1922, CJB Secretary Files, CJB Papers; Minutes of the GEB Meetings, 10–12 Aug. 1922, ACW Papers, box 164 folder 19.

83. Hillman to Schlossberg, 11 July 1919, ACW Papers, box 5 folder 22.

84. Rosenblum to Hillman, 24 Sept. 1920, ACW Papers, box 5 folder 7.

85. Philip Shieber to the GEB, 16 Nov. 1921; (Report of the special committee to investigate the grievances arising from transfers), (1922), both in CJB Secretary Files, CJB Papers. See also Albert Goldman to the Executive Board of Local 39, 17 Apr. 1923, ACW Papers, box 167 folder 11; *Documentary History*, 1920–1922, 413. The transferred shop chairman was Jerome Posner, who, together with Philip Aronberg and other communists, signed a protest against Local 39's officers in May 1922.

86. Peter Garafolo to the GEB, 27 June 1925; Fisch to Potofsky, 16 July 1925, 31 Aug. 1925, both in ACW Papers, box 20 folder 28.

87. Resolution of protest adopted by Local 269, 6 June 1919, ACW Papers, box 40 folder 8.

88. Philip Aronberg et al. to the Board of Directors, Chicago Joint Board, 22 May 1922, CJB Secretary Files, CJB Papers.

89. Resolution of protest adopted by Local 269, 6 June 1919.

90. *Advance*, 25 Nov. 1927.

91. Ibid., 13 Dec. 1929.

92. The quotations are from *Advance*, 17 Apr. 1925, 29 May 1925. See also ibid., 19 June 1925.

93. Ibid., 24 July 1925, 31 July 1925, 18 Sept. 1925, 23 Oct. 1925.

94. *Documentary History*, 1924–1926, 249–260, 323–335, 352–354.

95. Ibid., 351.

96. Minutes of the Membership Meetings, Local 61, 6 Mar. 1928; Minutes of the Executive Board Meetings, Local 61, 13 Mar. 1928, both in CJB Papers.

97. Chicago Joint Board Appeal Board case no. 10, 4 Oct. 1928, CJB Secretary Files, CJB Papers.

98. *Advance*, 28 Aug. 1925, 18 Sept. 1925, 25 Sept. 1925; *Documentary History*, 1924–1926, 78–84; Levin to Hillman, 2 July 1925, ACW Papers, box 3 folder 26; *Daily News Record*, 30 June 1925, newspaper scraps in ACW Papers, box 322, Red Books, III: 403; Josephson, *Hillman*, 283–289.

99. *Documentary History*, 1924–1926, 20–21, 120–122; ibid., 1928–1930, 70; *Advance*, 22 Apr. 1927, 9 Dec. 1927, 16 Mar. 1928, 6 Apr. 1928, 29 Mar. 1929, 3 May 1929, 12 July 1929, 13 Sept. 1929, 1 Nov. 1929.

100. Membership of the Amalgamated Clothing Workers of America (1920),

no date; Census of Membership as of July 1, 1925 (including members eighteen months in arrears), no date; Membership, Amalgamated Clothing Workers of America, July 1915–July 1925, no date, all in ACW Papers, box 246 folder 2.

101. Bernstein, *Lean Years*, pt. 1, 45–243. See also "Irving Bernstein's Labor History."

102. Bernstein, *Lean Years*, 97–103.

103. *Chicago Daily News*, 15 Mar. 1927, 30 Apr. 1928, newspaper scraps in ACW Papers, box 322, Red Books, III: 177, 181. See also *Advance*, 16 Mar. 1928.

104. *Clothing Workers of Chicago*, 231.

105. See, for example, Christie, *Empire in Wood*.

106. Brody, *Workers in Industrial America*, chs. 5 and 6, 173–257. The quotation is from 201.

107. Brody, *In Labor's Cause*, ch 6., 221–250. The quotation is from 242. See also Amberg, "CIO Political Strategy."

108. Dubofsky, *State and Labor*, ch. 5, 107–135.

109. Lichtenstein, *Labor's War at Home*, ch. 10, 178–202.

110. Tomlins, *State and the Unions*, pt. 3, 247–328.

CHAPTER 6. THE UNION IN THE CASH NEXUS

1. *Daily Jewish Courier*, 9 May 1922, Press Survey, reel 33.

2. Bernstein, *Lean Years*, 88.

3. Perlman, *Theory*, 155–162, 169–176.

4. Forbath, *Law and the Labor Movement*; Hattam, *Labor Visions and State Power*. See also Tomlins, "How Who Rides Whom."

5. Fink, *In Search of the Working Class*, ch. 4, 144–171; Oestreicher, "Rules of the Game."

6. See Dawson, "History and Ideology."

7. Oestreicher, "Urban Working-Class Political Behavior." For a broader discussion, see Moody and Kessler-Harris, eds., *Perspectives on American Labor History*; Dubofsky, "Lost in a Fog"; Katznelson, "'Bourgeois' Dimension."

8. Perlman, *Theory*, 254–272.

9. Philpott, *Slum and the Ghetto*, ch. 4, 89–109; Hines, *Burnham of Chicago*, especially ch.14, 312–345; Wilson, *City Beautiful Movement*, chs. 3–4, 53–95, and 281–285. For a broader context of Burnham's plan, see Boyer, *Urban Masses and Moral Order*; Gilbert, *Perfect Cities*; Miller, *American Apocalypse*; Smith, *Urban Disorder and the Shape of Belief*.

10. Burnham and Bennett, *Plan of Chicago*, 32.

11. Ibid., 108.

12. Condit, *Chicago*, 249–252, 253 ff.; Mayer and Wade, *Chicago*, 272–326.

13. "Ten Years of the Chicago Plan Commission, 1909–1919," *The Commercial Club of Chicago Year Book, 1919–20* (no place: The Executive Committee of the Commercial Club of Chicago, 1920), 273–303; "Status of Plan of Chicago Improvements," ibid., 304–329.

14. Philpott, *Slum and the Ghetto*, 139–145.

15. *Denni Hlasatel*, 20 Sept. 1914, 12 Oct. 1922, reel 1; ibid., 7 Mar. 1916, reel 5; ibid., 13 May 1917, reel 6, all in Press Survey; Spelman, *Town of Cicero*, 15.

16. *Reform Advocate*, 42 (23 Sept. 1911), reel 38, and 74 (27 Aug. 1927), reel 37; *Sinai Congregation Annual Meeting*, 4 May 1915, reel 38; Chicago Hebrew Institute *Observer*, Dec. 1916, reel 38 and Dec. 1918–Jan. 1919, reel 34; *Forward*, 7 Aug. 1920, reel 38; *American Jewish Year Book, 1918–19*, 326–327, reel 36, all in Press Survey.

17. *Dziennik Zwiazkowy*, 27 Feb. 1917, and *Dziennik Zjednoczenia*, 22 Sept. 1921, both in Press Survey, reel 55; "The Story of Milwaukee Avenue," Logan Square Community Collection, Neighborhood History Research Collection (hereafter Neighborhood History), box 1 folder 29. The ratio of the Polish population in Avondale is based on "Avondale," in *Local Community Fact Book, 1938*, ed. Wirth and Furez; Kantowicz, *Polish-American Politics*, 25, 165–168.

18. Nelli, *Italians in Chicago*, 36–40, 204–207.

19. Anna Miles, interview, JEPP.

20. Rosenblum to Hillman, 20 Apr. 1918, ACW Papers, box 5 folder 7.

21. Board of Arbitration for the Agreements between the Amalgamated Clothing Workers of America and Chicago Clothing Manufacturers, Decision of December 22, 1919, ACW Papers, box 38 folder 16.

22. Burgess, "Wage-Earning Families in Chicago," 185–186.

23. Morris Ginsburg, interview, JEPP.

24. The Family Status of Clothing Workers, ACW Papers, box 38 folder 18. See also Summary of Dependent Schedules, ACW Papers, box 38 folder 12; H. K. Hewitt to Potofsky, 10 Jan. 1923, ACW Papers, box 246 folder 2.

25. See Potofsky to McDonald's City Directory, 8 May 1915, ACW Papers, box 38 folder 9.

26. A. N. Fisher to Potofsky, 16 Dec. 1917, ACW Papers, box 20 folder 29.

27. Minutes of the GEB Meetings, 4–(?) May 1920, ACW Papers, box 16 folder 11. For educational work of the Baltimore ACW organization in the late 1910s, see Argersinger, *Making the Amalgamated*, 73–82.

28. Handout of the CJB Educational Committee (1920), ACW Papers, box 40 folder 3.

29. Ibid.; *Social Activities of the Chicago Joint Board, A. C. W. of A.*, red scrapbook in CJB Papers. For Frank Walsh, see Stromquist, "Class Wars"; Greene, "Negotiating the State."

30. Fisch to Potofsky, 27 Nov. 1920, ACW Papers, box 20 folder 28.

31. Ibid. See also the evening school handout in ACW Papers, box 40 folder 3.

32. Handout of the CJB Educational Committee (1921), ACW Papers, box 40 folder 3.

33. Handout of the CJB Educational Committee (1922), *Social Activities of the Chicago Joint Board*, CJB Papers.

34. Handout of the CJB Educational Committee (1924), ibid.

35. See handouts in *Social and Organizational Activities of Locals, A. C. W. of A.*, red scrapbook in CJB Papers.

36. Fisch to Potofsky, 27 Dec. 1919, ACW Papers, box 20 folder 28.

37. For the voting rates in the twenties, see CJB Staff Elections, 1919–1929, CJB Secretary Files, CJB Papers; Fisch to Wolman, 23 Sept. 1921, and Table Showing Membership and Arrears, both in ACW Papers, box 38 folder 12.

38. Minutes of Shop Meetings and Grievance Board Meetings of Hart, Schaffner and Marx Cutters, Oct. 1925–Dec. 1928, 26 Apr. 1926, CJB Papers.

39. See *Social and Organizational Activities of Locals*, CJB Papers.

40. Tuttle, *Race Riot*, especially 242–268; Philpott, *Slum and the Ghetto*, chs. 6–8, 146–200. See also Hirsch, *Making the Second Ghetto.*

41. Among the expanding literature on working-class racism, particularly relevant to my conception are the following works: Arnesen, *Waterfront Workers of New Orleans* and "Up from Exclusion"; Hill, "Myth-Making as Labor History" and "Race in American Labor History"; Lott, *Love and Theft*; Nelson, "Class, Race, and Democracy in the CIO"; Painter, "New Labor History and the Historical Moment"; Roediger, *Wages of Whiteness* and *Abolition of Whiteness*; Trotter, *Coal, Class, and Color.*

42. Cohen, *Making a New Deal*, especially ch. 3, 99–158. See also Edsforth, *Class Conflict and Cultural Consensus*; Fox and Lears, eds., *Culture of Consumption*; Susman, *Culture as History*; Taylor, ed., *Inventing Times Square*; Leach, *Land of Desire*; Lears, *Fables of Abundance.*

43. Spelman, *Town of Cicero*, 15; "North Lawndale" and "Avondale," in *Local Community Fact Book, 1938*, ed. Wirth and Furez.

44. *Dziennik Zjednoczenia*, 22 Sept. 1921, reel 55; *Forward*, 2 May 1919, reel 38, both in Press Survey.

45. *Denni Hlasatel*, 12 Oct. 1922, Press Survey, reel 1.

46. *Daily Jewish Courier*, 6 Apr. 1922, Press Survey, reel 32. See also ibid., 24 Aug. 1922, Press Survey, reel 32.

47. Barrett and Roediger, "Inbetween Peoples." See also Orsi, "Religious Boundaries"; Higham, *Strangers in the Land.*

48. *Denni Hlasatel*, 13 Oct. 1915, Press Survey, reel 6. See also ibid., 5 June 1918, 4 Sept. 1921, Press Survey, reel 6.

49. *Przebudzenie*, 3, 1 (6 June 1929), Press Survey, reel 55.

50. Oney Fred Sweet, "New, Growing, Thrifty, Clean—That's Cicero," *Chicago Tribune*, 21 July 1929, Newspaper Clippings Files, Chicago Historical Society, Chicago, Illinois, file "Towns. Cicero."

51. "The Czechs in Chicago," *Interpreter*, June 1936, 13–14, Press Survey, reel 6.

52. Sweet, "New, Growing, Thrifty, Clean."

53. *Lawndale* (Chicago: Lakeside, 1875); *Lawndale News*, 2 May 1946, both in Chicago Historical Society. See also *Denni Hlasatel*, 9 Mar. 1903, 15 Sept. 1913, reel 6; *Daily Jewish Courier*, 27 Oct. 1911, reel 33; ibid., 13 Dec. 1912, reel 38; ibid., 13 Feb. 1914, reel 32, all in Press Survey.

54. Chicago Plan Commission, *Housing in Chicago Communities: Community Area No. 29* (Chicago: Chicago Plan Commission, 1940), 1, 4. See also *Daily News*, 31 May 1941, Newspaper Clippings Files, Chicago Historical Society, file "North Lawndale."

55. *Forward*, 2 May 1919, Press Survey, reel 38.

56. *Daily Jewish Courier*, 17 Oct. 1916, Press Survey, reel 37.

57. Introduction to Logan Square Community Collection, Neighborhood History; "The Story of Milwaukee Avenue"; Chicago Plan Commission, *Housing in Chicago Communities: Community Area No. 21* (Chicago: Chicago Plan Commission, 1940), 11; "Avondale," in *Local Community Fact Book, 1938*, ed. Wirth and Furez.

58. *Dziennik Zwiazkowy*, 27 Feb. 1917, Press Survey, reel 55.

59. *Dziennik Zjednoczenia*, 22 Sept. 1921, Press Survey, reel 55.

60. See, for example, Berger, *Working-Class Suburb*; Gans, *Levittowners*; Kornblum, *Blue Collar Community*.

61. See Thernstrom, *Poverty and Progress* and *Other Bostonians*.

62. Zunz, *Changing Face of Inequality*, 402.

63. *Daily Jewish Courier*, 1 Apr. 1910, 2 May 1913; *Sunday Jewish Courier*, 26 May 1913, all in Press Survey, reel 36.

64. *Dziennik Zwiazkowy*, 29 Sept. 1910, Press Survey, reel 54.

65. Ibid., 14 Dec. 1910, 15 Dec. 1910, 20 Dec. 1910, 21 Dec. 1910, 26 Sept. 1916, Press Survey, reel 54.

66. *Daily Jewish Courier*, 4 May 1917; *Sunday Jewish Courier*, 26 May 1913, both in Press Survey, reel 36.

67. *Denni Hlasatel*, 1 Apr. 1912, 4 June 1914, Press Survey, reel 5.

68. Ibid., 23 Mar. 1914, 18 Jan. 1918, Press Survey, reel 5.

69. *Daily Jewish Courier*, 7 Nov. 1913, 9 Mar. 1914, 2 Dec. 1914, 3 Sept. 1916, Press Survey, reel 36.

70. *Denni Hlasatel*, 22 Nov. 1914, Press Survey, reel 5. See also Beito, *Mutual Aid*, ch. 3, 130–142.

71. *Daily Jewish Courier*, 30 May 1913, Press Survey, reel 36.

72. *Denni Hlasatel*, 20 Jan. 1918, 3 Feb. 1918, Press Survey, reel 5.

73. Ibid., 18 Jan. 1918, Press Survey, reel 5.

74. Ibid., 7 Apr. 1918, reel 5; ibid., 9 Sept. 1918, reel 1, both in Press Survey.

75. See, for example, *Daily Jewish Courier*, 8 May 1919, Press Survey, reel 36.

76. *Denni Hlasatel*, 3 Sept. 1914, 21 Oct. 1921, Press Survey, reel 5.

77. *Forward*, 19 Aug. 1919, reel 36; *Denni Hlasatel*, 11 Jan. 1920, reel 5, both in Press Survey.

78. *Denni Hlasatel*, 11 Aug. 1918, Press Survey, reel 5.

79. Ibid., 11 Jan 1920, Press Survey, reel 5.

80. *Sunday Jewish Courier*, 17 Aug. 1919, Press Survey, reel 36.

81. *Denni Hlasatel*, 8 Aug. 1920, Press Survey, reel 5.

82. Italo-American National Union *Bulletin*, Jan. 1933; *Mens Italica*, Dec. 1937, both in Press Survey, reel 30.

83. *Denni Hlasatel*, 21 Oct. 1921, Press Survey, reel 5.

84. See, for instance, *Denni Hlasatel*, 1 Sept. 1918, Press Survey, reel 5.

85. Ibid., 25 Feb. 1917, Press Survey, reel 5.

86. *Zgoda*, 8 Jan. 1931, Press Survey, reel 55.

87. *Denni Hlasatel*, 10 July 1910, 6 May 1914, 4 June 1914, 29 Aug. 1918, 12 Jan. 1920, 20 Oct. 1921, reel 5; ibid, 11 Dec. 1922, reel 4; *Il Bolletino Sociale*, 20 Mar. 1929, reel 30, all in Press Survey.

88. *Denni Hlasatel*, 3 Jan. 1921, 9 Apr. 1921, reel 5; ibid., 9 Dec. 1922, reel 4; *Forward*, 22 Feb. 1919, reel 36, all in Press Survey.

89. *Denni Hlasatel*, 21 Oct. 1921, reel 5; ibid., 22 Aug. 1922, reel 4; Italo-American National Union *Bulletin*, Dec. 1923, Feb. 1925, reel 30, all in Press Survey.

90. *Daily Jewish Courier*, 19 Jan. 1923, Press Survey, reel 38.

91. *Denni Hlasatel*, 6 May 1917, 27 Jan. 1918, Press Survey, reel 5.

92. Ibid., 20 Jan. 1918, 10 Feb. 1918, Press Survey, reel 5.

93. Ibid., 3 Feb. 1918, Press Survey, reel 5.

94. Ibid., 20 Jan. 1918, Press Survey, reel 5.

95. Ibid., 22 July 1922, Press Survey, reel 4.

96. Ibid., 2 Dec. 1917, Press Survey, reel 6.

97. *Forward*, 7 Jan. 1919, 12 Sept. 1920, reel 33; *Denni Hlasatel*, 5 March. 1921, reel 1, all in Press Survey. See also *Forward*, 13 Dec. 1920, 31 Dec. 1920, Press Survey, reel 37.

98. *Forward*, 28 Apr. 1919, 9 June 1919, 24 June 1919, 25 June 1919, 19 July 1919, 3 Apr. 1920, 12 Aug. 1921, 28 Nov. 1921, 8 Feb. 1922, reel 33; *La Parola del Popolo*, 28 Jan. 1922, reel 30, all in Press Survey.

99. *Forward*, 15 Feb. 1921, 9 Oct. 1922, reel 33; ibid., 1 Sept. 1922, 17 July 1924, reel 34; ibid., 21 Nov. 1923, reel 36; *La Parola del Popolo*, 14 Jan. 1922, 8 July 1922, 10 Feb. 1923, reel 30, all in Press Survey.

100. *La Parola del Popola*, 3 Mar. 1923, 24 Mar. 1923, reel 30; *Forward*, 22 Sept. 1922, reel 33, all in Press Survey.

101. See, for example, *Daily Jewish World*, 27 Oct. 1927; *Forward*, 29 Oct. 1927, both in Press Survey, reel 36.

102. Ginsburg, interview.

103. Jack Mitchell, interview by Morris Vogel, JEPP.

104. Lottie Spitzer, interview, JEPP.

105. Ibid.

106. *Record-Herald*, 25 Sept. 1905, reel 33; *Chicago Chronicle*, 17 Nov. 1905, reel 33; *Dziennik Ludowy*, 4 Nov. 1908, 7 Nov. 1908, reel 50, all in Press Survey.

107. *Denni Hlasatel*, 9 Sept. 1918, Press Survey, reel 1.

108. Oestreicher, "Urban Working-Class Political Behavior." The quotation is from 1269.

109. *Denni Hlasatel*, 4 Jan. 1906, Press Survey, reel 6.

110. Levin to Hillman, 3 July 1918, ACW Papers, box 3 folder 25.

APPENDIX. THE SPATIAL CONTEXT OF HISTORY

1. Soja, *Postmodern Geographies*, 31. See also Harvey, *Condition of Postmodernity*, ch. 15, 240–259; Sack, *Conceptions of Space in Social Thought*, ch. 1, 3–31; Bochner, "Space."

2. Braudel, *The Mediterranean*. The quotation is from 23.

3. Bailyn, "Braudel's Geohistory." See also Harsgor, "Total History"; Baker, "Historical Geography and the *Annales* School."

4. Braudel, *The Mediterranean*, 16. Braudel has since retreated farther, in *Civilization and Capitalism* restricting mention of space to the geographical boundaries of the world economy and of the national market in terms of transport technology. See vol. 1 *Structures of Everyday Life*, 415–430; vol. 3 *Perspective of the World*, 21–45, 315–322. The reason is in part that his general framework and major concepts are borrowed from Immanuel Wallerstein, who refers to the division of labor, not space itself, in spatial terms core and periphery. See Wallerstein, *Modern World-System I*, 15–16, 100–103, 116–117, 347–357.

5. Baker, "Historical Geography." The quotation is from 561. For detailed information, see Darby, "Relations of Geography and History"; Baker, "Ideology and Historical Geography"; Earle, *Geographical Inquiry*, 1–23; Norton, *Historical Analysis in Geography*, chs. 2–4, 17–61; Gregory, *Ideology, Science, and Human Geography*.

6. Frisby, *Simmel and Since*, ch. 6, 98–117.

7. Lefebvre, *Survival of Capitalism*, 19, 21, 83. See also Lefebvre, *Production of Space*; Gregory, *Geographical Imaginations*, ch. 6, 348–416; Soja, *Postmodern Geographies*, ch. 3, 76–93; Merrifield, "Place and Space"; Martins, "Theory of Social Space."

8. Castells, *Urban Question*, 430.

9. Harvey, *Social Justice and the City*, 10–11, 13.

10. The quotation is from Harvey, *Limits to Capital*, 234, and *Consciousness and the Urban Experience*, 36. See also Harvey, *Urbanization of Capital*; Gregory, *Geographic Imaginations*, ch. 6, 348–416.

11. Editors' Introduction, *Radical History Review* 21 (Fall 1979): 3–9. The quotation is from 5.

12. Rosenzweig, *Eight Hours for What We Will*. See also Rosenzweig and Blackmar, *Park and the People*.

13. Blackmar, *Manhattan for Rent*, chs. 1–3, 14–108.

14. Amsden, "Historians and the Spatial Imagination." The quotation is from 12, 14.

15. Merriman, *Margins of City Life*. The quotation is from 195, 200, 227.

16. Urry, "Social Relations, Space and Time."

17. Gregory and Urry, "Introduction," in *Social Relations and Spatial Structures*, ed. Gregory and Urry, 1–8. The quotation is from 3. See also Gregory, "Human Agency and Human Geography."

18. Giddens, *Constitution of Society* and *Central Problems in Social Theory*. The quotation is from Giddens, *Constitution of Society*, xxviii.

19. Thrift, "Determination of Social Action."

20. Soja, *Postmodern Geographies*, chs. 3–5, 76–137. The quotation is from 7, 129.

21. Sayer, "Difference that Space Makes."

22. Soja and Hadjimichalis, "Geographical Materialism and Spatial Fetishism."

23. Saunders, "Space, the City and Urban Sociology."

24. Harvey, "Geopolitics of Capitalism"; Massey, "New Directions in Space."

25. Zunz, *Changing Face of Inequality*.

26. Tuan, *Space and Place*. See also Samuel, *Theatres of Memory*, vol. 2 *Island Stories*, especially 351–369, where the late historian discusses the built environment as historical memory.

BIBLIOGRAPHY

A. MANUSCRIPTS

Addams, Jane Papers, 1860–1960 (microfilm ed.). Widener Library, Harvard University.
Amalgamated Clothing Workers of America Papers, 1910–1975. Labor-Management Documentation Center, Catherwood Library, Cornell University.
Chicago Foreign Language Press Survey (microfilm ed.). Chicago Historical Society.
Commons, John R. Papers (microfilm ed.). Widener Library, Harvard University.
Illinois. General Assembly. Senate. Special Committee to Investigate the Garment Workers' Strike. Proceedings. 3 vols. 47th General Assembly, 1911. Illinois State Archives, Springfield, Ill.
Morgan, Thomas J. Papers. Illinois Historical Survey, University of Illinois at Urbana-Champaign.
Neighborhood History Research Collection. Chicago Public Library.
(Papers of Hart, Schaffner and Marx). Hartmarx Corporation, Chicago, Ill.
Papers of Hart, Schaffner and Marx Labor Agreement. Regenstein Library, the University of Chicago.
Papers of the Chicago and Central States Joint Board, the Amalgamated Clothing and Textile Workers' Union. Chicago Historical Society.
(Papers of the Chicago Joint Board, the Amalgamated Clothing Workers of America). Chicago Historical Society (now integrated with the above papers).
Papers of the Women's Trade Union League and Its Principal Leaders (microfilm ed.). Schlesinger Library, Radcliffe College.
Papers of William Z. Ripley. Harvard University Archives.

B. INTERVIEWS

Brandzel, Sol. Interview by author. Tape recording, Chicago, Ill., 13 July 1987.
Hart, Max A. Interview by author. Tape recording, Chicago, Ill., 21 July 1987.
Interviews Conducted by N. N. Gold for the Oral History Research Office of Columbia University in 1963 and 1964, New York Times Oral History Program: Columbia University Collection (microfilm ed.). Transcript, Widener Library, Harvard University.
Italians in Chicago Oral History Project. Transcript, University of Illinois at Chicago Library.

Oral History Archives of Chicago Polonia. Transcript, Chicago Historical Society.
Oral History Project in Immigration and Labor History. Transcript, Downtown Library, Roosevelt University, Chicago, Ill.
Wadopian, Albert. Interview by author. Tape recording, Chicago, Ill., 2 July 1987.

C. PUBLICATIONS OF THE AMALGAMATED CLOTHING WORKERS OF AMERICA

Advance (official English organ). 1917–1929.
Clothing Workers of Chicago, 1910–1922, The. Chicago: Chicago Joint Board, the Amalgamated Clothing Workers of America, 1922.
Documentary History of the Amalgamated Clothing Workers of America. 1914–1930.
Marimpietri, Anzuino D. *From These Beginnings: The Making of the Amalgamated.* Chicago: Chicago Joint Board, the Amalgamated Clothing Workers of America, no date.
Schlossberg, Joseph. *The Rise of the Clothing Workers.* Amalgamated Educational Pamphlet no. 1, New York: Amalgamated Clothing Workers of America, 1921.
Wolman, Leo. *A Proposal for an Unemployment Fund in the Men's Clothing Industry.* Amalgamated Educational Pamphlet no. 5, New York: Amalgamated Clothing Workers of America, 1922.

D. PUBLIC DOCUMENTS

Chicago Plan Commission. *Housing in Chicago Communities: Community Area No. 21.* Chicago: Chicago Plan Commission, 1940.
———. *Housing in Chicago Communities: Community Area No. 29.* Chicago: Chicago Plan Commission, 1940.
Illinois. Bureau of Labor Statistics. *Seventh Biennial Report.* 1893.
Illinois. Factory Inspectors. *Eighth Annual Report.* 1901.
———. *First Special Report on Small-Pox in the Tenement House Sweat-Shops of Chicago.* 1894.
Illinois. General Assembly. Senate. *Report of the Illinois Senate Vice Committee.* 49th General Assembly. 1916.
Illinois. Health Insurance Commission. *Report.* 1919.
U.S. Commission on Industrial Relations. *Final Report and Testimony.* Vol. 1. S. Doc. 415, 64th Cong., 1st sess., 1916.
U.S. Congress. House. *Report of the Committee on Manufactures on the Sweating System.* H. Rept. 2309, 52d Cong., 2d sess., 1893.
———. *Eleventh Special Report of the Commissioner of Labor: Regulation and Restriction of Output.* H. Doc. 734, 58th Cong., 2d sess., 1904.
U.S. Congress. Senate. *Report on Condition of Woman and Child Wage-Earners in the United States.* Vol. 2: *Men's Ready-Made Clothing.* S. Doc. 645, 61st Cong., 2d sess., 1911.

U.S. Department of Commerce. Bureau of Foreign and Domestic Commerce. *The Men's Factory-Made Clothing Industry: Report on the Cost of Production of Men's Factory-Made Clothing in the United States*. Miscellaneous Series no. 34, 1916.

U.S. Department of Commerce and Labor. Bureau of the Census. *Census of Manufactures: 1914*. Vol. 2: *Reports for Selected Industries and Detail Statistics for Industries, By States*. 1919.

———. *Manufactures: 1905*, Pt. 1: *United States by Industries*. 1907.

U.S. Department of Labor. *Bulletin*, no. 4 (May 1896). H. Doc. 33, pt. 4, 54th Cong., 1st sess., 1896.

U.S. Department of the Interior. Census Office. *Report on the Manufactures of the United States at the Tenth Census (June 1, 1880): General Statistics*. 1883.

———. *Report on Manufacturing Industries in the United States at the Eleventh Census: 1890*, Pt. 2: *Statistics of Cities*. 1895.

U.S. Immigration Commission. *Reports*. Vol. 11: *Immigrants in Industries: Pt. 5, Silk Goods Manufacturing and Dyeing—Pt. 6, Clothing Manufacturing—Pt. 7, Collar, Cuff, and Shirt Manufacturing*. S. Doc. 633, 61st Cong., 2d sess., 1911.

———. *Reports*. Vol. 26: *Immigrants in Cities*. S. Doc. 338, 61st Cong., 2d sess., 1911.

U.S. Industrial Commission. *Reports*. Vol. 15: *Immigration and Education*, 1901.

Wirth, Louis, and Margaret Furez, eds. *Local Community Fact Book, 1938*. Chicago: Chicago Recreation Commission, 1938.

E. PERIODICALS

Chicago Daily Socialist. 1910–1911.

Chicago Times. 1888.

Chicago Tribune. 1910–1911.

International Socialist Review. 1910–1911.

Monthly Labor Review. 1917–1919.

Survey. 1910–1911.

F. BOOKS AND ARTICLES

Amberg, Stephen. "The CIO Political Strategy in Historical Perpective: Creating a High-Road Economy in the Postwar Era." In Boyle, ed., *Organized Labor and American Politics*, 159–194.

Amsden, Jon. "Historians and the Spatial Imagination," *Radical History Review* 21 (Fall 1979): 11–30.

Anderson, Perry. *Arguments Within English Marxism*. London: Verso, 1980.

Andreas, Alfred T. *History of Chicago*. 3 vols. Chicago, 1884–1886; reprint ed., New York: Arno, 1975.

Argersinger, Jo Ann E. *Making the Amalgamated: Gender, Ethnicity, and Class in the Baltimore Clothing Industry, 1899–1939*. Baltimore: Johns Hopkins University Press, 1999.

Arnesen, Eric. *Waterfront Workers of New Orleans: Race, Class, and Politics, 1863–1923*. Urbana, Ill.: University of Illinois Press, 1994; originally published in 1991.

———. "Up from Exclusion: Black and White Workers, Race, and the State of Labor History," *Reviews in American History* 26, 1 (Mar. 1998): 146–174.

———, Julie Greene, and Bruce Laurie, eds. *Labor Histories: Class, Politics, and the Working-Class Experience*. Urbana, Ill.: University of Illinois Press, 1998.

Asher, Robert. "Union Nativism and the Immigrant Response," *Labor History* 23, 3 (Summer 1982): 325–348.

Auten, Nellie Mason. "Some Phases of the Sweating System in the Garment Trades of Chicago," *American Journal of Sociology* 6 (Mar. 1901): 602–645.

Bailyn, Bernard. "Braudel's Geohistory—A Reconsideration," *Journal of Economic History* 11, 3 (Summer 1951): 277–282.

Baker, Alan R. H. "Reflections on the Relations of Historical Geography and the *Annales* School of History." In Baker and Gregory, eds., *Explorations in Historical Geography*, 1–27.

———. "On Ideology and Historical Geography." In Baker and Billinge, eds., *Period and Place*, 233–243.

———. "Historical Geography: A New Beginning," *Progress in Human Geography* 3, 4 (Dec. 1979): 560–570.

———, and Derek Gregory, eds. *Explorations in Historical Geography: Interpretative Essays*. Cambridge: Cambridge University Press, 1984.

———, and Mark Billinge, eds. *Period and Place: Research Methods in Historical Geography*. Cambridge: Cambridge University Press, 1982.

Balch, Emily Greene. *Our Slavic Fellow Citizens*. New York: Charities Publication Committee, 1910.

Banfield, Edward C. *The Moral Basis of a Backward Society*. Glencoe, Ill.: Free Press, 1958.

Baron, Salo W. *The Russian Jew under Tsars and Soviets*. New York: Macmillan, 1964.

Barrett, James R. *Work and Community in the Jungle: Chicago's Packinghouse Workers, 1894–1922*. Urbana, Ill.: University of Illinois Press, 1987.

———. "Boring from Within and Without: William Z. Foster, the Trade Union Education League, and American Communism." In Arnesen et al., eds., *Labor Histories*, 309–339.

———, and David Roediger. "Inbetween Peoples: Race, Nationality and the 'New Immigrant' Working Class," *Journal of American Ethnic History* 16, 3 (Spring 1997): 3–44.

Barton, Josef. *Peasants and Strangers: Italians, Rumanians, and Slovaks in an American City, 1890–1950*. Cambridge, Mass.: Harvard University Press, 1975.

Beito, David T. *From Mutual Aid to the Welfare State: Fraternal Societies and Social Services, 1890–1967*. Chapel Hill: University of North Carolina Press, 2000.

Bell, Rudolph M. *Fate and Honor, Family and Village: Demographic and Cultural Change in Rural Italy since 1800*. Chicago: University of Chicago Press, 1979.

Bender, Thomas. *Community and Social Change in America*. Baltimore: Johns Hopkins University Press, 1982.

Benson, Susan Porter. *Counter Cultures: Saleswomen, Managers, and Customers in American Department Stores, 1890–1940*. Urbana, Ill.: University of Illinois Press, 1986.

Berend, Iván T., and György Ránki. *Economic Development in East-Central Europe in the 19th and 20th Centuries*. New York: Columbia University Press, 1974.

Berger, Bennett M. *Working-Class Suburb: A Study of Auto Workers in Suburbia*. Berkeley: University of California Press, 1960.

Bernstein, Irving. *The Lean Years: A History of the American Worker, 1920–1933*. Boston: Houghton Mifflin, 1960.

Bing, Alexander M. *War-Time Strikes and Their Adjustment*. New York: E. P. Dutton, 1921.

Blackmar, Elizabeth. *Manhattan for Rent, 1785–1850*. Ithaca: Cornell University Press, 1989.

Blewett, Mary B. *Men, Women, and Work: Class, Gender, and Protest in the New England Shoe Industry*. Urbana, Ill.: University of Illinois Press, 1988.

Bloch, Marc. *Feudal Society*. Chicago: University of Chicago Press, 1961.

Blum, Jerome. *The End of the Old Order in Rural Europe*. Princeton: Princeton University Press, 1978.

———. "The European Village as Community: Origins and Functions," *Agricultural History* 45, 3 (July 1971): 157–178.

———. "The Internal Structure and Polity of the European Village Community from the Fifteenth to the Nineteenth Century," *Journal of Modern History* 43, 4 (Dec. 1971): 541–576.

Blumin, Stuart M. *The Emergence of the Middle Class: Social Experience in the American City, 1760–1900*. New York: Cambridge University Press, 1989.

Bobinska, Celina, and Pilch, Andrzej, eds. *Employment-Seeking Emigrations of the Poles World-Wide XIX and XX C*. Cracow: Uniwersytet Jagiellonski, 1975.

Bochner, Salomon. "Space." In *Dictionary of the History of Ideas* IV, 295–307. New York: Charles Scribner's Sons, 1973.

Bodnar, John. *The Transplanted: A History of Immigrants in Urban America*. 1st Midland Book ed., Bloomington, Ind.: Indiana University Press, 1987; originally published in 1985.

———. "Ethnic Fraternal Benefit Associations: Their Historical Development, Character, and Significance." In *Records of Ethnic Fraternal Benefit Associations in the United States: Essays and Inventories*. St. Paul, Minn.: Immigration History Research Center, University of Minnesota, 1981.

Boyer, Paul. *Urban Masses and Moral Order in America, 1820–1920*. Cambridge, Mass.: Harvard University Press, 1978.

Boyle, Kevin, ed. *Organized Labor and American Politics, 1894–1994: The Labor-Liberal Alliance*. Albany: State University of New York Press, 1998.

Brandes, Stuart D. *American Welfare Capitalism, 1880–1940*. Chicago: University of Chicago Press, 1976.
Braudel, Fernand. *Civilization and Capitalism*. 3 vols. New York: Harper & Row, 1979–1984.
———. *The Mediterranean and the Mediterranean World in the Age of Philip II*. 2 vols. New York: Harper & Row, 1972.
Braverman, Harry. *Labor and Monopoly Capital: The Degradation of Work in the Twentieth Century*. New York: Monthly Review Press, 1974.
Bregstone, Philip P. *Chicago and Its Jews: A Cultural History*. Private publication, 1933.
Briggs, John W. *An Italian Passage: Immigrants to Three American Cities, 1890–1930*. New Haven: Yale University Press, 1978.
Brody, David. *In Labor's Cause: Main Themes on the History of the American Worker*. New York: Oxford University Press, 1993.
———. *Workers in Industrial America: Essays on the Twentieth Century Struggle*. New York: Oxford University Press, 1980.
———. *Labor in Crisis: The Steel Strike of 1919*. Philadelphia: J. B. Lippincott, 1965.
———. *The Butcher Workmen: A Study of Unionization*. Cambridge, Mass.: Harvard University Press, 1964.
———. *Steelworkers in America: The Nonunion Era*. Cambridge, Mass.: Harvard University Press, 1960.
Browning, William C. "The Clothing and Furnishing Trade." In *One Hundred Years of American Commerce*, ed. Chauncey M. Depew. New York: D. O. Haynes, 1895, 561–565.
Budish, J. M., and George Soule. *The New Unionism in the Clothing Industry*. New York: Harcourt, Brace and Howe, 1920.
Buhle, Mari Jo. "Socialist Women and the 'Girl Strikers,' Chicago, 1910," *Signs* 1, 4 (Summer 1976): 1039–1051.
Burnham, Daniel, and Edward Bennett. *Plan of Chicago*. Chicago: The Commercial Club of Chicago, 1909.
Calhoun, C. J. "Community: Toward a Variable Conceptualization for Comparative Research," *Social History* 5, 1 (Jan. 1980): 105–129.
———. "History, Anthropology and the Study of Communities: Some Problems in Macfarlane's Proposal," *Social History* 3, 3 (Oct. 1978): 363–373.
Cameron, Ardis. "Bread and Roses Revisited: Women's Culture and Working-Class Activism in the Lawrence Strike of 1912." In Milkman, ed., *Women, Work and Protest*, 42–61.
Candeloro, Dominic. "Chicago's Italians: A Survey of the Ethnic Factor, 1850–1990." In Holli and Jones, eds., *Ethnic Chicago*, 4th ed., 229–259.
Capek, Thomas. *The Czechs (Bohemians) in America: A Study of Their National, Cultural, Political, Social, Economic and Religious Life*. Boston: Houghton-Mifflin, 1920.
Carsel, Wilfred. *A History of the Chicago Ladies' Garment Workers' Union*. Chicago: Normandie House, 1940.
Castells, Manuel. *The Urban Question: A Marxist Approach*. Cambridge, Mass.: MIT Press, 1977.

Christie, Robert A. *Empire in Wood: A History of the Carpenters' Union.* Ithaca: Cornell University Press, 1956.

Clarke, John, Chas Critcher, and Richard Johnson, eds. *Working-Class Culture.* London: Hutchinson, 1979.

Clawson, Mary Ann. *Constructing Brotherhood: Class, Gender, and Paternalism.* Princeton: Princeton University Press, 1989.

Cobrin, Harry A. *The Men's Clothing Industry: Colonial Times Through Modern Times.* New York: Fairchild Publications, 1970.

Cohen, Lizabeth. *Making a New Deal: Industrial Workers in Chicago, 1919–1939.* New York: Cambridge University Press, 1990.

The Commercial Club of Chicago Year Book, 1919–20. No place: The Executive Committee of the Commercial Club of Chicago, 1920.

Condit, Carl W. *Chicago, 1910–20: Building, Planning, and Urban Technology.* Chicago: University of Chicago Press, 1973.

Conner, Valerie Jean. *The National War Labor Board: Stability, Social Justice, and the Voluntary State in World War I.* Chapel Hill: University of North Carolina Press, 1983.

Conzen, Katheleen N., David A. Gerber, Ewa Morawska, George Pozzetta, and Rudolph J. Vecoli. "The Invention of Ethnicity: A Perspective from the U.S.A.," *Journal of American Ethnic History* 12, 1 (Fall 1992): 3–41.

Cooper, Patricia A. *Once a Cigar Maker: Men, Women and Work Culture in American Cigar Factories, 1900–1919.* Urbana, Ill.: University of Illinois Press, 1987.

Cronin, James E., and Carmen Sirianni, eds. *Work, Community, and Power: The Experience of Labor in Europe and America, 1900–1925.* Philadelphia: Temple University Press, 1983.

Cronon, William. *Nature's Metropolis: Chicago and the Great West.* New York: W. W. Norton, 1991.

Cutler, Irving. "The Jews of Chicago: From Shtetl to Suburb." In Holli and Jones, eds., *Ethnic Chicago*, 4th ed., 122–172.

Darby, H. C. "On the Relations of Geography and History," *Transactions and Papers of the Institute of British Geographers* 19 (1954): 1–11.

Davies, Norman. *God's Playground: A History of Poland.* 2 vols. New York: Columbia University Press, 1982.

Davis, Natalie Zemon. *Society and Culture in Early Modern France.* Stanford: Stanford University Press, 1975.

Dawley, Alan. *Class and Community: The Industrial Revolution in Lynn.* Cambridge, Mass.: Harvard University Press, 1976.

Dawson, Andy. "History and Ideology: Fifty Years of 'Job Consciousness'," *Literature & History* 8 (Autumn 1978): 233–241.

Draper, Theodore. *American Communism and Soviet Russia: The Formative Period.* New York: Viking Press, 1960.

Dublin, Thomas. *Women at Work: The Transformation of Work and Community in Lowell, Massachusetts, 1826–1860.* New York: Columbia University Press, 1979.

Dubofsky, Melvyn. *The State and Labor in Modern America.* Chapel Hill: University of North Carolina Press, 1994.

———. *We Shall Be All: A History of the* Industrial Workers of the World. Chicago: Quadrangle Books, 1969.

———. *When Workers Organize: New York City in the Progressive Era.* Amherst, Mass.: University of Massachusetts Press, 1968.

———. "Lost in a Fog: Labor Historians' Unrequited Search for a Synthesis," *Labor History* 32, 2 (Spring 1991): 295–300.

———. "Abortive Reform: The Wilson Administration and Organized Labor, 1913–1920." In Cronin and Siriani, eds., *Work, Community, and Power,* 197–220.

Duby, Georges. *The Early Growth of the European Economy: Warriors and Peasants from the Seventh to the Twelfth Century.* Ithaca: Cornell University Press, 1974.

Dye, Nancy Schrom. *As Equals and As Sisters: Feminism, the Labor Movement, and the Women's Trade Union League of New York.* Columbia, Mo.: University of Missouri Press, 1980.

Earle, Carville. *Geographical Inquiry and American Historical Problems.* Stanford: Stanford University Press, 1992.

Edsforth, Ronald. *Class Conflict and Cultural Consensus: The Making of a Mass Consumer Society in Flint, Michigan.* New Brunswick: Rutgers University Press, 1987.

Edwards, Richard. *Contested Terrain: The Transformation of the Workplace in the Twentieth Century.* New York: Basic Books, 1979.

Einhorn, Robin G. *Property Rules: Political Economy in Chicago, 1833–1872.* Chicago: University of Chicago Press, 1991.

Englander, Ernest J. "The Inside Contract System of Production and Organization: A Neglected Aspect of the History of the Firm," *Labor History* 28, 4 (Fall 1987): 429–446.

Ewen, Elizabeth. *Immigrant Women in the Land of Dollars: Life and Culture on the Lower East Side, 1890–1925.* New York: Monthly Review Press, 1985.

Fink, Leon. *In Search of the Working Class: Essays in American Labor History and Political Culture.* Urbana, Ill.: University of Illinois Press, 1994.

———. *Workingmen's Democracy: The Knights of Labor and American Politics.* Urbana, Ill.: University of Illinois Press, 1983.

Forbath, William. *Law and the Shaping of the American Labor Movement.* Cambridge, Mass.: Harvard University Press, 1991.

Fox, Richard Wightman. "Epitaph for Middletown: Robert S. Lynd and the Analysis of Consumer Culture." In *The Culture of Consumption: Critical Essays in American History, 1880–1980,* ed. Richard Wightman Fox and T. J. Jackson Lears. New York: Pantheon Books, 1983, 101–141.

Fraser, Steven. *Labor Will Rule: Sidney Hillman and the Rise of American Labor.* New York: Free Press, 1991.

———. "Combined and Uneven Development in the Men's Clothing Industry," *Business History Review* 57, 4 (Winter 1983): 522–547.

———. "The 'New Unionism' and the 'New Economic Policy.'" In Cronin and Siriani, eds., *Work, Community, and Power,* 173–196.

———. "Dress Rehearsal for the New Deal: Shop-Floor Insurgents, Political Elites, and Industrial Democracy in the Amalgamated Clothing Workers." In

Working-Class America: Essays on Labor, Community, and American Society, ed. Michael H. Frisch and Daniel J. Walkowitz. Urbana, Ill.: University of Illinois Press, 1983, 212–255.

Frisby, David. *Simmel and Since: Essays on Georg Simmel's Social Theory*. London: Routledge, 1992.

Frisch, Michael. *Town into City: Springfield, Massachusetts, and the Meaning of Community, 1840–1880*. Cambridge, Mass.: Harvard University Press, 1972.

Gabaccia, Donna. *Militants and Migrants: Rural Sicilians Become American Workers*. New Brunswick: Rutgers University Press, 1988.

———. *From Sicily to Elizabeth Street: Housing and Social Change Among Italian Immigrants, 1880–1930*. Albany: State University of New York Press, 1984.

———. "Neither Padrone Slaves nor Primitive Rebels: Sicilians on Two Continents." In *"Struggle a Hard Battle": Essays on Working-Class Immigrants*, ed. Dirk Hoerder. DeKalb, Ill.: Northern Illinois University Press, 1986, 95–117.

Gabin, Nancy F. *Feminism in the Labor Movement: Women and the United Auto Workers, 1935–1975*. Ithaca: Cornell University Press, 1990.

Gans, Herbert J. *The Levittowners: Ways of Life and Politics in a New Suburban Community*. New York: Pantheon, 1967.

———. "Comment: Ethnic Invention and Acculturation, a Bumpy-Line Approach," *Journal of American Ethnic History* 12, 1 (Fall 1992): 42–52.

Gerstle, Gary. *Working-Class Americanism: The Politics of Labor in a Textile City, 1914–1960*. New York: Cambridge University Press, 1989.

Giddens, Anthony. *The Constitution of Society: Outline of the Theory of Structuration*. Berkeley: University of California Press, 1984.

———. *Central Problems in Social Theory: Action, Structure and Contradiction in Social Analysis*. Berkeley: University of California Press, 1979.

Gierke, Otto von. *Community in Historical Perspective*. Ed. Anthony Black. New York: Cambridge University Press, 1990.

Gilbert, James. *Perfect Cities: Chicago's Utopia of 1893*. Chicago: University of Chicago Press, 1991.

Ginzburg, Carlo. *The Cheese and the Worms: The Cosmos of a Sixteenth-Century Miller*. London: Routledge & Kegan Paul, 1980.

Gitelman, H. M. "Welfare Capitalism Reconsidered," *Labor History* 33, 1 (Winter 1992): 5–31.

Glenn, Susan A. *Daughters of the Shtetl: Life and Labor in the Immigrant Generation*. Ithaca: Cornell University Press, 1990.

Glickman, Lawrence. "Inventing the 'American Standard of Living': Gender, Race and Working-Class Identity, 1880–1925," *Labor History* 34, 2–3 (Spring-Summer 1993): 221–235.

Gordon, Colin. *New Deals: Business, Labor, and Politics in America, 1920–1935*. New York: Cambridge University Press, 1994.

Gormly, Matthew E. "Trade Agreements in the Men's Clothing Industry of New York City," *Monthly Labor Review* 6, 1 (Jan. 1918): 18–26.

Gramsci, Antonio. *Selections from the Prison Notebooks of Antonio Gramsci*. Ed. and trans. Quintin Hoare and Geoffrey Nowell Smith. New York: International Publishers, 1971.

Greene, Julie. "Negotiating the State: Frank Walsh and the Transformation of Labor's Political Culture in Progressive America." In Boyle, ed., *Organized Labor and American Politics*, 71–102.

Greene, Victor R. *The Slavic Community on Strike: Immigrant Labor in Pennsylvania Anthracite.* South Bend: Notre Dame University Press, 1968.

Gregory, Derek. *Geographical Imaginations.* Cambridge, Mass.: Blackwell, 1994.

———. *Ideology, Science and Human Geography.* London: Hutchinson, 1978.

———. "Human Agency and Human Geography," *Transactions of the Institute of British Geographers*, NS 6, 1 (1981): 1–18.

———, and John Urry, eds. *Social Relations and Spatial Structures.* London: Macmillan, 1985.

Greven, Philip J., Jr. *Four Generations: Population, Land, and Family in Colonial Andover, Massachusetts.* Ithaca: Cornell University Press, 1970.

Gutman, Herbert G. *Work, Culture, and Society in Industrializing America: Essays in American Working-Class and Social History.* New York: Vintage Books, 1977.

Halpern, Rick. *Down on the Killing Floor: Black and White Workers in Chicago's Packinghouses, 1904–1954.* Urbana, Ill.: University of Illinois Press, 1997.

Handlin, Oscar. *The Uprooted: The Epic Story of the Great Migrations That Made the American People.* Boston: Little, Brown and Co., 1951.

Harsgor, Michael. "Total History: The *Annales* School," *Journal of Contemporary History* 31, 1 (Jan. 1978): 1–13.

Harris, Howell John. *The Right to Manage: Industrial Relations Policies of American Business in the 1940s.* Madison: University of Wisconsin Press, 1982.

Hart, Sara L. *The Pleasure Is Mine: An Autobiography.* Chicago: Valentine-Newman, 1947.

(Hartmarx). "The Hartmarx and Hart, Schaffner & Marx Centennial Celebration." (1987).

Harvey, David. *The Condition of Postmodernity: An Enquiry in the Origins of Cultural Change.* New York: Basil Blackwell, 1989.

———. *The Urbanization of Capital: Studies in the History and Theory of Capitalist Urbanization.* Baltimore: Johns Hopkins University Press, 1985.

———. *Consciousness and the Urban Experience.* New York: Basil Blackwell, 1985.

———. *The Limits to Capital.* New York: Basil Blackwell, 1982.

———. *Social Justice and the City.* London: Edward Arnold, 1973.

———. "The Geopolitics of Capitalism." In Gregory and Urry, eds., *Social Relations and Spatial Structures*, 126–163.

Hattam, Victoria C. *Labor Visions and State Power: The Origins of Business Unionism in the United States.* Princeton: Princeton University Press, 1993.

Herlihy, David. *Medieval Households.* Cambridge, Mass.: Harvard University Press, 1985.

Higham, John. *Strangers in the Land: Patterns of American Nativism 1860–1925.* College ed. New York: Atheneum, 1973.

———. "From Process to Structure: Formulations of American Immigration History." In Kivisto and Blanck, eds., *American Immigrants and Their Generations*, 11–41.

Hill, Herbert. "The Importance of Race in American Labor History," *International Journal of Politics, Culture and Society* 9, 2 (Winter 1995): 317–343.

———. "Myth-Making as Labor History: Herbert Gutman and the United Mine Workers of America," *International Journal of Politics, Culture and Society* 2, 2 (Winter 1988): 132–200.

Hines, Thomas S. *Burnham of Chicago: Architect and Planner*. Phoenix ed. Chicago: University of Chicago Press, 1979; originally published in 1974.

Hirsch, Arnold R. *Making the Second Ghetto: Race & Housing in Chicago, 1940–1960*. New York: Cambridge University Press, 1983.

Hobsbawm, Eric, and Terence Ranger, eds. *The Invention of Tradition*. Cambridge: Cambridge University Press, 1983.

Holli, Melvin G., and Peter d'A. Jones, eds. *Ethnic Chicago: A Multicultural Portrait*. 4th ed. Grand Rapids: William B. Eerdmans, 1995.

———, eds. *Ethnic Chicago*. Revised and expanded ed. Grand Rapids: William B. Eerdmans, 1977.

Hounshell, David A. *From the American System to Mass Production, 1800–1932*. Baltimore: Johns Hopkins University Press, 1984.

Howard, Earl Dean. "Cooperation in the Clothing Industry," *Proceedings of American Academy of Political Science* 9, 4 (Jan. 1922): 69–74.

Hyman, Collette A. "Labor Organizing and Female Institution-Building: The Chicago Women's Trade Union League, 1904–24." In Milkman, ed., *Women, Work and Protest*, 22–41.

Ignatiev, Noel. *How the Irish Became White*. New York: Routledge, 1995.

"Irving Bernstein's Labor History: A Symposium," *Labor History* 37, 1 (Winter 1995–1996): 75–99.

Jacobson, Matthew Frye. *Whiteness of a Different Color: European Immigrants and the Alchemy of Race*. Cambridge, Mass.: Harvard University Press, 1998.

Jaher, Frederic Cople. *The Urban Establishment: Upper Strata in Boston, New York, Charleston, Chicago, and Los Angeles*. Urbana, Ill.: University of Illinois Press, 1982.

Janowitz, Morris. *The Community Press in an Urban Setting: The Social Elements of Urbanism*. 2nd ed. Chicago: University of Chicago Press, 1967.

Jensen, Joan M., and Sue Davidson, eds. *A Needle, a Bobbin, a Strike: Women Needleworkers in America*. Philadelphia: Temple University Press, 1984.

Johnson, Richard. "Culture and the Historians." In Clarke et al., eds., *Working-Class Culture*, 41–71.

———. "Three Problematics." ibid., 201–237.

———. "Edward Thompson, Eugene Genovese, and Socialist-Humanist History," *History Workshop Journal* 6 (1978): 79–100.

Joseph Schaffner, 1848–1918: Recollections and Impressions of His Associates. Chicago: private publication, 1920.

Josephson, Matthew. *Sidney Hillman: Statesman of American Labor*. Garden City, N.Y.: Doubleday, 1952.

Joyce, Patrick. "Languages of Reciprocity and Conflict: A Further Response to Richard Price," *Social History* 9, 2 (May 1984): 225–231.

———. "Labour, Capital and Compromise: A Response to Richard Price," *Social History* 9, 1 (Jan. 1984): 67–76.

Kantowicz, Edward R. *Polish-American Politics in Chicago, 1888–1940*. Chicago: University of Chicago Press, 1975.

———. "Polish Chicago: Survival through Solidarity." In Holli and Jones, eds., *Ethnic Chicago*, 4th ed., 173–198.

Katznelson, Ira. *City Trenches: Urban Politics and the Patterning of Class in the United States*. New York: Pantheon Books, 1981.

———. "The 'Bourgeois' Dimension: A Provocation about Institutions, Politics, and the Future of Labor History," *International Labor and Working-Class History* 46 (Fall 1994): 7–32.

Kazal, Russell A. "Revisiting Assimilation: The Rise, Fall, and Reappraisal of a Concept in American Ethnic History," *American Historical Review* 100, 2 (Apr. 1995): 437–471.

Keating, Ann Durkin. *Building Chicago: Suburban Developers & the Creation of a Divided Metropolis*. Columbus: Ohio State University Press, 1988.

Keller, Morton. *The Life Insurance Enterprise, 1885–1910: A Study in the Limits of Corporate Power*. Cambridge, Mass.: Harvard/Belknap, 1963.

Kennedy, David M. *Over Here: The First World War and American Society*. New York: Oxford University Press, 1980.

Kessler-Harris, Alice. *Out to Work: A History of Wage-Earning Women in the United States*. New York: Oxford University Press, 1982.

———. "Where Are the Organized Women Workers?" *Feminist Studies* 3, 1–2 (Fall 1975): 92–110.

Kessner, Thomas. *The Golden Door: Italian and Jewish Immigrant Mobility in New York City, 1880–1915*. New York: Oxford University Press, 1977.

Kieniewicz, Stefan. *The Emancipation of the Polish Peasantry*. Chicago: University of Chicago Press, 1969.

Kivisto, Peter, and Dag Blanck, eds., *American Immigrants and Their Generations*. Urbana, Ill.: University of Illinois Press, 1990.

Kornblum, William. *Blue Collar Community*. Chicago: University of Chicago Press, 1974.

Kuznets, Simon. "Immigration of Russian Jews to the United States: Background and Structure," *Perspectives in American History* 9 (1975): 35–124.

Leach, William. *Land of Desire: Merchants, Power, and the Rise of a New American Culture*. New York: Vintage Books, 1993.

Lears, T. J. Jackson. *Fables of Abundance: A Cultural History of Advertising in America*. New York: Basic Books, 1994.

Lefebvre, Henri. *The Production of Space*. New York: Oxford University Press, 1991.

———. *The Survival of Capitalism: Reproduction of the Relations of Production*. New York: St. Martin's, 1976.

Levin, Nora. *Jewish Socialist Movements, 1871–1917: While Messiah Tarried*. London: Routledge & Kegan Paul, 1978.

Levine, Susan. *Labor's True Woman: Carpet Weavers, Industrialization, and Labor Reform in the Gilded Age.* Philadelphia: Temple University Press, 1984.

Levitats, Isaac. *The Jewish Community in Russia, 1772–1844.* Studies in History, Economics and Public Law no. 505, New York: Columbia University Press, 1943.

Lichtenstein, Nelson. *Labor's War ar Home: The CIO in World War II.* New York: Cambridge University Press, 1982.

Lockridge, Kenneth A. *A New England Town: The First Hundred Years, Dedham, Massachusetts, 1636–1736.* New York: W. W. Norton, 1970.

Lott, Eric. *Love and Theft: Blackface Minstrelsy and the American Working Class.* New York: Oxford University Press, 1995.

Lynd, Robert S., and Helen Merrell Lynd. *Middletown: A Study in American Culture.* New York: Harcourt, Brace & World, 1929.

McCarthy, Kathleen D. *Noblesse Oblige: Charity & Cultural Philanthropy in Chicago, 1849–1929.* Chicago: University of Chicago Press, 1982.

McCreesh, Carolyn Daniel. *Women in the Campaign to Organize Garment Workers: 1880–1917.* New York: Garland Publishing, 1985.

Macfarlane, Alan. "History, Anthropology and the Study of Communities," *Social History* 5 (May 1977): 631–652.

Mack Smith, Denis. *Modern Sicily after 1713.* London: Chatto & Windus, 1968.

McLennan, Gregor. "Thompson and the Discipline of Historical Context." In *Making Histories: Studies in History Writing and Politics*, ed. Richard Johnson, Gregor McLennan, Bill Schwarz, and David Sutton. Minneapolis: University of Minnesota Press, 1982, 96–130.

Macullar, Parker & Company. Cambridge, Mass.: Moses King, 1884.

Martins, Mario Rui. "The Theory of Social Space in the Work of Henri Lefebvre." In *Urban Political Economy and Social Theory: Essays in Urban Studies*, ed. Ray Forrest, Jeff Henderson, and Peter Williams. Aldershot: Gower, 1982, 160–185.

Marx, Karl. *Capital: A Critique of Political Economy*, vol. 1. Trans. Ben Fowkes. New York: Vintage Books, 1977.

Massey, Doreen. "New Directions in Space." In Gregory and Urry, eds., *Social Relations and Spatial Structures*, 9–19.

Matthews, Fred. "Paradigm Changes in Interpretations of Ethnicity, 1930–1980: From Process to Structure." In Kivisto and Blanck, eds., *American Immigrants and Their Generations*, 167–188.

Mayer, Harold M., and Richard C. Wade. *Chicago: Growth of a Metropolis.* Chicago: University of Chicago Press, 1969.

Mazur, Edward. "Jewish Chicago: From Diversity to Community." In Holli and Jones, eds., *Ethnic Chicago*, revised and expanded ed., 46–68.

Mendelsohn, Ezra. *Class Struggle in the Pale: The Formative Years of the Jewish Workers' Movement in Tsarist Russia.* New York: Cambridge University Press, 1970.

Merrifield, Andrew. "Place and Space: A Lefebvrian Reconciliation," *Transactions of the Institute of the British Geographers*, NS 18 (1993): 516–531.

Merriman, John. *The Margins of City Life: Explorations on the French Urban Frontier, 1815–1851*. New York: Oxford University Press, 1991.

Meyer, Stephen, III. *The Five Dollar Day: Labor Management in the Ford Motor Company, 1908–1921*. Albany: State University of New York Press, 1981.

Milkman, Ruth, ed. *Women, Work and Protest: A Century of US Women's Labor History*. London: Routledge & Kegan Paul, 1985.

Miller, Ross. *American Apocalypse: The Great Fire and the Myth of Chicago*. Chicago: University of Chicago Press, 1990.

Millis, H. A. "Unemployment Insurance in the Men's Clothing Industry of Chicago," *University Journal of Business* 2, 2 (Mar. 1924): 157–168.

Montgomery, David. *The Fall of the House of Labor: The Workplace, the State and American Labor Activism, 1865–1925*. Cambridge: Cambridge University Press, 1987.

———. *Workers' Control in America: Studies in the History of Work, Technology, and Labor Struggles*. Cambridge: Cambridge University Press, 1979.

Moody, J. Carroll, and Alice Kessler-Harris, eds. *Perspectives on American Labor History: The Problems of Synthesis*. DeKalb: Northern Illiniois University Press, 1990.

Morawska, Ewa. *For Bread with Butter: Life-Worlds of East Central Europeans in Johnstown, Pennsylvania, 1890–1940*. New York: Cambridge University Press, 1985.

———. "The Sociology and Historiography of Immigration." In *Immigration Reconsidered*, ed. Virginia Yans-McLaughlin. New York: Oxford University Press, 1990, 187–238.

Nadworny, Milton J. *Scientific Management and the Unions, 1900–1932: A Historical Analysis*. Cambridge, Mass.: Harvard University Press, 1955.

Nelli, Humbert S. *Italians in Chicago, 1880–1930: A Study in Ethnic Mobility*. New York: Oxford University Press, 1970.

Nelson, Bruce. "Class, Race and Democracy in the CIO: The 'New' Labor History Meets the 'Wages of Whiteness'," *International Review of Social History* 41 (Dec. 1996): 351–374.

Nelson, Daniel. *Frederick W. Taylor and the Rise of Scientific Management*. Madison: University of Wisconsin Press, 1980.

———. *Managers and Workers: Origins of the New Factory System in the United States, 1880–1920*. Madison: University of Wisconsin Press, 1975.

———. *Unemployment Insurance: The American Experience, 1915–1935*. Madison: University of Wisconsin Press, 1969.

Nestor, Agnes. *Women's Labor Leader: An Autobiography of Agnes Nestor*. Rockford, Ill.: Bellevue Books, 1954.

Nisbet, Robert A. *The Quest for Community: A Study in the Ethics of Order and Freedom*. New York: Oxford University Press, 1953.

Norton, William. *Historical Analysis in Geography*. London: Longman, 1984.

Nugent, Walter. *Crossings: The Great Transatlantic Migrations, 1870–1914*. Bloomington, Ind.: Indiana University Press, 1992.

Nystrom, Paul. *The Economics of Fashion*. New York: Ronald, 1928.

Oestricher, Richard Jules. *Solidarity and Fragmentation: Working People and*

Class Consciousness in Detroit, 1875–1900. Urbana, Ill.: University of Illinois Press, 1986.

———. "The Rules of the Game: Class Politics in Twentieth Century America." In Boyle, ed., *Organized Labor and American Politics*, 19–50.

———. "Urban Working-Class Political Behavior and Theories of American Electoral Politics, 1870–1940," *Journal of American History* 74, 4 (Mar. 1988): 1259–1286.

Orsi, Robert. "The Religious Boundaries of an Inbetween People: Street *Feste* and the Problem of the Dark-Skinned 'Other' in Italian Harlem, 1920–1990," *American Quarterly* 44, 3 (Sept. 1992): 313–347.

Pacyga, Dominic A. *Polish Immigrants and Industrial Chicago: Workers on the South Side, 1880–1922*. Columbus: Ohio State University Press, 1991.

———. "Chicago's Ethnic Neighborhoods: The Myth of Stability and the Reality of Change." In Holli and Jones, eds., *Ethnic Chicago*, 4th ed., 604–617.

Painter, Nell Irvin. "The New Labor History and the Historical Moment," *International Journal of Politics, Culture and Society* 2, 3 (Spring 1989): 367–370.

Park, Robert E., Ernest W. Burgess, and Roderick D. McKenzie. *The City*. Chicago: University of Chicago Press, 1925.

Payne, Elizabeth Anne. *Reform, Labor, and Feminism: Margaret Drier Robins and the Women's Trade Union League*. Urbana, Ill.: University of Illinois Press, 1988.

Perlman, Selig. *A Theory of the Labor Movement*. New York: Augustus M. Kelley, 1949; originally published in 1928.

Philpott, Thomas Lee. *The Slum and the Ghetto: Neighborhood Deterioration and Middle-Class Reform, Chicago, 1880–1930*. New York: Oxford University Press, 1978.

Pierce, Bessie Louise. *A History of Chicago*. 3 vols. New York: Alfred A. Knopf, 1937–1957.

Pilch, Andrzej. "Migrations of the Galician Populace at the Turn of the Nineteenth and Twentieth Centuries." In Bobinska and Pilch, eds., *Employment-Seeking Emigrations of the Poles*, 77–101.

Pope, Eliphalet. *The Clothing Industry in New York*. Columbia, Mo.: E. W. Stephens, 1905.

Popkin, Martin E. *Organization, Management and Technology in the Manufacture of Men's Clothing*. London: Sir Isaac Pitman & Sons, 1929.

Pounds, Norman J. G. *An Historical Geography of Europe, 1800–1914*. Cambridge: Cambridge University Press, 1985.

Price, Richard. "Theories of Labour Process Transformation," *Journal of Social History* 18, 1 (Fall 1984): 91–110.

———. "The Labour Process and Labour History," *Social History* 8, 1 (Jan. 1983): 57–75.

Reddy, William R. *The Rise of Market Culture: The Textile Trade & French Society, 1750–1900*. Cambridge: Cambridge University Press, 1984.

Rischin, Moses. *The Promised City: New York's Jews, 1870–1914*. Cambridge, Mass.: Harvard University Press, 1962.

Robinson, William Jay. "Helping Each Other!: The Story of the Landsmanshaften." In *History of Chicago Jewry, 1911–1961*, ed. Sheila R. Turner, Bob Gale, and Ellen Mayron. Chicago: Sentinel Publishing Co., 1961, 198–199.

Rodgers, Daniel T. "Tradition, Modernity, and the American Industrial Worker: Reflections and Critique," *Journal of Interdisciplinary History* 7, 4 (Spring 1977): 665–681.

Roediger, David. *Towards the Abolition of Whiteness: Essays on Race, Politics, and Working-Class History*. London: Verso, 1994.

———. *The Wages of Whiteness: Race and the Making of the American Working Class*. London: Verso, 1991.

Rosenzweig, Roy. *Eight Hours for What We Will: Workers & Leisure in an Industrial City, 1870–1920*. New York: Cambridge University Press, 1983.

———, and Elizabeth Blackmar. *The Park and the People: A History of Central Park*. Ithaca: Cornell University Press, 1992.

Rudolph, Richard L. *Banking and Industrialization in Austria-Hungary: The Role of Banks in the Industrialization of the Czech Crownlands, 1873–1914*. Cambridge: Cambridge University Press, 1976.

Ryan, Mary P. *Cradle of the Middle Class: The Family in Oneida County, New York, 1790–1865*. New York: Cambridge University Press, 1981.

Sack, Robert David. *Conceptions of Space in Social Thought*. Minneapolis: University of Minnesota Press, 1980.

Samuel, Raphael. *Theatres of Memory*. 2 vols. London: Verso, 1994–1998.

Saunders, Peter. "Space, the City, and Urban Sociology." In Gregory and Urry, eds., *Social Relations and Spatial Structures*, 67–89.

Sayer, Andrew. "The Difference that Space Makes." Ibid., 49–66.

Schiavo, Giovanni E. *The Italians in Chicago: A Study in Americanization*. Chicago: Italian American Publishing Co., 1928; reprint ed., New York: Arno, 1975.

Schofield, Ann. "The Uprising of the 20,000: The Making of a Labor Legend." In Jensen and Davidson, eds., *A Needle, a Bobbin, a Strike*, 167–182.

Scott, Joan Wallach. *Gender and the Politics of History*. New York: Columbia University Press, 1988.

Seidman, Joel. *The Needle Trades*. New York: Farrar & Rinehart, 1942.

Sennett, Richard. *Families against the City: Middle Class Homes of Industrial Chicago*. Cambridge, Mass.: Harvard University Press, 1970.

Simmel, Georg. *The Sociology of Georg Simmel*. Trans. and ed. Kurt H. Wolff. New York: Free Press, 1950.

Sive-Tomashefsky, Rebecca. "Identifying a Lost Leader: Hannah Shapiro and the 1910 Chicago Garment Workers' Strike," *Signs* 3, 4 (Summer 1978): 936–939.

Smith, Carl. *Urban Disorder and the Shape of Belief: The Great Chicago Fire, the Haymarket Bomb, and the Model Town of Pullman*. Chicago: University of Chicago Press, 1995.

Smith, Judith E. *Family Connections: A History of Italian and Jewish Immigrant Lives in Providence, Rhode Island, 1900–1940*. Albany: State University of New York Press, 1985.

Smith, Richard M. "'Modernization' and the Corporate Medieval Village Community in England: Some Sceptical Reflections." In Baker and Gregory, eds., *Explorations in Historical Geography*, 140–179.

Soffer, Benson. "A Theory of Trade Union Development: The Role of the 'Autonomous' Workman," *Labor History* 1, 2 (Summer 1960): 141–163.

Soja, Edward W. *Postmodern Geographies: The Reassertion of Space in Critical Social Theory*. London: Verso, 1989.

———, and Costis Hadjimichalis. "Between Geographical Materialism and Spatial Fetishism," *Antipode* 11, 3 (1979): 3–11.

Sollors, Werner, ed. *The Invention of Ethnicity*. New York: Oxford University Press, 1989.

Sorin, Gerald. *A Time for Building: The Third Migration, 1880–1920*. Baltimore: Johns Hopkins University Press, 1992.

Soule, George. *Sidney Hillman: Labor Statesman*. New York: Macmillan, 1939.

Spelman, Walter Bishop. *The Town of Cicero: History, Advantages, and Government*. Chicago: no publisher, 1923.

Stalson, J. Owen. *Marketing Life Insurance: Its History in America*. Harvard Studies in Business History no. 6, Cambridge, Mass.: Harvard University Press, 1942.

Stankiewicz, Zbigniew. "The Economic Emigration from the Kingdom of Poland Portrayed on the European Background." In Bobinska and Pilch, eds., *Employment-Seeking Emigrations of the Poles*, 27–52.

Stansell, Christine. *City of Women: Sex and Class in New York, 1789–1860*. Illinni Books ed. Urbana, Ill.: University of Illinois Press, 1987; originally published in 1986.

Stein, Leon, ed. *Out of the Sweatshop: The Struggle for Industrial Democracy*. New York: Quadrangle, 1977.

Stewart, Bryce M. "A Plan of Unemployment Insurance By Industry: The Administration of the Plan Inaugurated in 1923 by the Men's Clothing Industry of Chicago," *Taylor Society Bulletin* 12, 4 (Aug. 1927): 471–477.

Stone, Katherine. "The Origins of Job Structures in the Steel Industry," *Review of Radical Political Economics* 6, 2 (Summer 1972): 113–173.

Stonewell, Charles Jacob. "The Journeymen Tailors' Union of America," *University of Illinois Studies in the Social Sciences* 7, 4 (Dec. 1918): 435–571.

Stromquist, Shelton. "Class Wars: Frank Walsh, the Reformers, and the Crisis of Progressivism." In Arnesen et al., eds., *Labor Histories*, 97–124.

Susman, Warren I. *Culture as History: The Transformation of American Society in the Twentieth Century*. New York: Pantheon Books, 1984.

Suttles, Gerald D. *The Social Construction of Communities*. Chicago: University of Chicago Press, 1972.

Tax, Meredith. *The Rising of the Women: Feminist Solidarity and Class Conflict, 1880–1917*. New York: Monthly Review Press, 1980.

Taylor, Frederick W. *Scientific Management*. New York: Harper & Row, 1947.

Taylor, William R., ed. *Inventing Times Square: Commerce and Culture at the Crossroads of the World*. Baltimore: Johns Hopkins University Press, 1991.

Tentler, Leslie W. *Wage-Earning Women: Industrial Work and Family Life in the United States, 1900–1930*. New York: Oxford University Press, 1979.

Theibault, John. "Community and *Herrschaft* in the Seventeenth-Century German Village," *Journal of Modern History* 64, 1 (March 1992): 1–21.

Thernstrom, Stephan. *The Other Bostonians: Poverty and Progress in the American Metropolis, 1880–1970*. Cambridge, Mass.: Harvard University Press, 1973.

———. *Poverty and Progress: Social Mobility in a Nineteenth Century City*. Cambridge, Mass.: Harvard University Press, 1964.

Thomas, William I., and Florian Znaniecki. *The Polish Peasantry in Europe and America*. 2 vols. Chicago: University of Chicago Press, 1918.

Thompson, E. P. *Customs in Common: Studies in Traditional Popular Culture*. New York: New Press, 1993.

———. *The Poverty of Theory and Other Essays*. New York: Monthly Review Press, 1978.

———. *The Making of the English Working Class*. Vintage ed. New York: Vintage Books, 1966; originally published in 1963.

———. "Eighteenth-Century English Society: Class Struggle without Class?" *Social History* 3 (1978): 133–165.

Thrift, Nigel. "On the Determination of Social Action in Space and Time," *Environment and Planning D: Society and Space* 1 (1983): 23–57.

Tomlins, Christopher. *The State and the Unions: Labor Relations, Law, and the Organized Labor Movement in America, 1880–1960*. New York: Cambridge University Press, 1985.

———. "How Who Rides Whom: Recent 'New' Histories of American Labor Law and What They May Signify," *Social History* 20, 1 (Jan. 1995): 1–21.

Tönnies, Ferdinand. *Community and Society*. Trans. and ed. Charles P. Loomis. New York: Harper & Row, 1963.

Towers, Frank. "Projecting Whiteness: Race and the Unconscious in the History of 19th-Century American Workers," *Journal of American Culture* 21, 2 (Summer 1998): 47–57.

Trebilcock, Clive. *The Industrialization of the Continental Powers, 1780–1914*. London: Longman, 1981.

Trotter, Joe William, Jr. *Coal, Class, and Color: Blacks in Southern West Virginia, 1915–32*. Urbana, Ill.: University of Illinois Press, 1990.

Tuan, Yi-Fu. *Space and Place: The Perspective of Experience*. Minneapolis: University of Minnesota Press, 1977.

Tuttle, William M., Jr. *Race Riot: Chicago in the Red Summer of 1919*. New York: Atheneum, 1970.

Urry, John. "Social Relations, Space and Time." In Gregory and Urry, eds., *Social Relations and Spatial Structures*, 20–48.

Vecoli, Rudolph J. "*Contadini* in Chicago: A Critique of *The Uprooted*," *Journal of American History* 51, 3 (Dec. 1964): 404–417.

Waldinger, Roger. "Another Look at the International Ladies' Garment Workers' Union: Women, Industry Structure and Collective Action." In Milkman, ed., *Women, Work and Protest*, 86–109.

Wallerstein, Immanuel. *The Modern World-System I: Capitalist Agriculture and the Origins of the European World-Economy in the Sixteenth Century*. Orlando: Academic Press, 1974.

Wandycz, Piotr S. *The Lands of Partitioned Poland, 1795–1918*. Seattle: University of Washington Press, 1974.

Waugh, Joan. "Florence Kelley and the Anti-Sweatshop Campaign of 1892–1893," *UCLA Historical Journal* 3 (1982): 21–35.

Weiler, N. Sue. "Walkout: The Chicago Men's Garment Workers' Strike, 1910–1911," *Chicago History* 8, 14 (1979–1980): 238–249.

Weinryb, Bernard D. *The Jews of Poland: A Social and Economic History of the Jewish Community in Poland from 1100 to 1800*. Philadelphia: Jewish Publication Society of America, 1972.

Weinstein, James. *The Decline of Socialism in America, 1912–1925*. New Brunswick: Rutgers University Press, 1984; originally published in 1967.

Wilentz, Sean. *Chants Democratic: New York City & the Rise of the American Working Class, 1788–1850*. Paperback ed. New York: Oxford University Press, 1986; originally published in 1984.

Willett, Mabel Hurd. *The Employment of Women in the Clothing Trade*. Studies in History, Economics and Public Law, vol. 16, no. 2. New York: Columbia University Press, 1902.

Wilson, William H. *The City Beautiful Movement*. Baltimore: Johns Hopkins University Press, 1989.

Wirth, Louis. *The Ghetto*. Chicago: University of Chicago Press, 1928.

———. "Urbanism as a Way of Life," *American Journal of Sociology* 44 (July 1938): 1–24.

Wolf, Eric R. *Europe and the People Without History*. Berkeley: University of California Press, 1982.

Wolman, Leo. "Value of the Unemployment Insurance Scheme in the Clothing Industry." New York, Department of Labor, *Eighth Industrial Conference*, 1924, 137–144.

Wood, Ellen Meiksins. "The Politics of Theory and the Concept of Class: E. P. Thompson and His Critics," *Studies in Political Economy* 9 (1982): 45–75.

Woolf, Stuart. *A History of Italy 1700–1860: The Social Constraints of Political Change*. London: Methuen, 1979.

Wytrwal, Joseph A. *America's Polish Heritage: A Social History of the Poles in America*. Detroit: Endurance Press, 1961.

Yans-McLaughlin, Virginia. *Family and Community: Italian Immigrants in Buffalo, 1880–1930*. Ithaca: Cornell University Press, 1977.

Zaretz, Charles Elbert. *The Amalgamated Clothing Workers of America: A Study in Progressive Trades-Unionism*. New York: Ancon Publishing, 1934.

Zborowski, Mark, and Elizabeth Herzog. *Life Is With People: The Culture of the Shtetl*. 1st Schocken Paperback ed. New York: Schocken Books, 1962; originally published in 1952.

Zunz, Olivier. *The Changing Face of Inequality: Urbanization, Industrial Development, and Immigrants in Detroit, 1880–1920*. Chicago: University of Chicago Press, 1982.

G. UNPUBLISHED THESES

Horak, Jacub. "Assimilation of Czechs in Chicago." Ph.D., University of Chicago, 1920.

McCarthy, Eugene Ray. "The Bohemians in Chicago and Their Benevolent Societies: 1875–1946." M.A., University of Chicago, 1950.

Myers, Howard Barton. "The Policing of Labor Disputes in Chicago: A Case Study." Ph.D., University of Chicago, 1929.

Myers, Robert J. "The Economic Aspects of the Production of Men's Clothing (with Particular Reference to the Industry in Chicago)." Ph.D., University of Chicago, 1937.

Passero, Rosara Lucy. "Ethnicity in the Men's Ready-Made Clothing Industry, 1880–1950: The Italian Experience In Philadelphia." Ph.D., University of Pennsylvania, 1978.

INDEX